Network Analysis Using Wireshark Cookbook

Over 80 recipes to analyze and troubleshoot network problems using Wireshark

Yoram Orzach

BIRMINGHAM - MUMBAI

Network Analysis Using Wireshark Cookbook

First published: December 2013

Production Reference: 1171213

Published by Packt Publishing Ltd.
Livery Place
35 Livery Street
Birmingham B3 2PB, UK.

ISBN 978-1-84951-764-5

www.packtpub.com

Cover Image by iStockPhoto

Credits

Author
Yoram Orzach

Reviewers
Charles L. Brooks
Praveen Darshanam
Ritwik Ghoshal
Gilbert Ramirez

Acquisition Editors
Nikhil Chinnari
Akram Hussain
Antony Lowe

Lead Technical Editor
Ritika Dewani

Copy Editors
Roshni Banerjee
Janbal Dharmaraj
Brandt D'Mello
Kirti Pai
Shambhavi Pai
Alfida Paiva
Lavina Pereira
Sayanee Mukherjee
Karuna Narayanan

Technical Editors
Vrinda Nitesh Bhosale
Amit Ramadas
Pratik More
Anita Nayak

Project Coordinator
Anugya Khurana

Proofreader
Bridget Braund

Indexers
Monica Ajmera Mehta
Rekha Nair
Priya Subramani

Graphics
Disha Haria
Abhinash Sahu

Production Coordinator
Nitesh Thakur

Cover Work
Nitesh Thakur

About the Author

Yoram Orzach gained his Bachelor's degree in Science from the Technion in Haifa, Israel, and worked in Bezeq as a systems engineer in the fields of transmission and access networks from 1991 to 1995. In 1995, he joined Netplus from the Leadcom group as technical manager, and since 1999 he has worked as the CTO of NDI Communications (www.ndi-com.com), involved in the design, implementation, and troubleshooting of data communication networks worldwide. Yoram's experience is both with corporate networks, service providers, and Internet service provider's networks, and among his customers are companies such as Comverse, Motorola, Intel, Ceragon networks, Marvel, HP, and others. Yoram's experience is in design, implementation, and troubleshooting, along with training for R&D, engineering, and IT groups.

Acknowledgments

First and foremost, I would like to thank my family: my parents Israel and Selma; my father, the smartest man on earth, who survived the holocaust weighing 35 kilos alone in the world, and 40 years later became a leading expert in telecommunications; my mother, who taught me so many things; my amazing wife Ena, who has been tolerating me being at work over the last 20 years and more; my children Nadav, Dana, and Idan, whose achievements made my work look so simple. Thanks to my sister Hana, her husband Ofer, and their children.

I would also like to thank many colleagues. First, Reuven Matzliach, who started the Comverse IP college with me in the later 90s, transferring Comverse from TDM to IP networks, and helped me through some difficult times. Along with him, I would like to thank Omer Fuchs and Moshe Sakal for their assistance in this great project. Thanks to many colleagues and friends, who this paper is too short to mention.

Thanks to Lior Tzuberi, for many tips and case studies. Hanan Man, for a very interesting network. Yoel Saban and Rami Kletshevsky for very interesting network designs; your design groups are one of the best I've ever seen. Zvi Shacham, for the data-communication teaching experience I've gained from him. Asi Alajem for a very interesting network and Oren Gerstner for very interesting wireless cases. Chen Heffer, the best security expert I've ever known. Yoni Zini, for helping me with the system part. Ibrahim Jubram, for very interesting cellular cases. Ofer Sela, for very interesting projects. Amir Lavi and Eran Niditz, for very interesting cases. Dimitrios Liappis, for interesting cellular cases. Avner Mimon, for great tips and so many others.

Thanks to many training professionals that I've learned so much from. Thirty years ago I thought giving courses is fun; you taught me it's a profession. Harriet Rubin, Merav Sagi, Rvital Keinan, Guy Einav, Raanan Dagan, and many others.

Special thanks to Yoav Nokrean and his son Eran, who assisted me with many ideas, giving me assistance in all possible ways.

I would also like to thank the many colleagues who worked with me over the years; to customers at home, in Europe, North America, Eastern Asia, and other exotic places. Troubleshooting a network is always the same, the only question is, is it snowing outside or is there an exotic coast nearby with tequila?

Special thanks to the many designers that designed bad networks, to developers that wrote strange implementations for TCP/IP, to IT guys who connected the wrong cables, to engineering departments who thought that you just connect the cables to the boxes and it works. That's the best way to learn networking.

To many thousands of students, thanks to all of them for all the hard questions and the interesting cases that you brought with you; I've learned new things in every course. There is nothing that is more fun than connecting to networks and fixing problems in real time.

My admiration to the networking and security pioneers—Vint Cerf, Bob Kahn, Radia Perlman, Adi Shamir, Ronald Rivest, Van Jacobson, Steven McCanne, and so many others. Without you, we wouldn't have all this.

And lastly to Packt Publishing, for coming up with the idea to write this book and very patiently accompanying me through the process.

About the Reviewers

Charles L. Brooks is the founder and principal consultant at Security Technical Education, where he offers services in technical writing, reviewing, instructional design, and education. Charles also facilitates online courses at Boston University in data communications and networking, and teaches courses in network security, secure software development, securing virtualized and cloud infrastructures at Brandeis University, Rabb School of Graduate Professional Studies, in the MS in Information Security program. Prior to founding Security Technical Education (`www.securityteched.com`), Charles worked at EMC and at RSA as a senior technical education consultant, developing courseware for storage security, Big Data, network security analysis, and network forensics. Prior to EMC, Charles worked for many years as a software engineer, team leader, and software architect; and most recently as a systems architect for a managed VPN service offered by GTE Internetworking and Genuity.

Charles earned a BS and MA degree in English from Clark University, a MSCIS degree from Boston University, and holds several industry certifications including the CISSP, CEH, and CHFI.

> I want to thank Helyn Pultz for her encouragement, support, and timely counsel for all these many years.

Praveen Darshanam has over seven years of experience in Information Security with companies such as McAfee, Cisco Systems, and iPolicy Networks. His core expertise and passions are vulnerability research, signature development, Snort, application security, and malware analysis. He pursued B.Tech in Electrical Engineering (EE) and ME/M.Tech in Control and Instrumentation; EE from one of the premier institutes of India. He holds industry certifications such as CHFI, CEH, and ECSA.

Ritwik Ghoshal is a Senior Security Analyst at Oracle Corporation, responsible for Oracle software and hardware security assurance. His primary work areas are network security, operating systems, and virtualization. Before coming to Oracle in 2010, when the company acquired Sun Microsystems, he had been working at Sun since 2008 as a part of the Sun security engineering team and the Solaris team. At Oracle, Ritwik continues to be responsible for all Sun systems products and Oracle Linux and Virtualization products.

Ritwik earned a Bachelor's degree in Computer Science and Engineering in 2008 from Heritage Institute of Technology, Kolkata, India.

I'm heavily indebted to my parents and Sara E Taverner for their continuous help and support.

Gilbert Ramirez is a long-time contributor to Wireshark, starting when it was first released. He has added protocol dissectors, core routines such as the display filter engine, as well as the initial port to Windows. He works at Cisco Systems, where he handles software build systems as well as other software tools.

Gilbert has authored books on Wireshark, including *Wireshark & Ethereal Network Protocol Analyzer Toolkit*, *Ethereal Packet Sniffing*, and *Nessus, Snort, & Ethereal Power Tools*, all published by *Syngress Publishing Inc.*

www.PacktPub.com

Support files, eBooks, discount offers and more

You might want to visit www.PacktPub.com for support files and downloads related to your book.

Did you know that Packt offers eBook versions of every book published, with PDF and ePub files available? You can upgrade to the eBook version at www.PacktPub.com and as a print book customer, you are entitled to a discount on the eBook copy. Get in touch with us at service@packtpub.com for more details.

At www.PacktPub.com, you can also read a collection of free technical articles, sign up for a range of free newsletters and receive exclusive discounts and offers on Packt books and eBooks.

http://PacktLib.PacktPub.com

Do you need instant solutions to your IT questions? PacktLib is Packt's online digital book library. Here, you can access, read and search across Packt's entire library of books.

Why Subscribe?

- ▶ Fully searchable across every book published by Packt
- ▶ Copy and paste, print and bookmark content
- ▶ On demand and accessible via web browser

Free Access for Packt account holders

If you have an account with Packt at www.PacktPub.com, you can use this to access PacktLib today and view nine entirely free books. Simply use your login credentials for immediate access.

Table of Contents

Preface

Wireshark has long become the market standard for network analysis, and with the growth of the Internet and TCP/IP-based networks, it became very popular for network analysis, troubleshooting, as well as for R&D engineers to understand what is actually running over the network and what are the problems that we face.

This book is written from a practical point of view. The first part of it, from *Chapter 1, Introducing Wireshark*, to *Chapter 6, Using the Expert Infos Window*, describes the Wireshark software and how to work with it. This includes how to start it, where to locate it in the network, how to work with statistical tools, and how to use the Expert system. The second part, from *Chapter 7, Ethernet, LAN Switching, and Wireless LAN*, to *Chapter 14, Understanding Network Security*, describes how to use it for the analysis and troubleshooting of common networking protocols; among them, the TCP/IP protocol stack with emphasis on TCP performance issues, common Internet protocols such as HTTP, SMTP, POP and DNS, databases, Citrix and Microsoft Terminal Server, IP telephony, and multimedia applications. The last chapter is about network security. It describes how to locate security breaches and other problems in your network.

As the name of the book implies, this is a Cookbook. It is a list of effective, targeted recipes of how to analyze networks. Every recipe comes with a specific issue, how to use Wireshark for it, where to look and what to look for, and what is the reason for what you see. To complete the picture, every recipe provides the theoretical foundations of the subject, in order to give the reader the required theoretical background.

You will see many examples in the book, and all of them are real cases. Some of them took me minutes to solve, some hours, and some of them took many days. There is one thing common to all of them: work systematically, use the proper tools, try to get inside the head of the application writer, and like someone told me once, "Try to think like the network". Do this, use Wireshark, and you will get results. The purpose of this book is to try and get you there. Have fun!

What this book covers

Chapter 1, Introducing Wireshark, starts with introducing Wireshark, explaining where to locate it for effective network analysis. We will learn how to configure the basic parameters, the start window, the time values, and the coloring rules; and most importantly, we will learn how to use the Preferences window.

Chapter 2, Using Capture Filters, explains how to use capture filters which are used in order to define what data will be captured. This chapter explains how to configure these filters and how to use them in order to capture only the desired data.

Chapter 3, Using Display Filters, explains how to configure display filters which are used in order to display only the desired data, after the data is captured. This chapter explains how to configure these filters and how they can assist us in network troubleshooting.

Chapter 4, Using Basic Statistics Tools, explains how to work with the basic Wireshark statistical features, starting from the simple tables that provides us with "who is talking" information, conversations and HTTP statistics, and others.

Chapter 5, Using Advanced Statistics Tools, explains how to work with the advanced Wireshark statistical features, including the IO graphs and TCP stream graphs that provides us with powerful capabilities for network and application performance analysis.

Chapter 6, Using the Expert Infos Window, explains how to work with the Expert system, which is a powerful tool that pinpoints various types of events, such as TCP retransmissions, zero-window, low TTL and routing loops, out-of-order segments, and other events that might influence the behavior of our network.

Chapter 7, Ethernet, LAN Switching, and Wireless LAN, explains the Ethernet protocol and LAN switching, along with problems that might occur in this layer. It also focuses on Wireless LAN (WiFi), how to test it, and how to resolve problems in these networks.

Chapter 8, ARP and IP Analysis, explains about ARP, IP, and how to analyze IP connectivity and routing problems. This chapter also explains how to find duplicate IP addresses, DHCP problems, and other related issues.

Chapter 9, UDP/TCP Analysis, focuses on layer 4 protocols, TCP, and UDP, with emphasis on TCP performance issues. It provides recipes for allocation of TCP performance problems, such as retransmission, duplicate ACKs, sliding-window problems such as window-full and zero-window, resets, and other related issues.

Chapter 10, HTTP and DNS, focuses on DNS, HTTP, and HTTPs. In this chapter, we will see how they work and what can go wrong in these protocols.

Chapter 11, Analyzing Enterprise Applications', Behavior, talks about other applications such as FTP, mail protocols, terminal services, and databases. We will see how they are affected by network problems and how we can solve network-related problems in these applications.

Chapter 12, SIP, Multimedia, and IP Telephony, is about voice and video over IP, including recipes for finding VoIP SIP connectivity problems, RTP/RTCP performance problems, and video problems such as picture freezing and bad picture quality.

Chapter 13, Troubleshooting Bandwidth and Delay Problems, provides recipes for finding problems caused by low-bandwidth, high-delay, and high-jitter networks. The chapter explains the behavior of TCP over high-delay, high-jitter networks, and what we can do in order to improve this behavior.

Chapter 14, Understanding Network Security, focuses on TCP/IP-based network security, and it includes recipes for finding network scanning, SYN attacks, DOS/DDOS, and other attacks that can harm the network. This chapter provides recipes for finding various attack patterns and what causes them.

Appendix, Links, Tools, and Reading, provides references to some useful links from which you can get further information about Wireshark: learning sources, additional software, and so on.

What you need for this book

For working with this book, you will need to install the Wireshark software that can be downloaded from `www.wireshark.org`.

Who this book is for

This book is aimed at R&D, engineering and technical support, IT, and communication managers who are using Wireshark for network analysis and troubleshooting. It requires basic understanding of the networking concepts, but does not require specific and detailed technical knowledge of the protocols or vendor implementations.

Conventions

In this book, you will find a number of styles of text that distinguish between different kinds of information. Here are some examples of these styles, and an explanation of their meaning.

Code words in text are shown as follows: "Add the string `tcp.window_size` to view the TCP window size".

A block of code is set as follows:

```
[not] primitive [and|or [not] primitive ...]
proto [Offset in bytes from the start of the header : Number of bytes
to check]
```

Any command-line input or output is written as follows:

```
Reply from 173.194.35.148: bytes=32 time=98ms TTL=51
Request timed out.
Reply from 173.194.35.148: bytes=32 time=124ms TTL=51
Request timed out.
Reply from 173.194.35.148: bytes=32 time=134ms TTL=51
Request timed out.
Reply from 173.194.35.148: bytes=32 time=582ms TTL=51
Request timed out.
```

New terms and **important words** are shown in bold. Words that you see on the screen, in menus or dialog boxes for example, appear in the text like this: "clicking the **Next** button moves you to the next screen".

> Warnings or important notes appear in a box like this.

> Tips and tricks appear like this.

Reader feedback

Feedback from our readers is always welcome. Let us know what you think about this book—what you liked or may have disliked. Reader feedback is important for us to develop titles that you really get the most out of.

To send us general feedback, simply send an e-mail to feedback@packtpub.com, and mention the book title via the subject of your message.

If there is a topic that you have expertise in and you are interested in either writing or contributing to a book, see our author guide on www.packtpub.com/authors.

Customer support

Now that you are the proud owner of a Packt book, we have a number of things to help you to get the most from your purchase.

Piracy

Piracy of copyright material on the Internet is an ongoing problem across all media. At Packt, we take the protection of our copyright and licenses very seriously. If you come across any illegal copies of our works, in any form, on the Internet, please provide us with the location address or website name immediately so that we can pursue a remedy.

Please contact us at `copyright@packtpub.com` with a link to the suspected pirated material.

We appreciate your help in protecting our authors, and our ability to bring you valuable content.

Questions

You can contact us at `questions@packtpub.com` if you are having a problem with any aspect of the book, and we will do our best to address it.

1
Introducing Wireshark

In this chapter you will learn:

- ▶ Locating Wireshark
- ▶ Starting the capture of data
- ▶ Configuring the start window
- ▶ Using time values and summaries
- ▶ Configuring coloring rules and navigation techniques
- ▶ Saving, printing, and exporting data
- ▶ Configuring the user interface in the **Preferences** menu
- ▶ Configuring protocols preferences

Introduction

In this chapter, we will cover the basic tasks related to Wireshark. In the *Preface* of this book, we discussed network troubleshooting and the various tools that can help us in the process. After reaching the conclusion that we need to use the Wireshark protocol analyzer, it's time to locate it for testing in the network, to configure it with basic configurations, and to adapt it to be user friendly.

While setting Wireshark for basic data capture is considered to be very simple and intuitive, there are many options that we can use in special cases; for example, when we capture data continuously over a connection and we want to split the capture file into small files, when we want to see names of the devices participating in the connection and not only IP addresses, and so on. In this chapter we will learn how to configure Wireshark for these special cases.

Another important issue is where to locate Wireshark to capture data. Will it be before a firewall or after it? On which side of the router should we connect it? On the LAN side or on the WAN side? What should we expect to receive in each one of them? All these issues and more will be covered in the *Locating Wireshark* recipe in this chapter, along with recommendations on how to do it.

Another important issue that will be covered in this chapter is how to configure time values, that is, how you would like Wireshark to present the arrival time of captured packets. This is significantly important when we capture data of time-sensitive applications, when it is important to see the timing of packets inside a TCP connection or a UDP flow.

The next recipe will be on file manipulations, that is, how to save the captured data, whether we want to save the whole of it or part of it, save only filtered data, export that data into various formats, merge files (for example, when you want to merge captured files on two different router interfaces), and so on.

One more issue that will be discussed in this chapter is how to configure coloring rules. That is, how to configure Wireshark to present different packets and protocols in different colors. While Wireshark by default has its coloring scheme, we might want to configure it for special cases, for example, to give a special color to a specific protocol that we monitor or to a specific error or event that we expect. The *Configuring coloring rules and navigation techniques* recipe discusses these issues.

The last two recipes of the chapter will cover the configuration of the Wireshark preferences. These recipes discuss how to configure the user interface, that is, to configure the Wireshark windows, the columns and what to see in each one of them, text formats, and so on, along with specific protocol configurations; for example, which TCP ports should be resolved by default as a proxy service, whether or not to validate a protocol checksum, whether or not to calculate TCP timestamps, how to decode fields in the protocol header, and so on.

Locating Wireshark

After understanding the problem and deciding to use Wireshark, the first step would be to decide where to locate it. For this purpose, we need to have a precise network diagram (at least the part of the network that is relevant to our test).

The principle is to locate the device that you want to monitor, connect your laptop to the same switch that it is connected to, and configure a port mirror or monitor to the monitored device. This operation enables you to see all traffic coming in and out of the monitored device.

You can monitor a LAN port, WAN port, server or router port, or any other device connected to the network.

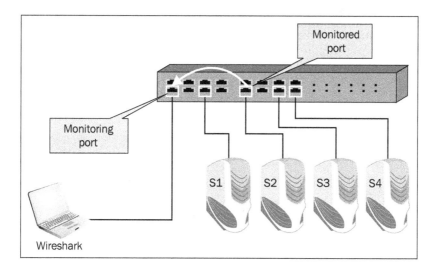

In the preceding diagram, the Wireshark software (installed on the PC on the left) and the port mirror, also called port monitor (configured on the switch in the direction as in the diagram), will monitor all the traffic coming in and out of server S2. Of course, we can also install Wireshark directly on the server itself, and by doing so, we will be able to watch the traffic directly on the server.

Some LAN switch vendors also enable other features such as:

 ▶ **Monitoring a whole VLAN**: We can monitor a server's VLAN, Telephony VLAN, and so on. In this case you will see all the traffic on a specific VLAN.

 ▶ **Monitoring several ports to a single analyzer**: We can monitor traffic on servers **S1** and **S2** together.

 ▶ **Filtering**: Filtering means choosing and accordingly configuring whether to monitor incoming traffic, outgoing traffic, or both.

Getting ready

To start working with Wireshark, go to the the Wireshark website, and download the latest version of the tool.

An updated version of Wireshark can be found on the website at `http://www.wireshark.org/`, under the **Download** heading. Download the latest Wireshark stable release that is available at `http://www.wireshark.org/download.html`.

Each Wireshark Windows package comes with the latest stable release of WinPcap, which is required for live packet capture. The WinPcap driver is a Windows version of the UNIX Libpcap library for traffic capture.

How to do it...

Let's take a look at the typical network architecture and network devices, how they work, how to configure them when required, and where to locate Wireshark.

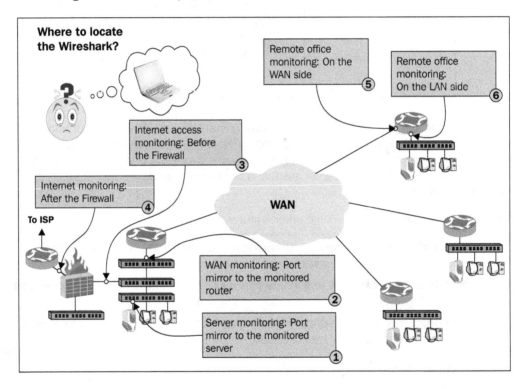

Let's have a look at the simple and common network architecture in the preceding diagram.

Monitoring a server

This will be one of the most common requirements that we will have. It can be done by either configuring the port monitor to the server (numbered as **1** in the preceding diagram), or installing Wireshark on the server itself.

Monitoring a router

In order to monitor a router, we can monitor a LAN port (numbered as **2** and **6** in the preceding diagram), or a WAN port (numbered as **5** in the preceding diagram). To monitor a LAN port is easy—simply configure the port monitor to the port you wish to monitor. In order to monitor a WAN port, you can connect a switch between the router port and the **Service Provider** (**SP**) network, and configure the port monitor on this switch, as in the following illustration.

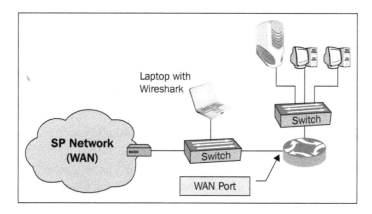

Connecting a switch between the router and the service provider is an operation that breaks the connection; however, when you prepare for it, it should take less than a minute.

When monitoring a router, don't forget—not all packets coming in to a router will be forwarded. Some packets can be lost, dropped on the router buffers, or routed back on the same port that they came in from.

Two additional devices that you can use are TAPs and Hubs.

- ► **TAPs**: Instead of connecting a switch on the link you wish to monitor, you can connect a device called **Test Access Point** (**TAP**), which is a simple three-port device that, in this case, will play the same role as that of the switch. The advantage of a TAP over a switch is its simplicity and price. TAPs also forward errors that can be monitored on Wireshark, unlike a LAN switch that drops them. Switches, on the other hand, are much more expensive, take a few minutes to configure, but provide you with additional monitoring capabilities, for example, **Simple Network Management Protocol** (**SNMP**). When you troubleshoot a network, it is better to have an available managed LAN switch, even a simple one.

- ► **Hubs**: You can simply connect a hub in parallel to the link you want to monitor, and since a hub is a half-duplex device, every packet sent between the router and the SP device will be watched on your Wireshark. The biggest con of this method is that the hub itself slows the traffic, and it therefore influences the test. In many cases you also want to monitor 1 Gbps ports, and since there is no hub available for this, you will have to reduce the speed to 100 Mbps, which again will influence the traffic. Therefore, hubs are not commonly used.

Monitoring a firewall

When monitoring a firewall, it differs depending on whether you monitor the internal port (numbered **3** in the diagram) or the external port (numbered **4** in the diagram). On the internal port you will see all the internal addresses and all traffic initiated by the users working in the internal network, while on the external port you will see the external addresses that we go out with (translated by NAT from the internal addresses); you will not see requests from the internal network that were blocked by the firewall. If someone is attacking the firewall from the Internet, you will see it (hopefully) only on the external port.

How it works...

To understand how the port monitor works, it is first important to understand the way that a LAN switch works. A LAN switch forwards packets in the following way:

1. The LAN switch continuously learns about the MAC addresses of the devices connected to it.

2. Now, if a packet is sent to a destination MAC, it will be forwarded only to the physical port that the switch knows this MAC address is coming from.

3. If a broadcast is sent, it will be forwarded to all the ports of the switch.

4. If a multicast is sent and **Cisco Group Management Protocol** (**CGMP**) or **Internet Group Management Protocol** (**IGMP**) is disabled, it will be forwarded to all the ports of the switch (CGMP and IGMP are protocols that enable multicast packets to be forwarded only to devices on a specific multicast group).

5. If a packet is sent to a MAC address that the switch does not know about (which is a very rare case), it will be forwarded to all the ports of the switch.

Therefore, when you configure a port monitor to a specific port, you will see all the traffic coming in and out of it. If you connect your laptop to the network, without configuring anything, you will see only the traffic coming in and out of your laptop, along with broadcasts and multicasts from the network.

There's more...

When capturing data, there are some tricky scenarios that you should be aware of.

One such scenario is monitoring a VLAN. When monitoring a VLAN, you should be aware of several important issues. The first issue is that even when you monitor a VLAN, the packet must physically be transferred through the switch you are connected to, in order to see it. If, for example, you monitor VLAN-10 that is configured across the network, and you are connected to your floor switch, you will not see the traffic that goes from other switches to the servers on the central switch.

This is because when building a network, the users are usually connected to floor switches in single or multiple locations in the floor, that are connected to the building central switch (or two redundant switches). For monitoring all traffic on a VLAN, you have to connect to a switch on which all traffic of the VLAN goes through, and this is usually the central switch.

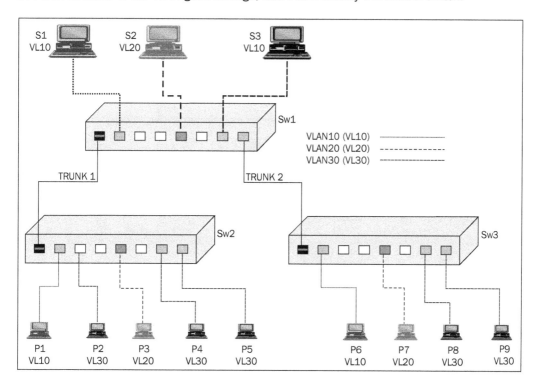

In the preceding diagram, if you connect Wireshark to Switch SW2, and configure a monitor to VLAN30, you will see all the packets coming in and out of **P2**, **P4**, and **P5**, inside or outside the switch. You will not see packets transferred between devices on **SW3** and **SW1**, or packets between **SW1** and **SW3**.

Another issue when monitoring a VLAN is that you might see duplicate packets. This is because when you monitor a VLAN, and packets are going in and out of the VLAN, you will see the same packet when it is comes in, and then when it goes out of the VLAN.

You can see the reason in the following illustration. When, for example, **S4** sends a packet to **S2**, and you configure the port mirror to VLAN30, you will see the packet once when sent from **S4** passing through the switch and entering the VLAN30, and then when leaving VLAN30 and coming to **S2**.

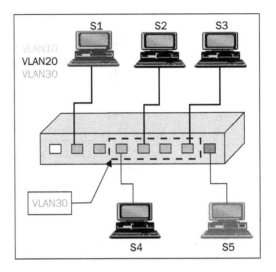

See also

For information on how to configure the port mirror, refer to the vendor's instructions.
It can be called **port monitor**, **port mirror**, or **SPAN** (**Switched Port Analyzer** from Cisco).

There are also advanced features such as remote monitoring (monitoring a port that is not directly connected to your switch), advanced filtering (such as filtering specific MAC addresses), and so on. There are also advanced switches that have capture and analysis capabilities on the switch itself. It is also possible to monitor virtual ports (for example, LAG or Ether channel groups). For all cases, refer to the vendor's specifications.

Starting the capture of data

In this recipe, we will learn how to start capturing data, and what we will get in various capture scenarios, after we have located Wireshark in the network.

Getting ready

After you install Wireshark on your computer, the only thing to do will be to start the analyzer from the desktop, program files, or the quick start bar.

When you do so, the following window will be opened (Version 1.10.2):

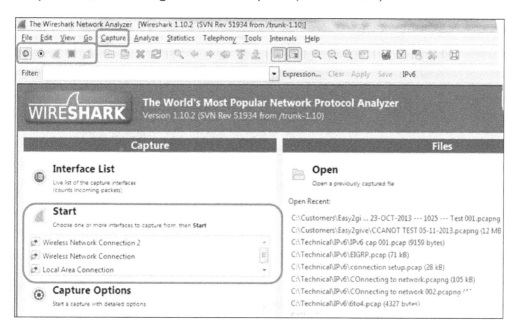

How to do it...

You can start the capture from the upper bar **Capture** menu, or from the quick-launch bar with the capture symbol, or from the center-left capture window on the Wireshark main screen. There are options that you can choose from.

How to choose the interface to start the capture

If you simply click on the green icon, third to the right, in Wireshark and start the capture, Wireshark will start the capture on the default interface as configured in the software (explained later in the chapter in the recipe *Configuring the user interface in the Preferences menu*). In order to choose the interface you want to capture on, click on the **List the available capture interfaces** symbol, and the **Wireshark Capture Interfaces** window will open.

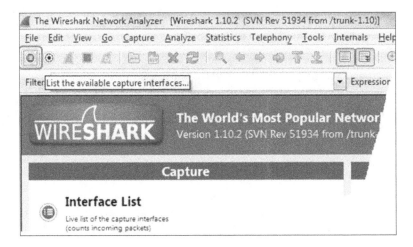

The best way to see which interface is active is simply to look at the right of the window of the interface on which you see the traffic running. There you will see the number of total **Packets** seen by Wireshark, and the number of **Packets/sec** in each interface.

In Wireshark Version 1.10.2 and above, you can choose one or more interfaces for the capture. This can be helpful in many cases; for example, when you have multiple physical NICs, you can monitor the port on two different servers, two ports of a router, or other multiple ports at the same time. A typical configuration is seen in the following screenshot:

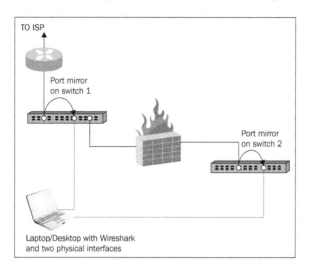

How to configure the interface you capture data from

To configure the interface you capture data from, choose **Options** from the **Capture** menu. The following window will appear:

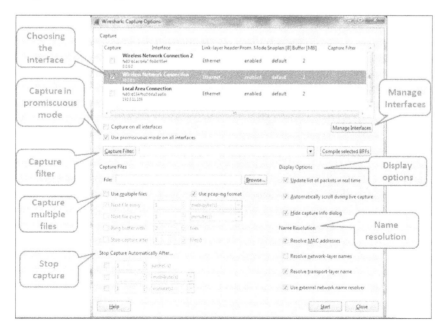

In the preceding window you can configure the following parameters:

1. On the upper side of the window, choose the interface you want to capture the data from.

2. On the left side of the window, you have the checkbox **Use promiscuous mode on all interfaces**. When checked, Wireshark will capture all the packets that the computer receives. Unchecking it will capture only packets intended for the computer.

3. In some cases, when this checkbox is checked, Wireshark will not capture data in the wireless interface; so if you start capturing data on the wireless interface and see nothing, uncheck it.

4. On the mid-left area of the window, you have the **Capture Files** field. You can write a file name here, and Wireshark will save the captured file under this name, with extensions 0001, 0002, and so on under the path you specify. This feature is extremely important when capturing a large amount of data; for example, when capturing data over a heavily-loaded interface, or over a long period of time. You can tell the software to open a new file after a specific interval of time, file size, or number of packets.

5. On the bottom left of the window, you have the area marked as **Stop Capture Automatically** in the preceding screenshot. In this area, you can tell the software to stop capturing data after a specific interval of time, file size, or number of packets.

6. On the mid-right area of the window, you can change the **Display** option and select the checkboxes **Update list of packets in real time**, **Automatically scroll during live capture**, and **Hide capture info dialog**, which close the annoying capture window (a pop up that appears the moment you start capture). In most of the cases you don't have to change anything here.

7. On the bottom right of the window, you configure the resolving options for MAC addresses, IP DNS names, and TCP/UDP port numbers. The last checkbox, **Use external network name resolver**, uses the system's configured name resolver (in most of the cases, DNS), to resolve network names.

How it works...

Here the answer is very simple. When Wireshark is connected to a wired or wireless network, there is a software driver that is located between the physical or wireless interface and the capture engine. In Windows we have the **WinPcap** driver, in Unix platforms the **Libpcap** driver, and for wireless interfaces we have the **AirPcap** driver.

There's more...

In cases where the capture time is important, and you wish to capture data on one interface or more, and be time-synchronized with the server you are monitoring, you can use **Network Time Protocol** (**NTP**) to synchronize your Wireshark and the monitored servers with a central time source.

This is important in cases when you want to go through the Wireshark capture file in parallel to a server logfile, and look for events that are shown on both. For example, if you see retransmissions in the capture file at the same time as a server or application error on the monitored server, you will know that the retransmissions are because of server errors and not because of the network.

The Wireshark software takes its time from the OS clock (Windows, Linux, and so on) For configuring the OS to work with a time server, go to the relevant manuals of the operating system that you work with.

In Microsoft Windows7, configure it as follows:

1. Go the **Control Panel**.
2. Choose **Clock, Language, and Region**.
3. Under **Date and Time**, Choose **Set the time and date** and change to the **Internet time** tab.
4. Click on the **Change Settings** button.
5. Change the server name or the IP address.

 In Microsoft Windows7 and later versions, there is a default setting for the time server. As long as all devices are tuned to it, you can use it as any other time server.

NTP is a network protocol used for time synchronization. When you configure your network devices (routers, switches, FWs, and so on) and servers to the same time source, they will be time synchronized to this source. The accuracy of the synchronization depends on the accuracy of the time server that is measured in levels or stratums. The higher the level, the more accurate it will be. Level 1 is the highest. Usually you will have levels 2 to 4.

NTP was first standardized in RFC 1059 (NTPv1), and then in RFC 1119 (NTPv2); the common versions in the last years are NTPv3 (RFC1305) and NTPv4 (RFC 5905).

You can get a list of NTP servers on various web sites, among them `http://support.ntp.org/bin/view/Servers/StratumOneTimeServers` and

`http://wpollock.com/AUnix2/NTPstratum1PublicServers.htm`.

See also

You can get more information about Pcap drivers at:

- For WinPcap visit: `http://www.winpcap.org`
- For Libpcap visit: `http://www.tcpdump.org`

Configuring the start window

In this recipe we will see some basic configurations for the start window. We will talk about configuring the main window, file formats, and viewing options.

Getting ready

Start Wireshark, and you will get the start window. There are several parameters you can change here in order to adapt the capture window to meet your requirements:

- Toolbars configuration
- Main window configuration
- Time format configuration
- Name resolution
- Colorize packet list
- Auto scroll in live capture
- Zoom
- Columns configuration
- Coloring rules

First, let's have a look at the toolbars that are used by the software:

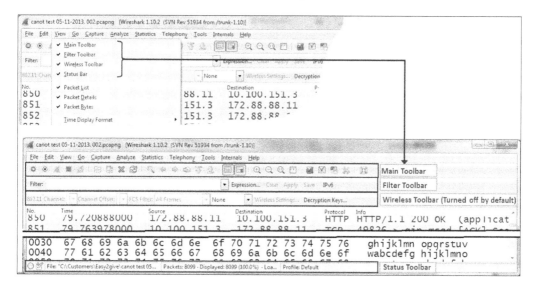

For operations with the other toolbars as follows, which are covered in the coming subsections in this recipe:

- ▸ Main Toolbar
- ▸ Display Filter Toolbar
- ▸ Status Bar

Main Toolbar

In the main toolbar you have the icons shown in the following screenshot:

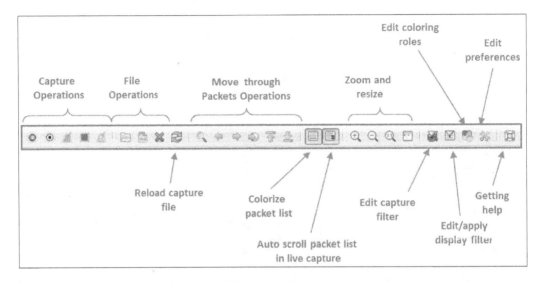

The five leftmost symbols are for capture operations, then you have symbols for file operations, zoom and "go to packet" operations, colorize and auto-scroll, zoom and resize, filters, preferences, and help.

Display Filter Toolbar

In the filter toolbar, you have the following fields:

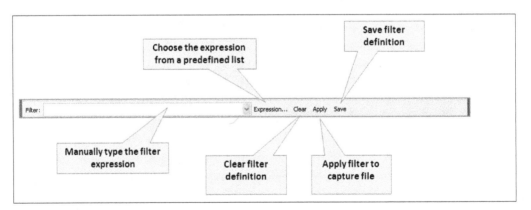

Status Bar

In the status bar on the lower side of the Wireshark window, you can see the data shown in the following screenshot:

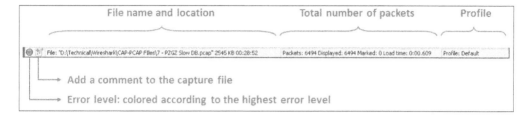

In the preceding screenshot you can see the following:

▶ Errors in the expert system

▶ The option to add a comment to the file

▶ The name of the captured file (during capture, it will show you a temporary name assigned by the software)

▶ Total number of captured packets, displayed packets (those which are actually displayed on the screen), and marked packets (those that you have marked).

How to do it...

In this part we will go step by step and configure the main menu.

Configuring toolbars

Usually for regular packet capture, you don't have to change anything. This is different when you want to capture wireless data over the network (not only from your laptop); you will have to enable the wireless toolbar, and this will be done by clicking on it under the view menu, as shown in the following screenshot:

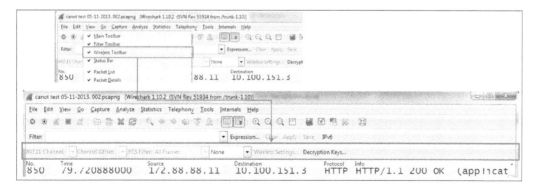

Configuring the main window

To configure the main menu for capturing, you can configure Wireshark to show the following windows:

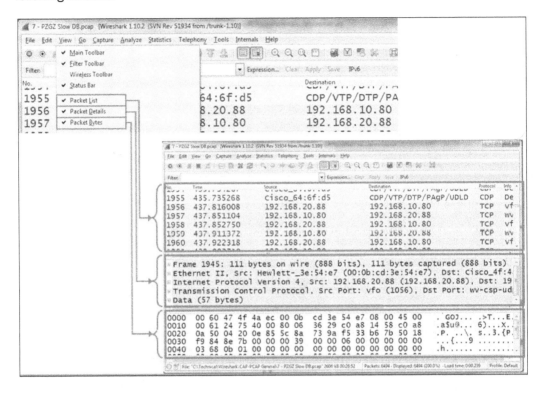

In most of the cases you will not need to change anything here. In some cases, you can cancel the packet bytes when you don't need to see them, and you will get more "space" for the packet list and details.

Name Resolution

Name Resolution is the translation of layer 2 (MAC addresses), layer 3 (IP addresses), and layer 4 (Port numbers) into meaningful information.

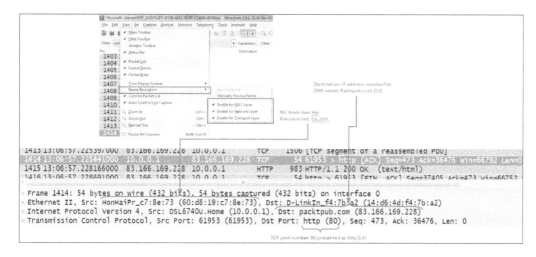

In the preceding screenshot, we see the MAC address **60:d8:19:c7:8e:73** (from **Hon Hai Precision Ind.**, used by Lenovo), the website (that is, `Packtpub.com`), and the HTTP port number (that is 80).

Colorizing the packet list

Usually you start a capture in order to establish a baseline profile of what normal traffic looks like on your network. During the capture, you look at the captured data and you might find a TCP connection, IP or Ethernet connectivity that are suspects, and you want to see them in another color.

To do so, right-click on the packet that belongs to the conversation you want to color, choose Ethernet, IP, or TCP/UDP (the appearance of TCP or UDP will depend on the packet), and choose the color for the conversation.

In the example you see that we want to color a **Transport Layer Security** (**TLS**) conversation.

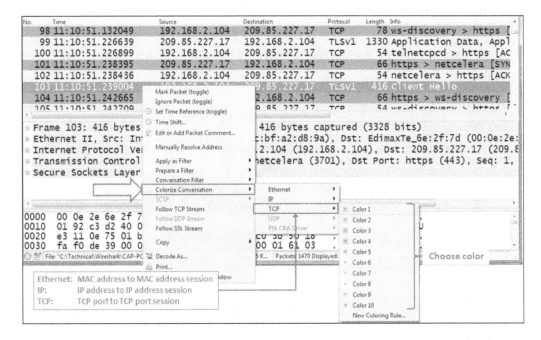

For canceling the coloring rule:

1. Go to the **View** menu.

2. In the lower part of the menu, choose **Reset Coloring 1-10** or simply click on *Ctrl* + Space bar.

Auto scrolling in live capture

To configure Wireshark to auto-scroll the packets as it captures them, do the following:

1. Go to the **View** menu.

2. Mark the **Auto Scroll in Live Capture** item.

3. Zoom

For zooming in and out:

1. Go to the **View** menu.

2. Click on **Zoom In** or press *Ctrl* + + to zoom in.

3. Click on **Zoom Out** or press *Ctrl* + - to zoom out.

Using time values and summaries

Time format configuration is about how the time column (second from the left on default configuration) will be presented. In some scenarios, there is a significant importance given to this; for example, in TCP connections that you want to see time intervals between packets, when you capture data from several sources and you want to see the exact time of every packet, and so on.

Getting ready

To configure the time format, go to the **View** menu, and under **Time Display Format** you will get the following window:

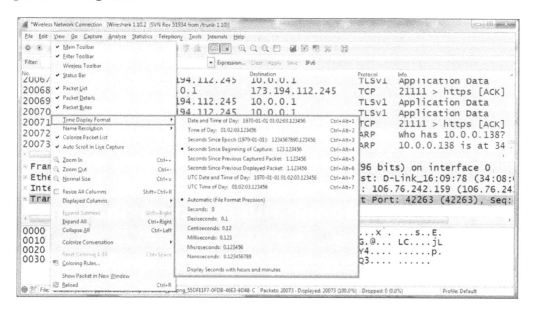

How to do it...

You can chose from the following options:

  ▶ **Date and Time of Day (the first two options)**: This will be good to configure when you troubleshoot a network with time-dependent events, for example, when you know about an event that happens at specific times, and you want to look at what happens on the network at the same time.

- **Seconds Since Epoch**: Time in seconds since January 1, 1970. Epoch is an arbitrary date chosen as a reference time for a system, and January 1, 1970 was chosen for Unix and Unix-like systems.

- **Seconds Since Beginning of Capture**: The default configuration.

- **Seconds Since Previous Captured Packet**: This is also a common feature that enables you to see time differences between packets. This can be useful when monitoring time-sensitive traffic (when time differences between packets is important), such as TCP connections, live video streaming, VoIP calls, and so on.

- **Seconds Since Previous Displayed Packet**: This is a useful feature that can be used when you configure a display filter, and only a selected part of the captured data is presented (for example, a TCP stream). In this case, you will see the time difference between packets that can be important in some applications.

- **UTC Date and Time of Day**: Provides us with relative UTC time.

The lower part of the submenu provides the format of the time display. Change it only if a more accurate measurement is required.

You can also use *Ctrl + Alt +* any numbered digit key on the keyboard for the various options.

How it works...

This is quite simple. Wireshark works on the system clock and presents the time as it is in the system. By default you see the time since the beginning of capture.

Configuring coloring rules and navigation techniques

Coloring rules define how Wireshark will color protocols and events in the captured data. Working with the coloring rules will help you a lot with network troubleshooting, since you are able to see different protocols in different colors, and you can also configure different colors for different events.

Coloring rules enable you to configure new coloring rules according to various filters. It will help you to configure different coloring schemes for different scenarios and save them in different profiles. In this way you can configure coloring rules for resolving TCP issues, rules for resolving Sip and Telephony problems, and so on.

 You can configure Wireshark Profiles in order to save Wireshark configuration; for example, predefined colors, filters, and so on. To do so, navigate to **Configuration Profiles** from the **Edit** menu.

Getting ready

To start with the coloring rules, proceed as follows:

1. Go to the **View** menu.
2. On the lower part of the menu, choose **Coloring Rules**. You will get the following window:

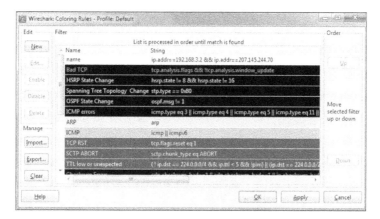

How to do it...

We will now move on to the coloring rules:

Click on the **New** button, and you will get the following window:

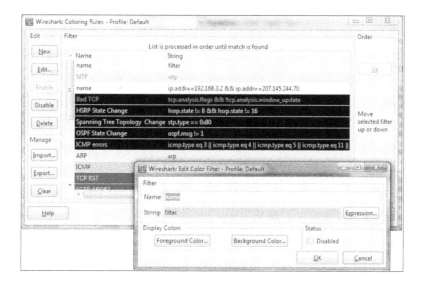

In order to configure a new coloring rule, follow these steps:

1. In the **Name** field, fill in the name of the rule. For example, fill in NTP for the Network Time Protocol.

2. In the **String** field, fill in the filter string, that is, what you want the rule to show (we will talk about display filters in *Chapter 3, Using Display Filters*). You can click on the expression button and get a list of preconfigured filters.

3. Click on the **Foreground Color** button and choose the foreground color for the rule. This will be the foreground color of the packet in the packet list.

4. Click on the **Background Color** button and choose the background color for the rule. This will be the background color of the packet in the packet list.

5. Click on the **Edit** button if you want to edit an existing rule. You can also either click on the **Import** button to import an existing coloring scheme, or click on the **Export** rule for exporting the current scheme.

There is an importance to the order of the coloring rules. Make sure the order that the coloring rules are in is the order of implementation. For example, application layer protocols should come before TCP or UDP, so that Wireshark colors them in their color and not the regular TCP or UDP color.

How it works...

Like many operations in Wireshark, you can configure various operations on the data that is filtered. The coloring rules mechanism simply applies a coloring rule to a predefined filter.

See also

You can find various types of coloring schemes at http://wiki.wireshark.org/ColoringRules, along with many other examples, in a simple Internet search.

Saving, printing, and exporting data

In this recipe we will talk about file operations such as save, export, print, and others.

Getting ready

Start Wireshark or open a saved file.

How to do it...

We can save a whole file, and export specific data in various formats and file types. In the following paragraphs we will see how to do it.

To save a whole file with captured data, perform the following steps:

1. In the **File** menu, click on **Save** (or press *Ctrl + S*) for saving the file with its own name.

2. In the **File** menu, click on **Save as** (or press *Shift + Ctrl + S*) for saving the file with a new name.

For saving a part of a file, for example, only the displayed data:

1. Navigate to **Export Specified Packets** under the **File** menu. You will get the following window:

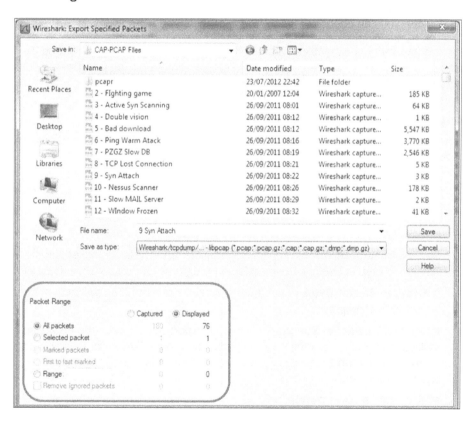

2. At the bottom-left side of the window, you will see that you can choose which part of the data you want to save.

3. For saving all the captured data, select **All packets** and **Captured**.

4. For saving only the displayed data, choose **All packets** and **Displayed**.

5. For saving only selected packets from the file (a selected packet is simply a packet that you clicked on), choose **Selected packet**.

6. For saving marked packets (that is, packets that were marked by right-clicking on it in the packet list window, and choosing the **Marked packet** toggle from the menu), choose **Marked packet**.

7. For saving packets between two marked packets select the **First to last marked** option.

8. For saving a range of packets, select **Range** and specify the range of packets you want to save.

9. In the packet list window, you can manually choose to ignore a packet. In the **Export** window you can choose to ignore these packets and not save them.

In all the options mentioned, you can choose the packets from the entire captured file, or from the packets displayed on the screen (packets displayed on the packet list after a displayed filter has been applied).

Saving data in various formats

You can save the data captured by Wireshark in various formats, for further analysis with other tools.

You can save the file in the following formats:

▶   **Plain text** (`*.txt`): export packet data into a plain text ASCII file.

▶   **PostScript** (`*.ps`): export packet data into PostScript format.

▶   **Comma Separated Values**: Packet Summary (`*.csv`): export packet summary into CSV file format, to use it with spreadsheet programs (such as Microsoft Excel).

▶   **C Arrays to Packet Bytes** (`*.c`): export packet bytes into C-Arrays so that it can be imported by C programs.

▶   **PSML or XML Packet Summary** (`*.psml`): export packet data into PSML, an XML-based format including only the packet summary. Further details about this format can be found at `http://www.nbee.org/doku.php?id=netpdl:psml_specification`.

▶   **PDML - XML Packet Details** (`*.pdml`): export packet data into PDM, an XML-based format including the packet details. Further details about this format can be found at `http://www.nbee.org/doku.php?id=netpdl:pdml_specification`.

To save the file, select **Export Packet Dissections** from the **File** menu, and you will get the following window:

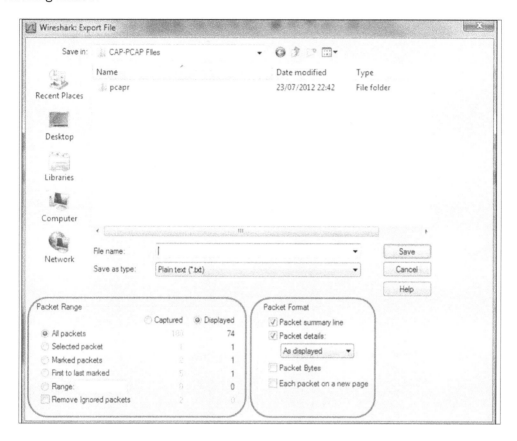

In the preceding screenshot, in the marked box on the left-hand side, you choose the packets you want to save. The process is the same as in the previous recipe. In the marked box on the right-hand side, you choose the format of the file to be saved.

How to print data

In order to print data, click on the **Print** button from the **File** menu, and you will get the following window:

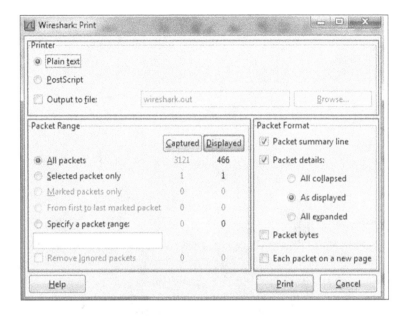

In the Wireshark **Print** window, you have the following choices:

▶   In the upper window, you choose the file format to be printed

▶   In the lower-left window, you choose the packet to print (like in the Export window)

▶   In the lower-right window, you choose the format of the printed data, and the data panes to print from the Wireshark window:

    ❑   The **Packet Summary** pane

    ❑   The **Packet Details** pane

    ❑   The **Packet Byte** pane

How it works...

The data can be printed in a text format, postscript (for postscript-aware printers), or to a file. After configuring this window and clicking on print, the regular printing window will appear and you can choose the printer.

Configuring the user interface in the Preferences menu

There are a large number of parameters you can change in the **Preferences** window, including what data is presented, where files are saved by default, what is the default interface that Wireshark captures data from, and many more.

What we will refer to in this chapter are the common parameters that when changed will help us with various capture scenarios.

Getting ready

For configuring **User Interface**, we will choose the **Preferences** option from the **Edit** menu. You will get the following window:

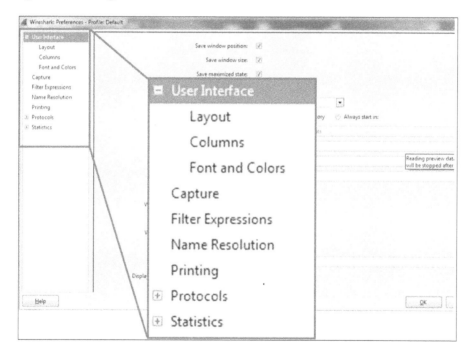

We will look at the configuration of the following parameters:

- ▸ **Columns**
- ▸ **Capture**
- ▸ **Name Resolution**

How to do it...

In this section we will see how to change parameters that will help in working with Wireshark.

Changing and adding columns

The default columns that we see in the packet pane are the number, time, source and destination addresses, protocol, length, and information columns, as shown in the following screenshot:

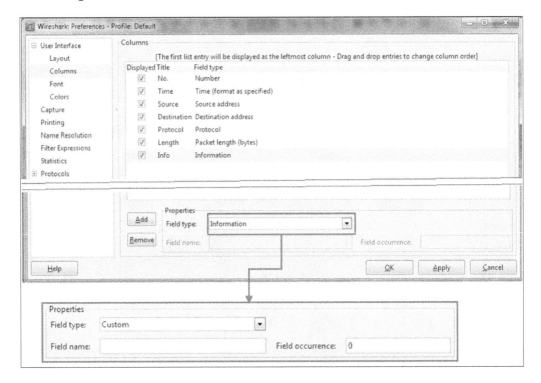

To add a new column to the packet pane:

1. You can choose one of the predefined parameters to be added as a new column from the **Field type**. Among these parameters are time delta, IP DSCP value, port numbers, and others.

2. A very important feature comes up when you fill in **Custom** in the field type. In this case, you can fill in any filter string for **Field name**. You can, for example, add the following:

    1. Add the string `tcp.window_size` to view the TCP window size (that influences performance).

    2. Add the string `ip.ttl` to view the IP **TTL (Time-To-Live)** parameter of every packet.

    3. Add `rtp.marker` to view every instance of a marker set in an RTP packet.

    4. As we will see in the later chapters, this feature will assist us a lot for fast resolutions of network problems.

Changing the capture configuration

There are some parameters that can be configured before capturing data. In the **Preferences** window choose the **Capture** menu, and the following window will come up:

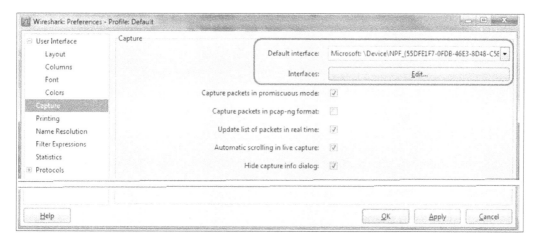

For changing the default interface that the capture will start from, just click on the **Edit** button, and mark the interface you would like to be the default. Of course you can change it every time you start a new capture, this is only the default.

Configuring the name resolution

Wireshark supports **Name Resolution** in three layers:

- **Layer 2**: by resolving the first part of the MAC addresses to the vendor name. For example, **14:da:e9** will be presented as AsusTeckC (ASUSTeK Computer Inc.).
- **Layer 3**: by resolving IP addresses to the DNS names. For example, **157.166.226.46** will be resolved to www.edition.cnn.com.
- **Layer 4**: by resolving TCP/UDP port numbers to port names. For example, port 80 will be resolved as HTTP, and port 53 as DNS.

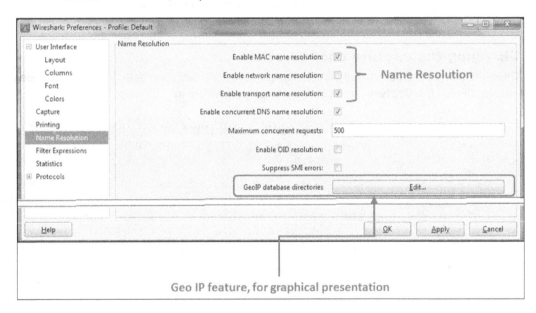

Geo IP feature, for graphical presentation

 In TCP and UDP, there is a meaning only to the destination port that the client initially opens the session to. The source port that the connection is opened from is a random number (higher than 1024), and therefore there is no meaning to its translation to a port name.

The Wireshark default is to resolve layer-2 MAC addresses and layer-4 TCP/UDP port numbers. Resolving IP addresses can slow down Wireshark due to a large amount of DNS queries that it uses; therefore, use it carefully.

How it works...

Very simple. This is the configuration menu for the Wireshark. Here you can configure parameters as described in this recipe, along with some other parameters. You can refer to Wireshark manuals at `www.wireshark.org` for further information.

Configuring protocol preferences

Configuring protocol preferences provides us with capabilities to change the way that Wireshark captures and presents common protocols. In this recipe we will learn how to configure the most common protocols.

Getting ready

1. Go to **Preferences** under the **Edit** menu, and you will see the following window:

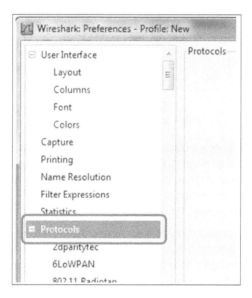

2. Click on the **+** sign on the left side of the protocols, and a protocol list will be opened. Under the protocol list you will find the common and lesser-common protocols. In this part we will talk about the common configurations, and we'll get into protocol details in the protocols chapters that is, *Chapter 7, Ethernet, LAN Switching, and Wireless LAN*, to *Chapter 14, Understanding Network Security*.

How to do it...

In this recipe, we will talk about the following basic protocols (basic means that they are used everywhere, not that they are simple):

▶ IPv4 and IPv6

▶ TCP and UDP

Configuring of IPv4 and IPv6 Preferences

When you choose to configure the IPv4 or IPv6 parameters, you will get the following window:

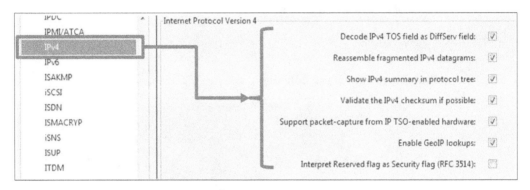

The parameters that you may change are:

▶ **Decode IPv4 ToS field as DiffServ Field**: the original IP protocol came out with a field called **Type Of Service (ToS)**, for enabling the IP quality of service through the network. In the early 90s the **Differentiated Services (DiffServ)** standard changed the way that an IP device looked on this field. Unchecking this checkbox will show this field as in the original IP standard.

▶ **Enable GeoIP lookups**: GeoIP is a database that enables Wireshark to present IP addresses as geographical locations. Enabling this feature in IPv4 and IPv6 will enable this presentation. This feature involves name resolutions and can therefore slow down packet capture in real time.

Configuring TCP and UDP

In UDP, there is not much to change. A very simple protocol, with a very simple configuration. In TCP on the other hand, there are some parameters that can be changed.

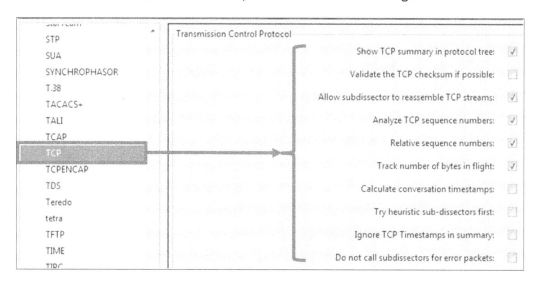

Most of the changes you can do in the TCP preferences are in the way that Wireshark dissects the captured data.

- ▶ **Validate the TCP checksum if possible**: in some NICs, you may see many "checksum errors". This is due to the fact that TCP Checksum offloading is often being implemented on some NICs. The problem here might be that the NIC actually adds the checksum AFTER Wireshark captures the packet, so if you see many TCP checksum errors, the first thing to do will be to disable this checkbox and verify that this is not the problem.

- ▶ **Analyze TCP Sequence numbers**: this checkbox must be checked for Wireshark to provide TCP analysis, which is one of its main and most important features.

- ▶ **Relative Sequence Numbers**: when TCP opens a connection, it starts from a random sequence number. When this checkbox is checked, the Wireshark will normalize it to "0", so what you will see are not the real numbers, but numbers starting from "0" and increasing. In most of the cases the relative numbers are much easier to handle.

- ▶ **Calculate conversations timestamps**: When checking this checkbox, the TCP dissector will show you the time since the beginning of the connection in every packet. This can be helpful in cases of very fast connection when times are critical.

How it works...

Using the **Protocols** feature from the **Preferences** menu adds more analysis capabilities to the Wireshark software. Just be careful here to not add too many capabilities that will slow down the packet capture and analysis.

There's more...

You can get more information on GeoIP at `http://wiki.wireshark.org/HowToUseGeoIP`.

2

Using Capture Filters

In this chapter, we will cover the following topics:

- ► Configuring capture filters
- ► Configuring Ethernet filters
- ► Configuring hosts and networks filters
- ► Configuring TCP/UDP and port filters
- ► Configuring compound filters
- ► Configuring byte-offset and payload matching filters

Introduction

In the first chapter we talked about how to install Wireshark, how to configure it for basic operations, and where to locate it in the network. In this chapter and the next one we will talk about capture filters (*Chapter 2, Using Capture Filters*) and display filters (*Chapter 3, Using Display Filters*).

It is important to distinguish between these two types of filters:

- ► Capture filters are configured before we start to capture data, so only data that is approved with the filters will be captured. All other data will be lost. These filters are described in this chapter.
- ► Display filters are filters that filter data after it has been captured. In this case, all data is captured, and you configure what data you wish to display. These filters are described in *Chapter 3, Using Display Filters*.

Capture filters are based on the `tcpdump` syntax presented in the `libpcap/WinPcap` library, while the display filters syntax was presented some years later. Therefore, keep in mind that the display and capture filters have different syntaxes!

In some cases, you need to configure Wireshark to capture only a part of the data that it sees over the interface, for example, cases such as:

▶ When there is a large amount of data running over the monitored link, and you want to capture only the data you care about

▶ When you want to capture data only going in and out of a specific server on a VLAN that you monitor

▶ When you want to capture data only of a specific application or applications (for example, you suspect that there is a DNS problem in the network, and you want to analyze only DNS queries and responses that go to and from the Internet)

There are many other cases in which you want to capture only specific data and not all that runs on your network. When using the capture filters, only predefined data will be captured, and all other packets will be ignored, so you will get only the desired data.

 Be careful when using capture filters. In many cases in networking, there are dependencies between different applications and servers that you are not always aware of; so, when you use Wireshark with capture filters for troubleshooting a network, make sure that you don't filter out some of the connections that will cause some problems to disappear. A common and simple example of this is to filter only traffic on TCP port 80 for monitoring suspected slow HTTP responses, while the problem could be due to a slow or non-responsive DNS server that you will not see.

In this chapter we will describe how to configure simple, structured, byte offset, and payload matching capture filters.

Configuring capture filters

We recommend that before configuring a capture filter, you will carefully design what you want to capture, and prepare your filter for this. Don't forget—what doesn't pass the filter, will be lost.

There are some Wireshark predefined filters that you can use, or you can configure it yourself as described in the next recipe.

Getting ready

For configuring capture filters, open Wireshark, and follow the steps in the recipe.

How to do it...

For configuring capture filters before starting with the capture, go through the following steps:

1. For configuring a capture filter, click on the **Show the capture options...** button, second from the left, as shown in the following screenshot:

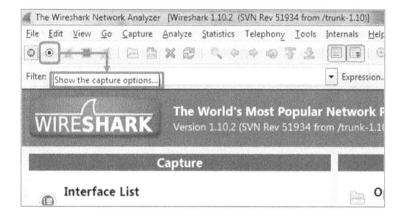

2. The **Wireshark: Capture Options** window will open as you see in the following screenshot:

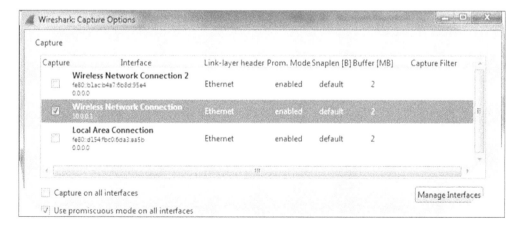

3. Double-click on the interface on which you want to configure the capture filter (you can verify which interface is the active one, as described in *Chapter 1, Introducing Wireshark*).

4. The **Edit Interface Settings** window will open up, as in the following screenshot:

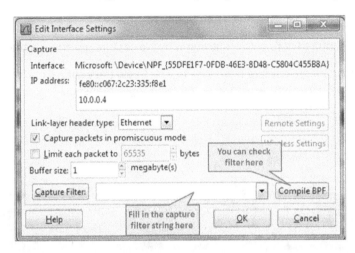

5. Now, we can configure the capture filters by simply writing the filter string in the **Wireshark: Capture Filter** window, or click on the **Capture Filter:** button; the following window will open:

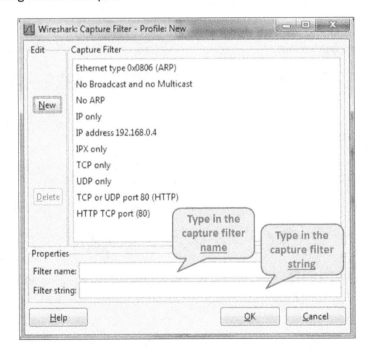

How it works...

The **Wireshark: Capture Filter** window enables you to configure filters according to **Berkeley Packet Filter** (**BPF**). After writing a filter string, you can click on the **Compile BPF** button, and the BPF compiler will check your syntax, and if it's wrong you will get an error message.

In addition to this, when you type a filter string in the capture filter text box, and the filter string is correct, it will become green, and if not, it will become red.

The BPF filter only checks if the syntax is right. It does not check if the condition is correct. For example, if you type the string `host` without any parameter, you will get an error and the string will become red, but if you type `host 192.168.1.1000`, it will pass and the window will become green.

> BPF is a syntax coming from the paper *The BSD Packet Filter: A New Architecture for User-level Packet Capture* by *Steven McCanne* and *Van Jacobson* from the Lawrence Berkeley Laboratory at Berkeley University from December 1992. The document can be seen at: `http://www.tcpdump.org/papers/bpf-usenix93.pdf`.

Capture filters are made out of a string containing a filtering expression. This expression selects the packets which will be captured and which packets will be ignored. Filter expressions consist of one or more primitives. Primitives usually consist of an identifier (name or number) followed by one or more qualifiers. There are three different kinds of qualifiers:

- **Type**: These qualifiers say what kind of thing the identifier name or number refers to. Possible types are `host` for host name or address, `net` for network, `port` for TCP/UDP port, and so on.
- **Dir (direction)**: These qualifiers specify a particular transfer direction to and/or from ID. For example `src` indicates source, `dst` indicates destination, and so on.
- **Proto (protocol)**: These are the qualifiers that restrict the match to a particular protocol. For example, `ether` for Ethernet, `ip` for Internet Protocol, `arp` for Address Resolution Protocol, and so on.

Identifiers are the actual condition that we test. Identifier can be the address 10.0.0.1, port number 53, or network address 192.168.1 (this is an identifier for network 192.168.1.0/24).

For example, in the filter `tcp dst port 135`, we have:

- `dst` is the dir qualifier
- `port` is the type qualifier
- `tcp` is the Proto qualifier

There's more...

You can configure different capture filters on different interfaces:

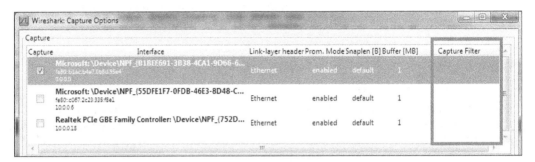

This can be used when you capture traffic on two interfaces of a device, and want to check for different packets on the two sides.

The capture filters are stored in a file named `cfilters` under the Wireshark directory. In this file you will find the predefined filters, along with the filters you have configured, and you will be able to copy the file to other computers. The location of this directory will change depending on how Wireshark is installed and on what platform.

See also

1. The Wireshark Capture Filters are based on the `tcpdump` program. You can find the reference at `http://www.tcpdump.org/tcpdump_man.html`.

2. You can also find helpful information on the Wireshark manual pages at `http://wiki.wireshark.org/CaptureFilters`.

Configuring Ethernet filters

When talking about Ethernet filters, we refer to Layer-2 filters that are MAC address-based filters. In this recipe we will refer to these filters and what we can do with them.

Getting ready

The basic Layer 2 filters are:

▶ `ether host <Ethernet host>`: To get the Ethernet address

▶ `ether dst <Ethernet host>`: To get the Ethernet destination address

▶ `ether src <Ethernet host>`: To get the Ethernet source address

- ▶ `ether broadcast`: To capture all Ethernet broadcast packets
- ▶ `ether multicast`: To capture all Ethernet multicast packets
- ▶ `ether proto <protocol>`: To filter only the protocol type indicated in the protocol identifier
- ▶ `vlan <vlan_id>`: To pass only packets from a specific VLAN that is indicated in the identifier field

For negating a filter rule, simply type the word `not` or `!` in front of the primitive. For example:

`Not ether host <Ethernet host>` or `! Ether host <Ethernet host>` will capture packets that are not from/to the Ethernet address specified in the identifier field.

How to do it...

Let's look at the following diagram, in which we have a server, PCs, and a router, connected to a LAN switch. Wireshark is running on the laptop connected to the LAN switch, with port mirror to the entire switch (to VLAN1).

The `/24` notation in the drawing refers to a subnet mask of 24 bits, that is, 11111111.11111 111.11111111.00000000 in binary or 255.255.255.0 in decimal.

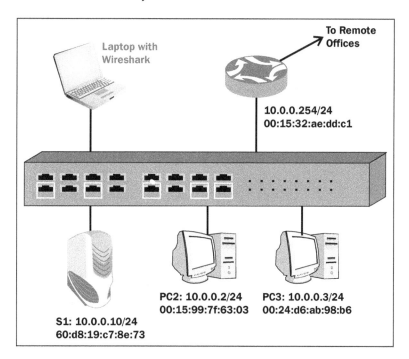

Follow the instructions in the *Configuring capture filters* recipe, and configure filters as follows:

1. To capture packets only from/to a specific MAC address, for example of PC3 in the preceding image, configure `ether host 00:24:d6:ab:98:b6`.

2. To capture packets going to a destination MAC address, for example of PC3 in the preceding image, configure `ether dst 00:24:d6:ab:98:b6`.

3. To capture packets coming from a source MAC address, for example of PC3 in the preceding image, configure `ether src 00:24:d6:ab:98:b6`.

4. To capture broadcast packets, configure `ether broadcast` or `ether dst ff:ff:ff:ff:ff:ff`.

5. To capture multicast packets, configure `ether multicast`.

6. To capture a specific Ether Type (number in Hexadecimal value), configure `ether proto 0800`.

How it works...

The way capture filters work with source host and destination host is simple—the capture engine simply compares the condition with the actual MAC addresses, and passes only what is relevant.

A broadcast address is an address in which the destination address is all 1's, that is, `ff:ff:ff:ff:ff:ff`, therefore when you configure a broadcast filter, only these addresses will pass the filter. Broadcast addresses can be:

▶ L3 IPv4 broadcast that is converted to L2 broadcast; for example, IP packet to 10.0.0.255 (class C subnet, as in the previous illustration), which will be converted to L2 broadcast in the destination MAC field.

▶ A network-related broadcast; for example, IPv4 ARP (Address Resolution Protocol) that sends a broadcast as a part of network operation.

> Network-related broadcasts are broadcasts that are sent for the regular operation of the network. Among these are ARPs, routing updates, discovery protocols, and so on.

In a multicast filter, there are IPv4 and IPv6 multicasts:

▶ In IPv4, a multicast MAC address is transmitted when the MAC address starts with the string `01:00:5e`. Every packet with a MAC address that starts with this string will be considered a multicast.

▶ In IPv6, a multicast address is transmitted when the MAC address starts with the string `33:33`. Every packet with a MAC address that starts with this string will be considered a multicast.

Ethernet protocol refers to the ETHER-TYPE field in the Ethernet packet that indicates what will be the upper Layer protocol. Common values here are `0800` for IPv4, `86dd` for IPv6, and `0806` for ARP.

There's more...

- To configure filter for a specific VLAN, use `vlan <vlan number>`
- To configure filter on several VLANs, use `vlan <vlan number>` and `vlan <vlan number>` and `vlan <vlan number>`...

See also

There are around a hundred ETHER-TYPE codes, most of them not in use. You can refer to `http://www.mit.edu/~map/Ethernet/Ethernet.txt` for additional codes, or simply browse the Internet for Ethernet code.

Configuring host and network filters

When talking about host and network filters, we refer to Layer 3 filters that are IP address-based filters. In this recipe we will refer to these filters and what we can do with them.

Getting ready

The basic Layer 3 filters are:

- `ip` or `ip6`: To capture IP or IPv6 packets.
- `host <host>`: To get host name or address.
- `dst host <host>`: To get destination host name or address.
- `src host <host>`: To get source host name or address.

> Host can be an IP address or a host name related with this number. You can type, for example, a filter host `www.packtpub.com` that will show you all packets to/from the IP address related to the Packt website.

- `gateway <Host name or address>`: It captures traffic to or from the hardware address but not to the IP address of the host. This filter captures traffic going through the specified router. This filter requires a host name that is used and can be found by the local system's name resolution process (for example, DNS).

▶ `net <net>`: All packets to or from the specified IPv4/IPv6 network.

▶ `dst net <net>`: All packets to the specified IPv4/IPv6 destination network.

▶ `src net <net>`: All packets to the specified IPv4/IPv6 destination network.

▶ `net <net> mask <netmask>`: All packets to/from the specific network and mask. This syntax is not valid for the IPv6 network.

▶ `dst net <net> mask <netmask>`: All packets to/from the specific network and mask. This syntax is not valid for the IPv6 network.

▶ `src net <net> mask <netmask>`: All packets to/from the specific network and mask. This syntax is not valid for the IPv6 network.

▶ `net <net>/<len>`: All packets to/from the `<net>` network with `<len>` length in bits.

▶ `dst net <net>/<len>`: All packets to/from the `<net>` network with `<len>` length in bits.

▶ `dst net <net>/<len>`: All packets to/from the `<net>` network with `<len>` length in bits.

▶ `broadcast`: All broadcast packets.

▶ `multicast`: All multicast packets.

▶ `ip proto <protocol code>`: It captures packets while the IP protocol field equals to the `<protocol>` identifier. There can be various protocols, such as, TCP (Code 6), UDP (Code 17), ICMP (Code 1), and so on.

▶ `ip6 proto <protocol>`: It captures IPv6 packets with protocol as indicated in the type field. Note that this primitive does not follow the IPv6 extension headers chain.

 In IPv6 header, there is a field in the header that can point to an optional extension header, which points to the next extension header, and so on. In the current version, Wireshark capture filter does not follow this structure.

▶ `icmp[icmptype]==<identifier>`: It captures ICMP packets, while the identifier is ICMP codes, such as `icmp-echo` and `icmp-request`.

How to do it...

Follow the instructions mentioned in the *Configure capture filters* recipe, and configure filters as follows:

1. For capturing packets to/from host `10.10.10.1`, configure `host 10.10.10.1`.

2. For capturing packets to/from host at `www.cnn.com`, configure `host www.cnn.com`.

3. For capturing packets to host `10.10.10.1`, configure `dst host 10.10.10.1`.

4. For capturing packets from host `10.10.10.1`, configure `src host 10.10.10.1`.

5. For capturing packets to/from network `192.168.1.0/24`, configure `net 192.168.1` or `net 192.168.1.0 mask 255.255.255.0` or `net 192.168.1.0/24`.

6. For capturing all data without broadcasts or without multicasts, configure `not broadcast` or `not multicast`.

7. For capturing packets to/from the IPv6 network 2001::/16, configure `net 2001::/16`.

8. For capturing packets to IPv6 host 2001::1, configure `host 2001::1`.

9. For capturing only ICMP packets, configure `ip proto 1`.

10. For filtering only ICMP Echo's pings, you can use ICMP messages or message codes. configure `icmp[icmptype]==icmp-echo` or `icmp[icmptype]==8`.

How it works...

For host filtering, when you type a host name, Wireshark will translate the name to an IP address, and capture packets that refer to this address. For example, if you configure a filter host `www.cnn.com`, it will be translated by a name resolution service (mostly DNS) to an IP address, and will show you all packets going to and from this address. Note that in this case, if CNN website will forward you to other websites on other addresses, only packets to the first address will be captured.

There's more...

Some more useful filters:

- `ip multicast`: IP multicast packets
- `ip broadcast`: IP broadcast packets
- `ip[2:2] == <number>`: IP packet size
- `ip[8] == <number>`: TTL (Time To Live) value
- `ip[9] == <number>`: Protocol value
- `(ip[12:4] = ip[16:4])`: IP source equal to IP destination address
- `ip[2:2]==<number>`: Total length or IP packet
- `ip[9] == <number>`: Protocol identifier

These filters are further explained in the *Configuring byte offset and payload matching filters* recipe at the end of this chapter. The principle, as illustrated in the following diagram, is that the first number in the brackets defines how many bytes are from the beginning of the protocol header, and the second number indicates how many bytes to watch.

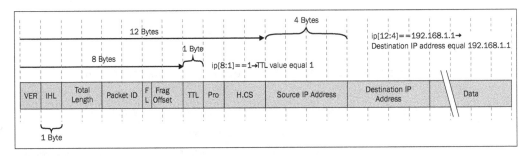

See also

For more filters, refer to the tcpdump manual pages at `http://www.tcpdump.org/ tcpdump_man.html`.

Configuring TCP/UDP and port filters

In this recipe we will present Layer 4 TCP/UDP port filters and how we can use them with capture filters.

Getting ready

The basic Layer 4 filters are:

▸ `port <port>`: When the packet is a Layer 4 protocol, such as TCP or UDP, this filter will capture packets to/from the port indicated in the identifier field

▸ `dst port <port>`: When the packet is a Layer 4 protocol, such as TCP or UDP, this filter will capture packets to the destination port indicated in the identifier field

▸ `src port <port>`: When the packet is a Layer 4 protocol, such as TCP or UDP, this filter will capture packets to the source port indicated in the identifier field

The port-range matching filters are:

- ▸ `tcp portrange <p1>-<p2>` or `udp portrange <p1>-<p2>`: TCP or UDP packets in the port range of p1 to p2

- ▸ `tcp src portrange <p1>-<p2>` or `udp src portrange <p1>-<p2>`: TCP or UDP packets in the source port range of p1 to p2

- ▸ `tcp dst portrange <p1>-<p2>` or `udp src portrange <p1>-<p2>`: TCP or UDP packets in the destination port range of p1 to p2

How to do it...

Follow the instructions in the *Configuring capture filters* recipe, and configure filters as follows:

1. To capture packets to port 80 (HTTP), configure `dst port 80` or `dst port http`.

2. To capture packets to or from port 5060 (SIP), configure `port 5060`.

3. To capture packets to or from port 5060 (SIP), configure `port 5060`.

4. To capture the start (SYN flag) and end (FIN flag) packets of all TCP connections, configure `tcp[tcpflags] & (tcp-syn|tcp-fin) != 0`.

 In `tcp[tcpflags] & (tcp-syn|tcp-fin) != 0`, it is important to note that this is a bitwise and operation, not a logical and operation. For example, 010 or 101 equals 111, and not 000.

5. To capture all TCP packets with RST (Reset) flag set to 1, configure `tcp[tcpflags] & (tcp-rst) != 0`.

6. Length filters are configured in the following way:

   - ❏ `less <length>`: It captures only packets with length less than or equal to length identifier. This is equivalent to `len <= <length>`.

   - ❏ `greater <length>`: It captures only packets with length greater than or equal to length identifier. This is equivalent to `<len >= length>`.

   For example,

   - ❏ `tcp portrange 2000-2500`
   - ❏ `udp portrange 5000-6000`

Port range filters can be used for protocols that work in a range of ports rather than specific ones.

How it works...

Layer 4 protocols, mostly TCP and UDP, are the protocols that connect between end applications. The end node on one side (for example, a web client) sends a message to the other side (for example, a web server), requesting to connect to it. The codes of the processes that send the request and the processes that receive the request are called port numbers. Further discussion on this issue is provided in *Chapter 9, UDP/TCP Analysis*.

Both in TCP and UDP, the port numbers indicate the application codes. The difference between them is that TCP is a connection-oriented, reliable protocol, while UDP is a connectionless unreliable protocol. There is an additional Layer 4 protocol called **Stream Control Transport Protocol** (**SCTP**) that you can refer to as an advanced version of TCP, which also uses port numbers.

TCP flags are sent in packets in order to establish, maintain, and close connections. A signal is set when a specific bit in the packet is set to 1. The most common flags that are in use are:

- **SYN**: A signal sent in order to open a connection
- **FIN**: A signal sent in order to close a connection
- **ACK**: A signal sent to acknowledge received data
- **RST**: A signal sent for immediate close of a connection
- **PSH**: A signal sent for pushing data for processing by the end process (application)

Using capture filters you can filter packets to/from specific applications, along with filtering packets with specific flags turned on.

There's more...

Some problematic scenarios (mostly attacks...) are:

- `tcp[13] & 0x00 = 0`: No flags set (null scan)
- `tcp[13] & 0x01 = 1`: **FIN** set and **ACK** not set
- `tcp[13] & 0x03 = 3`: **SYN** set and **FIN** set
- `tcp[13] & 0x05 = 5`: **RST** set and **FIN** set
- `tcp[13] & 0x06 = 6`: **SYN** set and **RST** set
- `tcp[13] & 0x08 = 8`: **PSH** set and **ACK** not set

In the following diagram you can see how it works. `tcp[13]` is the number of bytes from the beginning of the protocol header, when the values `0,1,3,5,6,` and `8` refer to the flag locations.

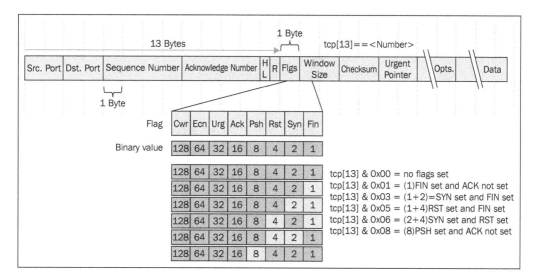

See also

A deeper description of UDP and TCP is provided in *Chapter 9, UDP/TCP Analysis*.

Configuring compound filters

Structure filters are simply made for writing filters out of several conditions. It uses simple conditions, such as `not`, `and`, and `or` for creating structured conditions.

Getting ready

Structured filters are written in the following format:

    [not] primitive [and|or [not] primitive ...]

The following modifiers are commonly used in the Wireshark capture filters:

- ▸   `!` or `not`
- ▸   `&&` or `and`
- ▸   `||` or `or`

How to do it...

To configure structured filters, you simply write the conditions according to what we learned in the previous recipes, with conditions to meet your requirements.

Some common filters are:

1. For capturing only unicast packets, configure `not broadcast and not multicast`.

2. For capturing HTTP packets to `www.youtube.com`, configure `host www.youtube.com and port 80`.

3. A capture filter for telnet that captures traffic to and from a particular host, configures `tcp port 23 and host 192.180.1.1`.

4. For capturing all telnet traffic not from `192.168.1.1`, configure `tcp port 23 and not src host 192.168.1.1`.

How it works...

Some examples for structured filters:

For capturing data to tcp port 23 (Telnet) from source port range of 5000-6000, configure `tcp dst port 23 and tcp src portrange 5000-6000`.

There's more...

Some interesting examples are as follows:

▶ `host www.mywebsite.com and not (port 80 or port 23)`

▶ `host 192.168.0.50 and not tcp port 80`

▶ `host 10.0.0.1 and not host 10.0.0.2`

See also

For more examples, you can take a look at:

▶ `http://www.packetlevel.ch/html/tcpdumpf.html`

▶ `http://www.packetlevel.ch/html/txt/tcpdump.filters`

Configuring byte offset and payload matching filters

Byte offset and payload matching filters come to provide us with a flexible tool for configuring self-defined filters (filters for fields that are not defined in the Wireshark dissector and filters for proprietary protocols). By understanding the protocols that we work with and understanding their packet structure, we can configure filters that will watch a specific string in the captured packets, and filter packets according to it. In this recipe we will learn how to configure these types of filters, and we will also see some common and useful examples of the subject.

Getting ready

To configure byte offset and payload matching filters, start Wireshark and follow the instructions in the *Configuring capture filters* recipe in the beginning of this chapter.

How to do it...

1. String matching filters comes to check a specific string in the packet header. It comes in the following format:

   ```
   proto [Offset: bytes]
   ```

   With this filter we can create filters for strings over IP, TCP, and UDP.

2. For IP string-matching filters you can create the following filter:

   ```
   ip [Offset:Bytes]
   ```

3. For matching application data, that is, to look into the application data that is carried by TCP or UDP, the most common uses of it are: `tcp[Offset:Bytes]` Or `udp[Offset:Bytes]`.

How it works...

The general structure of offset filter is:

```
proto [Offset in bytes from the start of the header : Number of bytes
to check]
```

Common examples for string matching filters are:

1. For filtering destination TCP ports between 50 and 100, configure `(tcp[2:2] > 50 and tcp[2:2] < 100)`.

    Here we count two bytes from the beginning of the TCP header, and check the next two bytes to be lower than 100 and higher than 50.

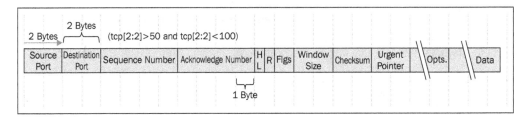

2. For checking TCP window size smaller then 8192, configure `tcp[14:2] < 8192`.

    Here we count two bytes from the beginning of the TCP header, and check the next two bytes (the window size) to be less than 8192.

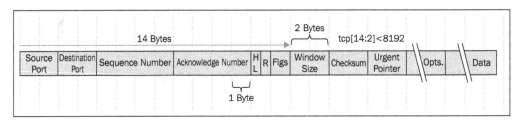

There's a nice string-matching capture filter generator in `http://www.wireshark.org/tools/string-cf.html`

There's more...

You can also see additional filters in the `tcpdump` man pages:

1. To print all IPv4 HTTP packets to and from port 80, (that is to print only packets that contain data, not, for example, SYN, FIN or ACK-only packets), configure the following filter: `tcp port 80 and (((ip[2:2] - ((ip[0]&0xf)<<2)) - ((tcp[12]&0xf0)>>2)) != 0)`.

2. To print the start and end packets (the SYN and FIN packets) of each TCP conversation that involves a non-local host, configure `tcp[tcpflags] & (tcp-syn|tcp-fin) != 0 and not src and dst net <localnet>`.

3. To print IP broadcast or multicast packets that were not sent via Ethernet broadcast or multicast, configure `ether[0] & 1 = 0 and ip[16] >= 224`.

4. To print all ICMP packets that are not echo requests/replies (that is, not ping packets), configure `icmp[icmptype] != icmp-echo and icmp[icmptype] != icmp-echoreply`.

See also

▶ There is a string calculator at `http://www.wireshark.org/tools/string-cf.html`.

  It doesn't always provide working results, but it might be a good place to start from.

▶ Another interesting blog can be found on `http://www.packetlevel.ch/html/txt/byte_offsets.txt`.

3
Using Display Filters

In this chapter you will learn the following:

- ▶ Configuring display filters
- ▶ Configuring Ethernet, ARP, host, and network filters
- ▶ Configuring TCP/UDP filters
- ▶ Configuring specific protocol filters
- ▶ Configuring substring operator filters
- ▶ Configuring macros

Introduction

In this chapter we will learn how to work with display filters. Display filters are filters that we apply after capturing data (filtered by capture filters or not), and when we wish to display only part of the data.

Display filters can be implemented in order to locate various types of data:

- ▶ Parameters such as the IP address, TCP or UDP port numbers, URLs, and server names
- ▶ Conditions such as "packet length shorter than..." and the TCP port range
- ▶ Phenomena such as TCP retransmissions, duplicate and other types of ACKs, various protocol error codes, and flag existence
- ▶ Various applications parameters such as Short Message Service (SMS) source and destination numbers and Server Message Block (SMB) server names

Any data that is sent over the network can be filtered, and when filtered, you can create statistics and graphs according to it.

As we will describe in the recipes in this chapter, there are various ways to configure display filters: from predefined menus, from the packet pane, or by writing the syntax directly.

 While using display filters, don't forget that all the data was already captured and the display filters only decide what to display. Therefore, after filtering data, the capture file still contains the original data that was captured. You may later save the complete data or only the displayed data.

Configuring display filters

In order to configure display filters, you can choose one of the several options:

- ▸ Choosing from the filters menus
- ▸ Writing the syntax directly into the display filter window (while working with Wireshark; after a while this will become your favorite)
- ▸ Choosing a parameter in the packet pane and defining it as a filter
- ▸ Using `tshark` or `wireshark` with command line ; this will be discussed in *Appendix*

This chapter discusses the first three options.

Getting ready

In general, a display filter string takes the form of a series of primitive expressions connected by conjunctions (and, or, or something else) and optionally preceded by `not`:

`[not] Expression [and|or] [not] Expression...`

While `Expression` can be any filter expression, such as `ip.src==192.168.1.1` for the source address, `tcp.flags.syn==1` for TCP SYN flag presence, and `tcp.analysis. retransmission` for TCP retransmissions, `and|or` are conjunctions that can be used in any combinations of expression, including brackets, multiple brackets, and any lengths of strings.

There are several conditions to these. They can be one of the following:

C-like Syntax	Shortcut	Description	Example
`==`	**eq**	Equal	`ip.addr == 192.168.1.1` or `ip.addr eq 192.168.1.1`
`!=`	**ne**	Not equal	`!ip.addr==192.168.1.1`, `ip.addr != 192.168.1.1`, or `ip.addr ne 192.168.1.1`

C-like Syntax	Shortcut	Description	Example
>	**gt**	Greater than	`frame.len > 64`
<	**lt**	Less than	`frame.len < 1500`
>=	**ge**	Greater than or equal to	`frame.len >= 64`
<=	**le**	Less than or equal to	`frame.len <= 1500`
	is present	A parameter is present	`http.response`
	contains	Contains a string	`http.host contains cisco`
	matches	A string matches the condition	`http.host matches www.cisco.com`

You can insert a space character between parameters and operators or leave it without spaces.

Wireshark colorizes the display filter area in yellow whenever you use the `!=` operator for combined expressions such as `eth.addr`, `ip.addr`, `tcp.port`, and `udp.port`, but this will not work due to the following reason.

When you type a filter expression such as `ip.addr != 192.168.1.100`, you will see **The packet contains the field ip.addr with a value different from 192.168.1.100**. Because an IP datagram contains both a source and a destination address, the expression will evaluate to `true` whenever at least one of the two addresses differs from 192.168.1.100. For this reason you should write `!(ip.addr == 192.168.1.100)`; this will display **Show me all the packets for which it is not true that a field ip.addr have the value of 1.2.3.4**.

There are several operators. They can be as follows:

C-like Syntax	Shortcut	Description	Example
&&	and	Logical AND	`ip.src==10.0.0.1 and tcp.flags.syn==1`
			All SYN flags sent from IP address 10.0.0.1 practically and all connections opened (or tried to be opened) from 10.0.0.1.
||	or	Logical OR	`ip.addr==10.0.0.1 or ip.addr==10.0.02`
			All the packets going in or out the two IP addresses.
!	not	Logical NOT	`not arp and not icmp`
			All the packets that are neither ARP nor ICMP.

How to do it...

To configure display filters, you can choose any one of the methods mentioned earlier.

Choosing from the filters menu

For choosing from the filters menu, navigate to the display filter pane on the upper side of the window and click on the **Expression...** button as you see in the following screenshot:

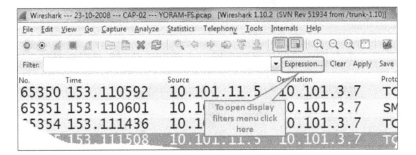

When you click on the **Expression...** button, the following window will open:

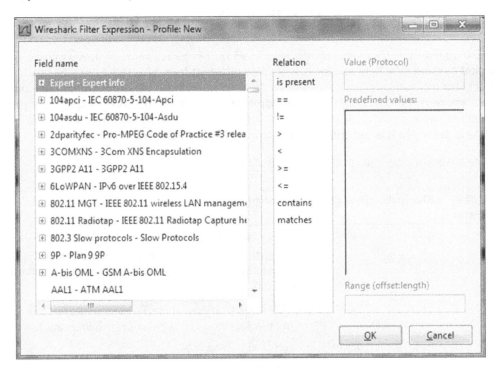

There are five important panes in the filters menu:

- ▶ **Field name**: In this pane you configure the filter parameter. You can go to the protocol by typing its name, and get to the protocol parameter by clicking on the **+** sign to the left of the list.

  One example for this would be: type `ipv4` to get to the **IPv4** protocol, click on the **+** sign to expand the protocol parameters (or press *Enter* twice) and choose **ip.addr** to filter a specific IP address.

  Another example would be to type `tcp` to get to the **TCP** protocol, click on the **+** sign to the left of the protocol parameter and choose **tcp.port** for the source or destination port number.

- ▶ **Relation**: This is the pane from where you choose the operator. You can choose `==` for equal, `!=` for not equal, and so on.

  An example for this would be: type `sip` to get to the **SIP** protocol, choose **sip.Method**, and choose **==** from the **Relation** pane. Type `invite` in the **Value (Protocol)** pane. This will filter all the SIP INVITE methods.

- ▶ **Value**: Here you enter the value of the field that you have chosen before.

  An example for this would be: type `tcp` to get to the **TCP** protocol, click on the **+** sign to go to the protocol parameter, choose **tcp.flags.syn** for the TCP SYN flag, and enter `1` in the **Value** field.

- ▶ **Predefined values**: When the value of the field you chose is not Boolean, there might be a list of options in this field.

  An example for this would be: under **TCP**, there is an option named **tcp.option_kind**. This option is related to **TCP** options (for more details, refer to *Chapter 9, UDP/TCP Analysis*). You will get a list of values that are possible.

- ▶ **Range (offset: length)**: This field provides you the length of the string in the `offset:length` format.

Writing the syntax directly into the display filter window

After you get used to the display filters syntax, you may find it easier to type the filter string directly into the filter window:

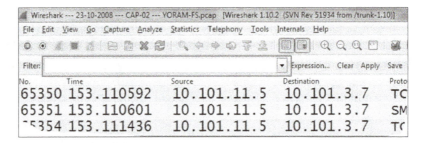

In this case, when you write a filter string into the window, the window will light up in one of the following three colors:

- **Green**: This is when the filter is correct and you can apply it.

- **Red**: This indicates a wrong string. Fix the string before you apply it.

- **Yellow**: Whenever you use the ! = operator, the display filter area will turn yellow. It doesn't mean your filter will not work, it is just a warning that it *may not* work.

Choosing a parameter in the packet pane and defining it as a filter

This is a very convenient option. You can choose any field from the packet detail pane in the captured file; right-click on it and you will get a few options, as illustrated in the following screenshot:

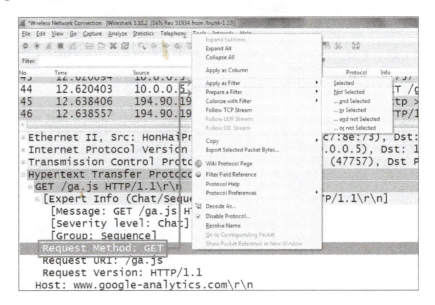

A couple of options are as follows:

- ▶ **Apply as Filter**: This will set a filter according to the field you choose and apply it to the captured data.

- ▶ **Prepare a Filter**: This will prepare a filter but not apply it. It will be applied when you click on the **Apply** button on the right-hand side of the filter window.

In both the options, you can choose to configure a filter:

- ▶ **Selected**: This will choose the selected field and parameter

- ▶ **Not Selected**: This will choose the the field and parameter that are not selected

For example, right-clicking on the field `http.request.method` and choosing **Selected** will come with the filter string `http.request.method == GET`; while, choosing **Not Selected** will come with the string `!(http.request.method == "GET")`.

You can also choose the options **... and selected, ... or selected, ... and not selected**, or **... or not selected** for structured filters.

How it works...

The display filter is a proprietary Wireshark language. There are many places where display filters can be used that will be discussed in the later chapters. Additional filters will be introduced in the upcoming recipes of this chapter.

You can always use the autocomplete feature to complete filter strings. For example, if you type in `tcp.f`, as shown in the following screenshot, the autocomplete feature lists possible display filter values that can be created beginning with `tcp.f`, that is, TCP flags (SYN, FIN, RST, and so on).

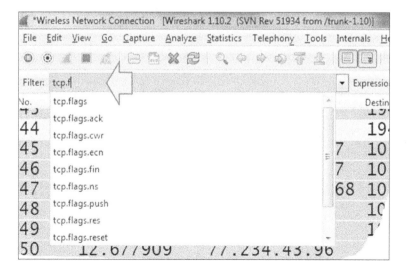

There's more...

Now we will cover some additional helpful features.

What is the parameter we filter?

Anytime you mark a specific field in the packet details pane, you will see the correlating filter string in the status bar at the bottom-left corner of the Wireshark window.

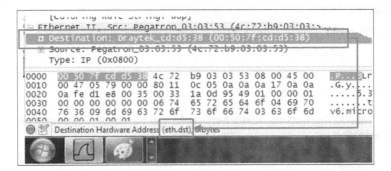

Adding a parameter column

You can also right-click on a parameter in the packet pane and choose **Apply as Column**. This will add a column with the specific parameter. For example, you can choose the parameter `tcp.window_size_value` and add it as a column to the packet list pane, so you will be able to watch the TCP window size online. This influences TCP performance, as we will learn in *Chapter 9, UDP/TCP Analysis*.

Saving the displayed data

To save the displayed data, you can navigate to **File | Export Specified Packets...** and choose which packets to save.

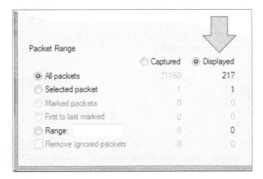

Configuring Ethernet, ARP, host, and network filters

In this recipe we will discuss how to configure filters of layers 2 and 3, that is, Ethernet- and IP-based filters respectively. We will also discuss **Address Resolution Protocol** (**ARP**) filters.

Getting ready

In layer 2 we will configure Ethernet-based filters, while in layer 3 we will configure IP-based filters. In Ethernet we have filters based on the Ethernet frame and the MAC address, while in IP we have filters based on the IP packet and address.

The common frame delta filters are as follows:

 ▶ `frame.time_delta`: This is used for the time delta between the current and previously captured frames; this will be used in statistical graphs displayed in *Chapter 5, Using Advanced Statistics Tools*

 ▶ `frame.time_delta_displayed`: This is used for the time delta between current and previously displayed frames; this will be used in statistical graphs displayed in *Chapter 5, Using Advanced Statistics Tools*

Since the time between frames can influence TCP performance significantly, we will use the `frame.time_delta` parameters in statistical graphs for monitoring TCP performance.

The common layer 2 (Ethernet) filters are as follows:

 ▶ `eth.addr == <MAC Address>`: This is used to display a specific MAC address

 ▶ `eth.src == <MAC Address>`: This is used to get the source MAC address

 ▶ `eth.dst == <MAC Address>`: This is used to get the destination MAC address

 ▶ `eth.type == <Protocol Type (Hexa)>`: This is used to get the Ethernet protocol types

The common ARP filters are as follows:

 ▶ `arp.opcode == <value>`: This is used for ARP requests/responses

 ▶ `arp.src.hw_mac == <MAC Address>`: This is used to capture the ARP address of the sender

The common layer 3 (IP) filters are as follows:

 ▶ `ip.addr == <IP Address>`: This is used to get the source or destination IP address

- ▶ `ip.src == <IP Address>`: This is used to get the source IP address
- ▶ `ip.dst == <IP Address>`: This is used to get the destination IP address
- ▶ `ip.ttl == <value>`, `ip.ttl < value`, or `ip.ttl > <value>`: This is used to get IP TTL (Time To Live) values
- ▶ `ip.len = <value>`, `ip.len > <value>`, or `ip.len < <value>`: This is used to get IP packet length values
- ▶ `ip.version == <4/6>`: This is used to get the IP protocol version (Version 4 or Version 6)

How to do it...

Here we will see some common examples for layer 2 and 3 filters.

Address format	Syntax	Example
Ethernet (MAC) address	`eth.addr == xx:xx:xx:xx:xx:xx` Here, x = 0 to f.	`eth.addr == 00:50:7f:cd:d5:38`
	`eth.addr == xx-xx-xx-xx-xx-xx` Here, x = 0 to f.	`eth.addr == 00-50-7f-cd-d5-38`
	`eth.addr == xxxx.xxxx.xxxx` Here x = 0 to f.	`eth.addr == 0050.7fcd.d538`
Broadcast MAC address	`Eth.addr == ffff.ffff.ffff`	
IPv4 host address	`ip.addr == x.x.x.x` Here, x = 0 to 255.	`Ip.addr == 192.168.1.1`
IPv4 network address	`ip.addr == x.x.x.x/y` Here x = 0 to 255, y = 0 to 32.	`ip.addr == 192.168.200.0/24` This covers all the addresses in the network 192.168.200.0 mask 255.255.255.0.

IPv6 host address	`ipv6.addr == x:x:x:x:x:x:x:x`
	 `ipv6.addr == x::x:x:x:x`
	 Here in the format of nnnn, n = 0 to f (Hex).
		`ipv6.addr == fe80::85ab:dc2e:ab12:e6c7`

IPv6 network address	`ipv6.addr == x::/y` Here x = 0 to f (Hex) and y = 0 to 128.	`ipv6.addr == fe80::/16` This covers all the addresses that start with the 16 bits `fe80`.

The table refers to `ip.addr` and `ipv6.addr` filter strings. The value for any field that has an IP address value can be written the same way.

Ethernet filters

These are classified into two categories:

▸ To display only packets sent from or to specific MAC addresses, use something like these: `eth.src == 10:0b:a9:33:64:18` and `eth.dst == 10:0b:a9:33:64:18`

▸ To display only broadcasts, use `Eth.dst == ffff.ffff.ffff`

ARP filters

These are classified into two categories:

▸ To display only ARP requests, use `arp.opcode == 1`

▸ To display only ARP responses, use `arp.opcode == 2`

IP and ICMP filters

▸ To display only packets from a specific IP address, use something like this: `ip.src == 10.1.1.254`

▸ To display only packets that are not from a specific address, use something like this: `!ip.src == 64.23.1.1`

▸ To display only packets between two hosts, use something like these: `ip.addr == 192.168.1.1` and `ip.addr == 200.1.1.1`

▸ To display only packets that are sent to multicast IP addresses, use something like this: `ip.dst == 224.0.0.0/4`

▸ To display only packets coming from the network 192.168.1.0/24 (mask 255.255.255.0), use `ip.src==192.168.1.0/24`

▸ To display only IPv6 packets to/from specific addresses, use something like the following:

  ❏ `ipv6.addr == ::1`

  ❏ `ipv6.addr == 2008:0:130F:0:0:09d0:666A:13ab`

  ❏ `ipv6.addr == 2006:0:130f::9c2:876a:130b`

  ❏ `ipv6.addr == ::`

Complex filters

▶ To check for packets sent from the network 10.0.0.0/24 to a website that contains the word `packt`, use `ip.src == 10.0.0.0/24` and `http.host contains "packt"`

▶ To check for packets sent from the network 10.0.0.0/24 to websites that end with `.com`, use `ip.addr == 10.0.0.0/24` and `http.host matches "\.com$"`

▶ To check for all the broadcasts from the source IP address 10.0.0.0, use `ip.src == 10.0.0.0/24` and `eth.dst == ffff.ffff.ffff`

▶ To check for all the broadcasts that are not ARP requests, use `not arp` and `eth.dst == ffff.ffff.ffff`

▶ To check for all the packets that are not ICMP, use `!arp || !icmp`, and to check for all the packets that are not ARP, use `not arp or not icmp`

How it works...

Here are some explanations to the filters we saw in the *How to do It...* section of this recipe.

Ethernet broadcasts

In Ethernet, broadcasts are packets that are sent to addresses with all 1s in the destination field and this is why, to find all broadcasts in the network, we insert the filter `eth.dst == ffff.ffff.ffff`.

IPv4 multicasts

IPv4 multicasts are packets that are sent to an address in the address range 224.0.0.0 to 239.255.255.255 that is in binary of the address range 11100000.00000000.00000000.00000000 to 11101111.11111111.11111111.11111111.

If you look at the binary representation, a destination multicast address is an address that starts with three 1s and a 0, and therefore, a filter to IPv4 multicast destinations will be `ip.dst == 224.0.0.0/4`. That is, an address that starts with four 1s (224), and a subnet mask of 4 bits (`/4`) will indicate a network address ranger from 224 to 239 that will filter multicast addresses.

IPv6 multicasts

IPv6 multicasts are packets that are sent to an address that starts with ff (first two hex digits = `ff`), then one-digit flags, and scope. Therefore when we write the filter `ipv6.dst == ff00::/8`, it means to display all the packets in IPv6 that are sent to an address that starts with the string `ff`, that is, IPv6 multicasts.

See also

▸ For more information on Ethernet, refer to *Chapter 7, Ethernet, LAN Switching, and Wireless LAN*

Configuring TCP/UDP filters

TCP and UDP are the main protocols in layer 4 that provide connectivity between end applications. Whenever you start an application from one side to another, you start the session from a source port, usually a random number equal or higher than 1,024, and connect to a destination port, which is a well-known or registered port that waits for the session on the other side. These are the port numbers that identify the application that works over the session.

Other types of filters refer to other fields in the UDP and TCP headers. In UDP we have a very simple header with very basic data, while in TCP we have a more complex header that we can get much more information from.

In this recipe we will concentrate on the possibilities while configuring TCP and UDP display filters.

Getting ready

As done earlier, we should plan precisely what we want to display and prepare the filters accordingly.

For TCP or UDP port numbers use the following display filters:

▸ `tcp.port == <value>` or `udp.port == <value>`: This is used for specific TCP or UDP ports (source or destination)

▸ `tcp.dstport == <value>` or `udp.dstport == <value>`: This is used for specific TCP or UDP destination ports

▸ `tcp.srcport == <value>` or `udp.srcport == <value>`: This is used for specific TCP or UDP destination ports

In UDP, the header structure is very simple: source and destination ports, packet length, and checksum. Therefore, the only significant information here is the port number.

TCP on the other hand is more complex and uses connectivity and reliability mechanisms that can be monitored by Wireshark. Using `tcp.flags`, `tcp.analysis`, and other smart filters will help you resolve performance problems (retransmissions, duplicate ACKs, zero windows, and so on), protocol operation issues such as resets, half-opens, and so on.

Common display filters in this category are as follows:

- ▶ `tcp.analysis`: This is used for TCP analysis criteria such as retransmission, duplicate ACKs, or window issues. Examples for this filter are as follows (you can use the autocomplete feature to get the full list of available filters):

  - ❑ `tcp.analysis.retransmission`: This is used to display packets that were retransmitted.

  - ❑ `tcp.analysis.duplicate_ack`: This is used to display packets that were acknowledged several times.

  - ❑ `tcp.analysis.zero_window`: This is used to display packets when a device on the connection end sends a zero-window message (that tells the sender to stop sending data on this connection, until window size increases again).

 The `tcp.analysis` filters do not analyze the TCP header; they provide a protocol analysis through the Wireshark expert system.

- ▶ `tcp.flags`: These are used to find out if a flag(s) is set or not. Examples of this filter are as follows:

  - ❑ `tcp.flags.syn == 1`: This is used to check if the SYN flag is set.

  - ❑ `tcp.flags.reset == 1`: This is used to check if the RST flag is set.

  - ❑ `tcp.flags.fin == 1`: This is used to check if the FIN flag is set.

 For TCP flags, the `tcp.flags` filter will be used to find out whether a specific flag is set or not.

- ▶ `tcp.window_size_value < <value>`: This is used to look for small TCP window sizes that are in some cases indications for slow devices.

How to do it...

Some examples for filters in TCP/UDP filters:

- ▶ To filter all the packets to the HTTP server, use `tcp.dstport == 80`

- ▶ To filter all the packets from the network 10.0.0.0/24 to the HTTP server, use `ip.src==10.0.0.0/24` and `tcp.dstport == 80`

- ▶ For all the retransmissions in a specific TCP connection, use `tcp.stream eq 16 && tcp.analysis.retransmission`

To isolate a specific connection, place the mouse on a packet in the connection you want to watch, right-click on it, and choose **Follow TCP Stream**. A TCP stream is the data that is transferred between the two ends of the connection from the connection establishment to the connection tear down. The string `tcp.stream eq <value>` will appear in the display filter window. This is the stream you can work on now. In the preceding example, it came out as stream `16`, but it can be any stream number (starting the count from stream `1` in the capture file).

Retransmissions are TCP packets that are sent again. It can be due to several reasons, as explained in *Chapter 9, UDP/TCP Analysis*.

 While monitoring phenomena such as retransmissions, duplicate ACKs, and others that influence performance, it is important to remember that these phenomena refer to a specific TCP connection.

Other examples of the types of TCP filters are as follows:

- To transfer all the window problems in a specific connection:
    - `tcp.stream eq 0 && (tcp.analysis.window_full || tcp.analysis.zero_window)`
    - `tcp.stream eq 0 and (tcp.analysis.window_full or tcp.analysis.zero_window)`
- To transfer all the packets from 10.0.0.5 to the DNS server: `ip.src == 10.0.0.5 && udp.port == 53`
- To transfer all the packets or protocols in TCP (for example HTTP) that contains the string `cacti` (case sensitive): `tcp contains "cacti"`
- To check all the packets that are retransmitted from 10.0.0.3: `ip.src == 10.0.0.3 and tcp.analysis.retransmission`
- To transfer all the packets to any HTTP server: `tcp.dstport == 80`
- To check all the connections opened from a specific host (if in a form of scan, can be a worm!): `ip.src==10.0.0.5 && tcp.flags.syn==1 && tcp.flags.ack==0`
- To check all the cookies sent from and to a client: `ip.src==10.0.0.3 && (http.cookie || http.set_cookie)`

How it works...

The following are illustrations of the IP and TCP header structures respectively. UDP is quite simple; it has only source and destination port numbers, length, and checksum. In the following diagram we see the IP header structure:

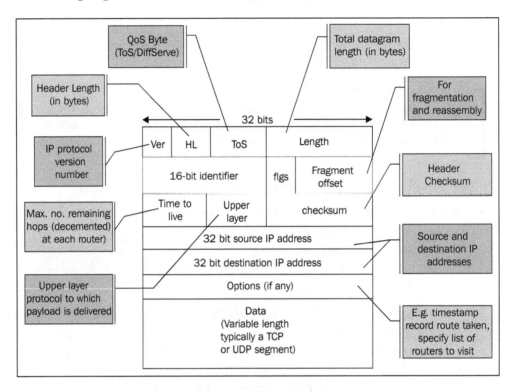

Some important factors in the IP packet are as follows:

▶ **Ver**: The version is either 4 or 6.

▶ **Header length (HL)**: The header length is 20 to 24 bytes, with options.

▶ **Type of Service (ToS)**: This is usually implemented with **Differentiated Services** (**DiffServ**) and provides priority to preferred services.

> IP standard (RFC 791 from September 1981) has named this field Type of Service (ToS) and defined its structure. The standards for Differentiated Services were published later (RFCs 2474, 2475 from December 1998 and others) and are used for the implementation of the ToS byte in majority of the applications.

- **Length**: This field indicates the total datagram length in bytes.

- **16-bit identifier, flgs, and Fragment offset**: Every packet has it's own packet ID. When fragmented along with the flags and offset, these will enable the receiver to reassemble it.

- **Time to live (TTL)**: This starts with 64, 128, or 256 (depending on the operation system that sends the packet), when every router on the way decrements the value by one. This comes to prevent packets from traveling endlessly through the network. The router that sees 1 in the packet decrements it to 0 and drops the packet.

- **Upper layer**: This field consists of upper-layer protocols such as TCP, UDP and ICMP.

- **Checksum**: This field represents the packet checksum. The idea here is that the sender uses an error-checking mechanism to calculate a value over the packet. This value is set in the checksum field while the receiver of the packet calculates it again. If the sent value is not equal to the received value, it will be considered as a checksum error.

- **32-bit source and destination IP addresses**: As the names suggest, these are source and destination IP addresses.

- **Options**: This field is usually not in use in IPv4. In the following diagram you see the TCP header:

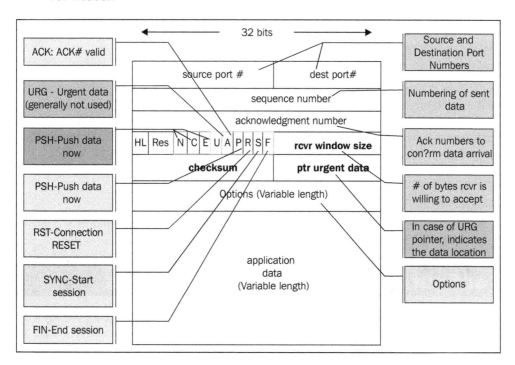

Some important factors in the TCP packet are as follows:

- **Source and destination ports**: These are the applications codes on either end.
- **Sequence number**: This field counts the bytes that the sender sends to the receiver.
- **Acknowledgement number**: This field indicates the ACK's received bytes. We will discuss this in detail in *Chapter 9, UDP/TCP Analysis*.
- **HL**: This is the header length field and it indicates whether we use the **Options** field or not.
- **Res**: This field is reserved for future flags.
- **Flags**: This field indicates flags to start a connection (SYN), close a connection (FIN), reset a connection (RST), and push data for fast processing (PSH). We will discuss this in detail in *Chapter 9, UDP/TCP Analysis*.
- **Rcvr window size**: This field indicates the buffer that the receiver has allocated to the process.
- **Checksum**: This field indicates the packet checksum.
- **Options**: Timestamps and receiver window enhancement (RFC 1323), and MSS extension. **Maximum Segment Size** (**MSS**) is the maximum side of the TCP payload. It is indicated in this field. Further discussion on this will be done in *Chapter 9, UDP/TCP Analysis*.

There's more...

The TTL field in IP is quite a helpful field. While checking a TTL value, it explicitly indicates how many routers the packet has passed. Since operating system defaults are 64, 128, or 256, and the maximum number of hops that a packet will cross through the Internet are 30 (in private networks it is much less). For example, if we see a value of 120, the packet has passed 8 routers, and a value of 52 indicates that the packet has passed 12 routers.

See also

- For further information on the TCP/IP protocol stack, refer to *Chapter 9, UDP/TCP Analysis*

Configuring specific protocol filters

In this recipe we will have a look at the instructions and examples to configure display filters for common protocols such as DNS, HTTP, and FTP.

The purpose of this recipe is to learn how to configure filters that will help us in network troubleshooting. We will learn about network troubleshooting in the upcoming chapters.

To perform this recipe, you will need a running Wireshark software capture; there are no other prerequisites.

In this recipe we will see the display filters for some common protocols.

HTTP display filters

The following are some common HTTP display filters:

- To display all the HTTP packets going to <`"host name"`>, use `http.request.method == <"Request methods">`
- To display packets with the HTTP `GET` method, use `http.request.method == "GET"`
- To display the URI requested by client, use `http.request.method == <"Full request URI">`; for example, `http.request.uri == "/v2/rating/mail.google.com"`
- To display the URI requested by the client that contains a specific string (all requests to Google in the preceding example), use `http.request.uri contains "URI String"`; for example, `http.request.uri contains "mail.google.com"`
- To check all the cookie requests sent over the network (note that cookies are always sent from the client to the server), use `http.cookie`
- To check all the cookie set commands sent from the server to the client, use `http.set_cookie`
- To check all the cookies sent by Google servers to your PC, use `(http.set_cookie) && (http contains "google")`
- To check all the HTTP packets that contain a ZIP file, use `http matches "\.zip" && http.request.method == "GET"`

DNS display filters

Here, we will look at some common DNS display filters.

To display DNS queries and responses, use:

- `dns.flags.response == 0 for DNS queries`
- `dns.flags.response == 1 for DNS response`

To display only DNS responses with four answers or more, use `dns.count.answers >= 4`.

FTP display filters

Some common FTP display filters are as follows:

- To fetch FTP request commands, use `ftp.request.command == <"requested command">` - `ftp.request.command == "USER"`

- To fetch FTP commands from port 2, use `ftp`, and to fetch FTP data from port 20 or any other configured port, use `ftp-data`

How it works...

The Wireshark regular expression syntax for display filters uses the same syntax as regular expressions in Perl.

Some common modifiers are as follows:

- `^`: This is used to match the beginning of the line

- `$`: This is used to match the end of the line

- `|`: This is used for alternation purposes

- `()`: This is used for grouping purposes

- `*`: This is used to match either 0 or more times

- `+`: This is used to match 1 or more times

- `?`: This is used to match 1 or 0 times

- `{n}`: This is used to match exactly n times

- `{n, }`: This is used to match at least n times

- `{n,m}`: This is used to match at least n but not more than m times

You can use these modifiers to configure more complex filters. Have a look at the following examples:

- To look for HTTP GET commands that contain ZIP files, use `http.request.method == "GET" && http matches "\.zip" && !(http.accept_encoding == "gzip, deflate")`

- To look for HTTP GET commands that contain ZIP files, use `http.request.method == "GET" && http matches "\.zip" && !(http.accept_encoding == "gzip, deflate")`

- To look for HTTP messages that contain websites that end with `.com`, use `http.host matches "\.com$"`

See also

▸   The Perl regular expression syntax list can be found at `http://www.pcre.org/`, and the manual pages can be found at `http://perldoc.perl.org/perlre.html`

Configuring substring operator filters

Offset filters are filters in which you actually say, "Go to field x in the protocol header and check if the next y bytes equal to....".

These filters can be used in many cases in which a known string byte appears somewhere in the packet and you want to display packets that contain it.

Getting ready

To step through this recipe, you will need a running Wireshark software and a running capture; there are no other prerequisites. The general representation for offset filters is:

Protocols[x:y] == <value>

Here, x refers to the bytes from the beginning of the header and y refers to the number of bytes to check.

How to do it...

Examples for filters that use substring operators are as follows:

▸   **Packets to IPv4 multicast addresses**: `eth.dst[0:3] == 01:00:5e` (RFC 1112, section 6.4 allocates the MAC address space of 01-00-5E-00-00-00 to 01-00-5E-FF-FF-FF for multicast addressing)

▸   **Packets to IPv6 multicast addresses**: `eth.dst[0:3] == 33:33:00` (RFC 2464, section 7 allocates the MAC address space that starts with 33-33 for multicast addressing)

How it works...

Wireshark enables you to look into protocols and search for specific bytes in it. This is specifically practical for well-known strings in protocols, such as Ethernet in the given example.

Configuring macros

Display filter macros are used to create shortcuts for complex display filters, which you can configure once and use later.

Getting ready

To configure display filter macros, navigate to **Analyze | Display Filter Macros | New**.

You will get the following window:

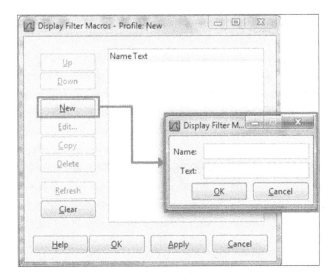

How to do it...

1. In order to configure a macro, you give it a name and fill the textbox with the filter string.

2. In order to activate the macro, you simply write `$(macro_name:parameter1;para mater2;parameter3 ...)`.

3. Let's configure a simple filter name, `test01`, which takes the following parameters as values:

   ❑ `ip.src == <value>`

   ❑ `tcp.dstport == <value>`

This will be a filter that looks for packets from a specific source network that go out to the HTTP port.

A macro that takes these two parameters will be: `ip.src==$1 && tcp.dstport==$2`.

4. Now, in order to get the filter results for the parameters `ip.src == 10.0.0.4` and `tcp.dstport == 80`, we should write the string `${test01:10.0.0.4;80}` in the display window bar.

How it works...

Macros work in a simple way; you write a filter string with the sign `$` ahead of every positional parameter. While running the macros, it will accept the parameters in order.

4

Using Basic Statistics Tools

In this chapter you will learn:

- ▶ Using the **Summary** tool from the **Statistics** menu
- ▶ Using the **Protocol Hierarchy** tool from the **Statistics** menu
- ▶ Using the **Conversations** tool from the **Statistics** menu
- ▶ Using the **Endpoints** tool from the **Statistics** menu
- ▶ Using the **HTTP** tool from the **Statistics** menu
- ▶ Configuring **Flow Graph** for viewing TCP flows
- ▶ Creating IP-based statistics

Introduction

One of Wireshark's strengths is the statistical tools. While using Wireshark, we have various types of tools starting from simple tools for listing end nodes and conversations to the more sophisticated tools such as Flow and IO graphs.

In the next two chapters we will learn how to use these tools. In this chapter we will look at the simple tools that provide us with basic network statistics; that is, who talks to whom over the network, which are the "chatty" devices, what packet sizes run over the network, while in the next chapter we'll get into tools such as IO and Stream graphs, which provide us with much more information about the behavior of the network.

There are some tools that we will not talk about; those that are quite obvious (for example, **Packet sizes**), and those that are less common (such as **ANSP**, **BACnet**, and others).

To use the **Statistics** tool, start Wireshark and choose **Statistics** from the main menu.

Using the Summary tool from the Statistics menu

In this recipe we will learn how to get general information about the data that runs over the network.

Getting ready

Start Wireshark, click on **Statistics**.

How to do it...

To use the **Summary** tool from the **Statistics** menu, follow the ensuing steps:

1. From the statistics menu, choose **Summary**.

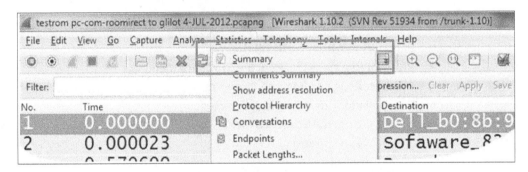

What you will get is the **Summary** window (displayed in the following two screenshots).

2. As shown in the following screenshot, in the upper side of the window, you will see:

   - **File**: This part of the window provides file data, such as file name and path, length, and so on
   - **Time**: This part on the window displays the start time, end time, and duration of capture

❑ **Capture**: This part of the window shows on which interface the file was captured and also displays a remark window

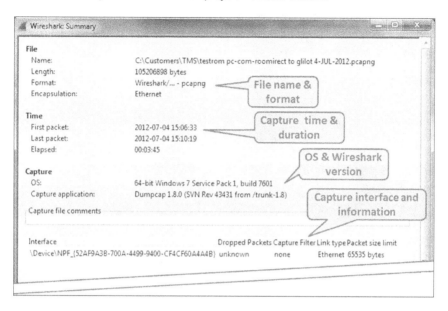

3. In the lower part of the window is the **Display** window, where you will get a summary of the capture file statistics; this includes:

❑ The number of packets that were captured: their total number and percentage

❑ The number of packets displayed (after passing the **Display Filter**)

❑ The number of packets that are marked

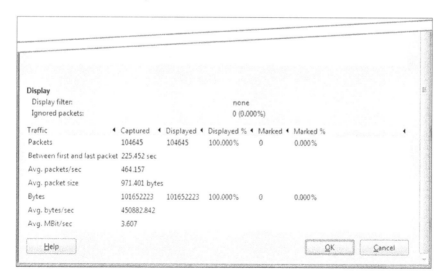

How it works...

This menu simply collects all the captured data, and when a filter is defined, it presents the filtered data. When the question is, "how do I use Wireshark simply to know what is the average packets or bytes per second?", this is your answer.

There's more...

From the **Summary** window, you can get the average packets/second and bits/second of the entire captured file and also for the displayed data.

Using the Protocol Hierarchy tool from the Statistics menu

In this recipe, we will learn how to get protocol hierarchy information of the data that runs over the network.

Getting ready

Start Wireshark, click on **Statistics**.

How to do it...

To use the **Protocol Hierarchy** tool from the statistics menu, go through the following steps:

1. From the statistics menu, choose **Protocol Hierarchy**.

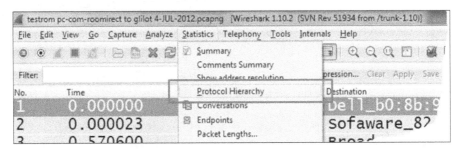

2. What you will get here is data about the protocol distribution in the captured file. You will get the protocol distribution of the captured data, as shown in the following screenshot:

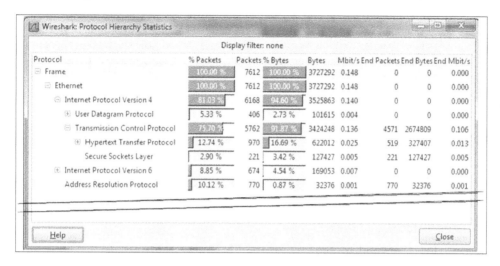

3. You will get the following fields in the **Protocol Hierarchy** window:

- ❏ **Protocol**: This field specifies the protocol name
- ❏ **% Packets**: This field specifies the percentage of protocol packets from the total captured packets
- ❏ **Packets**: This field specifies the number of protocol packets from the total captured packets
- ❏ **% Bytes**: This field specifies the percentage of protocol bytes from the total captured packets
- ❏ **Bytes**: This field specifies the number of protocol bytes from the total captured packets
- ❏ **Mbit/s**: This field specifies the bandwidth of this protocol in relation to the capture time
- ❏ **End Packets**: This field specifies the total number of packets in this protocol (for the highest protocol in the decode file)
- ❏ **End Bytes**: This field specifies the absolute number of bytes of this protocol (for the highest protocol in the decode file)
- ❏ **End Mbit/s**: This field specifies the bandwidth of this protocol relative to the capture packets and time (for the highest protocol in the decode file)

> The **End Packets**, **End Bytes**, and **End Mbits/s** columns are those in which the protocol in this line is the last protocol in the packet (that is, when the protocol comes at the end of the packet, and there is no higher layer information). These can be, for example, TCP packets with no payload (for example, SYN packets), which do not carry any upper layer information. That is why you see a **0** count for Ethernet and IPv4 and UDP end packets because there are no frames where these protocols are the last protocol in the frame.

How it works...

In simple terms, it calculates statistics over the captured data. Some important things to notice are:

- The percentage always refers to the same layer protocols. For example, we see in the previous example that IPv4 has 81.03 percent of the packets, IPv6 has 8.85 percent of the packets, and ARP has 10.12 percent of the packets; a total of 100 percent of the protocols over layer-2.

- On the other hand, we see that TCP has 75.70 percent of the data, and within TCP, only 12.74 percent of the packets are HTTP, and there is nearly nothing more. This is because Wireshark counts only the packets with the HTTP headers. It doesn't count for example, the acknowledge packets or data packets that doesn't have HTTP header.

There's more...

In order to ensure that Wireshark will also count the data packets, for example, the data packets of HTTP within the TCP packet, disable the **Allow sub-dissector** option to reassemble the TCP streams. You can do this from the **Preferences** menu or by right-clicking on the TCP in the **Packet Details** pane.

Using the Conversations tool from the Statistics menu

In this recipe, we will learn how to get information about conversations that runs over the network.

Getting ready

Start Wireshark, click on **Statistics**.

How to do it...

To use the **Conversations** feature from the **Statistics** menu, follow the ensuing steps:

1. From the statistics menu, choose **Conversations**.

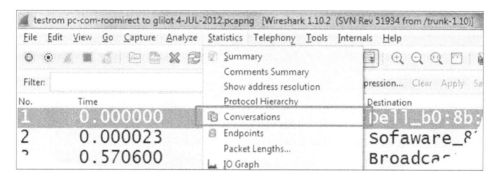

2. The following window will come up:

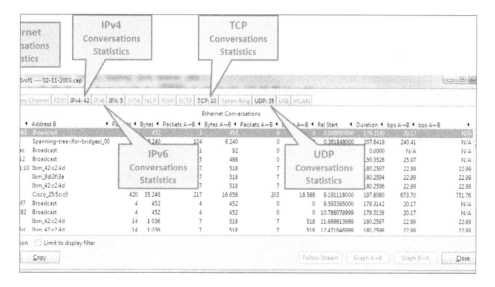

3. You can choose between layer 2 Ethernet statistics, layer 3 IP statistics, or layer 4 TCP or UDP statistics.

4. You can use these statistics tools:

   ❑ **On layer 2 (Ethernet):** To find and isolate broadcast storms or

   ❑ **On layer 3 or 4 (TCP/IP):** To connect in parallel with the Internet router port and check who is loading the line to the ISP

If you see that there is a lot of traffic going out to port 80 (HTTP) on a specific IP address on the Internet, you just have to copy the address to your browser and see access to which website is most "popular" with your users.

If you don't get anything, simply go to a standard DNS resolution website (just Google *DNS lookup*) and find out which is the traffic that loads your Internet line.

5. You can also limit the conversations statistics to a display filter by selecting the **Limit to display filter** checkbox located down in the down to the left of the window. In this way, statistics will be presented on all the packets passing the display filter.

6. For viewing the IP addresses as names, you can select the **Name resolution** checkbox. For viewing the name resolution, you will have to first enable it by navigating to **View | Name Resolution | Enable for Network layer**.

7. For TCP or UDP, you can mark a specific packet in the **Packet list** and then select **Follow TCP Stream** or **Follow UDP Stream** (depending on whether it is a UDP or TCP packet) from the menu that appears on the screen. This will define a display filter that will show you the specific stream of data.

How it works...

A network conversation is the traffic between two specific endpoints. For example, an IP conversation is all the traffic between two IP addresses and TCP conversations represent all the TCP connections.

There's more...

There are many network problems that will simply "pop up" while using the **Conversations** list.

Ethernet conversations statistics

In the Ethernet conversations statistics, look for the following problems:

▸   Large amount of broadcasts: you might be viewing a broadcast storm (a minor one. In a major one, you might not see anything.)

What usually happens in a severe broadcast storm is that due to thousands, and even tens of thousands, of packets sent and received per second by Wireshark, the software simply stops showing us the data and the screen freezes. Only when you disconnect Wireshark from the network will you see it.

▶ If you see a lot of traffic coming from a specific MAC address, look at the first part of the conversation; this is the vendor ID that will give you a hint about the troublemaker.

 Even though the first half of a MAC address identifies the vendor, it does not necessarily identify the PC itself. This is because the MAC address belongs to the Ethernet chip vendor that is installed on the PC or laptop board and is not necessarily from the PC manufacturer. If you are unable to identify the address where the traffic is arriving from, you can ping the suspect and get its MAC address by ARP, find the MAC address in the switches, and if you have a management system, use a simple `find` command to locate it.

IP conversations statistics

In the IP conversations statistics, look for the following problems:

▶ Look for IP addresses with a lot of traffic going in or out of them. If it is a server you know (and probably you remember the server's address or address range), then it is OK; but it might also be that someone scanned the network, or just a PC that generated too much traffic.

▶ Look for scanning patterns (presented in detail in *Chapter 14, Understanding Network Security*). It can be a good scan, such as an SNMP software that sends a ping to discover the network, but usually the scans in the network are not good.

▶ You can see a typical scan pattern in the following screenshot:

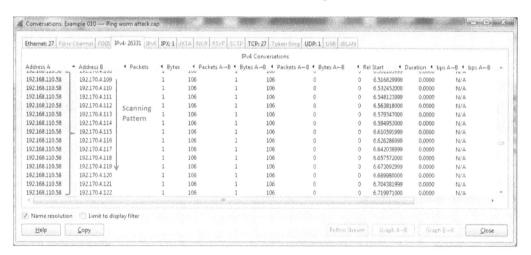

In this example, there is a scan pattern. A single IP address, **192.168.110.58**, sends ICMP packets to **192.170.3.44**, **192.170.3.45**, **192.170.3.46**, **192.170.3.47**, and so on (in the screenshot we see only a very small part of the scan). In this case we had a worm that infected all PCs on the network, and the moment it infects a PC, it starts to generate ICMP requests and sends them to the network; such narrow band links (for example, WAN connections) can easily be blocked.

TCP/UDP conversations statistics:

▸ Look for devices with too many open TCP connections. 10 to 20 connections per PC are reasonable, hundreds are not.

▸ Look and try to find unrecognized port numbers. It might be OK, but it can mean trouble. In the following screenshot, you can see a typical TCP scan:

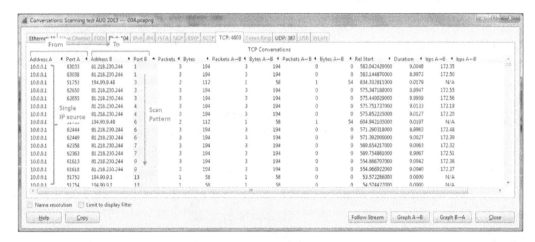

Using the Endpoints tool from the Statistics menu

In this recipe we will learn how to get statistics on endpoints information of the captured data.

Getting ready

Start Wireshark, click on **Statistics**.

How to do it...

To view the endpoint statistics, follow these steps:

1. From the statistics menu, click on **Endpoints**.

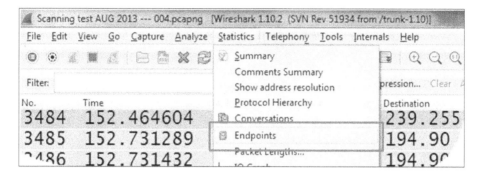

2. The following window will come up:

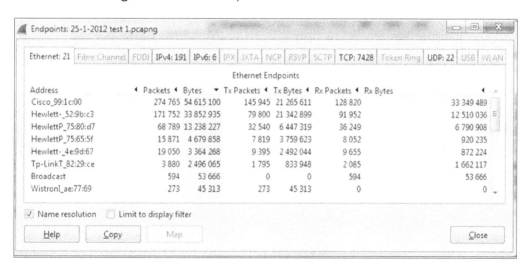

3. In this window, you will be able to see layers 2 and 3 and 4 endpoints, which are Ethernet, IP, and TCP or UDP.

How it works...

It simply gives statistics on all the endpoints that Wireshark has discovered. It could be any of the situations here:

> ▶ Few Ethernet endpoints (these are MAC addresses) with many IP end nodes (these are IP addresses): This will be the case where, for example, we have a router that sends/receives packets from many remote devices, and what we will see is the MAC address of the router and many IP addresses coming/going through it.

> ▶ Few IP end nodes with many TCP end nodes: this will be the case for many TCP connections per host. It can be a regular operation of a server with many connections, and it can also be a kind of attack that comes through the network (for example, an SYN attack).

There's more...

Here you see an example for a capture file taken from a network center, and what we can get from it.

In the following screenshot, we see an internal network with four HP servers and a single Cisco router. We can see this from the first part of the MAC address that is resolved to vendor names:

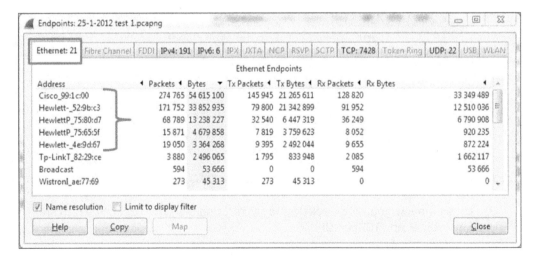

When we choose to see the endpoints under **IPv4: 191**, we see many endpoints coming from the networks **192.168.10.0**, **192.168.30.0**, and also other networks.

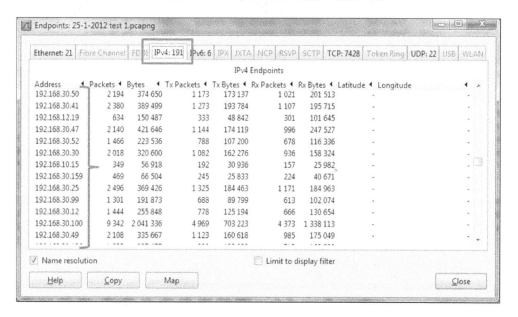

Using the HTTP tool from the Statistics menu

In this recipe we will learn how to use HTTP statistical information of the data that runs over the network.

Getting ready

Start Wireshark, click on **Statistics**.

How to do it...

To view the HTTP statistics follow these steps:

From the **Statistics** menu, select **HTTP**. The following window will appear:

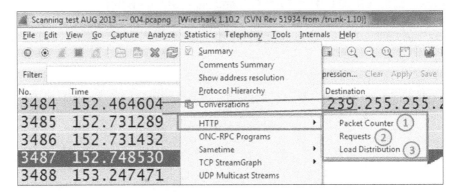

In the **HTTP** submenu, we have the following:

- **Packet Counter (marked as 1 in the preceding screenshot)**: This provides us with the number of packets to each website. This will help us to identify how many requests and responses we have had.

- **Requests (marked as 2 in the preceding screenshot)**: This is used to see request distribution to websites.

- **Load Distribution (marked as 3 in the preceding screenshot)**: This is used to see load distribution between websites.

We will perform the following steps to view the **Packet Counter** statistics:

1. Navigate to **Statistics | HTTP | Packet Counter**.

2. The following filter window will open:

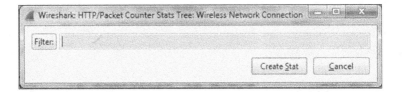

3. In this window, you configure a filter to see the statistics that are applied to these filters. If you want to see statistics over the whole captured file, leave it blank. This will show you statistics over IP, that is, all the HTTP packets.

4. Click on the **Create Stat** button, and you will get the following window:

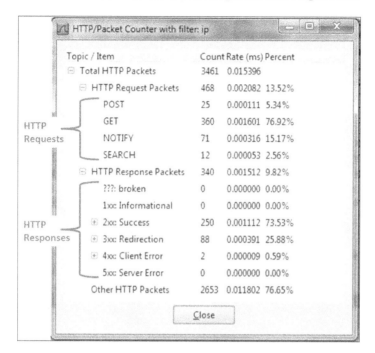

In order to see the HTTP statistics for a specific node, you can configure a filter for it using a display filter format.

We will perform the following steps to view HTTP Requests statistics:

1. Navigate to **Statistics | HTTP | Requests**. The following window will appear:

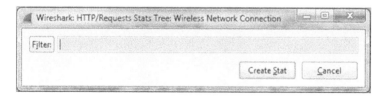

2. Choose the filter you need. For all data, leave blank.

3. Click on the **Create Stat** button and the following window will come up:

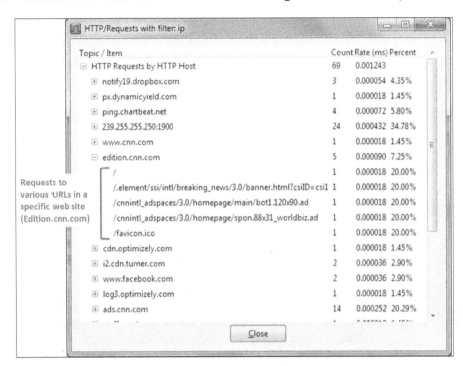

4. To get statistics for a specific HTTP host, you can set a filter `http.host contains <host_name>` or `http.host==<host_name>` (depends on whether you need a hostname with a specific name or a hostname that contains a specific string), and you will see statistics to this specific host.

5. For example, by configuring the filter `http.host contains ndi-com.com`, you will get the statistics for the website `www.ndi-com.com` (shown in the following screenshot):

6. What you will get is:

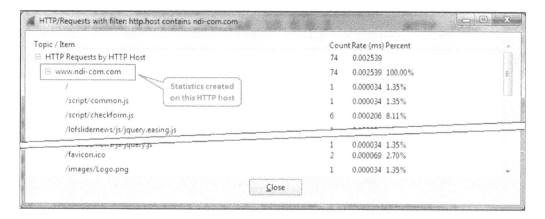

To see **Load Distribution** on the Web or a specific website:

1. Navigate to **Statistics | HTTP | Packet Counter**.

2. The following window will appear:

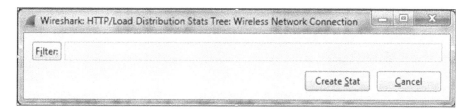

3. Choose the filter you need. For all data, leave it blank.

4. Click on the **Create Stat** button and the following window will come up:

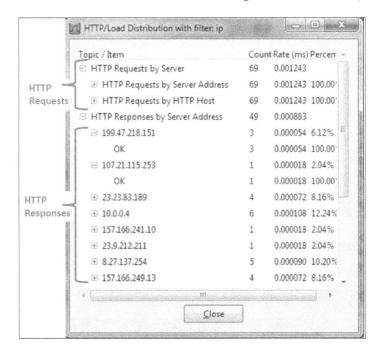

How it works...

When we open a website, it usually sends requests to several URLs. In this example, one of the websites we opened was www.cnn.com, which took us to edition.cnn.com, where we have sent several requests: to the root URL, to the breaking_news URL, and to two other locations on the home page.

There's more...

For deeper HTTP analysis, you can use purpose-specific tools. One of the most common ones is **Fiddler**. You can find it at http://www.fiddler2.com/fiddler2/

Fiddler is a software tool developed for HTTP troubleshooting and therefore it provides more data with a better user interface for HTTP.

Configuring Flow Graph for viewing TCP flows

In this recipe we will learn how to use the Flow Graph feature.

Getting ready

Open Wireshark and from the **Statistics** menu choose **Flow Graph**. The following window will open:

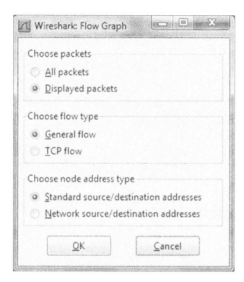

How to do it...

You can choose several options in the **Flow Graph** window, such as:

- ▸ What to view:
    - ❑ Choose **All packets**: for viewing all captured packets
    - ❑ Choose **Displayed packets**: for viewing only filtered packets
- ▸ Flow type:
    - ❑ General flow will show all captured or displayed packets (for what you choose before).
    - ❑ TCP flow will show only TCP flags, sequence, and ACK numbers. This graph provides a very partial picture of the flow.

How it works...

Simply by creating simple statistics from the captured file: nothing special to say here.

There's more...

Understanding TCP problems is sometimes quite complex. The best way to do it most of the time is to use graphical software that have better graphical interface, or simply take a piece of paper along with different colored pens and draw it yourself.

A friendly software that can do the job is the **Cascade Pilot** package by the developers of Wireshark which can be found at `http://www.riverbed.com/us/products/cascade/wireshark_enhancements/cascade_pilot_personal_edition.php`

You can see an example of a self-made graph in the following image:

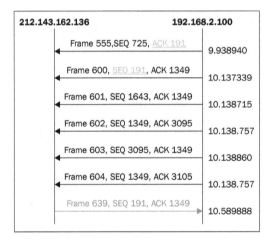

After preparing a few graphs, you will know them like the back of your hand.

Creating IP-based statistics

In this recipe we will learn how to create some IP-based statistics. We will discuss the following statistics tools:

- ▶ IP Addresses
- ▶ IP Destinations
- ▶ IP Protocols Types

Getting ready

Open Wireshark and click on the **Statistics** menu.

How to do it...

To get IP addresses statistics, perform the following steps:

1. Navigate to **Statistics | IP Addresses**.

2. In the window that comes up, select the filter you want to use by clicking on the **Filter** button:

3. If you want to see statistics of the whole captured file, leave it blank and all the IP packet statistics will be shown.

4. If you want to see only statistics up to a specific IP address, type the filter in the display filter syntax. For example, the filter `ip.addr==10.0.0.2` will show you only IP packets sent to or from this address.

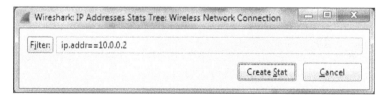

5. After typing in the filter, you will get the following statistics:

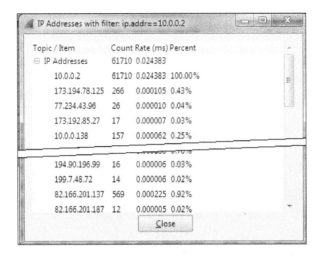

To get IP and TCP/UDP destination statistics, perform the following steps:

1. Navigate to **Statistics | IP Destinations**.
2. In the following window, choose the filter you want to use:

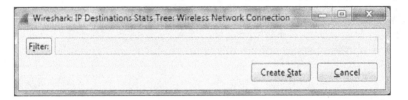

3. This window will show you all those IP addresses to whose destination IPs it has sent packets, and on what protocols.

4. You will get the following statistics:

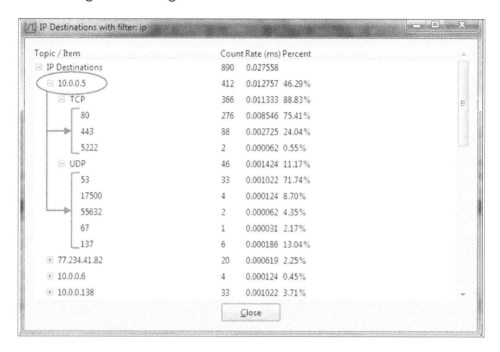

5. In this statistics table, you can see that host **10.0.0.5** has sent TCP packets to port **80**, **443**, and **5222**, and UDP packets to ports **53** and some others.

This is one of the tools that brings up suspected issues; for example, when you see a suspected port with too many packets sent to it, start looking for a reason. To get IP protocol types:

1. Navigate to **Statistics | IP Protocol Types**.

2. In the following window, choose the filter you want to use:

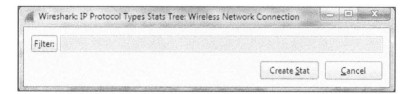

3. You will get the statistics of the protocols that run over IP that are mostly TCP and UDP.

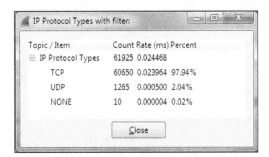

How it works...

Simply by creating statistics over the captured file.

There's more...

There are various options in Wireshark that give you quite similar statistics; these are **Conversations**, **Protocol Hierarchy**, and **Endpoint**, which were discussed at the beginning of this chapter. You can use them in conjunction with the methods we learned in this recipe.

5
Using Advanced Statistics Tools

In this chapter we will learn the following:

- ▶ Configuring IO Graphs with filters for measuring network performance issues
- ▶ Throughput measurements with IO Graph
- ▶ Advanced IO Graph configurations with advanced Y-Axis parameters
- ▶ Getting information through TCP stream graphs – the Time-Sequence (Stevens) window
- ▶ Getting information through TCP stream graphs – the Time-Sequence (tcp-trace) window
- ▶ Getting information through TCP stream graphs – the Throughput Graph window
- ▶ Getting information through TCP stream graphs – the Round Trip Time window
- ▶ Getting information through TCP stream graphs – the Window Scaling Graph window

Introduction

In *Chapter 4*, Using *Basic Statistics Tools*, we discussed the basic statistics tools such as lists of end users, conversations, capture summary, and more. In this chapter we will look at the advanced statistical tools such as the IO Graph, TCP stream graphs, and in brief, the UDP multicast streams as well.

The tools we will talk about here enable us to have a better look at the network. Here we have two major tools:

▶ The IO Graph tool enables us to view statistical graphs for any predefined filter; for example, the throughput on a single IP address, the load between two or more hosts, the application throughput, the TCP phenomena distribution, and more

▶ We will have a deeper look at a single TCP connection using the TCP stream graphs, with the ability to isolate TCP problems and their causes

In this chapter we will learn how to use the tools, and in the next chapters we will use them to isolate and solve networking problems.

Configuring IO Graphs with filters for measuring network performance issues

In this recipe we will learn how to use the IO Graph tool and how to configure it for network troubleshooting.

Getting ready

Under the **Statistics** menu, open the IO Graph tool by clicking on **IO Graph**. You can do this during an online file capture or on a file you've captured before. While using the IO Graph tool on a live capture, you will get live statistics on the captured data.

How to do it...

Run the IO Graph tool and you will get the following window:

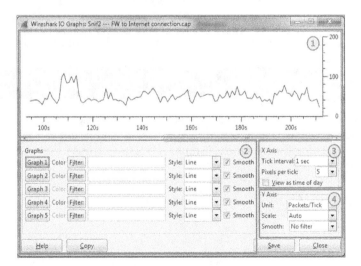

On the upper part of the window, you will get the graph highlighted as area **1**. On the lower-left part, highlighted as area **2**, you will get the filters that enable you to configure display filters, which will enable specific graphs. On the right-hand side of the window, highlighted as areas **3** and **4**, you will get the **X-Axis** and **Y-Axis** configuration. Let's see what we can configure and how to do it.

Filter configuration

1. In the filter window, fill in a filter in the display-filter format. Only the packets that pass this filter will be taken into account for this graph. You have five optional filters to configure here.

2. Choose the type of graph you want to present: **Line**, **Impulse**, **FBar**, or **Dot**.

3. Click on the **Graph** button. This is required in order to activate the filter graph. Don't forget it.

X-Axis configuration

1. Choose a value to enter in **Tick interval:**. The scale can be between 0.001 seconds and 10 minutes.

 If, for example, we get a peak of 1,000 packets/second when the tick interval X Axis is configured with 1-second intervals, it means that in the last second we've got 1,000 packets. When we change the tick interval for X Axis to 0.1-second intervals, the peak will be different because now we see how many packets were captured in the last 0.1 second.

2. Choose the **Pixels per tick:** value to configure the pixels per tick interval.

3. Mark the **View as time of day** button for choosing the time of day format instead of time since the beginning of capture.

Y-Axis configuration

1. Choose the value for **Unit:** from **Packets/Tick**, **Bytes/Tick**, **Bits/Tick**, or **Advanced...** for choosing the Y-Axis scale.

2. Choose **Scale:** for the Y Axis. You can choose it to be **Linear** or change it to **Logarithmic**. You can also leave it as **Automatic** or change it to manual values when required.

3. Choose a value for **Smooth:** if you want to see a running average; that is, in every tick interval you will see the average of the past ticks. You can choose values from 4 to 1,024 to smooth the graph.

How it works...

The **IO Graphs** feature is one of the important Wireshark tools that enable us to monitor online performance along with offline capture file analysis.

While you are using this tool, it's important to configure the right filter with the right X-Axis and Y-Axis parameters.

Let's have a look at the next two graphs, in which a PC with an IP address of 10.0.0.2 is browsing the Internet. In these two IO graphs, we have configured two filters:

  ▸ The first graph is the upload (upstream) traffic graph, which indicates all the traffic from the IP address 10.0.0.2; this is the filter `ip.src==10.0.0.2`, colored in red.

  ▸ The second graph is the download (downstream) traffic graph, which indicates all the traffic to the IP address 10.0.0.2; this is the filter `ip.dst==10.0.0.2`, colored in green.

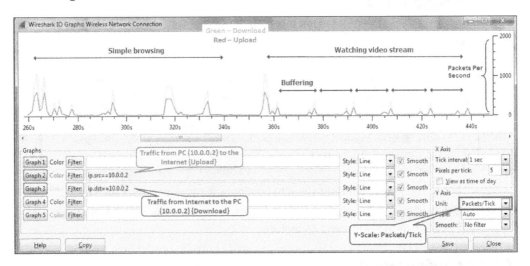

In the first graph, we see that we've measured the traffic when the X Axis is configured to a tick interval of one second and the Y-Axis scale is configured to packets/tick. The result that we've got is that while browsing (on the left-hand side of the graph) or while watching a movie (on the right-hand side of the graph), the upload and download traffic is nearly identical.

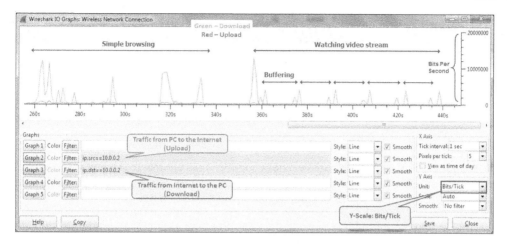

In the second graph, we see the traffic in bits/sec. Here, we see the bandwidth required from the network while using it to connect to the Internet; that is, an asymmetrical bandwidth when most of the traffic is in the download direction.

There's more...

Let's have a look at another example here. This is an example of a file download in FTP when 10.0.52.164 downloads a file. Again, you can see that in order to get the traffic on the network, we changed **Unit:** under **Y-Axis** to **Bits/Tick**. **Packets/Tick** is also important and we will see implementations for it in the applications chapters (chapters 7-14) later in the book.

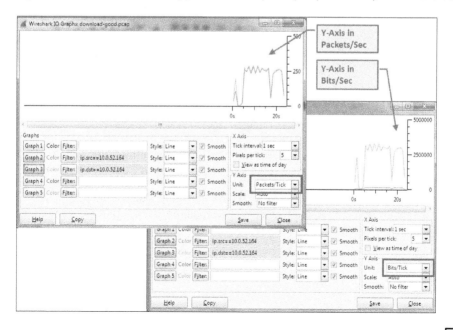

Throughput measurements with IO Graph

IO Graph is a convenient tool for measuring the throughput of a network. Using it, we can measure the traffic and throughput of any predefined filter. In this recipe we will see some examples for measuring the throughput of a network.

Getting ready

Connect your laptop with Wireshark to a network with a port mirror to the link you want to measure, as you learned in *Chapter 1, Introducing Wireshark*. Start a new capture or open an existing file, and open the **IO Graphs** tool from the **Statistics** menu.

While measuring the throughput, we can measure the throughput on a communication line between end devices (PC to server, phone to phone, PC to the Internet, and so on) or to a specific application.

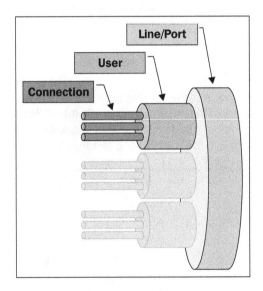

The process of isolating network problems starts from measuring traffic over a link between end devices on single connections and seeing where it comes from.

Some typical measurements are host-to-host traffic, all the traffic to a specific server, all the traffic to a specific application on a specific server, all the TCP performance phenomena on a specific server, and more.

How to do it...

In this recipe, we will provide some basic filters for measuring traffic in the network.

Measuring throughput between end devices

To measure the throughput between end devices, simply configure a display filter between their IP addresses.

For example, to see the traffic between 10.2.10.101 and 10.2.10.240, configure the filter:

```
ip.add req 10.2.10.240 and ip.add req 10.2.10.240.
```

You can either type the filter in the IO Graph's **Filter:** box or perform the following steps:

1. Place the cursor on a packet in a specific connection.
2. Right-click on it and navigate to **Conversation filter | IP**. The filter string will appear in the upper display filter box.
3. Copy the filter string from the upper display filter box to one of the IO Graph **Filter:** boxes.
4. Click on the filter bow button in the **IO Graphs** window to activate it.

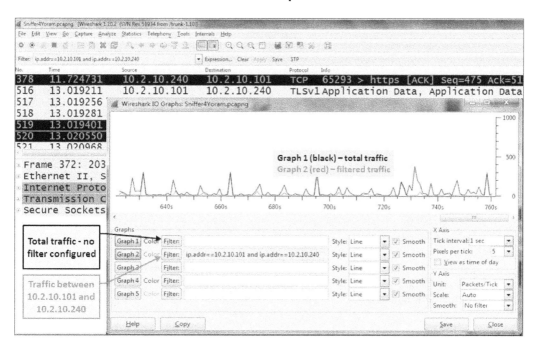

Measuring application throughput

In order to configure the performance measurement of a specific application, you can configure a filter that contains specific port numbers or a specific connection.

There are several ways to isolate an application graph. Here's one of them:

1. In the captured data, click on any packet that belongs to the traffic stream. In TCP it will be a specific connection; in UDP it will be just a stream between two IP/Port pairs.

2. Right-click on it and choose **Follow TCP stream** or **Follow UDP stream**. You will get `tcp.streameq<number>` or `udp.streameq<number>`. `<number>` is simply the number of the stream in the capture file.

3. Copy the string to the filter window in the **IO Graphs** window and you will get the graph of the specific stream.

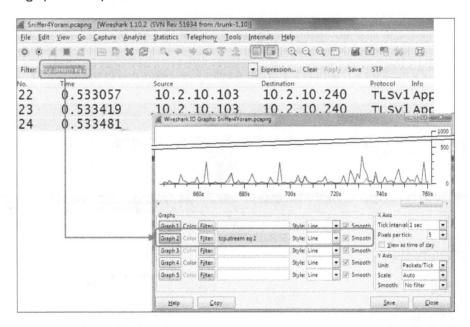

If you want a graph for specific data on the stream, add information to the filter. For example (in the previous illustration):

▸ `tcp.streameq 2` and `tcp.analysis.retransmissions` will give all the TCP retransmissions on the specific stream (indicating, for example, a slow network, errors, or packet loss)

▸ `tcp.streameq 2` and `tcp.analysis.zero_window` will give all the TCP zero window phenomena on the specific stream (indicating a slow end device)

How it works...

The power of the IO Graph tool comes from the fact that you can configure any display filter and see it as a graph in various shapes and configurations. Any parameter in a packet can be filtered and monitored in this way.

There's more...

Some examples for parameters that can be monitored are explained in this section.

Graph SMS usage – finding SMS messages sent by a specific subscriber

1. To configure the filter, choose **SMPP** (**Short Message Peer to Peer protocol**) packets with the command `Submit_SM`. This is the SMPP command that sends the SMS.

2. Type `smpp.destination_addr == "phone number"` in the filter. The filter `smpp.destination_addr == "972527098241"` was configured in the example.

Graphing number of accesses to the Google web page

1. Open the **IO Graphs** window. You can do it during the capture to view online statistics or open a saved capture file.

2. Configure the filter `http.host contains "<name>"`, in our case, `http.host contains "google"`.

3. In the packet list you will see (while configuring the same filter) the information shown in the following screenshot:

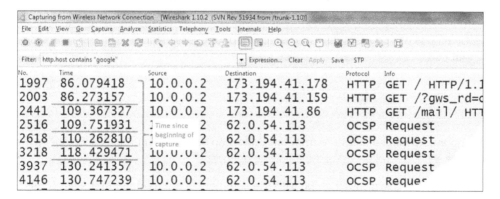

4. In the **IO Graphs** window, you will see the following graph:

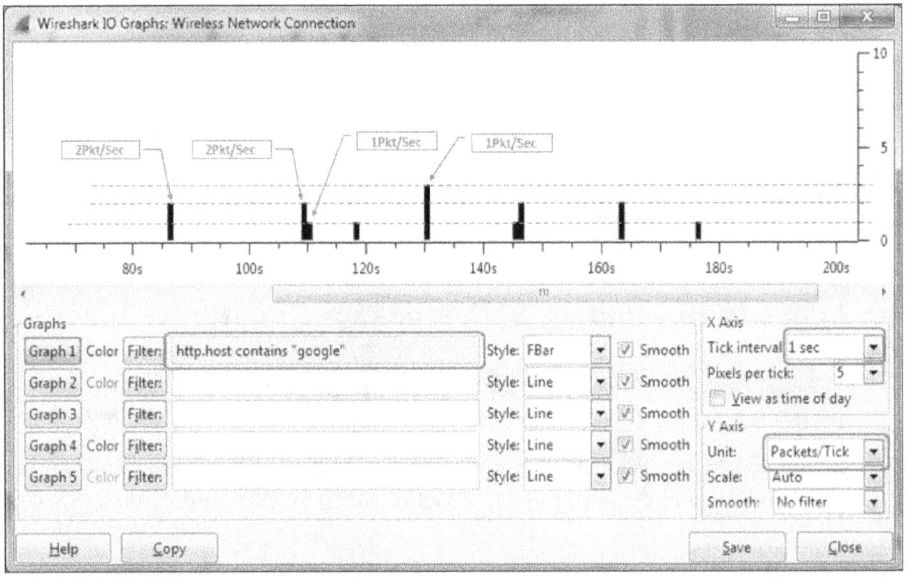

In the packet capture pane, you can see that we've had two accesses to Google after around 86 seconds, the next two after around 109 seconds, and so on.

Advanced IO Graph configurations with advanced Y-Axis parameters

In standard measurements with the IO Graph tool, we measure the performance of the network in units of packets/second, bytes/second, or bits/second. There are some types of data that cannot be measured with these parameters, and this is the reason we have the **Advanced...** feature in the **Y-Axis** options.

Getting ready

Choosing the **Advanced...** feature from the **Unit:** drop-down menu under **Y-Axis** opens a wider **IO Graphs** window, and provides the following options:

- ▶ **SUM (*)**: This draws a graph with the summary of a parameter in the tick interval
- ▶ **COUNT FRAMES (*)**: This draws a graph that counts the occurrence of the filtered frames in the tick interval
- ▶ **COUNT FIELDS (*)**: This draws a graph that counts the occurrence of the filtered field in the tick interval

- ► **MAX (*)**: This draws a graph with the maximum of a parameter in the tick interval
- ► **MIN (*)**: This draws a graph with the minimum of a parameter in the tick interval
- ► **AVG (*)**: This draws a graph with the average of a parameter in the tick interval
- ► **LOAD (*)**: This is used for response time graphs

How to do it...

To start using the **IO Graphs** window with the **Advanced** feature, perform the following steps:

1. Start the **IO Graphs** window from the **Statistics** menu.
2. In the **Unit:** drop-down menu under **Y-Axis**, choose the **Advanced...** option. You will get the following window:

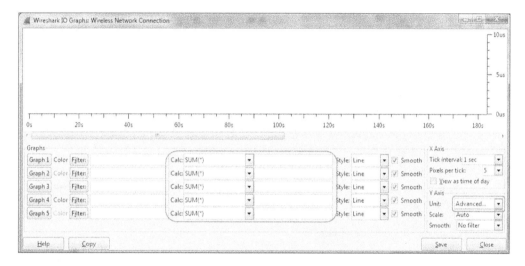

3. You will see new drop-down menus with the string **SUM(*)**.
4. Choose **SUM(*)/COUNT FRAMES (*)/COUNT FIELDS (*)/MAX(*)/MIN(*)/AVG(*)/ LOAD(*)**, and configure the appropriate filters. In the next recipes we will see some useful examples.

How to monitor inter-frame time delta statistics

The time delta between frames can influence TCP performance, and there are cases in which we would like to correlate these with the performance we get from the network.

Let's look at the following capture file:

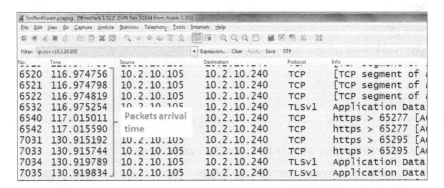

Here, we see packets sent from the source IP 10.2.10.105 as configured in the display filter.

To view the time variance between frames, configure the following parameters:

- To view the maximum `frame.time_delta` value, configure `ip.src == 10.2.10.105` in the field beside **Filter:** and choose **MAX(*)** and type `frame.time_delta` in the fields beside **Calc:**

- To view the average `frame.time_delta` value, configure `ip.src == 10.2.10.105` in the field beside **Filter:** and choose **AVG(*)** and type `frame.time_delta` in the fields beside **Calc:**

- To view the minimum `frame.time_delta` value, configure `ip.src == 10.2.10.105` in the field beside **Filter:** and choose **MIN(*)** and type `frame.time_delta` in the fields beside **Calc:**

The graph that we will get is as follows:

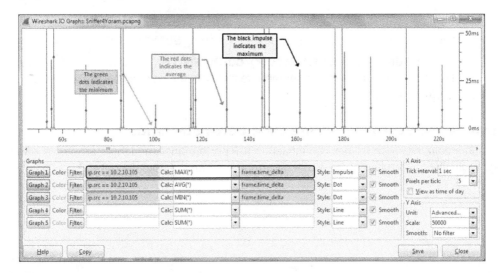

What we see in the screenshot is a graph of the minimum, average, and maximum time delta between frames. What do we do with it and how do we use it for network debugging? This will be covered in *Chapter 10, HTTP and DNS*.

How to monitor the number of TCP retransmissions in a stream

TCP events can be of many types: retransmissions, sliding window events, ACKs (or lack of them), and others. To see the number of TCP events over time, we can use the IO Graph tool with the **Advanced...** feature and the **COUNT(*)** parameter.

To do this, perform the following steps:

1. Open **IO Graphs** from the **Statistics** menu.

2. Under **Y-Axis**, choose **Advanced...** for **Unit:**.

3. Configure the filters as follows:

    ❑ IP source and destination filters in the fields beside the **Filter:** buttons

    ❑ TCP events in the fields to the left of **Style:**

    ❑ Choose **COUNT FRAMES (*)** in the **Calc:** field and type `tcp.analysis.retransmissions` in the filter field

In this example, filters were configured to monitor TCP retransmissions on three different TCP streams.

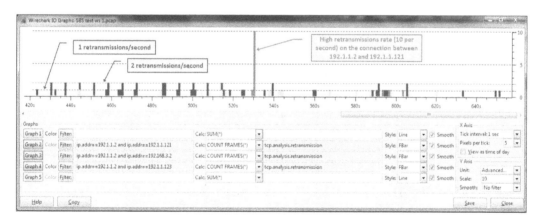

In the graph of the preceding screenshot, you can see that retransmissions from each TCP stream are presented in different colors.

How to monitor a number of field appearances

In various network protocols (mostly on those running over TCP), variations in time between frames (that is, the frame-time delta filter) can influence the performance significantly. One of the tools for viewing these changes in the **IO Graphs** window is the **Advanced...** configuration.

To do it, perform the following steps:

1. Right-click on a packet in the suspicious TCP stream and navigate to **Conversation filter | TCP**. A filter will appear in the main filter box.

2. Open **IO Graph** from the **Statistics** menu.

3. Under **Y-Axis**, choose **Advanced...** for **Unit:**.

4. Configure the filters as follows:

    ❏ Copy the filter definition from the upper filter box on the right-hand side to the IO Graph filter box on the left-hand side

    ❏ On the left-hand side, type the filter `frame.time_delta`

    ❏ Choose **AVG(*)** to see the average delta.

5. Choose the appropriate X-Axis resolution.

Here is an example. In the following screenshot, we see a packet list with time variations between frames (a second time column was added in order to see the real time and time variations):

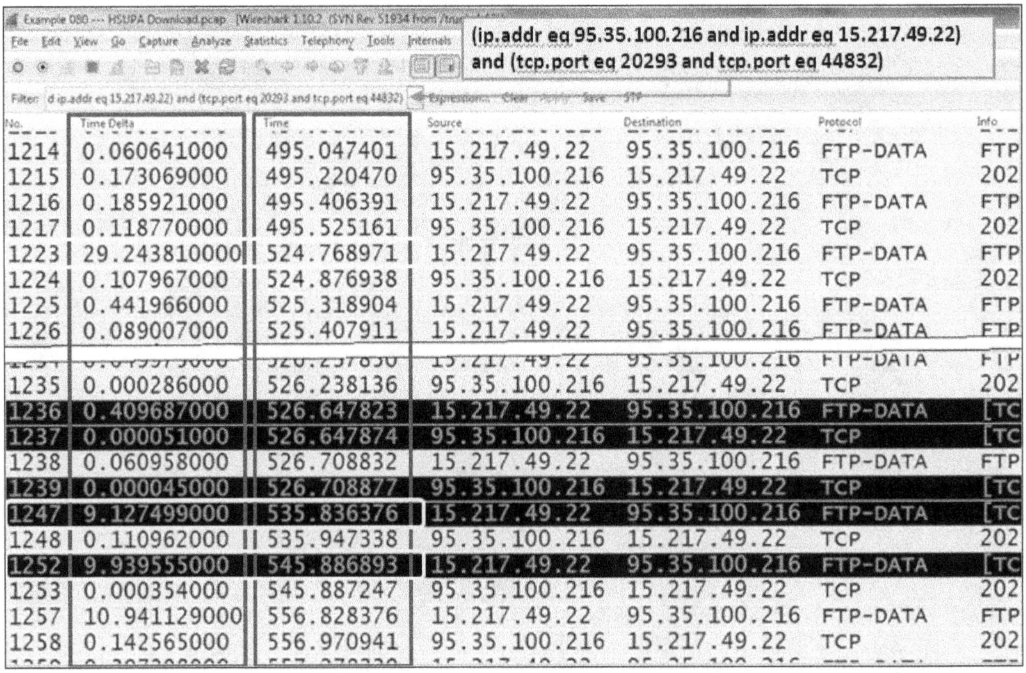

You see that there are some large time variations between frames; for example, 29.24 seconds in the frame 1,223, 9.12 seconds in the frame 1,247, and more.

In the **IO Graphs** window configured as described earlier, you will see the following:

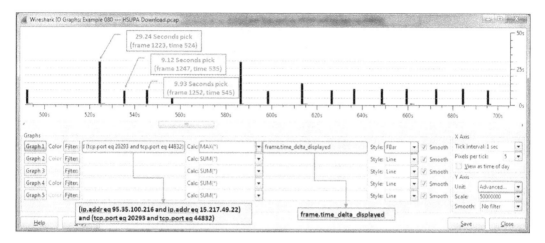

As you see here, there are variations in time between frames. Later in this book, we will learn to see what causes these problems and how to solve them.

How it works...

The IO Graph tool is one of the strongest and most efficient tools of Wireshark. While the standard IO Graph statistics can be used for basic statistics, the **Advanced...** feature can be used for in-depth monitoring of response times, TCP analysis of a single stream or several streams, and more.

When we configure a filter on the left, we will filter the traffic between hosts, traffic in a connection, traffic on a server, and so on. The **Advanced...** feature provides us with more details on traffic. Here are a few examples:

- ▶ On the left you see the TCP stream; on the right you see the time delta between frames in the stream

- ▶ On the left you see the video/RTP stream; on the right you see the occurrence of a marker bit

There's more...

You can always click on **IO Graph**, and it will bring you to the reference packet in the packet pane.

Getting information through TCP stream graphs – the Time-Sequence (Stevens) window

One of the tools in Wireshark that enables us to dig deeper into applications behavior is the TCP stream graphs. These graphs, as we will see in the following recipes, enable us to get the filling of the application behavior along with the possibility to locate problems in it.

Getting ready

Open an existing capture or start a new capture. Click on a specific packet in the capture file. Even though you can use this feature on a running capture, it is not meant for online statistics; so it is recommended that you start a capture, stop it, and then use this tool.

How to do it...

To view TCP stream graph statistics, perform the following steps:

1. Click on the packet of the stream you want to monitor.

The TCP Stream shows a directional graph, so when you click on a packet, it should be in the direction you want to view the statistics on. If, for example, you download a file and want to view the download statistics, click on a packet in the download direction.

2. From the **Statistics** menu navigate to **TCP StreamGraph | Time-Sequence Graph (Stevens)**. The following window will open up:

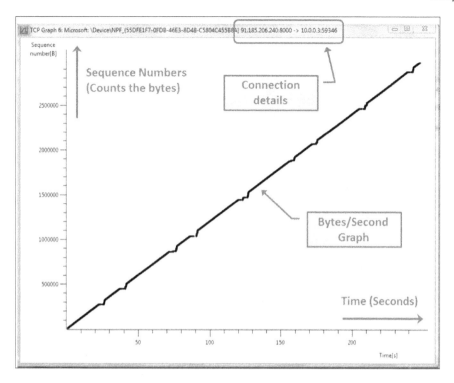

The graph actually shows the advance of byte transfer over time. In this example we see a continuous diagonal line, which is an indication of a good file transfer.

To measure the throughput of a file transfer, simply calculate the bytes transferred in a unit of time as shown in the following screenshot:

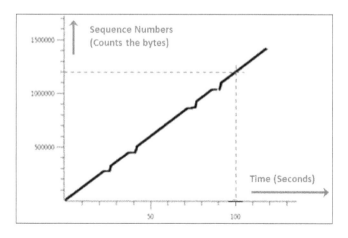

We see that the transfer rate is 1,200,000 bytes in 100 seconds, that is, 12,000 bytes/seconds or 95 Kbits/sec.

3. Clicking on a point in the graph using the scrollbar will magnify the graph around the point that you clicked on.

4. Right-clicking on a point in the graph will take us to the packet pane in the captured file.

5. For changing graph parameters, we have a small window opened parallel to the graph as shown in the following screenshot:

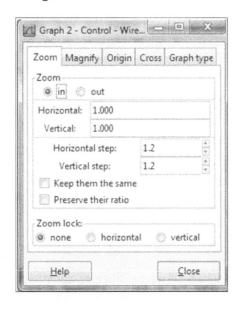

6. For changing from zoom in to zoom out, click on the **in** or **out** button.

How it works...

The Time-Sequence Graph (Stevens) is a simple graph that counts the TCP sequence numbers over time. Since TCP sequence numbers count the bytes sent by TCP, these are actually application bytes (including application headers) sent from one side to another.

This graph (as we will learn in the TCP and applications chapters) can give us a good indication of the application's behavior. For example, a diagonal line means a good file transfer, while a diagonal line with interrupts shows a problem in transfer. A diagonal line with a high gradient indicates fast data transfer, while a low gradient indicates a low rate of transfer (depends on the scale of course).

There's more...

Left-clicking on a point in the graph will take you to the packet in the packet pane. When you see a problem, zoom into it, left-click on it, and check what went wrong with the packets.

While viewing a graph, it is important to know what the application is. A graph that indicates a problem in one application can be a perfect network behavior for another application.

Getting information through TCP stream graphs – the Time-Sequence (tcp-trace) window

TCP time-sequence graphs based on the UNIX `tcpdump` command provide us with additional data on the connection that we monitor. In addition to the standard sequence/seconds in Time-Sequence (Stevens), we also get information on the ACKs that were sent, retransmissions, window size, and more details that enables us to analyze problems on the connection.

Getting ready

Open an existing capture or start a new capture. Click on a specific packet in the capture file. Even though you can use this feature on a running capture, it is not meant for online statistics; so it is recommended that you start a capture, stop it, and then use this tool.

How to do it...

To view TCP stream graph statistics, perform the following steps:

1. Click on a packet in the stream you want to monitor.

The TCP stream shows a directional graph, so when you click on a packet, it should be in the direction you want to view the statistics on. If, for example, you download a file and want to view the download statistics, click on a packet in the download direction.

2. From the **Statistics** menu navigate to **TCP StreamGraph | Time-Sequence Graph (tcp-trace)**. The following window will open up:

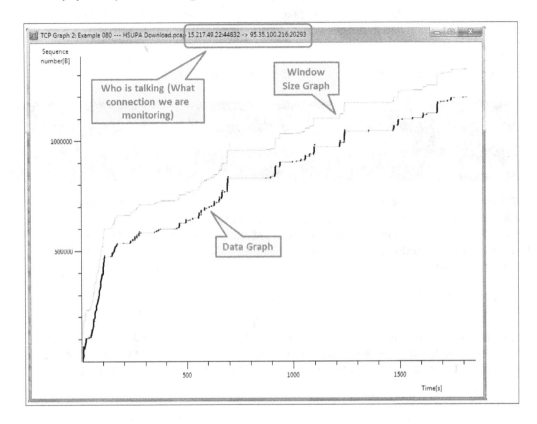

The graph shows the advance of byte transfer over time in the lower black graph and the window size in the upper gray graph. When there is space between the two, it means that there is some TCP buffering left and TCP will transfer bytes. Once they get closer and touch each other, it would be a window-full phenomenon that does not enable further data transfer.

3. We obtain the following screenshot when we zoom into a specific area:

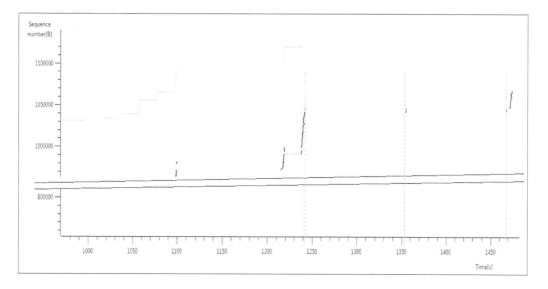

4. We obtain the following captured packets when we zoom into a particular area in the graph:

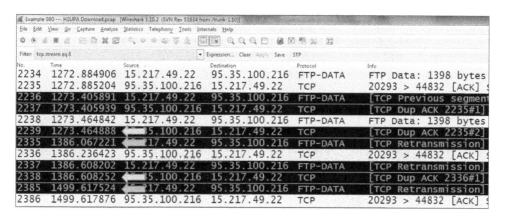

You can see that in the packet capture, there is a frame in time 1,273 (seconds after the beginning of the capture), a break, a packet in time 1,386, a break, and a packet in 1499.

In the TCP stream graph you see the breaks in transmission, and we can look for its reason when we are back to the packets pane.

How it works...

The **Time sequence (TCP-trace)** graph is taken from the UNIX `tcpdump` command, which also checks the window size published by the receiver (this is the buffer size allocated by the receiver to the process), along with retransmitted packets and ACKs.

Working with this graph provides us with a lot of information, which we will use later for network debugging. The phenomena from a window that is being filled faster than expected to a lot of retransmissions and others will become visual with this graph that will help us to solve them.

There's more...

The more we zoom in, the more details we will get as shown in the following screenshot:

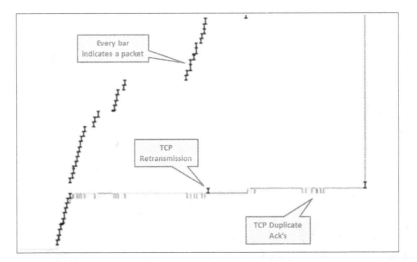

A bar is an indication of a packet that carries data between the initial and final sequence numbers. The bar that is not in the regular graph and looks like it runs away from it is a retransmission and the gray bar is a duplicate ACK. We will learn about these phenomena in *Chapter 9, UDP/TCP Analysis*.

Getting information through TCP stream graphs – the Throughput Graph window

The **Throughput Graph** window of the TCP stream graphs enables us to look at the throughput of a connection and check for instabilities.

Getting ready

Open an existing capture or start a new capture. Click on a specific packet in the capture file. Even though you can use this feature on a running capture, it is not meant for online statistics; so it is recommended that you start a capture, stop it, and then use this tool.

How to do it...

To view TCP stream graph statistics, perform the following steps:

1. Click on a packet in the stream you want to monitor.

2. From the **Statistics** menu, navigate to **TCP StreamGraph | Throughput Graph**. The following window will open up:

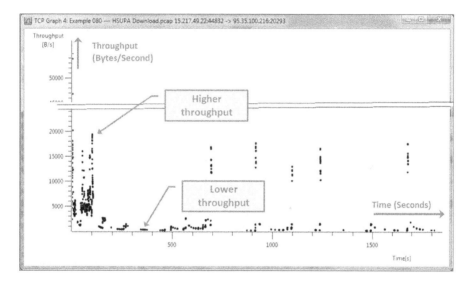

In the graph, we see that the throughput is not stable and varies between around 20,000 bytes/sec to 1000 bytes/sec. This can be due to an unstable file transfer (which is the case in this FTP download over the HSUPA cellular connection), or just an application that works this way (for example, browsing the Internet).

How it works...

The throughput graph simply counts the TCP sequence numbers over time and since sequence numbers are actually the application's data, this gives us the application throughput in bytes per second.

There's more...

A stable file transfer should look almost like a solid line, as shown in the following graph:

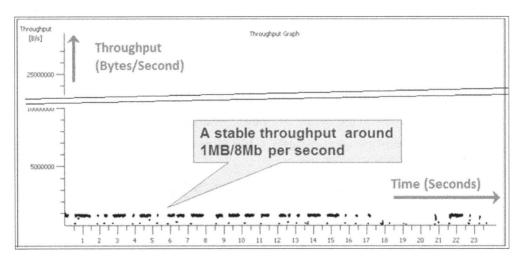

Here, MB is mega bytes and Mb is mega bits.

Getting information through TCP stream graphs – the Round Trip Time window

The **Round Trip Time** window of the TCP stream graphs enables us to look at the round trip between sequence numbers and the time they were acknowledged. Along with other graphs, it provides us with a look at the performance of the connection.

Getting ready

Open an existing capture or start a new capture. Click on a specific packet in the capture file. Even though you can use this feature on a running capture, it is not meant for online statistics, so it is recommended that you start a capture, stop it, and then use this tool.

How to do it...

To view the TCP stream graph statistics, perform the following steps:

1. Click on a packet in the stream you want to monitor.

2. From the **Statistics** menu navigate to **TCP StreamGraph** | **Round Trip Time Graph**. The following window will open up:

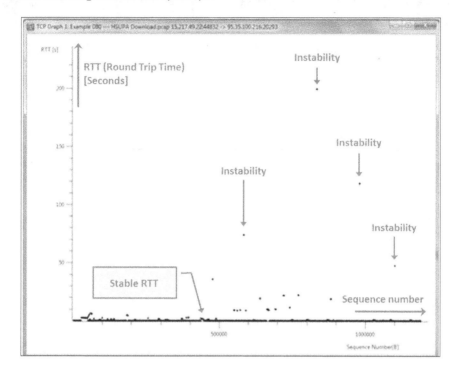

In the preceding graph, we see that most of the sequence numbers were acknowledged in a short time; however, there is some instability that will influence the TCP performance.

How it works...

What we see in the graph is a plot of TCP sequence numbers versus the time that took to acknowledge them. Actually, this is the time between a sent packet and the ACK received for that packet.

There's more...

When you see a graph that shows instabilities, it's not necessarily a problem. It can also be that this is how the application works. You can see that it took time to acknowledge a packet because there is a problem, or because a server is waiting for a response, or because a client is browsing a web server and the user is waiting between clicks on new links.

Getting information through TCP stream graphs – the Window Scaling Graph window

The Window Scaling Graph of the TCP stream graph enables us to look at the window size published by the receiving side, which is an indication of the receiver's ability to process data. Along with the other graphs, it provides us with a look at the performance of the connection.

Getting ready

Open an existing capture or start a new capture. Click on a specific packet in the capture file. Even though you can use this feature on a running capture, it is not meant for online statistics, so it is recommended that you start a capture, stop it, and then use this tool.

How to do it...

To view TCP stream graph statistics, perform the following steps:

1. Click on a packet in the stream you want to monitor.

2. From the **Statistics** menu navigate to **TCP StreamGraph | Window Scaling Graph**. The following window will open up:

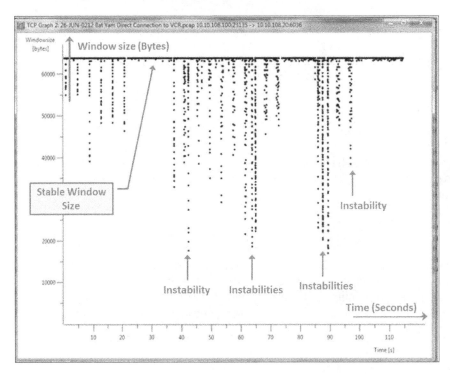

In this graph, we see the instability caused by one of the sides. This can be an indication of a slow server or client that cannot process all the data it receives and therefore, by reducing the received window size, it tells the other side to send less data.

How it works...

The software here simply watches the window size on the connection and draws it. In *Chapter 9, UDP/TCP Analysis*, we will get into the details.

There's more...

When the window size decreases, the application throughput should decrease as well. The window size is completely controlled by the two ends of a connection, for example, a client and a server; variations in the window size do not have anything to do with network performance.

6

Using the Expert Infos Window

In this chapter we will talk about the following:

- ▶ The **Expert Infos** window and how to use it for network troubleshooting
- ▶ Error events and understanding them
- ▶ Warnings events and understanding them
- ▶ Notes events and understanding them

Introduction

One of Wireshark's strongest capabilities is the ability to analyze network phenomena and suggest to us a probable cause for it. Along with other tools, it gives us detailed information on network performance and problems. In this chapter, we will learn about the Expert System. It is a tool that provides us with a deeper analysis of network phenomena, including events and problems. Later in this book, we will provide detailed recipes on how to use the **Expert Infos** window along with other tools to find and resolve network problems.

In the first recipe, we will learn how to work with the **Expert Infos** window. In the next recipes, we will learn about the probable causes for the majority of events that you can expect.

The Expert Infos window and how to use it for network troubleshooting

The **Expert Infos** window provides us with a list of events and network problems discovered by Wireshark. In this recipe, we will learn how to start the **Expert Infos** window and how to refer to the various events.

Getting ready

Start Wireshark, and start a live capture or open an existing file.

How to do it...

To start the **Expert Infos** window, perform the following steps:

Navigate to the **Analyze** menu and click on **Expert Info**. The following window will open:

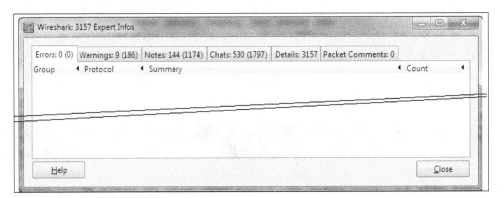

Now you can choose any one of the upper bars: **Errors:**, **Warnings:**, **Notes:**, **Chats:**, **Details:**, or **Packet Comments:**.

 The number at the right-hand side of the bar shows the number of events in this category.

The upper bars give you the following information:

▶ **Errors:** These are serious problems, mostly malformed packets or missing fields in a protocol header. These can be malformed packets of various types such as malformed SPOOLSS, GTP, or others. These can also be bad checksum errors such as IPv4 bad checksum.

In the following screenshot you can see malformed TCP and SSL packets:

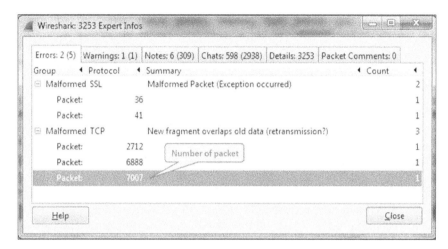

In the following screenshot, you can see another type of error, which is a protocol (in this case the **BOOTP/DHCP**) option error, that is, when Wireshark identifies a missing field in the packet:

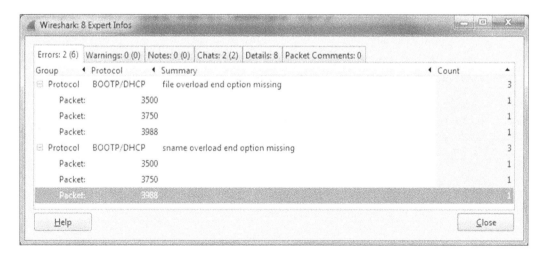

> ▶ **Warnings:** A warning indicates a problem in the application or in communication, things such as TCP zero window, TCP window full, previous segment not captured, out-of-order segment, and others that are unnatural to the protocol behavior. You can see an example of this in the following screenshot:

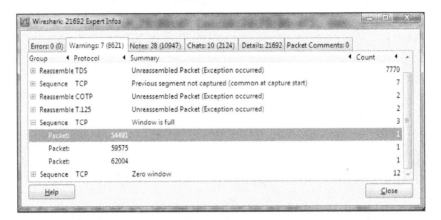

> ▶ **Notes:** A note is when Wireshark indicates an event that may cause a problem, but is still within the normal behavior of the protocol. TCP retransmission, for example, will be displayed here because even though it is a critical problem that slows down the network, it is still under the normal behavior of TCP. Other events here are duplicate ACK, fast retransmission, and so on.

> ▶ **Chats:** This tab provides information about the usual workflow, for example, TCP connection start (SYN), connection end (FIN), connection reset (RST), HTTP Post, HTTP codes, and so on.

> ▶ **Details:** This tab provides all the events in an ordered list. In older versions of Wireshark, this was directly under the **Analyze** menu.

> ▶ **Packet Comments:** You can manually add a comment to every packet. This column will show all the comments in the capture file.

To add a comment to a packet, right-click on it and choose **Packet Comment...**. A window will open in which you will be able to add or change your comment. You can see this in the following screenshot:

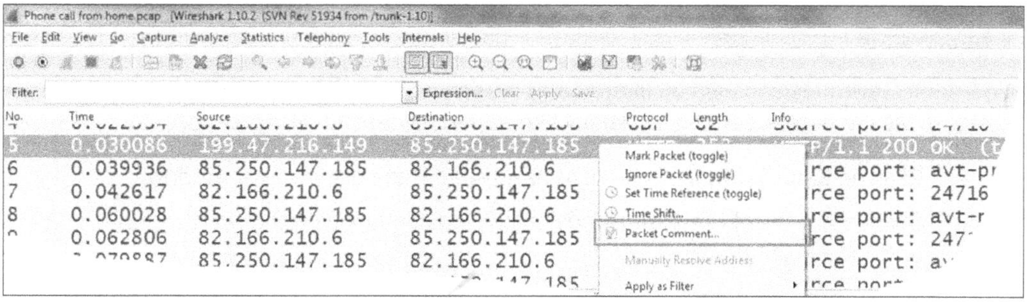

To go to the event in the packet capture pane, simply click on the packet under the event in the **Expert Infos** window, and it will lead you to it.

> It is important to note that although a warning event may have no importance, a note event can influence the network badly. Always get into the problem details, see where is it coming from, and what is its meaning.

How it works...

The Wireshark **Expert Infos** window is an expert system that provides us with information about problems in the network and also some suggestions to the probable cause of it in some cases. Although it gives reasonable results, always double-check its findings.

There are cases where Wireshark finds problems that are not genuine, and there are other cases where the real problems that exist do not show up.

> Don't forget that the best troubleshooting tool is your brain (and your knowledge of networking). Wireshark is a very smart tool, but still it is only a tool.

It can be that you started the capture during a data transfer; so you will see the previous segment's loss messages or even more sophisticated problems, when for some reason (good or not) you have captured only a part of the data, and Wireshark refers to it as a complete stream of data and displays many errors about it. We will see many examples of these issues later in the book.

There's more...

Expert Info severities can also be filtered and presented in the packet pane by displaying filters. To view events according to display filters, perform the following steps:

1. Click on **Expression...** on the right-hand side of the display filter window.

2. Scroll down to get the **Expert** messages (you can just type the word `expert` and you will get there).

    As illustrated in the following screenshot, you will get the following filters: `expert.message`, `expert.group`, and `expert.severity`:

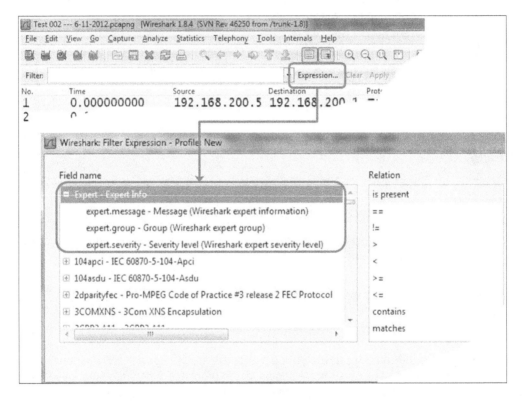

-   `expert.group` refers to expert message groups. This filter categorizes problems according to their types, for example, checksum problems, TCP sequence-related problems, and so on. Have a look at the following screenshot and you will see a list of these issues:

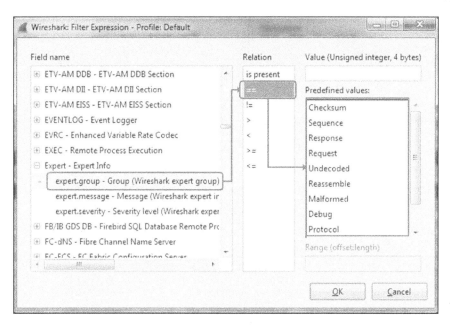

The main categories in `expert.group` are as follows:

- ❑ **Checksum**: This indicates an invalid checksum.

- ❑ **Sequence**: This indicates TCP sequence-related problems.

- ❑ **Response**: This indicates application response code problems
  (4xx response code files).

- ❑ **Request**: This indicates application requests.

- ❑ **Undecoded**: This indicates data that cannot be decoded by dissector.

- ❑ **Reassemble**: This indicates problems while reassembling (usually when
  a fragment is missing).

- ❑ **Malformed**: This indicates a malformed packet or dissector problem,
  and the dissection of this packet is aborted.

- ❑ **Debug**: This indicates debugging (should not occur in released versions).

- ❑ **Protocol**: This indicates the violation of protocol specification
  (for example, missing field, wrong length, and so on), dissection
  of this packet will probably be continued.

- ❑ **Comment**: This indicates packets with a comment added to them
  (comments can be added to a packet by right-clicking on it and choosing
  the **Packet comment ...** option.

❑ expert.message refers to specific messages. Here, for example, you can configure a filter that displays a message that contains or matches a specific string.

❑ expert.severity refers to messages with specific severities, that is error, warning, note and so on.

You can also choose to show events severities on the **Expert Info** window.

1. Navigate to **Edit | Preferences....**

2. Choose **User Interface**.

3. In the lower half of the right pane, mark the **Display LEDs in the Expert Infos dialog tab labels:** checkbox as presented in the following screenshot:

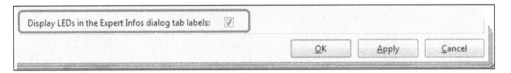

4. Click on **OK**.

5. Open the **Expert Infos** window and the severity LEDs will appear on each bar.

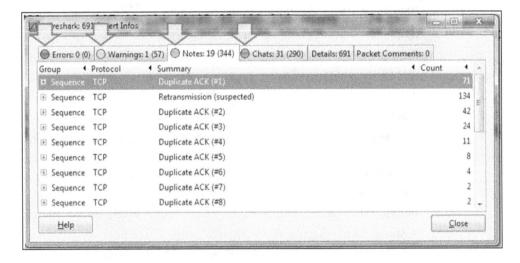

The severity level LED will also appear on the lower left corner of the Wireshark main window.

See also

▸   *Chapter 9, UDP/TCP Analysis*

Error events and understanding them

In this recipe, we will get into error and event types, checksum errors, malformed packets, and other types of errors, and what we can understand from them.

Getting ready

Start capturing or open an existing file, and then start the **Expert Infos** window.

How to do it...

1. From the **Analyze** menu, open **Expert Infos** by clicking on **Expert Info**.

2. Click on the **Errors:** bar (should be opened as default). You will get the following window (all events are examples):

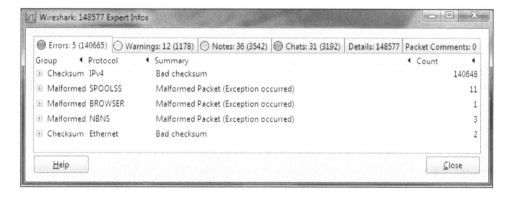

In the preceding window, you can see the following two types of errors:

❏   **Checksum errors**: These can be in Ethernet, IP, or other protocols. In this case, it can be because of real errors or offload.

❏   **Malformed packets**: These are usually in the application protocols. In this case also, it can be due to a real problem or a dissector error.

How it works...

Checksum is an error-checking mechanism that uses a byte or a sequence of bytes inserted in the packet in order to implement a frame verification algorithm. The principle of error-checking algorithms is to calculate a formula over the entire message (layer 4), packet (layer 3) or frame (layer 2), insert the result in bytes inside the packet, and when the packet arrives at the destination, it calculates the formula again. If we get the same result, it is a good packet; if not, there is an error. The error-checking mechanism can be calculated over the entire packet or only over the header, depending on the protocol.

Offload mechanisms are mechanisms on which the IP, TCP, and UDP checksums are calculated on the NIC just before they're transmitted to the wire. In Wireshark, these show up as corrupt packets because Wireshark captures packets before they are sent to the network adapter; therefore, it will not see the correct checksum because it has not been calculated yet.

For this reason, even though it might look like severe errors, in many cases checksum errors are actually Wireshark errors of misconfiguration. In cases where you see many checksum errors on packets that are sent from your PC, it is probably because of offload.

To cancel the checksum validation, you can do either of the following depending on your protocol:

- ▸ For IPv4, when you see many checksum errors and you are sure they are because of the offload, navigate to **Edit | Preferences...**. Further, navigate to **Protocols | IPv4** and uncheck the **Validate the IPv4 checksum if possible:** checkbox.

- ▸ For TCP, when you see many checksum errors and you are sure they are because of the offload, navigate to **Edit | Preferences...**. Further, navigate to **Protocols | TCP** and uncheck the **Validate the TCP checksum if possible:** checkbox.

There's more...

Malformed packets can be Wireshark bugs or real malformed packets. Use other tools for isolating the problem. Suspected bugs can be reported on the Wireshark website.

When you see a large amount of malformed packets of checksum errors, it is probably because of offload or dissector errors. Networks with more than 1-2 percent errors of any kind will cause many other events (retransmissions for example) and will become much slower than expected, and therefore, you cannot have a high error rate with a functioning network!

See also

▸   *Chapter 9, UDP/TCP Analysis*

Warning events and understanding them

As described earlier, warning events indicate problems in the application or in communication. In this recipe, we will describe the main events in this category.

Getting ready

Start capturing or open an existing file, and start the **Expert Infos** window.

How to do it...

1.   From the **Analyze** menu, open **Expert Infos** by clicking on **Expert Info**.

2.   Click on the **Warnings:** bar. You will get the following window (all events are examples):

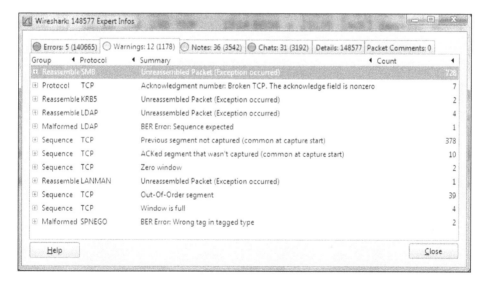

You will see here several event categories:

- ❏   **Reassembly problems**: These are mostly un-reassembled packets. These are usually indicated as Wireshark dissector problems.

- ❏   **TCP window problems**: These are mostly zero window and window full problems. These usually indicate slow-end devices (servers, PCs, and so on).

> ❑ **Segment loss, segments not in order**: These indicate previous segment losses and the ACKed segment that wasn't captured. These are usually TCP problems that are caused by network problems.

How it works...

Wireshark watches the parameters of the monitored packets as follows:

- ▶ It watches TCP window sizes and checks if the window size reduced to zero
- ▶ It looks for TCP packets (segments) that are out of order, that is, if they were sent before or after the expected time
- ▶ It looks for ACKs for TCP packets that were not sent

These parameters, along with many others, provide you with a good starting point to look for network problems. We will go into the details of it in *Chapter 9, UDP/TCP Analysis*.

There's more...

Don't forget that warning events are those that Wireshark refers to as important, but it is not necessarily so. If, for example, you have previous segment not captured, they will be under warnings, but it can be due to capture problems.

See also

- ▶ *Chapter 9, UDP/TCP Analysis*

Notes events and understanding them

As described earlier, when Wireshark indicates that an event may cause a problem but is still inside the normal behavior of the protocol, it will be under the **Notes** bar. TCP retransmission, for example, will be displayed under the **Notes** bar because even though it is a critical problem that slows down the network, it is still under the normal behavior of TCP.

Getting ready

Start capturing or open an existing file and start the **Expert Infos** window.

How to do it...

1. From the **Analyze** menu, open **Expert Infos** by clicking on **Expert Info**.
2. Click on the **Notes** bar. You will get the following window (all events are examples):

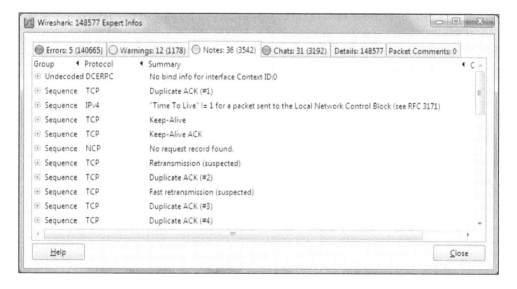

Insert image 76450S_01_08.png

You will see here several event categories:

- ❑ Retransmissions, duplicate ACKs, fast retransmissions that usually indicate slow network, packet loss, or very slow end devices or applications

- ❑ Keep-alives that indicate TCP or application problems

- ❑ Time to live and routing events that in most cases indicate routing problems

> Additional events will be discussed in *Chapter 9, UDP/TCP Analysis, Chapter 10, HTTP and DNS, Chapter 11, Analyzing Enterprise Applications', Behavior,* and *Chapter 12, SIP, Multimedia, and IP Telephony.*

How it works...

Wireshark watches the parameters of the monitored packets. It watches TCP sequences and acknowledges numbers while checking for retransmissions and other sequencing problems. It looks for IP **Time To Live** (**TTL**) with value of 1 coming from a remote network, and tells you it is a problem. It looks for keep-alives that may be in a normal condition but can also indicate a problem.

These parameters, along with many others, provide you with a good starting point to look for network performance problems.

There's more...

Many symptoms that are seen here can be an indication of several types of problems. For example, a packet can be retransmitted because of an error that caused the packet to be lost, because of bad network conditions (low bandwidth or high delay) that caused the packet not to arrive on time, and it can be also because of a nonresponsive server or client. The Expert Info system will give you the symptom. We will learn later in this book how to solve this problem.

See also

- ▶ You can read more on TCP performance issues in *Chapter 9, UDP/TCP Analysis.* It includes TCP retransmissions, fast retransmissions and why they happen, what are ACKs and duplicate ACKs, zero window, window changes and other TCP sliding windows issues, and more.

7
Ethernet, LAN Switching, and Wireless LAN

In this chapter we will cover the following topics:

- ▶ Discovering broadcast and error storms
- ▶ Analyzing Spanning Tree Protocols
- ▶ Analyzing VLANs and VLAN tagging issues
- ▶ Analyzing wireless (Wi-Fi) problems

Introduction

In this chapter, we will focus on how to find and resolve layer-2-based problems with the focus on Ethernet-based issues such as broadcast events and errors and how to find out where they are coming from. We will also focus on LAN protocols such as Spanning Tree, VLANs, and Wireless LAN.

These issues have to be resolved before we go up to layers 3, 4, and the Application layers, since layer 2 problems will be reflected in the upper layer protocols. For example, packet losses in layer 2 will cause retransmissions in TCP, which is a layer 4 protocol, and these can cause slow application response time in the upper layers.

Discovering broadcast and error storms

One of the most troublesome problems in communication networks is the **broadcast** and **error storms**. These problems can happen because of layer 2 loops, layer-2-based attacks, a problematic network adapter, or a service that sends packets to the network.

In this chapter we will provide some basic recipes on how to find, isolate, and solve these types of problems.

 A broadcast storm is when you get thousands and even tens of thousands of broadcasts per second. In most cases it would lock out the network completely.

Getting ready

In these types of problems, you will usually be called on to solve the *network is very slow* or *network has stopped working* problems.

Several important facts to remember are:

- Broadcasts are not forwarded by routers.
- Broadcasts are not forwarded between VLANs (this is why VLANs are called **broadcast domains**), so every VLAN is a single broadcast domain.
- Error packets are not forwarded by LAN switches (at least not through the good ones).
- Multicasts are forwarded through switches, unless configured otherwise.
- Multicasts are forwarded through routers only if the routers are configured to do so.
- A reasonable number of broadcasts are transmitted in every network. This is how networks work. Too many broadcasts could be a problem.

 There is a difference between too many broadcasts and a broadcast storm. Too many broadcasts (for example, a few hundred per second) can load the network but still, in most cases, users will not notice it. Broadcast storms will lock out the network completely.

How to do it...

To find out where the problem comes from, go through the following steps:

1. Since "slow network" is a problem sensed by users, start with asking the following questions:

    ❏ Is this problem in the HQ?

    ❏ In a single branch?

    ❏ All over the network or a specific VLAN?

    > Don't ask the users about VLANs, of course; users are not networking experts. Ask them about applications running on their group, on their department, and so on.

> In an organization network, VLAN will usually be configured per department (or several departments) and per geographical area (or several areas) or even per organization functionality; for example, HR VLAN, finance VLAN, users of a specific software VLAN, and so on. By asking if the problem is as per one of these characters, you will be able to narrow the area in which you need to look for the problem.

2. The next question should be a trivial one: "Is the network still working?" In a broadcast storm, the network will become very slow; in most cases, to the point that applications will stop functioning. In this case, you have the following typical problems:

    ❏ Spanning Tree Problems

    ❏ A device that generates broadcasts

    ❏ Routing loops (will be discussed in *Chapter 8, ARP and IP Analysis*)

> The question I'm always asked is: "How many broadcasts are too many?" Well, there are, of course, several answers for this. It depends on what the network devices are doing and the protocols that are running on them.
>
> A reasonable number of broadcasts should be from 1 to 2 up to 4 to 5 per device per minute. For example, if your network is built from 100 devices on a single VLAN, you should expect no more then 5-10 broadcasts per second (5 broadcasts x 100 devices gives 500 broadcasts per minute, that is, around 9-10 per second). More than these is also reasonable, as long as they are not coming in thousands and you know what they are.

Spanning Tree Problems

In Spanning Tree Problem, you will get thousands and even tens of thousands of broadcasts per second (refer to the *How it works...* section in this recipe to know why). In this case, your Wireshark, and probably your laptop, will freeze. Close Wireshark, disconnect cables to isolate the problem, and check the STP configuration in the switches.

A device that generates Broadcasts

A typical broadcast storm generated from a specific device will have the following characteristics:

- Significant number of broadcasts per second (thousands and more)
- In most cases, the broadcasts would be from a single source; but in case of attacks, they can be from multiple sources
- Usually in constant packet/second rate, that is, with intervals between frames that are nearly equal

We can see how we find a broadcast storm according to the parameters mentioned in the preceding list in the next three screenshots.

In the following screenshot we see a large number of broadcast packets sent from the source MAC (HP network adapter) to ff:ff:ff:ff:ff:ff:

In the preceding screenshot we just saw that the time column is configured in seconds since the previous displayed packet. You can configure it by navigating to **View | Time Display Format**.

The following screenshot shows the traffic on an IO Graph; we see that the total number of packets/second is 5,000:

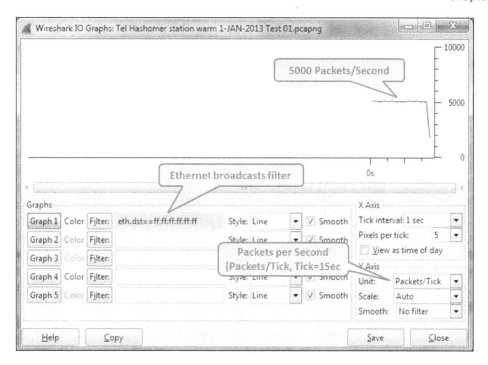

In the following screenshot we see what we will get in the **Conversations** window. Here, we will also get an enormous number of broadcasts that can be viewed in the Ethernet and the IPv4 statistics (I've captured data for 18 seconds).

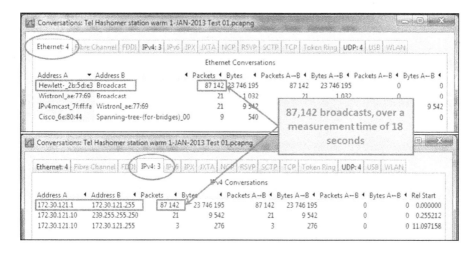

In the preceding case, the problem was a service called **SMB Mailslot Protocol**. Simple trial and error to find what this service is, and disabling it on the station that caused it solved the problem.

 It is important to note that when you disable a service (especially the one that belongs to the operating system), make sure that the system keeps functioning and stays stable over time. Don't leave the site before you have verified it!

Fixed pattern broadcasts

You can also have broadcasts in fixed patterns, for example, every fixed amount of time, as shown in the following screenshot:

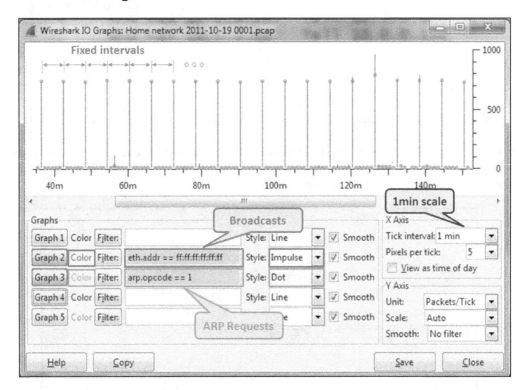

The graph is configured for **Tick interval:** (under **X Axis**) of **1 min**, and for the following filters:

- ▸ The red filter for all broadcasts in the network (eth.addr == ff:ff:ff:ff:ff:ff)

- ▸ The green filter for broadcasts that are ARP requests (arp.opcode ==1)

What we see here is that around every five minutes, there is a burst of ARP requests (the green dots). If we click on one of the dots in the graph, it will take us to the packet in the capture pane. In the following screenshot, we see the scan pattern that happens every five minutes:

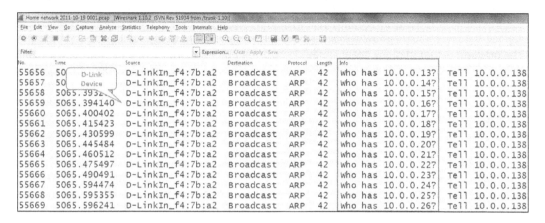

In the preceding screenshot, we can see that it is the D-Link router that scans the internal network. This can be good or bad, and we will get to the details later in *Chapter 14, Understanding Network Security*. In any case, it's good to check what is running in our network.

How it works...

Broadcasts in IPv4 networks are quite common, and these layer 3 broadcasts will be sent over layer 2 broadcasts. Every time a layer 3 device sends a broadcast to the network (an IP address that ends with all 1s, refer to *Chapter 8, ARP and IP Analysis*), it will be converted to layer 2's all fs destination address.

There are several families of broadcasts that you will see in IP-based networks. Some of them are as follows:

- TCP/IP-based network protocols such as ARP requests, DHCP requests, and others
- Network protocols such as **NetBIOS Name Service** (**NBNS**) queries, **NetBIOS Server Message Block** (**SMB**) announcements, **Network Time Protocol** (**NTP**), and others
- Applications that send broadcasts such as Dropbox, Microsoft Network Load Balancing, and others

In IPv6, we don't have broadcasts, but we have unicasts, multicasts, and anycasts. Since the protocol works with multicasts for discovery mechanisms, announcements, and other mechanisms, we will see a lot of them.

There's more...

A problem I come across in many cases is how to use the broadcast and multicast storm control definitions in LAN switches (the `storm-control broadcast level [high level] [lower level]` command in Cisco devices).

The problem is that in many cases, I see configurations that limit the number of broadcasts to 50, 100, or 200 broadcasts per second, and this is not enough. In a network, you could happen to install a software that sends broadcasts or multicasts to the network that crosses these values. Then, according to what you have configured in the switch, it will start sending traps to the management system or even disconnecting ports (the `storm-control action {shutdown | trap}` command in Cisco devices), depending on what you have configured.

The solution for this is simply to configure high levels of broadcasts as the threshold. When a broadcast storm happens, you will get thousands of broadcasts; so configuring a threshold level of 1,000 to 2,000 broadcasts or multicasts per second provides you with the same protection level, without any disturbances to the regular network operation.

See also

- ▶ For more information about IPv4 refer to *Chapter 8, ARP and IP Analysis*

Analyzing Spanning Tree Protocols

All of us have worked with, or at least heard about, **STP** (**Spanning Tree Protocol**). The reason I call this recipe *Analyzing Spanning Tree Protocols* is because there are three major versions of it as follows:

- ▶ **Spanning Tree Protocol (STP)**: This is an IEEE 802.1D standard from 1998 called 802.1D-1998
- ▶ **Rapid Spanning Tree Protocol (RSTP)**: This is an IEEE 802.1W standard from 2001, later added to 802.1D, called 802.1D-2004
- ▶ **Multiple Spanning Tree (MST)**: This was originally defined in IEEE 802.1S and later merged into IEEE 802.1Q

There are also some proprietary versions from Cisco and other vendors. In this recipe we will focus on the standard versions, and learn how to troubleshoot problems that might occur during STP/RSTP/MST operations.

Getting ready

The best way to find out STP problems is to log in to the LAN switches and use the vendor's commands (for example, Cisco IOS or Juniper JUNOS CLI) to find and fix the problem. If you have properly configured SNMP on your network device, you will get all the messages on the management console.

The purpose of this recipe is to see how to use Wireshark for this purpose, even though we still recommend to use it as a second line tool for this purpose.

So just open your laptop, start Wireshark, and start capturing data on the LAN.

How to do it...

There are several things to notice in a network regarding STP:

 ▸   Which STP version is running on the network?

 ▸   Are there any topology changes?

Which STP version is running on the network?

Wireshark will provide you with the version of the STP type (STP, RSTP, or MST) running on the network by looking at the **Bridge Protocol Data Units** (**BPDUs**). BPDUs are the update frames that are multicast between switches.

The protocol versions are:

 ▸   For STP, protocol version ID equals 0

 ▸   For RSTP/MST, the protocol version ID equals 3

In the standards you will not find the word "switch"; it will always be "bridge" or "multiport bridge". In this book, we will use the terms bridge and switch alternatively.

Are there too many topology changes?

When you monitor STP operations, you may be concerned when you see many topology changes. Topology changes are normal in STP, but too many of them can have an impact on network performances.

A topology change happens when a new device is connected to the network. You can see a topology change in the following screenshot:

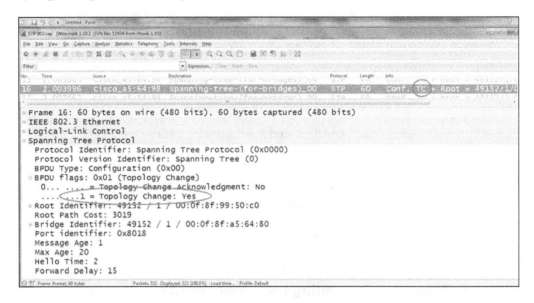

When you see too many topology changes, configure the LAN switch ports that are connected to hosts, which do not support STP, (typically, end stations that users frequently power on and off) with the portfast feature (applied for Cisco switches; for other vendors, check the vendor's manual).

In the old STP (IEEE 802.1d), after connecting a device to a switch port, it takes the switch around a minute to start and forward packets. This can be a problem when a client tries to log in to the network servers during this period of time. The portfast feature forces the port to start forwarding within a few seconds (usually 8 to 10), in order to prevent these kinds of problems.

If topology changes continue, check what can be the problem and who is causing it.

How it works...

Spanning Tree Protocol prevents a loop in the local area networks. A loop can happen if you connect two or more switches with multiple connections as shown in the following figure:

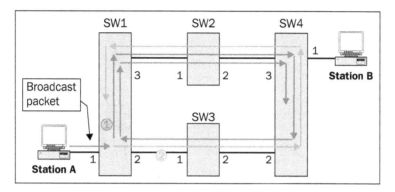

Let's see how a loop is created:

1. **Station A** sends a broadcast to the network. A broadcast can be an ARP, NetBIOS, or any other packet with all ffs in the destination MAC address.

2. Since broadcasts are forwarded to all ports of the switch, **SW 1** receives the broadcast from port **1** and forwards it to ports **2** and **3**.

3. **SW 1** and **SW 3** will forward the packets to their other ports, which will get them to ports **2** and **3** of **SW 4**.

4. **SW 4** will forward the packet from port **2** to port **3**, and the packet coming from port **3** to port **2**.

5. We will get two packets circling endlessly: the one that has been forwarded to port **3** (the red arrows), and the one that has been forwarded to port **2** (the green arrows) of **SW 1**.

6. Depending on the switch forwarding speed, we will get up to tens of thousands of packets that will block the network completely.

The Spanning Tree Protocol prevents this from happening by simply building a tree topology, that is, by defining a loop-free topology. Links are disconnected and brought back to service in the case of a failure.

In the following figure, we see how we initially connect all switches with multiple connections between them, and how STP creates the tree:

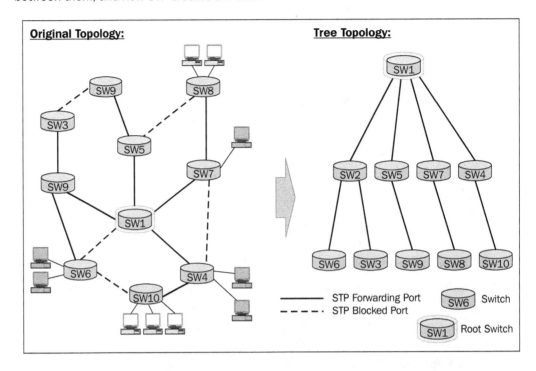

BPDUs are update frames that are sent by multicast between the LAN switches.

First, on the Ethernet level as we see in the following screenshot, the packet will be multicast from the source MAC of the switch sending the update:

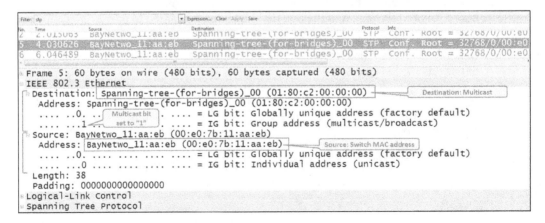

The BPDU is carried by Ethernet 802.3 frame has the format as shown in the next diagram:

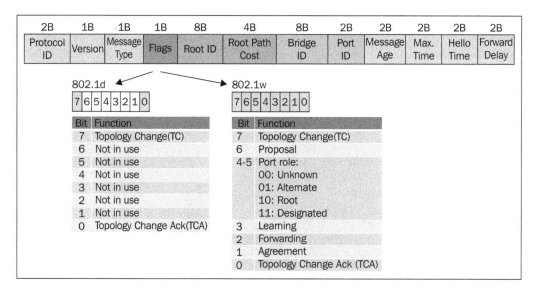

In the following table, you can see the fields in the STP frame:

Field	Bytes	What is it	Values	Display filter
Protocol ID	2	The protocol identifier.	Always 0	`stp.protocol`
Version	1	The protocol version.	For STP = 0 For RSTP = 2 For MST = 3	`stp.version`
Message Type	1	The BPDU type.	For STP = 0 For RSTP = 2 For MST = 2	`stp.type`
Flags	1	The protocol flags.	In the previous illustration.	`stp.flags`

Root ID	8	The root identifier (Root ID), that is, the bridge priority concatenated with the bridge hardware address (MAC).	The MAC address of the root bridge.	`stp.root.prio`
				`stp.root.ext`
				`stp.root.hw`

Field	Bytes	What is it	Values	Display filter
Root Path Cost	4	The path cost to the root.	Path cost as calculated by Spanning Tree. In case this is the root, path cost will be zero.	`stp.root.cost`

Bridge ID	8	The bridge identifier (Bridge ID), that is, the bridge priority concatenated with the bridge hardware address (MAC).	The bridge MAC address.	`stp.bridge.prio`
				`stp.bridge.ext`
				`stp.bridge.hw`

Port ID	2	The port identifier.	The identifier of the port from which the update was sent.	`stp.port`
Message Age	2	The **Message Age** field indicates the amount of time that has elapsed since a bridge sent the configuration message on which the current configuration message is based.	For every BPDU, the bridge that sends the frame sends a value of 0, incremented by 1 for every bridge that forwards it.	`stp.msg_age`
Max. Time	2	The maximum age, which is the maximum time (practically the number of bridges) that the frame can stay in the network.	Usually 20	`stp.max_age`
Hello Time	2	Time between BPDUs.	Usually 2 seconds	`stp.hello`
Forward Delay	2	The **Forward Delay** field indicates the length of time that bridges should wait before transitioning to a new state after a topology change.	Usually 15 seconds	`stp.forward`

Note that in the case of MST, an additional header will be added for the MST parameters.

Port states

In STP, the port states are as follows:

- ▸ **Disabled**: In this state no frames are forwarded and no BPDUs are heard
- ▸ **Blocking**: In this state no frames are forwarded, but BPDUs are heard
- ▸ **Listening**: In this state no frames are forwarded, but the port listens for frames
- ▸ **Learning**: In this state no frames are forwarded, but MAC addresses are captured
- ▸ **Forwarding**: In this state frames are forwarded, and MAC addresses are captured

The moment you connect a device to the LAN switch, the port goes through these stages and the time it takes is as follows:

- ▸ From Blocking to Listening takes 20 seconds
- ▸ From Listening to Learning takes 15 seconds
- ▸ From Learning to Forwarding takes 15 seconds

In RSTP and MST, the port states are as follows:

- ▸ **Discarding**: In this state frames are discarded
- ▸ **Learning**: In this frame no frames are forwarded, and MAC addresses are captured
- ▸ **Forwarding**: In this state frames are forwarded, and MAC addressesare captured

The entire port state transition from Discarding to Forwarding should take a few seconds, depending on the network topology and complexity.

There's more...

For Spanning Tree debugging, the best thing is to get the data from a direct connection to the LAN switches. A well-configured SNMP trap to a management system can also assist in this task.

Some examples of STP packets are as follows:

▸ In the following screenshot you see an STP frame. You can see that the source MAC address is a Nortel address, and in the BPDU itself you see that the root and the bridge identifiers are equal; this is because the bridge that sends the packet is the root. The port ID is 8003, which in Nortel switches indicates port number 3.

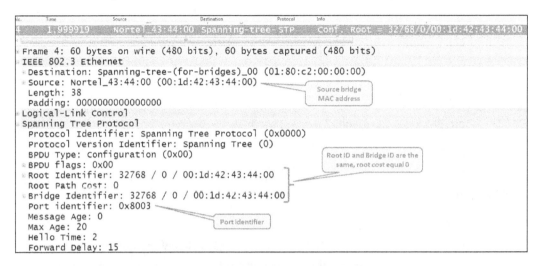

▸ In the following screenshot, you can see a Rapid STP BPDU. You can see here the protocol identifier that equals 2 and the port state that is designated.

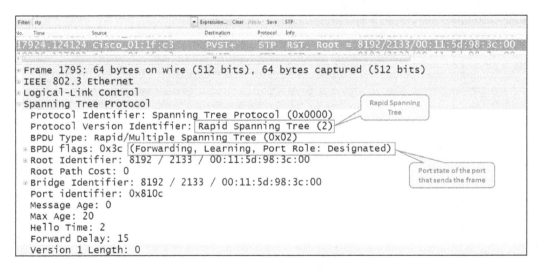

- ► In the previous screenshot, you can see an example for MST. Here we see the MST extension right after the standard STP frame.

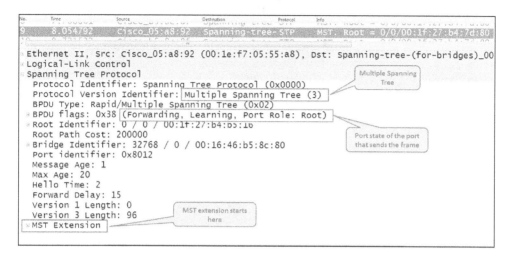

Analyzing VLANs and VLAN tagging issues

VLAN, or **Virtual LAN**, is a mechanism that divides a LAN into separate LANs without any connectivity between them, and this is where the name virtual comes from. In this section we will have a look at recipes to monitor VLAN traffic.

The purpose of this recipe is to give the reader a general description of how to use Wireshark for VLAN issues. An easier way to solve related problems is to use the vendor's CLI (Cisco IOS, Juniper JUNOS, and so on) for this purpose.

Getting ready

We will discuss two issues in this recipe:

- ► How to monitor traffic inside a VLAN
- ► How to view tagged frames going through a VLAN-tagged port

In the first case, a simple configuration is required. In the second case, there are some points to take care of.

While capturing on a VLAN, you won't necessarily see the VLAN tags in packets. The question of whether you will see the VLAN tags actually depends on the operating system you are running, and if your **Network Interface Card** (**NIC**) and the NIC driver supports this feature.

> The question of whether your OS and NIC supports VLAN tagging entirely depends on the OS and the NIC vendor. Go to the vendor's manuals or Goggle it to find out.

In the following figure you can see a typical topology with VLANs. The upper switch is connected by two trunks (these are ports that tag the Ethernet frames) to the lower switches. On this network you have VLANs 10, 20, and 30, while PCs connected to each of the VLANs will not be able to see PCs from other VLANs.

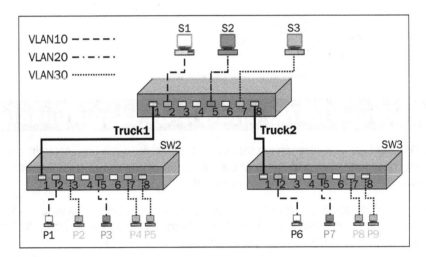

How to do it...

Connect Wireshark to the switch you want to monitor. Let's look at the preceding configuration (shown in the preceding figure).

Monitoring traffic inside a VLAN

In order to monitor traffic on an entire VLAN

1. Connect your laptop to the central switch and to one of the ports.

2. Configure the port mirror from the monitored VLAN to the port you are connected to. For example, if you connect your laptop to SW1 port 4, and you want to monitor traffic from VLAN10, the commands will be (in Cisco):

```
Switch(config)#monitor session 1 source vlan 10
```

```
Switch(config)#monitor session 1 destination interface
fastethernet 0/4
```

This will show you traffic from VLAN10 that is forwarded through the central switch, SW1.

For further information on how to configure port mirroring on various vendor websites, search for SPAN (in Cisco), port mirror, or mirroring (HP, DELL, Juniper, and others). While monitoring traffic in a blade center, usually, you can only monitor traffic on a physical port; however, there are applications that enable you to monitor traffic on only a specific server on a blade (for example, Cisco Nexus 1000V).

Viewing tagged frames going through a VLAN tagged port

Monitoring tagged traffic is not a straightforward mission. The issues of whether you see VLAN tags while capturing data with Wireshark or not will depend on the network adapter you have, the driver that runs over it, and what they do with VLAN tags.

The simplest way to verify that your laptop can capture tagged frames is as follows:

1. Start capturing the tagged port with the port mirror. If you see tags, continue with your work.

2. If you don't see any tags, go to the adapter configuration. In Windows 7, you will get there by clicking on Start and then navigating to **Control Panel | Network and Internet | View Network Status and Tasks | Change Adapter Settings | Local Area Connection**. Next, perform the steps as shown in the following screenshot:

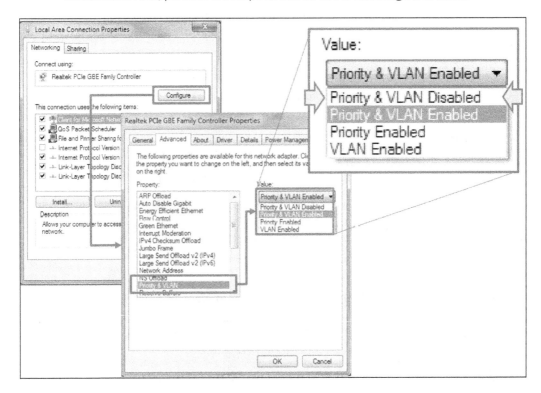

3. Configure the adapter with **Priority & VLAN Disabled**. This will move the tags for the WinPcap driver and for the Wireshark.

In the previous screenshot we see an example of a Lenovo laptop with Realtek NIC. The illustration gives an example on a popular device, but it can be different on other laptops or servers. The principle should be the same; disable the adapter by extracting the VLAN tag, so it will be forwarded to the WinPcap driver and presented on Wireshark.

How it works...

Tags are small pieces of data added to a packet in order to add VLAN information to it. The tag is a 4-byte long string (32 bits), as presented in one of the following diagrams.

Most network adapters and their drivers will simply pass VLAN tags to the upper layer to handle them. In these cases, Wireshark will see VLAN tags and present them.

In more sophisticated adapters and drivers, the VLAN tag will be handled in the adapter itself. This includes some of the most common adapters with Intel and Broadcom Gigabit chipsets. In these cases, you will have to disable the VLAN feature.

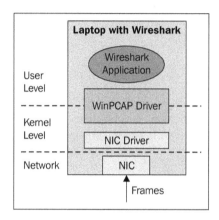

When configuring the NIC driver in order to ensure that it will not handle VLAN tags, packets will simply be forwarded to the WinPcap driver and presented by Wireshark.

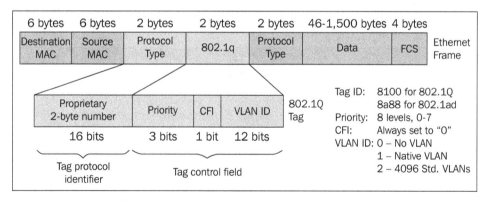

VLAN tagging

In the following screenshot you see an example for a tagged frame; the frame is tagged with VLAN ID = 20.

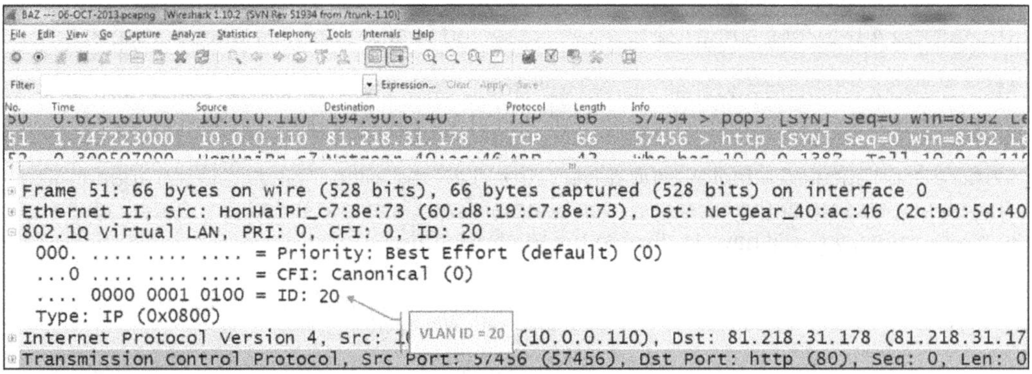

There's more...

Wireshark will also capture double tags, just like in the 802.1ad standard. These tags are what's called service tags and are added at the service provider edge, in order to divide between the provider and the customer tags. The provider tag is called **S-Tag** (802.1ad), and the customer tag is called **C-Tag** (802.1Q). It is also referred to as a QinQ mechanism.

See also

▸ For more information about WinPcap, go to the Winpcap home page at http://www.winpcap.org/

▸ For more information on the UNIX/Linux library, refer to the tcpdump home page at http://www.tcpdump.org/

Analyzing wireless (Wi-Fi) problems

Wireless LAN (**Wi-Fi**) became very popular in the last decade, starting from the old 802.11b through 802.11g and to the latest 802.11n standard for high-bandwidth wireless communications.

There are also the emerging standards such as IEEE 802.11ac with products coming in to the market, along with the 802.11ad, which is still under development.

In this recipe we will learn how to resolve Wi-Fi problems, and how to use Wireshark to capture Wi-Fi frames and for basic traffic analysis.

Getting ready

When users complain about bad performance when they connect through a Wi-Fi connection, go as close as you can with your laptop to the user location and verify that you have your Wi-Fi adapter enabled.

How to do it...

The basic tool is right in the laptop (as we can see in the following screenshot) where, you have the first indication for:

- ▸ The signal strength, that is the **Received Signal Strength Indicator** (**RSSI**). In some cases, you will see only the quality of signal; in other cases, you will also see the dBm number

- ▸ The access point ID, that is the **Service Set Identification** (**SSID**)

- ▸ The security protocol that is used

- ▸ Radio type (802.11n as shown in the following screenshot)

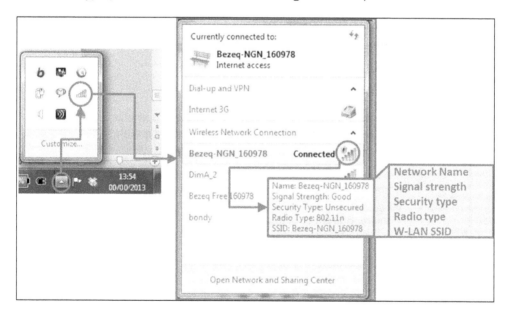

You can also use dedicated software, many of them being freeware, to discover available Wi-Fi networks and channels (some of them from the laptop vendors, and some from others). In the following screenshot you can see a list of wireless networks discovered by a software name WIFi Locator (`http://tcpmonitor.altervista.org/`); however, there are many other software with basic discovery features:

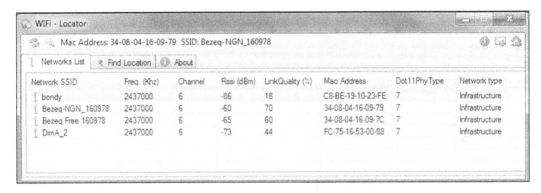

RSSI levels indicate that the higher the number is, the lower is the strength:

- **-60dBm and better**: This indicates a good signal level
- **-80dBm to -60dBm**: This indicates a reasonable signal level
- **-80 dBm to -90dBm**: This indicates a weak signal level
- **-90 dBm and lower**: This indicates a very weak signal

If you have RSSI in the reasonable range and above, the received level is usually enough, and you should look for frequency disturbances and other radio problems.

 A rule of thumb that I usually apply for wireless network design is that for standard enterprise applications, I require 75dBm and better, and for wireless networks that should also be used for VoIP, I require -65dBm or better.

If you want to check if there are any disturbances, you can use software that will discover RSSI over time, and will give you a more accurate picture of your network. In the following screenshot you see such a software, called **InSSIDer**; it gives you a more accurate picture about which access points are working and their details.

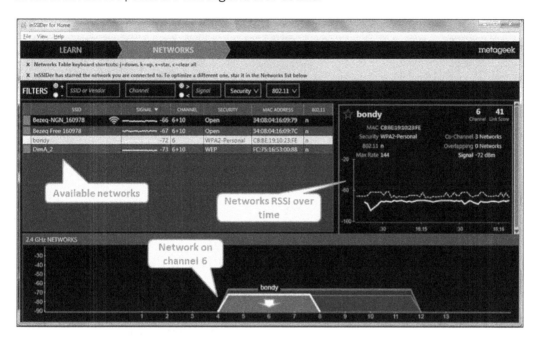

1. Try to find out the following problems:

   ❑ Different access points (APs) working on the same channel in the same area

   ❑ Low RSSI values (indicated in RSSI numbers lower than -90dBm)

2. The next step is to use spectrum analyzers to check which frequencies are used in your area. You can expect frequency disturbances in areas such as airports, seaports, and military. Spectrum analyzers are available from various vendors such as Fluke Networks, Agilent, and Anritsu.

3. Wireshark can be used to analyze Wi-Fi control frames. The first thing to look for is whether the APs are sending beacon frames. In the following screenshot, you can see these frames:

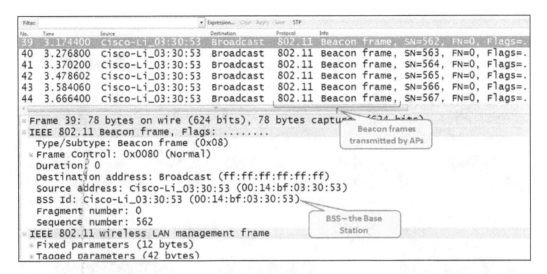

The stations can send beacon probe request frames to find a nearby access point.

 A probe request frame is sent by a station when it wants to obtain information from another Wi-Fi device, for example, to determine the access points within the range.

The station can also acknowledge the beacon frames coming from the access point in order to register to the AP.

 The access point periodically sends beacon frames to announce its presence and relay information. This information includes timestamps, SSIDs, and other parameters with regard to the access point. Radio wireless NICs continually scan all 802.11 radio channels and listen to beacons, in order to choose the best access point to associate with.

4. After accepting and acknowledging the beacon frame, a standard DHCP process will start, as described in *Chapter 8, ARP and IP Analysis*.

How it works...

The Wireless LAN standards are based on the IEEE 802.11 committee. The standards started with 802.11a, 802.11b, 802.11g, 802.11n, and lately 802.11ac and 802.11ad for higher bandwidth.

As seen in the following figure, Wireless LAN networks are based on access points (APs), and wireless clients connect to them.

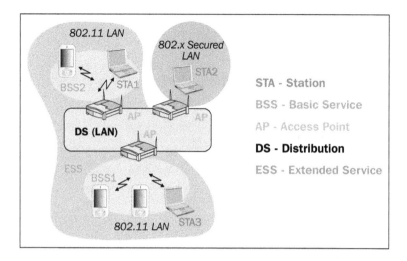

The most common wireless standard today is the 802.11n, which uses the advanced modulation **Multiple Input Multiple Output** (**MIMO**), to work with up to four antennas and some additional technologies, to increase bandwidth.

8
ARP and IP Analysis

In this chapter we will cover the following issues:

- ▸ Analyzing connectivity problems with ARP
- ▸ Using IP traffic analysis tools
- ▸ Using GeoIP to look up physical locations of the IP address
- ▸ Finding fragmentation problems
- ▸ Analyzing routing problems
- ▸ Finding duplicate IPs
- ▸ Analyzing DHCP problems

Introduction

In this chapter we will learn how to analyze Layer 3 (IP) and Layer 3 to Layer 2 resolution (ARP). We will discuss the **Internet Protocol (IP)**, **Address Resolution Protocol (ARP)**, **Dynamic Host Configuration Protocol (DHCP)**, routing issues and others, and the problems that you might face while troubleshooting these protocols.

We will start with presenting the protocol's normal behavior for the various protocols and continue with showing what can go wrong and how to solve it.

In general, when we analyze a network problem, we will go bottom up: if you cannot get connectivity, look for the problem in the following order:

1. **Layer 1**: Check if the cable is connected and the link LED on the switch and your PC is turned on. This step is to be executed manually.

2. **Layer 2**: Check if ARP has discovered the MAC address of the destination. In case of a remote location, check for connectivity between every two nodes/routers on the way. This can be executed with the command line (look at the ARP recipe following this).

3. **Layer 3**: Check by using the `ping` command to the destination, and if you do not receive a response, trace route to it. This can be executed with the command line and in some cases with Wireshark.

4. **Layer 4**: Check if the process/server on the other side is answering. This step is to be executed with Wireshark.

5. **Layers 5-7**: Check for application problems. This step is to be executed with Wireshark.

In *Chapter 7, Ethernet, LAN Switching, and Wireless LAN*, we talked about Layers 1 and 2. In this chapter we will talk about Layer 3, that is IP, and the resolving process between Layer 3 and Layer 2, that is ARP. In *Chapter 9, UDP/TCP Analysis*, we will talk about Layer 4, that is TCP and UDP, and in the rest of the book about application layers.

Analyzing connectivity problems with ARP

ARP is used by IP to resolve the destination MAC address out of the IP address of the device that we wish to communicate with. When we send packets to a destination, the first packet is the ARP request to find the MAC address of the destination. We get it from the destination and then send the other packets destined to it.

ARP operation is only local, that means the ARP request, which is a broadcast, will be sent only on the LAN. In case you send a packet to a device on your IP network (with the same IP network and mask), ARP will try to find its address. When you send a packet to someone out of your network, ARP will be sent to find out the default gateway MAC address.

Getting ready

We will use three methods to find the basic connectivity problems:

- The standard command line (In MS-Windows go to **Start** and in the command window type `run`. In Linux use any available Shell)
- Wireshark
- Connecting to a LAN switch or router directly and getting information from there

To connect to the communication devices (routers, switches, and so on), you first connect with a console cable (in Cisco, this is the light-blue flat cable); you configure the device with an IP address, and then you can access the device via Telnet, HTTP, or SNMP software. With all of these methods you can read the device counters that provide you with information of the traffic, errors, CPU utilization, and more.

In each one of the following recipes, we will see exactly what to use and where.

How to do it...

In this recipe, we will see several connectivity issues and how to deal with them. Let's look at the very simple network in the following figure. Here, we can see a typical network and discuss some of the connectivity problems that can happen on it.

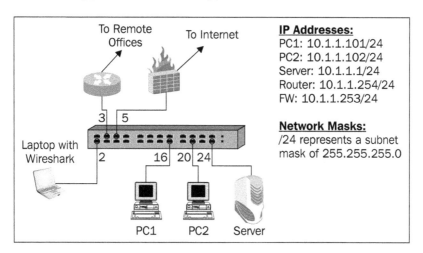

In the network, we can see two PCs, PC1 and PC2, that are connected to switch ports 16 and 20 respectively, a server connected to switch port 24, a router that connects us to the remote offices on switch port 3, and a firewall that connects us to the Internet on switch port 5. Our laptop with Wireshark installed on it is connected to port 2.

Let's see some of the problems that might occur here and how to solve them.

Let's consider case 1 when there is no connectivity from the PCs to the server:

1. Ping the server from PC1 and PC2.

2. If there is no answer, type ARP -a on the command line. In the ARP table, you should see the IP address of the server and its MAC address.

3. If you see the MAC address of the server, probably there is a firewall running on the server that blocks ICMP requests. For the test, disable the firewall and test again.

 A firewall, VPN client, or an antivirus software that comes with some firewall features can block ICMP requests. Don't forget it while testing network connectivity issues.

4. If you have pinged, but your application still doesn't work, go to *Chapter 9, UDP/TCP Analysis*, and continue from there.

   You've gone through steps 1 to 3 in case 1, and still don't get a ping response (you get request time out).

5. Connect to the LAN switch and get the list of MAC addresses that the switch has learned.

> In every managed switch, you will be able to see the list of MAC addresses that the switch has learned and on which ports the switch has learned them.
>
> In Cisco, the command for this will be show mac-address-table or show mac address table (depends on the IOS version).

6. If you don't see the addresses of your PC and the server, check for physical problems such as bad cable, adapter problem, and switch port problem. For doing so, you can simply switch cables or replace the switch for the test, replace ports on the switch and so on.

   Now let's see how to use Wireshark to resolve this problem.

7. When clients complain about connectivity problems to a specific device (server, printer, and so on), you connect Wireshark to the port (with port mirror), and you see many ARP requests and no answer. You can see an example of this in the following screenshot:

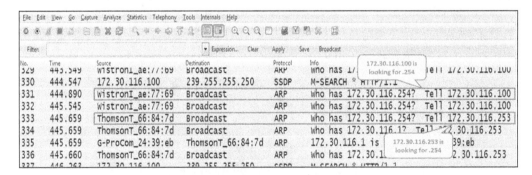

8. In this example, we see that both **172.30.116.100** and **172.30.116.253** are looking for the MAC address of **172.30.116.254**, but there is no reply.

9. In this case, check in the switch if the MAC address has been learned, and if not, check for physical problems.

ARP poisoning and Man-in-the-Middle attacks

One of the types of a Man-in-the-Middle attack is when an attacker poisons the ARP cache of the devices that he wants to listen to with the MAC address of his Ethernet NIC. Once the ARP cache has been successfully poisoned, each of the victim devices sends all their packets to the attacker while communicating with the other device. The attacker, of course, will resend it to them after reading the data.

This is called Man-in-the-Middle attack since it puts the attacker in the middle of the communication path between the two victim devices. It is also called ARP Poisoning since the attacker actually poisons the victim's ARP cache with wrong information.

In the following figure, we see an example of a Man-in-the-Middle attack:

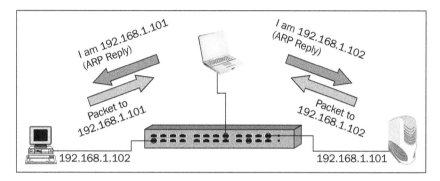

The following screenshot shows Wireshark:

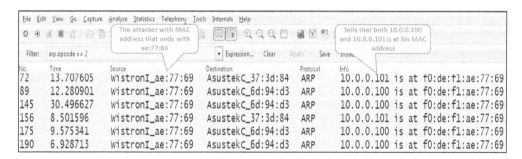

Gratuitous ARP

A gratuitous ARP takes place when a device wants to verify if some other device has its own IP address. In this case, you will see an ARP with the same source and destination address fields. There is nothing wrong with gratuitous ARPs. There are devices that work this way; for example, home routers that scan for attached devices.

No.	Time	Source	Destination	Protocol	Info
173	0.000000	AsustekC_6d:94:d3	Broadcast	ARP	Who has 10.0.0.7? Tell 10.0.0.1
925	7.271417	D-LinkIn_f4:7b:a2	HonHaiPr_c7:8e:7 ARP		who has 10.0.0.6? Tell 10.0.0.138
926	0.000020	HonHaiPr_c7:8e:73	D-LinkIn_f4:7b:a ARP		10.0.0.6 is at 60:d8:19:c7:8e:73

```
▸ Frame 173: 60 bytes on wire (480 bits), 60 bytes captured (480 bits) on interface 0
▸ Ethernet II, Src: AsustekC_6d:94:d3 (14:da:e9:6d:94:d3), Dst: Broadcast (ff:ff:ff:ff:ff:ff)
▾ Address Resolution Protocol (request)
    Hardware type: Ethernet (1)
    Protocol type: IP (0x0800)
    Hardware size: 6
    Protocol size: 4
    Opcode: request (1)
    Sender MAC address: AsustekC_6d:94:d3 (14:da:e9:6d:94:d3)
    Sender IP address: 10.0.0.1 (10.0.0.1)
    Target MAC address: 00:00:00_00:00:00 (00:00:00:00:00:00)
    Target IP address: 10.0.0.1 (10.0.0.1)
```

ARP sweeps

ARP sweep is used when, for some reason, we see a device that scans the network with ARPs, requests, or response in order to get information or attack the network.

While watching an ARP sweep, just check for the following:

▸ Is it requests or replies, and who is the sender?

▸ How many ARPs (per second)?

Requests or replies, and who is the sender

ARP requests and replies are a part of the regular network operation. Here are some rules of thumb to make sure they are actually so:

▸ Requests from different sources—no problem, this is how a network works (as long as there are not too many of them!)

▸ Many requests from a singles device—look at the source address and verify who is the device actually sending the requests to:

  ❑ It can be a management system that auto-discovers the network

  ❑ It can be a router that scans to see who is on the local network (see the previous screenshot)

❑ If you don't identify the source, it might be a problem, like a worm or ARP poisoning. Get into the details!

▸ If you see replies that are not to specific requests, it might be a problem. Get into the details!

How many ARPs

An ARP is sent when a device wishes to send data to a destination for the first time (see the *How it works...* section). It is difficult to estimate the exact number of ARPs per minute on a network, but this thumb rule gives you a general idea.

▸ Around 1-2 ARPs per device per minute is ok. If, for example, you have 100 devices (PCs, servers, printers, and so on) on your network, up to 200 ARPs per minute or 2-3 ARPs per second are still ok.

▸ Even if you have more than this, for example, 5 and even 10 per second for the network mentioned earlier, it is not necessarily a problem; it will be a good idea to just look for a suspicious pattern.

The number of ARPs on the network depends on what the devices on the network actually do. If all devices are connecting only to a single device (for example, to a router that connects them to the world), you will see a small number of ARPs. However, if devices, for example, send periodic messages to all their neighbors, you will see many ARPs. Don't forget, God is in the details!

How it works...

When we send a packet from our IP address to a destination IP address through the LAN, we send the data in an IP packet that is encapsulated in an Ethernet frame.

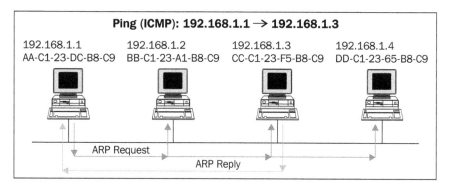

Let's say for example, we send a Ping (ICMP request) from **192.168.1.1** to **192.168.1.3** on the same LAN. To send the packet, we need the IP and the MAC addresses of the destination, but what we have is only its IP address. We know it because this is our destination.

In order to find out what is the MAC address of the destination, we simply send an ARP broadcast to the LAN, asking all devices attached to it: who has the IP address **192.168.1.3**? If the destination station is alive, it sends an ARP response with the MAC address of the destination.

From this moment, the source station holds the data in a cache, the **ARP Cache**, and the next time it wants to transmit, the station transmits the data directly to the destination address.

The ARP Cache remains in the host buffer for the next several minutes (how many minutes depends on the operating system). The ARP entry is flushed a few minutes after the last packet is sent to the destination.

The ARP request will be a broadcast sent to the LAN, as you see in the following screenshot:

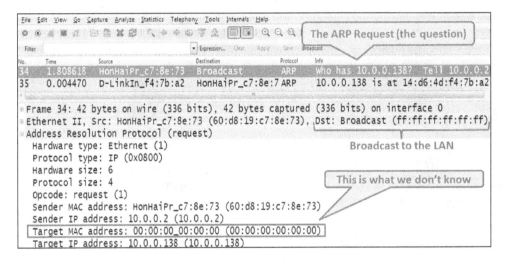

The ARP reply will be a packet sent from the destination that we looked for to the source with the required MAC address, as you see in the following screenshot:

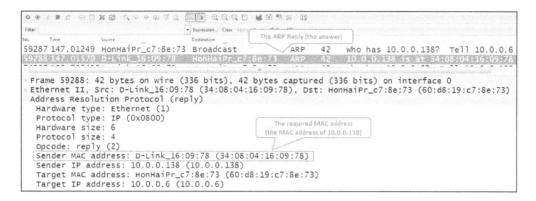

Anything that doesn't look like the standard and is a known exception (for example, gratuitous ARP, ARP sweep by router) should be checked!

There's more...

Here is a short example to understand the principle of ARP operation. In the following diagram, we see an interesting case: two devices attached to the same LAN with different subnets with a default gateway configured to their own IP address. The question is: will a Ping (or any communication) work between them?

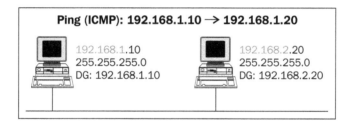

Well, intuitively, you will say no because these are two devices on different subnets and therefore require a router between them. But let's look at what actually happens over the wire:

▸ **192.168.1.10** wants to send a packet to **192.168.2.20**. Since the default gateway is configured to its own address, it thinks the destination is on the same LAN and sends an ARP request.

▸ Since we are on the same LAN as the destination, the destination receives the ARP request (because it is a broadcast) and answers to **192.168.1.10** with its MAC address.

▸ Now, the source has the MAC address of the destination. It sends the packet to it, and although not on the same IP subnet, the destination receives the packet.

Another important issue is Proxy ARP. While a proxy in communications is a device that performs an operation on behalf of someone else, Proxy ARP is the technique in which one host, usually a router, answers the ARP requests intended for another machine.

The proxy ARP concept is implemented in various cases, for example:

▸ While placing a device in front of a router, for example, WAN acceleration/ optimization device. When you configure this device in bridge (or transparent) mode, it will answer to the ARP requests intended for the router.

▸ Firewalls, web filters, and other devices that work in the transparent mode and are located in front of a server.

▸ In case of a software that requires an IP address in addition to the IP of the server it is installed on.

Using IP traffic analysis tools

IP is the network protocol in the TCP/IP protocol stack that carries all upper layer information. Whether it is HTTP, Video, IP Telephony, or other application, IP will be the Layer-3 protocol for all of them. In this section, we will look at some tools that will help us with the analyses of IP traffic.

Getting ready

Just open Wireshark, connect it to the network, configure port mirror to the device you want to test, and start it.

How to do it...

There are several tools and configurations that will help you with the analysis of IP traffic. Among them are:

▸ IP statistics

▸ IP name resolution

IP statistics tools

When you monitor a communication line, connectivity to a server, traffic to the Internet, or any other type of traffic, there are several tools for monitoring the source and destination IPs.

Following are the steps for seeing the source and destination IPs:

1. From the menu, choose **View | Name Resolution** and mark **Enable** for the Network layer. If you are watching an existing file, after you make the change, click on the **Reload** icon. The capture screen will be presented with DNS names in addition to IP addresses.

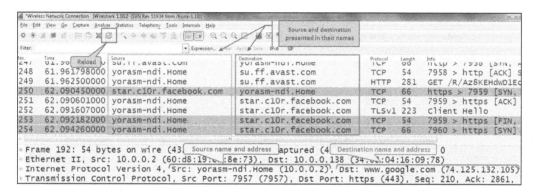

2. In order to see the statistics, choose from the **Statistics | Conversations** menu and mark **Name resolution** at the bottom-left corner of the window, as illustrated in the next screenshot:

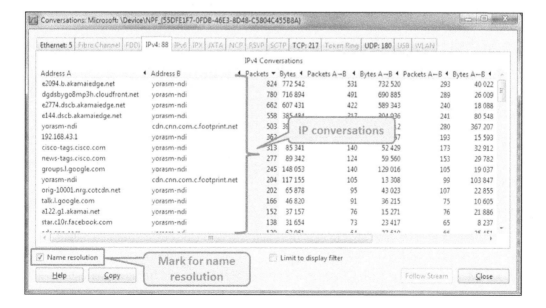

How it works...

This is very simple. Wireshark uses the DNS server configured on your laptop in order to translate the IP addresses to names. In some cases, it can be very helpful to find out problematic traffic patterns. These can be, for example:

▶ Traffic to websites that is not allowed according to company policy.

▶ Automatic software updates, for example, Anti-virus websites and Microsoft updates. The solution to this is the central servers that download the software while all company PCs get the software and updates from this server.

▶ Toolbar traffic can cause a huge amount of traffic if installed on organization devices (think about 50-100 opened connections on every device in your company in addition to regular traffic).

There's more...

You can see, for example, a browser configured with the Conduit toolbar. The moment you run it, you will see many connections to the websites that you know, and to the websites that you don't. Here, for example, you see connections to the Conduit website, and also to a **Content Delivery Network (CDN)** vendor.

No.	Time	Source	Destination	Protocol
145	51.908032000	fa-in-f125.1e100.net	10.0.0.5	TCP
146	52.168236000	10.0.0.5	fa-in-f125.1e100.net	TCP
147	53.346941000	component.usage.toolbar...s.com	10.0.0.5	TCP
148	53.347008000	10.0.0.5	component.usage.toolbar.conduit-services.com	TCP
149	53.347385000	10.0.0.5	component.usage.toolbar.conduit-services.com	HTTP
150	53.505912000	component.usage.toolbar.conduit-services.com	10.0.0.5	HTTP
151	53.506134000	10.0.0.5	component.usage.toolbar.conduit-services.com	TCP
152	53.514323000	10.0.0.5	component.usage....-services.com	TCP
153	53.667798000	component.usage.toolbar.conduit-services.com	10.0.0.5	TCP
154	54.105292000	10.0.0.5	LB140.TELA.COT	TCP
155	54.105434000	10.0.0.5	LB260.TELA.COT	TCP
156	54.122334000	LB140.TELA.COTENDO.net	10.0.0.5	TCP
157	54.122451000	10.0.0.5	LB140.TELA.COTENDO.net	TCP
158	54.123039000	LB260.TELA.COTENDO.net	10.0.0.5	TCP
159	54.123119000	10.0.0.5	LB260.TELA.COTENDO.net	TCP
160	54.123206000	10.0.0.5	LB140.TELA.COTENDO.net	HTTP

To see the exact website and pages, you can, of course, select **Statistics | HTTP** and choose the relevant feature (with IP configured as filter).

Some rules for efficient usage of toolbars:

▶ Have a policy about what to use and what not, and block users from installing toolbars that are not allowed

▶ Monitor your line to the Internet, and make sure where the traffic is going

Using GeoIP to look up physical locations of the IP address

Wireshark 1.1.2 and the higher versions can use GeoIP (commercial version) and GeoLite (free version) databases to look up the city, country, AS number, and other information for an IP address discovered by Wireshark.

Getting ready

1. Go to the following website: `http://dev.maxmind.com/geoip/geolite`.

2. For IPv4, download the following files (the binaries):

   - GeoLite Country
   - GeoLite City
   - GeoLite ASN

3. For IPv6, download the following files:

   - GeoLite Country (IPv6)
   - GeoLite City (IPv6)
   - GeoLite ASN (IPv6)

   You will get the binary files with the country, city, and Autonomous System (AS) numbers.

> Autonomous System (AS) is a term used in Exterior Gateway Protocols (EGPs), for identifying all routers under the control of the same network operator. When you connect to the Internet through two different Internet Service Providers (ISPs), you will get your own AS, while the two ISPs have their ASe While configuring connectivity to the Internet with two different Internet Service Providers (ISPs), ASs are configured along with an EGP routing protocol. The market standard for EGP protocol is Border Gateway Protocol version 4 (BGPv4).

How to do it...

After you have downloaded the files, follow these steps:

1. Put all of the files in the same directory (you can also put them in different directories, but it will be less convenient).

2. Now, you must tell Wireshark where the files are. Go to **Edit | Preferences | Name Resolution** and select **GeoIP database directories**.

3. Add the full path of the GeoIP directory, as shown in the following screenshot:

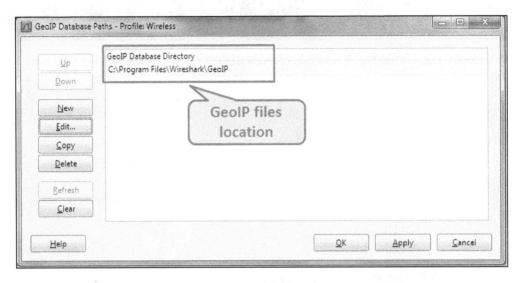

4. Click on **Apply** and close the window and restart Wireshark.

5. Now, start Wireshark (or open saved file), select **Statistics | Endpoints**, and see the GeoIP information in any of the tabs that contains the IP addresses:

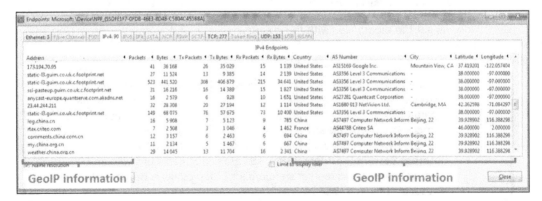

6. You can also see the GeoIP data in the IP packet detail tree. To enable this, go to **Edit | Preferences | Protocols | IP** and make sure that **Enable GeoIP lookup** is checked.

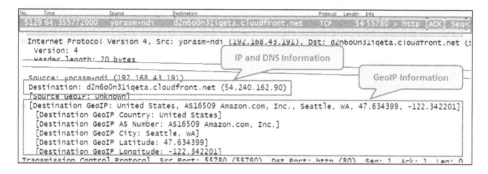

How it works...

The IP addresses are provided by **Internet Assigned Numbers Authority** (**IANA**), a suborganization of the Internet Standard Organization (ISO), to regional organizations called Regional Internet Registrars (RIPE-NCC, APNIC, AFRINIC, LACNIC, and ARIN), who then allocate them to national ISPs, and national ISPs allocate them to individual customers. GeoIP simply is a database of these locations, so it resolves the IP addresses that Wireshark captures according to this database.

The GeoLite files are free IP geographical location databases that are updated monthly. It can be found at `http://dev.maxmind.com/geoip/geolite#IP_Geolocation-1`.

There's more...

The GeoIP can be used for several reasons:

▸ To view the sites (websites, FTP servers, and so on), that people in your organization are connecting to

▸ To resolve source IP addresses of connections that are coming from the world to your organization

▸ For fun

Finding fragmentation problems

Fragmentation is a common mechanism in IP that takes a large IP packet and divides it into smaller-size packets that will fit in the Layer-2 Ethernet frames. In most of the cases, there shouldn't be any problems with the mechanism, but there might be performance issues due to this mechanism.

Getting ready

Just open Wireshark, connect it to the network, configure port mirror to the device that you want to test, and start it. Fragmentation will mostly influence interactive applications such as databases, and these are the places where we should look for problems.

How to do it...

When fragmentation takes place, you will see UDP or TCP packets along with fragmented IP Protocol packets, as shown in the following screenshot:

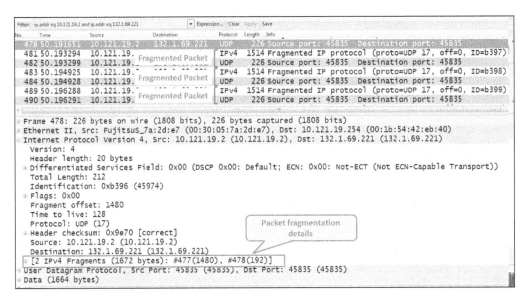

While suspecting performance problems, for example, a database client that experiences slow connectivity with the server, follow these steps to see if the problem is due to fragmentation:

1. Test the connectivity between clients and the server to verify that there are no other problems.

2. Look for fragmentation between the client and the server. Fragments will be shown as in the previous screenshot (IPv4 fragments).

3. In the case that you suspect fragmentation to be the reason for the problem, contact a good **Database Administrator** (**DBA**) that will tune the database to send out packets that do not cause fragmentation to the network.

4. The recommended packet size in Ethernet is not greater than 1460 bytes minus the TCP header size. Thus, the segments coming out of the interface should have a size of 1420-1440 bytes.

In cases where we need more bytes for the header, for example, when we use tunneling mechanisms and TCP options, the DBA will have to reduce this size even more. The best way will be simply to reduce it to such a size that you will not see any fragments.

How it works...

It is important to understand two terms that define the size of the data units that are sent over the network, as you see in the following diagram:

- **Maximum Transfer** (or **Transmission**) **Unit (MTU)**: This is the size of the IP packet including the header and the data
- **Maximum Segment Size (MSS)**: This is the maximum size of the TCP payload, that is, the size of the upper-layer protocol and data

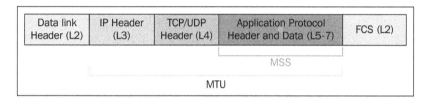

The fragmentation mechanism that is used in IPv4 works as shown in the following illustration:

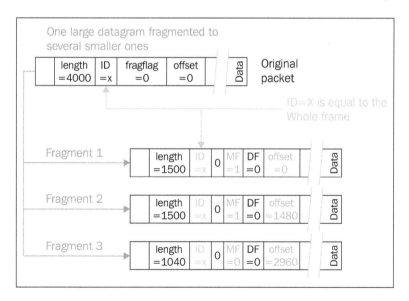

1. An original large packet enters the NIC or the router with a packet size that needs to be fragmented.

2. The packet is fragmented into several parts depending on the original size.

3. For the fragmentation, we have these fields:

- **ID**: This is identical to the ID of the original packet
- **Bit 0**: Always 0
- **Bit 1 (DF Bit)**: 0 = May Fragment, 1 = Don't Fragment.
- **Bit 2 (MF Bit)**: Don't Fragment: 0 = Last Fragment, 1 = More Fragments
- **Fragment offset**: This indicates the number of bytes from the beginning of the original packet

In IPv4, the NIC itself can fragment the packet along with every router on the way to the destination.

In IPv6, fragmentation can be done only by the sender and not by the routers to the destination. In IPv6, fragmentation is implemented by the extension headers.

There's more...

A packet can be fragmented several times on the way to the destination, while in any case, it will be reassembled by the end device only.

In the example in the following illustration, we see a part of a large network in which the customer has several hundred remote offices connection to a central data center through a **service provider** (**SP**) network.

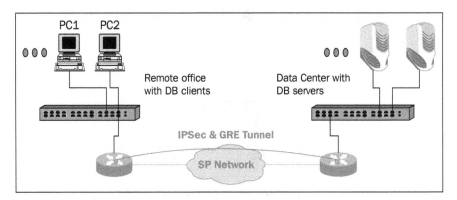

In the remote offices, there were 5 to 10 PCs with DB clients connecting to the DB servers in the central data center. IPSec and GRE tunnels were used for encrypting the data through the SP network.

The problem was that in some of the database applications, the database created frames of 1800 bytes that were fragmented:

- First, it was created in the NIC and sent out of it in two fragments: 1500 bytes and 300 bytes

- Second, it was created in the router because the tunnel required some bytes for itself that divided the 1500 bytes frame to 1420 bytes and 80 bytes frame

The bottom line is that for every packet sent by the PC the servers received 3 packets, and since the customer had several thousand clients and quite an old server, the whole thing worked very slowly.

In the next screenshot, you see the packets when they leave the client. In the first packet, which is the first fragment leaving the NIC, we see:

```
443  IPv4  Fragmented IP protocol (proto=UDP 17, off=0, ID=89a8) [Reassembled in #444]   Fragmented
444  UDP    Source port: 45835  Destination port: 45835                                  packet    1
445  IPv4  Fragmented IP protocol (proto=UDP 17, off=0, ID=89a9) [Reassembled in #446]   Fragmented
446  UDP    Source port: 45835  Destination port: 45835                                  packet

 Frame 443: 1514 bytes on wire (12112 bits), 1514 bytes captured (12112 bits)
 Ethernet II, Src: FujitsuS_7a:27:5e (00:30:05:7a:27:5e), Dst: Cisco_42:eb:40 (00:1b:54:42:eb:
 Internet Protocol Version 4, Src: 10.121.19.1 (10.121.19.1), Dst: 132.1.69.200 (132.1.69.200)
   Version: 4
   Header length: 20 bytes
   Differentiated Services Field: 0x00 (DSCP 0x00: Default; ECN: 0x00: Not-ECT (Not ECN-Capable
   Total Length: 1500
   Identification: 0x89a8 (35240)
   Flags: 0x01 (More Fragments)
     0... .... = Reserved bit: Not set
     .0.. .... = Don't fragment: Not set
     ..1. .... = More fragments: Set
   Fragment offset: 0
```

In the preceding screenshot, we see that packets 443 and 444 (1) are both fragments of the original packet. In packet 443, we see that the total length is 1500 bytes (2), the ID is 0x89a8 (3), more fragments flag is set (4), meaning that there are more fragments to follow, and the fragment offset is 0 (5), meaning that this is the first fragment in the stream.

In the next screenshot, we see the next fragment, that is, packet 444 in the capture file:

```
No.      Protocol    Info
443   IPv4    Fragmented IP protocol (proto=UDP 17, off=0, ID=89a8) [Reassembled in #444]   Fragmented
444   UDP     Source port: 45835  Destination port: 45835                          1      packet
445   IPv4    Fragmented IP protocol (proto=UDP 17, off=0, ID=89a9) [Reassembled in #446]   Fragmented
446   UDP     Source port: 45835  Destination port: 45835                                 packet

Frame 444: 226 bytes on wire (1808 bits), 226 bytes captured (1808 bits)
Ethernet II, Src: FujitsuS_7a:27:5e (00:30:05:7a:27:5e), Dst: Cisco_42:eb:40 (00:1b:54:42:eb:4
Internet Protocol Version 4, Src: 10.121.19.1 (10.121.19.1), Dst: 132.1.69.200 (132.1.69.200)
   Version: 4
   Header length: 20 bytes
   Differentiated Ser 2 es Field: 0x00 (DSCP 0x00: Default; ECN: 0x00: Not-ECT (Not ECN-Capable
   Total Length: 212
   Identification: 0x89a8 (35240)   3
   Flags: 0x00
       0... .... = Reserved bit: Not set
       .0.. .... = Don't fragment: Not set
       ..0. .... = More fragments: Not set      4
   Fragment offset: 1480
                                5
```

In packet 444, we see that the total length is 212 bytes (2), the ID is 0x89a8 (3), which is the same as in packet 443, more fragments flag is not set (4) meaning that this is the last fragment from the original packet, and the fragment offset is 1480 (5), meaning that this is the second fragment from the original packet.

Analyzing routing problems

One of the most critical issues in networks is routing. These include routing loops, no route to destination, and many more. Most of the routing problems will not require using Wireshark in order to solve them. In most of the cases, some knowledge of routing principles and protocols along with common sense will do the job. In this recipe, we will try to provide some basic tips along with some basic issues such that Wireshark can be of assistance.

Getting ready

First, make sure you are familiar with the very basic commands, Ping and Tracert (or Traceroute). In most of the cases, these commands along with logging in to the routers will help you with solving the problems.

In this recipe, we will show some important things on the captured file that can indicate a routing problem.

How to do it...

In this section, we will not give a recipe of what to do, like we usually do, but rather mention things to watch and notice.

Among the things you should notice, the crucial ones are:

▸ The first and most important, **Time To Live** (**TTL**) messages. A TTL value of 0 should raise an alert since the meaning of it in most of the cases is a loop. Wireshark will not tell you where the loop is coming from, but seeing these messages is an alert to something that went wrong. A typical message will be: TTL expired in transit.

▸ The following ICMP message should indicate a configuration problem in a router or in several routers:

❏ **Destination network unreachable**: It usually indicates a missing route in one of the network routers

❏ **Destination host unreachable**: It usually indicates a device (for example, a PC) on the destination network that is not connected to the network or a default gateway is not configured on it

▸ Another issue that should raise a flag is when you see packets going from a source IP address to the destination, back to the source, back to the destination, and so on, while the TTL value is reduced by one in every packet, which is a clear indication of a loop.

How it works...

The TTL is an 8-bit field in the IP header that is implemented in the following way:

▸ The sender inserts a number to it. The number value is usually 64, 128, or 256, depending on the operating system that sends the packet.

▸ Each router decrements this value by one. If, for example, a packet is sent with a value of 128 and crosses 10 routers, the TTL value will be 118.

▸ A router that will see a value of 1 in the TTL field will decrement it to 0 and drop the packet, as well as send an ICMP error message to the source address from which it has received the packet.

 The TTL field in the IP packet can tell us how many routers the packet has crossed on the way from the source to us. This is due to two assumptions: first, while sending a packet from end-to-end through the Internet, it will not cross more than 30 hops (routers); this is the way the Internet is planned, and second, the sender inserts a value of 64, 128, or 256 in the TTL field. If, for example, we see a TTL value of 110, the meaning is that it has crossed 18 routers on the way to us (128-110) because it cannot be that it has crossed 146 routers (256-110).

There's more...

A typical routing problem can be seen in the following illustration. In this network, we have a central data center with two remote offices. The network was built this way in order to provide redundancy from the remote offices to the central data center.

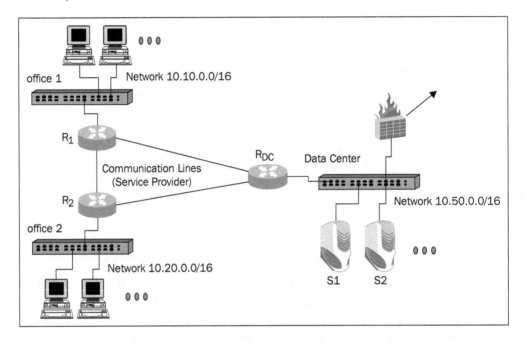

EIGRP is running in the routers, in addition to static routes to the Internet. A partial (and relevant to the case) routing table is presented in the following figure (only routes that are relevant to the example are resent):

Router	Destination Network	Next Hop	Admin Cost	Discovery Protocol
R_{DC}	10.10.0.0/16	R_1	5	EIGRP
	10.20.0.0/16	R_2	5	EIGRP
	0.0.0.0/0	FW	1	Static
R_1	10.50.0.0/16	R_{DC}	5	EIGRP
	0.0.0.0/0	R_{DC}	1	Static
R_2	10.50.0.0/16	R_{DC}	5	EIGRP
	0.0.0.0/0	R_{DC}	1	Static
FW	10.10.0.0/16	RDC	1	Static
	10.20.0.0/16	RDC	1	Static
	0.0.0.0/0	ISP	1	Static

The problem was that we've had a very rare case in which both lines to the center, R1 to RDC, and R2 to RDC were disconnected (a tractor that cut both in the last mile).

Of course, both offices were disconnected immediately. The question was why the central office that had several hundred PCs in addition to the data center became very slow, especially on the Internet.

When I connected Wireshark to the central switch with port mirror to the whole switch (port mirror to VLAN1), I saw the loop. Packets were traveling between the servers and firewall with TTL decrement in every packet. This is a loop.

What happened?

1. The moment the two lines were disconnected, EIGRP in router RDC stopped seeing R1 and R2.

2. When a server sends a packet to networks 10.10.0.0/16 or 10.20.0.0/16, the server sends it to its default gateway; that is, R_{DC}.

3. When the packet arrived to it, R_{DC} sent it to the firewall. This is the route to 0.0.0.0 that takes place if EIGRP becomes inactive.

4. The firewall gets the packet and sends it back to R_{DC}. This is what he has in his routing table.

5. All packets from servers in the data center that are sent to the remote locations start to ping-pong between the servers and the firewall, and that is enough traffic to slow down the servers and access to the Internet.

Finding duplicate IPs

One of the most annoying problems in IP networks is duplicate IP addresses. The funny thing is that if you are familiar with the problem, what causes it, and how to find it, it becomes one of the most simple ones to solve.

Getting ready

When you suspect a duplicate address in the network, the first thing to do will be to use the simple CLI commands—ARP and Ping. If you don't locate the problem, connect Wireshark to the switch and in a large network to every VLAN in the network and move step-by-step until you find the problem.

How to do it...

We start with the phenomena, such as slow access to a server or to another device, slow access to the Internet, and all the pings that you don't get replies to.

1. When you get slow access to a network device, one of the problems that might arise is that the IP address of this device collides with another address. To verify this, ping the IP address.

> In some devices, when their address collides with an identical address, the driver will simply be turned off (the little symbol at the bottom-left corner of the screen in the Windows operating system). In other devices, you will not get any notification for a conflict, and this is the place where problems will arise.

2. Type **arp –a** in the **Command Line Interface** (**CLI**). Use the command cmd in Windows (or any shell in Linux). If you get two lines for the IP address you've pinged with different MAC addresses, this is a duplicate.

3. Google the MAC addresses of the two devices, and the first part of the address will tell you who the vendor is. This will lead you to the trouble maker.

4. If you need the location of the device, log in to your LAN switch (when you have a managed switch, of course), and from the switch MAC address table, you will see the switch port that you are connected to.

> There is a software that shows you the list of devices that are connected to every switch along with their MAC address, IP address, DNS names, and more. Google for switch port mapper or switch port mapping tools and you will find lots of them.

5. If you don't get anything with Ping and ARP, simply start Wireshark and port mirror the network VLANs. Wireshark will show you a duplicate address error with the relevant details.

6. The error message that you will get will be as shown in the following screenshot:

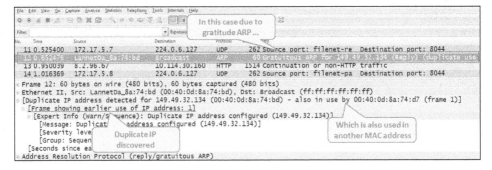

How it works...

When you ping an IP address that appears twice on your local network, the two devices (or more) that have the same IP address will answer to the ARP request that you sent, and your ARP cache will have two entries for the same IP address.

In many cases, your device will indicate it by closing its IP driver and notify you by a pop-up window or any other type of notification that you will be aware of.

In other cases, the colliding devices will not notify the conflict, and then you will find a problem only with Ping and ARP, as described before.

In any case, when you connect Wireshark to the network and see duplicate IP messages, don't ignore it.

There's more...

Duplicate IP usually happens when there are two identical addresses in the network, but it becomes even more interesting when you have three identical addresses.

You can see a funny example for this in the upcoming screenshot:

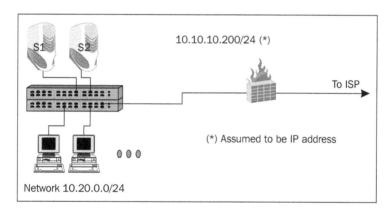

In this customer network, they've internal network of around 150 devices with connectivity to the Internet through a firewall. The problem was a very slow connection to the Internet.

When they did a ping to a server on the Internet (any server), they got the following responses:

```
Reply from 173.194.35.148: bytes=32 time=98ms TTL=51
Request timed out.
Reply from 173.194.35.148: bytes=32 time=124ms TTL=51
```

```
Request timed out.
Reply from 173.194.35.148: bytes=32 time=134ms TTL=51
Request timed out.
Reply from 173.194.35.148: bytes=32 time=582ms TTL=51
Request timed out.
```

The customer made some changes to the network, the network became even slower, and pinging the same server on the Internet got them the following response:

```
Reply from 173.194.35.148: bytes=32 time=98ms TTL=51
Request timed out.
Request timed out.
Reply from 173.194.35.148: bytes=32 time=124ms TTL=51
Request timed out.
Request timed out.
Reply from 173.194.35.148: bytes=32 time=134ms TTL=51
Request timed out
Request timed out....
```

When I came into the picture, the first thing I did was to ping the server on the Internet and type ARP -a to see what I got. And what I saw was the IP address 10.10.10.200 with three different MAC addresses. Of course, it was a three-time duplicate address, and digging into the problem showed me what actually happened there, as illustrated in the following figure:

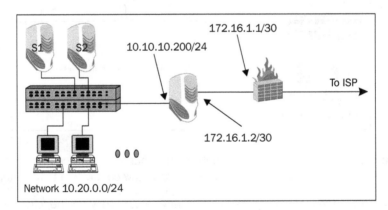

What happened was that the network default gateway to the Internet was not actually the firewall, but a web-filtering device that was located between the network and the firewall with the address 10.10.10.200, while the network between it and the firewall was **172.16.1.2/30**.

What actually happened is explained as follows:

1. In the first place, they configured the DHCP server on the network to exclude addresses 10.10.10.201-254, so the FW address was not excluded.

2. Then they connected a new LAN switch to the stack. The LAN switch was configured by default to receive the IP address by DHCP, so it received the address 10.10.10.200 and that was the first duplicate.

3. And the funniest thing was that the customer suspected a problem of connecting to the Internet, so they disconnected the web-filter server. The stupid problem was that they disconnected the external interface of the web-filter server and connected the internal interface to the switch while changing its address to the address of the firewall that was still connected to the network.

4. What they got is presented in the following illustration, that is, triple 10.10.10.200 addresses.

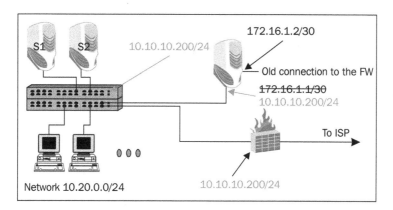

The conclusion from this case and from many other cases I've experienced is that one of the most important conclusions, is: *Always have an updated drawing of your network!!!*

Analyzing DHCP problems

Dynamic Host Configuration Protocol (**DHCP**) is the protocol that provides you with an IP address automatically while connecting to the network. In this recipe, we will learn how to locate some of the common DHCP problems.

Getting ready

When you have a DHCP server on your network, and PCs are not able to receive IP addresses automatically, just connect Wireshark with port mirror to the device that doesn't receive the address, connect and disconnect the device from the network, or simply use the `ipconfig / release` and `ipconfig /renew` commands. Now, we will have a look at what can go wrong.

How to do it...

Have a look at the DHCP procedure described in the *How it works ...* section. Anything that is not going according to this procedure is wrong, so check for the following:

1. Did the client send the `DHCP Discover` packet?

2. If it did, the client works fine.

3. If it didn't:
   - Something is wrong with the client. Check if the client is configured with DHCP (obtain an IP address automatically as marked in the TCP/IP configuration window).
   - It can be that the client is physically not connected to the network. It happens a lot with wireless communications (WiFi), where the client does not have connectivity to the network and therefore, does not send the `DHCP Discover` packet since it doesn't have a network to send it over.

4. The client sends `DHCP Discover` and receives `DHCP Offer` from a single server. This is ok; continue watching the wire.

5. The client sends `DHCP Discover` and receives `DHCP Offer` from two or more servers. This is a problem. You have more than one DHCP server on your LAN, and you might get different address allocations to clients on the LAN. Turn off one of the servers (at least the DHCP service on it).

6. You receive DHCP Discover and send DHCP Request; this is fine.
   - If you immediately receive `DHCP Ack` with the IP parameters, everything is fine.
   - If you don't receive anything, and you send another `DHCP Request`, it can be a slow or non-responsive server. Check it.

7. If you receive a DHCP Decline message, it is the server that has refused your request.
   1. It can be that the server does not have available addresses. In this case, extend your address range.
   2. It can be also that the server has allocated your previous IP address to someone else. This is a server configuration issue; so if you need this feature, configure the server to save IP addresses per clients.

How it works...

DHCP is considered to be a simple protocol, but actually it is very complex. When you connect a client to the network, it will go through the following steps:

1. `DHCP Discover`: The client initializes a limited version of TCP/IP and broadcasts a request looking for a DHCP server. The request is sent from UDP port 68 to UDP port 67.

2. `DHCP Offer`: DHCP servers listen on UDP port 67, and if a server receives the request, it answers with a DHCP offer, that is offering to provide the service of address assignment.

3. `DHCP Request`: The client receives the DHCP offer and sends back a request to receive information. The request will be, for example, the IP address that we requested before (because we had it before), for our MAC address so that the server will recognize us as a prior client with a saved IP address and other parameters.

4. `DHCP Ack`: Here the server sends the requested information, including the IP address, subnet mask, default gateway, DNS servers, and other parameters that are configured on the server.

In the next screenshot, we see a standard procedure of DHCP that works properly:

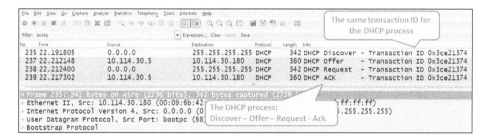

There's more...

A very common problem is when you connect a device to your network, you receive an IP address and you don't have any idea where it came from. Usually, this is because someone has connected a DHCP server to your LAN without telling you. In most of the cases, it will be a small Internet router. This is very simple to find out:

1. If you type `ipconfig` and get an address that you don't know, it might be a problem.

2. Since the router we suspect is connected to the network, assign your IP address, subnet mask, and a default gateway. When you ping your default gateway, you actually ping the router, which is likely to be the troublemaker.

3. Type `ARP -a` to give you the troublemaker's MAC address. This will tell you two things:

    ❑ Who is the vendor? When you know who is the vendor is (D-Link, Edimax, Netgear, and many others), you can simply go and look for it.

    ❑ By logging into the LAN switch, the MAC address will also tell you which port it is connected to. Go to your communications room and disconnect it.

4. Of course, while listening to the port with Wireshark, you will see the vendor MAC address easily.

9
UDP/TCP Analysis

This chapter contains the following recipes:

- ▶ Configuring TCP and UDP preferences for troubleshooting
- ▶ TCP connection problems
- ▶ TCP retransmissions – where they come from and why
- ▶ Duplicate ACKs and fast retransmissions
- ▶ TCP out-of-order packet events
- ▶ TCP Zero Window, Window Full, Window Change, and other Window indicators
- ▶ TCP resets and why they happen

Introduction

The goal of **Transmission Control Protocol** (**TCP**) and **User Datagram Protocol** (**UDP**) is to pass information between end applications, for example, from a web client to a web server, mail client to a mail server, and so on. This is done by providing identification to end applications and forwarding packets between them. These identifications are called port numbers, and a port number with its IP address is called a socket. In the following diagram you can see what happens when you open a connection from your browser to a web server. The web server listens on port 80 and you will open a connection, for example, from port 1024.

So, the server is listening to requests on port 80 and will send responses to you on port 1024.

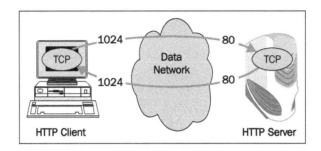

While TCP is a reliable, connection-oriented protocol, UDP does not support connectivity and reliability, but simply transfers datagrams between two end processes.

 There is an additional layer-4 protocol, which is called SCTP (Stream Control Transmission Protocol). This protocol can be considered as an improved version of TCP, and mostly used in a service provider's networks. SCTP is not included in the scope of this book.

In this chapter, we will focus on TCP, its behavior, various problems, and how to use Wireshark in order to isolate and solve them.

Configuring TCP and UDP preferences for troubleshooting

In most cases you can use the default Wireshark parameters for TCP and UDP network analysis, but there are also some changes that can be configured. The changes will be configured in the **Preferences** window.

Getting ready

For TCP or UDP configuration:

1. Start Wireshark, and from the **Edit** menu, choose **Statistics**.
2. Under **Protocols**, choose **TCP** or **UDP**.

How to do it...

In this section we will see how to configure TCP and UDP preferences.

UDP parameters

Let's see some parameters that can influence the capture of UDP:

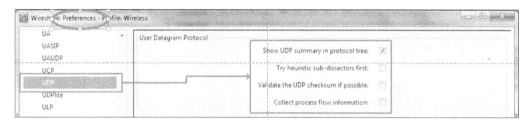

You can configure the following parameters in UDP:

▸ **Show UDP summary in protocol tree**: Mark this button if you want the UDP summary line to be shown in the protocol tree (set by default)

▸ **Try heuristic sub-dissectors first**: Try to decode a packet using the heuristic method before using a sub-dissector registered to the specific port

▸ **Validate the UDP checksum if possible**: Validates the UDP checksum

▸ **Collect process flow information**: Collects process flow information

By default only the first parameter is set. In most cases it is enough.

TCP parameters

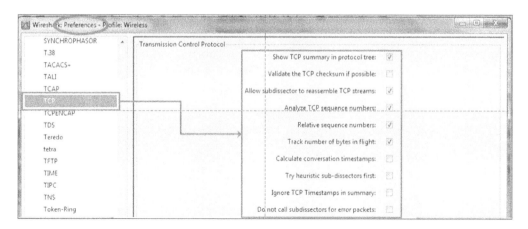

You can configure the following parameters in TCP:

▶ **Show TCP summary in protocol tree**: Mark this button if you want the TCP summary line to be shown in the protocol tree (set by default).

▶ **Validate the TCP checksum if possible**: This feature can slow down performance. In most cases it is not required.

▶ **Allow subdissector to reassemble TCP streams**: This option is for stream analysis (set by default).

▶ **Analyze TCP sequence numbers**: When this is set, Wireshark analyzes sequence numbers and track phenomena such as retransmission, duplicate ACKs, and so on, which is one of the important features of Wireshark.

▶ **Relative sequence numbers**: When this is set, Wireshark will show you every TCP connection that starts from Seq=0.

▶ **Track number of bytes in flight**: This setting enables Wireshark to track the number of unacknowledged bytes flowing on the network (set by default).

▶ **Calculate conversation timestamps**: This feature enables the calculations of TCP timestamps option.

▶ **Try heuristic sub-dissectors first**: Try to decode a packet using heuristic method before using a sub-dissector registered to the specific port.

▶ **Ignore TCP Timestamps in summary**: Ignore the timestamp option in the TCP header.

▶ **Do not call subdissector for error packets**: This option does not analyze erroneous TCP packets.

How it works...

There are some parameters in the TCP preferences that I would like to say a few words about.

Referring to **relative sequence numbers**, when you look at a TCP connection you see that it always starts with sequence numbers equal to zero. These are the relative numbers that are normalized to zero by Wireshark. The real numbers are numbers between 0 and 2^{32}, picked by the TCP process, which are difficult to follow. The TCP standard does not set any rule for picking this number.

The **calculating conversations timestamps** refers to the timestamp option of the TCP packet. The TCP timestamps option carries two 4-byte timestamp fields, as seen in the next diagram:

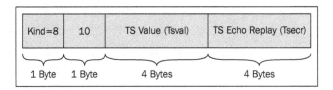

The problem that the timestamp option comes to solve is the sensitivity of TCP to delay variations. The solution, and written in RFC 1323, is to use TCP options in the following ways (for every TCP connection):

▸ The sender places a timestamp in each data segment that it sends (the Tsval field)

▸ The receiver reflects these timestamps in ACK segments (the Tsecr field)

Then, a single subtraction gives the sender an accurate RTT measurement for every ACK segment (which will correspond to every other data segment, with a sensible receiver). This mechanism is called **Round Trip Time Measurement** (**RTTM**).

There's more...

UDP is a very simple protocol with a very simple header that includes only four fields: source port, destination port, packet length, and checksum. Checksum is used by the receiver to check whether to accept the packet or drop it. In case of a packet drop, there is no recovery mechanism. In some cases, the application will recover it (for example, DNS that sends the request again), and in some cases it won't.

TCP is more sophisticated. It is a connection-oriented, reliable protocol, with sequencing mechanism, flow, and congestion control. These subjects will be discussed later in this chapter.

SCTP is a reliable, connection-oriented protocol that allows the transfer of multiple streams per connection, optional bundling of multiple user messages into a single SCTP packet, support for cookies, multi-homing, and other mechanisms. It was initially developed for carrying signaling messages in cellular networks, and later implemented with other application protocols.

TCP connection problems

When two TCP processes wish to communicate, they open the connection, send the data, and then close the connection. This happens when you open a browser to the Internet, connect from your mail client to the mail server, or connect with Telnet to your router or any other application that works over TCP.

When TCP opens the connection, it sends a request for open connection from the source port to destination port.

Some problems can occur during the establishment or closing of the application. Using Wireshark to locate and solve these problems is the goal of this recipe.

Getting ready

If you experience one of the following problems, use Wireshark in order to find out what is the reason for it.

These problems can be of many types. Of these:

- You try to run an application and it does not work. You try to browse the Internet and you don't get any response.

- You try to use your mail but you don't have a connection to the mail server.

- Problems can be due to simple reasons, such as the server being down, the application is not running on the server, or the network is down somewhere on the way to the server.

- Problems can be also due to more complicated reasons, such as DNS problems, insufficient memory on the server that does not enable you to connect (due to high memory consumption by an application, for example), duplicate IPs, and many others.

In this recipe we focus on these GO/NO-GO problems that are usually quite easy to solve.

How to do it...

Here you will see some indicators and what you can see when you use Wireshark for debugging TCP connectivity problems. Usually these problems result in trying to run an application and getting no results.

When you try to run an application, for example, a database client, a mail client, watching cameras servers, and so on, and you don't get any output, follow these steps:

1. Verify that the server and applications are running.

2. Verify if your client is running, you have an IP address configured (manually or by DHCP), and you are connected to the network.

3. Ping the server and verify you have connectivity to it.

In some cases, you will not have Ping to the server, but still have connectivity to the application. This can happen because a firewall is blocking the ICMP messages, so if you don't have Ping to a destination it doesn't necessarily mean that something is wrong. The firewall can be a dedicated device in the network or a windows (or Linux/UNIX) firewall installed on the end device.

4. In the capture file, look for one of the following patterns:

   ❑ Triple SYN messages with no response (in the following screenshot)

   ❑ SYN messages with a reset (RST) response

In both cases it can be that a firewall is blocking the specific application or the application is not running.

In the following screenshot, we see a simple case in which we simply don't get access to web server 81.218.31.171 (packets 61, 62, and 63). It can be because it is not permitted by a firewall, or simply because there is a problem with the server. We can also see that we have a connection to another website (108.160.163.43, packets 65, 66, and 67), so the connection problem is only to 81.218.31.171.

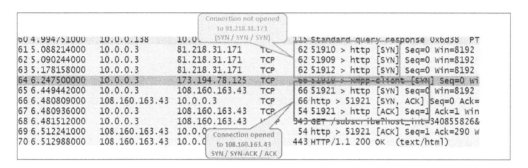

In the next screenshot we see a slightly more complex case of the same situation. In this case, we've had a cameras server that the customer wanted to log in to and watch the cameras on a remote site. The camera's server had the IP address 135.82.12.1 and the problem was that the customer was able to get the main web page of the server with the login window, but couldn't log into the system. In the following screenshot, we can see that we open a connection to the IP address 135.82.12.1. We see that a TCP connection is opened to the HTTP server, and at first it looks like there are no connectivity problems:

The problems arise when we filter all traffic to the IP address `135.82.12.1`, that is, the cameras server.

Here we see that when we try to connect to TCP port `6036`, we get an RST/ACK response, which can be:

- A firewall that blocks port `6036` (that was the case here)
- When port address translation (PAT) is configured, and we translate only port `80` and not `6036`
- The authentication of the username and password were done on TCP port `6036`, the firewall allowed only port `80`, the authentication was blocked, and the application didn't work

No.	Time	Source	Destination	Protocol	Length Info
2620	36.423135	10.0.0.3	135.82.12.1	TCP	54 62438 > http [ACK] Seq=915
2		10.0.0.3	135.82.12.1	TCP	66 62442 > 6036 [SYN] Seq=0 W
2 Connection Trials to		135.82.12.1	10.0.0.3	TCP	54 6036 > 62442 [RST, ACK] Se
2 TCP port 6036:		fe80::c067:2c23:335:ff02::c		SSDP	208 M-SEARCH * HTTP/1.1
2 • SYN request		10.0.0.3	194.90.1.5	ICMP	74 Echo (ping) request id=0x
2 • RST/ACK response		194.90.1.5	10.0.0.3	ICMP	74 Echo (ping) reply id=0x
2626	37.329129	10.0.0.3	135.82.12.1	TCP	62 62442 > 6036 [SYN] Seq=0 W
2627	37.369547	135.82.12.1	10.0.0.3	TCP	54 6036 > 62442 [RST, ACK] Se
2628	38.023274	10.0.0.3	194.90.1.5	ICMP	74 Echo (ping) request id=0x

To summarize, when you don't have connectivity to a server, check the server and the client if all TCP/UDP ports are forwarded throughout the network, and if you have any ports that you don't know about.

In some cases when you install new applications in your network, it is good to connect Wireshark on the client and the server, and check what is actually running between them. The software house will not always tell you what they are actually transferring over the network (sometimes this is because they are not aware of it!), and firewalls can block information that you are not aware of.

How it works...

Starting a TCP connection, as seen in the next screenshot, happens in three steps:

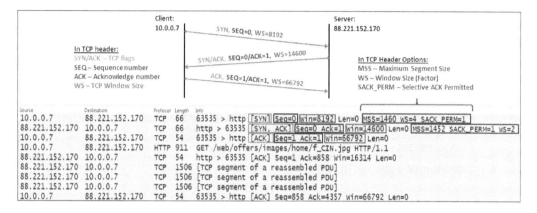

1. The TCP process on the client side sends an SYN packet. This is a packet with the SYN flag set to `1`. In this packet the client:

    ❑ Specifies its initial sequence number. This is the number of the first byte that the client sends to the server.

    ❑ Specifies its window size. This is the buffer the clients allocate to the process (the place in the client's RAM).

    ❑ Sets the options that will be used by it: MSS, Selective ACK, and so on.

2. When the server receives the request to establish a connection, the server:

    ❑ Sends an SYN/ACK packet to the client, confirming the acceptance of the SYN request.

    ❑ Specifies the server's initial sequence number. This is the number of the first byte that the server sends to the client.

    ❑ Specifies the server's window size. This is the buffer size that the server allocates to the process (the place in the server's RAM).

    ❑ Responds to the options requested and sets the options on the server side.

3. When receiving the server's SYN/ACK, the client:

    ❑ Sends an ACK packet to the server, confirming the acceptance of the SYN/ACK packet from the server.

    ❑ Specifies the client's window size. This is the buffer size that the client allocates to the process. Although this parameter was defined in the first packet (the SYN packet), the server will refer to this one since it is the latest window size received by the server.

In the options field of the TCP header, we have the following main options:

- **Maximum Segment Size (MSS)**: This is the maximum size of the TCP datagram, that is, the number of bytes from the beginning of the TCP header to the end of the entire packet.

- **Windows Size (WSopt)**: This factor is multiplied with the Window Size field in the TCP header to notify the receiver on a larger size buffer. Since the maximum window size in the header is 64 KB, a factor of 4 gives us 64 KB multiplied by 4, that is, a 256 KB window size.

- **SACK**: Selective ACK is an option that enables the two parties of a connection to acknowledge specific packets, so when a single packet is lost, only this packet will be sent again. Both parties of the connection have to agree on SACK in the connection establishment.

- **Timestamps options (TSopt)**: This parameter was explained earlier in this chapter, and refers to measurement of the delay between client and the server.

By this stage, both sides:

- Agree to establish a connection

- Know the other side's initial sequence number

- Know the other side's window size

 Anything but a full three-way handshake while establishing a connection should be considered as a problem. This includes SYN without a response, SYN and then SYN/ACK and no last ACK, SYN which is answered with a reset (RST flag equal 1), and so on.

There's more...

Some rules of thumb are as follows:

- In case an SYN packet is answered with RST, look for the firewall that blocks the port numbers.

- Triple SYN without any answer occurs either due to an application that didn't respond, or a firewall that blocks the request on a specific port.

- Always verify if you have Network Address Translation (NAT), port forwarding, and mechanisms that play with TCP or UDP ports. These mechanisms can interrupt with the standard operation of TCP.

TCP retransmission – where do they come from and why

When TCP sends a packet or a group of packets (refer to the *How it works...* section later in this recipe), it waits for acknowledgment to confirm the acceptance of these packets. Retransmissions, obviously, happen due to a packet that has not arrived, or acknowledgment that has not arrived on time. There can be various reasons for this, and finding the reason is the goal of this recipe.

Getting ready

When you see that the network becomes slow, one of the reasons for this can be retransmissions. Connect Wireshark in the port mirror to the suspicious client or server, and watch the results.

In this recipe, we will see some common problems that we encounter with Wireshark, and what they indicate.

How to do it...

Let's get started:

1. Start capturing data on the relevant interface.
2. Go to the **Analyze | Expert Info** menu.
3. Under **Notes**, look for **Retransmissions**.
4. You can click on the (**+**) sign and a list of retransmissions will open. A single mouse click on every line will bring you the retransmission in the packet capture pane.
5. Now comes the important question: how to locate the problem.

 When you capture packets over a communication line, server interface, link to the Internet, or any other line, you can have traffic from many IP addresses, many applications, and even specific procedures on every application, for example, accessing a specific table in a database application. The important thing here is to locate the TCP connections on which the retransmissions happen.

6. You can see where the retransmissions come from by:

   ❑ Moving packet-by-packet in the **Expert Info** window, and looking for what packets does it take you in the packet capture pane (good for experienced users)

   ❑ In the packet pane, configure the display filter `expert.message == "Retransmission (suspected)"`, and you will get all retransmissions in the capture file

   ❑ By applying the filter, and then checking the **Limit to display filter** section to the right-bottom corner of the window in the **Statistics à Conversations** window

Case 1 – retransmissions to many destinations

In the following screenshot, you see that we've got many retransmissions, spread between many servers, with destination ports 80 (HTTP). What we can also see from here is the `10.0.0.5` port sends the retransmission, so packets were lost on the way to the Internet, or acknowledgement was not sent back on time from the web servers.

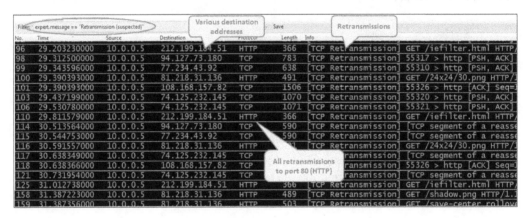

Well, obviously something is wrong on the line to the Internet. How can we know what it is?

1. From the **Statistics** menu, open **IO Graph**.

2. In this case (case 1), we see that the line is nearly empty. Probably it is an error, or another loaded line on the way to the Internet.

3. You can check packet losses and errors that cause them by logging into the communications equipment or by any SNMP browser (when the SNMP agent is configured on the equipment). Check the following screenshot for reference:

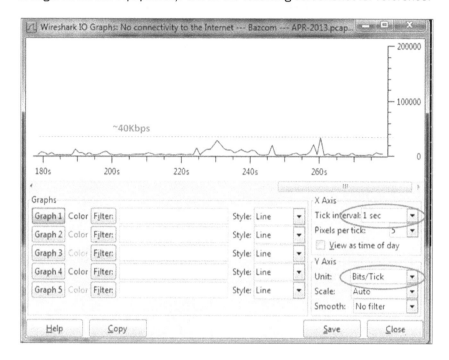

Case 2 – retransmissions on a single connection

If all retransmissions will be on a single IP, with a single TCP port number, it will be a slow application. We can see this in the following screenshot:

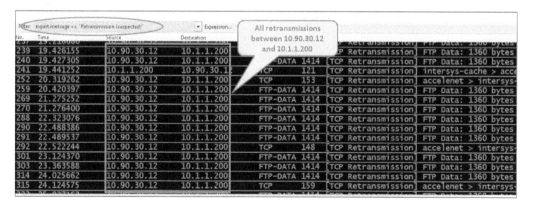

For retransmissions on a single connection, perform the following steps:

1. We can also verify this by opening **Conversations** from the **Statistics** menu, and by selecting the **Limit to display filter** checkbox, we will get all the conversations that have retransmissions, in this case, a single conversation.

2. By choosing the **IPv4** tab as shown in the following screenshot we will see from which IP addresses we get the retransmissions:

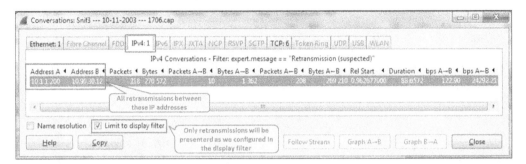

3. By choosing the **TCP** tab as shown in the following screenshot we will see from which port numbers (or applications) we get the retransmissions:

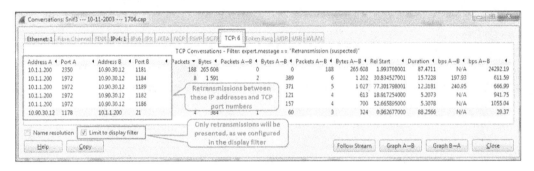

To isolate the problem, perform the following steps:

1. Look at the IO graph, and make sure that the line is not busy.

An indication of a busy communication line will be a straight line very close to the maximum bandwidth of the line. For example, if you have a 10 Mbps communication line, you port mirror it, and see in the IO graph a straight line which is close to the 10 Mbps, this is a good indication of a loaded line. A non-busy communication line will have many ups and downs, peaks and empty intervals.

2. If the line is not busy, it can be a problem on the server for the IP address `10.1.1.200` (`10.90.30.12` is sending most of the retransmissions, so it can be that `10.1.1.200` responds slowly).

3. From the packet pane we see that the application is FTP-DATA. It is possible that the FTP server works in an active mode. Hence we've opened a connection on one port (`2350`), and the server changed the port to `1972`, so it can be a slow non-responsive FTP software (that was the problem here eventually).

Case 3 – retransmission patterns

An important thing to watch for in TCP retransmissions is if the retransmissions have any pattern that you can see.

In the following screenshot, we see that all retransmissions are coming from a single connection, between a single client and NetBIOS Session Service (TCP port `139`) on the server.

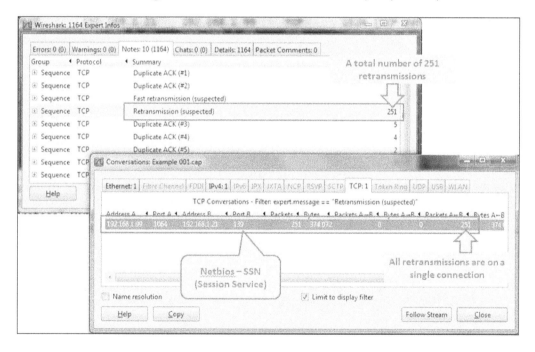

Looks like a simple server/application problem, but when we look at the packet capture pane, we see something interesting (refer to the following screenshot):

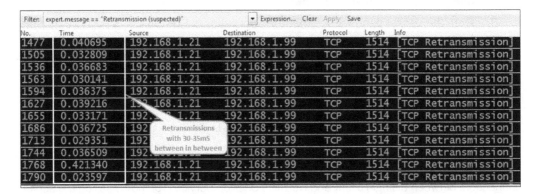

The interesting thing is that when we look at the pattern of retransmissions, we see that they occur cyclically every 30 ms. The time format here is seconds, since the previously displayed packet and the time scale is in seconds.

The problem in this case was a client that performed a financial procedure in the software that caused the software to slow down every 30-36 ms.

Case 4 – retransmission due to a non-responsive application

Another reason for retransmissions can be when a client or a server does not answer to requests. In this case, you will see five retransmissions, with an increasing time difference. After these five consecutive retransmissions, the connection is considered to be lost by the sending side (in some cases, reset will be sent to close the connection, depending on the software implementation). After the disconnection, two things may happen:

- ▶ An SYN request will be sent by the client, in order to open a new connection. What the user will see in this case is a freeze in the application, and after 15-20 seconds it will start to work again

- ▶ No SYN will be sent, and the user will have to run the application (or a specific part of it) again

In the following screenshot we can see a case in which a new connection is opened:

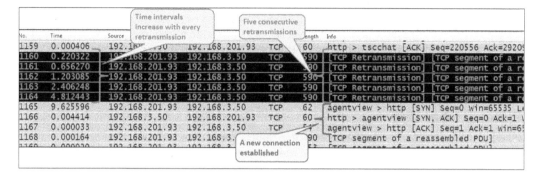

Case 5 – retransmission due to delayed variations

TCP is a protocol that is quite tolerant of delays, as long as the delay does not vary. When you have variations in delay, you can expect retransmissions. The way to find out if this is the problem is as follows:

1. The first thing to do is, of course, to ping the destination, and get the first information of the communications line delay. Look at the *How it works...* section to see how it should be.

2. Check for the delay variations, which can happen due to the following reasons:

   ❑ A delay can happen due to a non-stable or busy communication line. In this case, you will see delay variations using the Ping command. Usually it will happen on lines with a narrow bandwidth, and in some cases on cellular lines.

   ❑ A delay can happen due to a loaded or inefficient application. In this case, you will see many retransmissions on this specific application only.

   ❑ A delay can happen due to a loaded communication equipment (CPU load, buffer load, and so on). You can check this by accessing the communication equipment directly.

3. Use the Wireshark tools as explained in *Chapter 13, Troubleshooting Bandwidth and Delay Problems*.

The bottom line with TCP retransmissions is that retransmissions are a natural behavior of TCP as long as we don't have too many of them. Degradation in performance will start when the retransmissions are around 0.5 percent, and disconnections will start around 5 percent. It also depends on the application and its sensitivity to retransmissions.

Finding what it is

When you see retransmissions on a communication link (to the Internet, on a server, between sites, or any other link), perform the following:

1. Locate the problem—is it a specific IP address, specific connection, specific application, or some other problem.

2. Check if the problem is because of the communication link, packet loss, or a slow server or PC. Check if the application is slow.

3. If it is not due to any of the preceding reasons, check for delay variations.

How it works...

Let's see the regular operation of TCP, and what are the causes for problems that might happen.

Regular operation of the TCP Sequence/Acknowledge mechanism

One of the mechanisms that is built into TCP is the retransmission mechanism. This mechanism enables the recovery of data that is damaged, lost, duplicated, or delivered out of order.

This is achieved by assigning a sequence number to every transmitted byte, and expecting an acknowledgment (ACK) from the receiving party. If the ACK is not received within a timeout interval, the data is retransmitted.

At the receiver end, the sequence numbers are used in order to verify that the information comes in the order that it was sent. If not, rearrange it to its previous state.

This mechanism works as follows:

1. At the connection establishment, both sides tell each other what will be their initial sequence number.

2. When data is sent, every packet has a sequence number. The sequence number indicates the number of the first byte in the TCP payload. The next packet that is sent will have the sequence number of the previous one, plus the number of bytes in the previous packet, plus one (in the next screenshot).

3. When a packet is sent, the RTO (Retransmission Timeout) counter starts to count the time from the moment it was sent.

 The Retransmission Timeout timer is based on the Van Jacobson congestion avoidance and control algorithm, which basically says the TCP is tolerant to high delays, but not to fast delay variations.

4. When the receiver receives the packet, it answers with an ACK (Acknowledge) packet that tells the sender to send the next packet. In the following screenshot you will see how it works:

    1. You can see from here that 10.0.0.7 is downloading a file from 62.219.24.171. The file is downloaded via HTTP (the Wireshark window was configured to show tcp.seq and tcp.ack from the **Edit** | **Preferences** columns configuration, as described in *Chapter 1, Introducing Wireshark*).

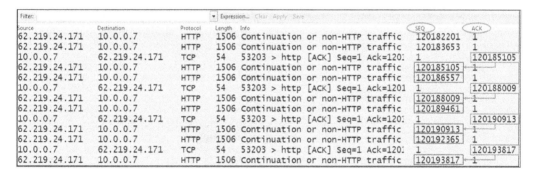

2. You can see from here that 62.219.24.171 sends a packet with a sequence number of 120185105, and then a packet with the sequence number 120186557. When receiving these two packets, the client 10.0.0.7 tells the server to send him the next packet with ACK = 120188009, after which the server sends the packet with the sequence number 120188009, and the next packet with sequence number 120189461, and so on.

You can see a diagram for this.

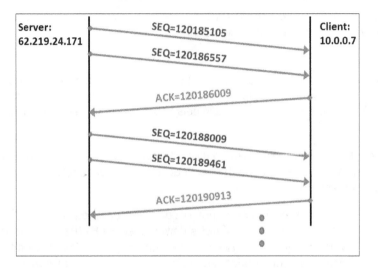

What are TCP retransmissions and what do they cause

When a packet acknowledgment is lost, or when an ACK does not arrive on time, the sender will perform two things:

1. Send the packet again, as described earlier in this recipe.

2. Decrease the throughput.

In the next screenshot we see an example of retransmissions that reduce the sender throughput (red thin lines added for clarity):

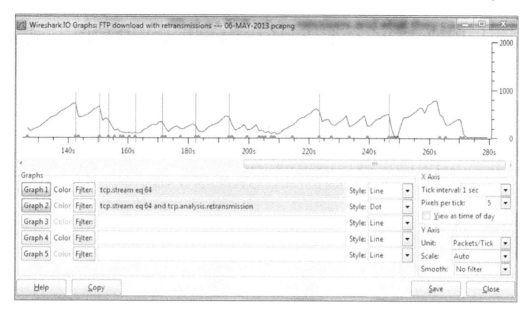

There's more...

TCP is tolerant of high delays, as long as they are reasonably stable. The algorithm that defines the TCP behavior under delay variations (among other things) is called the Van Jacobson algorithm (after the name of its inventor). The Van Jacobson algorithm enables tolerance of up to 3-4 times the average delay, so if for example, you have a delay of 100 ms, TCP will be tolerant to delays of up to 300-400 ms as long as they are not frequently changed.

See also

You can check the Van Jacobson algorithm at `http://ee.lbl.gov/papers/congavoid.pdf`.

Duplicate ACKs and fast retransmissions

Another phenomenon that you will see in TCP is what is called duplicate ACKs and fast retransmissions. This phenomenon also happens due to performance problems, and in this recipe we will focus on how to find them and what they indicate.

Getting ready

When you see that the network becomes slow, one of the reasons for this can be duplicate ACKs. Connect the Wireshark in the port mirror to the suspicious client or server and see the results.

How to do it...

In most cases, duplicate ACKs will happen because of high latency, delayed variations, or a slow end point that simply does not response to ACK requests.

When looking for a reason for slow communication, duplicate ACKs can be one of the reasons for it.

1. When you see a reasonable amount of duplicate ACKs, that is, 1 or 2 percent, this is probably not your problem.

2. When you see a huge number of duplicate ACKs (say ten of them), you might have:

   ❑ A very busy communication line that causes variations in delays

   ❑ A non-responsive server or client (depends on who is not responding)

3. A fast retransmission is a packet that is sent in response to the duplicate ACKs.

4. In the next screenshot you see an example of the problem. In the example you see how a fast retransmission is sent after 51 DupACKs (duplicate ACKs):

Source	Destination	Protocol	Length	Info
10.0.0.7	15.192.45.26	TCP	66	[TCP Dup ACK 19022#46] 56247 > 44600 [ACK] Seq=1 Ack=14593377 W
15.192.45.26	10.0.0.7	FTP-DATA	1506	FTP Data: 1452 bytes
10.0.0.7	15.192	TCP		TCP Dup ACK 19022#4	=1 Ack=14593377 W
15.192.45.26	10.0.0		06	FTP Data: 1452 bytes	Requesting for sequence
10.0.0.7	15.192			TCP Dup ACK 19022#4	number 14593377	Ack=14593377 W
15.192.45.26	10.0.0		506	FTP Data: 1452 bytes
10.0.0.7	15.192.45.26	TCP	66	[TCP Dup ACK 19022#49] 56247 > 44600 [ACK] Seq=1 Ack=14593377 W
15.192.45.26	10.0.0.7	FTP-DATA	1506	FTP Data: 1452 bytes
10.0.0.7	15.192.45.26	TCP	66	[TCP Dup ACK 19022#50] 56247 > 44600 [ACK] Seq=1 Ack=14593377 W
15.192.45.26	10.0.0.7	FTP-DATA	1506	FTP Data: 1452 bytes
10.0.0.7	15.192.45.26	TCP	66	[TCP Dup ACK 19022#51] 56247 > 44600 [ACK] Seq=1 Ack=14593377 W
15.192.45.26	10.0.0.7	FTP-DATA	1506	[TCP Fast Retransmission] FTP Data: 1452 bytes
10.0.0.7	15.192.45.26	TCP	54	56247 > 44600 [ACK] Seq=1 Ack=14687325 Win=261360 Len=0
15.192.45.26	10.0.0.7	FTP-DATA	1506	FTP Data: 1452 bytes

Duplicate Ack's number 46, 47, 48 ...51 for packet number 19022

Response packet (Fast Retransmission)

```
> Ethe          :7b:a2 (14:d6:4d:f4:7b:a2), Dst: HonHaiP          7:8e:73)
> Inte          Src: 15.192.45.26 (15.192.45.26), Dst: 10.0.0.7 (10.0.0.7)
> Trar          , Src Port: 44600 (44600), Dst Port: 56247 (56247), Seq: 14593377, Ack: 1, Len: 14
   Source port: 4400     (       )
   Destination port: 56      (56247)
   [Stream index: 64]
   Sequence number: 14593377    (relative sequence number)
   [Next sequence number: 14594829    (relative sequence number)]
   Acknowledgment number: 1    (relative ack number)
```

Fast Retransmission with the requested sequence number

5. Here is how you can solve the problem:

   ❏ If you have a small number of duplicate ACKs and retransmissions (less than 1 percent), it's tolerable.

   ❏ When you have this over cellular or wireless networks, or in connections over the Internet, the delay and delay variations are common to these networks, so there is really nothing much you can do about it.

   ❏ If you have it in your organization's network, it might be a problem. If it's on the LAN, check for severe problems, such as switch buffers and CPU load, very slow servers, and so on. If it's on the WAN, check for delays and loaded or unstable lines.

How it works...

A duplicate ACK happens if a packet is detected as missing (the expected sequence number was not received), or when an unexpected sequence number was received. In this case, the receiver generates an ACK indicating the next expected sequence number that it wishes to receive. The receiver will continue to generate ACKs requesting the missing segment, until it will receive it.

On the sender side, when it receives three identical ACKs (the original ACK and two duplicate ACKs) with the same value, it assumes there is a packet loss and it resends the missing packet, regardless of whether the RTO is expired or not. The packet that is sent again is called fast retransmission.

Duplicate ACKs also reduce the throughput that is sent over the network. How much throughput is reduced depends on the TCP version. In the earlier versions of TCP (that is Tahoe, Reno, and New-Reno) the idea was that in the appearance of a duplicate ACK, the sender reduces the throughput to half of what it was before. In case of many DupACKs, the throughput will be reduced to minimum.

In the next screenshot you see a typical example for what is caused by duplicate ACKs and retransmissions:

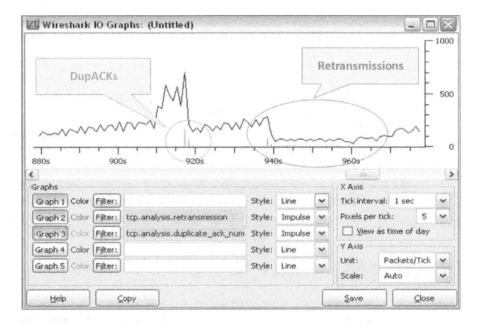

In this screenshot we see that first duplicate ACKs reduce the throughput to around 40 percent of what it was before, and then retransmissions reduce it to minimum.

There's more...

The mechanism that is used in duplicate ACKs is called fast recovery. In recent years some advanced versions of TCP were introduced, especially for cellular networks, in order to improve the behavior of TCP under high and changing delay conditions. In these examples, you might see some differences in the behavior of the sender and receiver, for example, lighter degradation in performance, faster recovery, and so on. Still, the characteristic behavior of TCP is maintained.

TCP out-of-order packet events

Another phenomenon that you will see in networks is **previous segment loss** and **out-of-order segments**. Both relate to packets arriving out of order, and in some cases indicate a problem.

When you see this on a network connection, it might happen due to network problems or an interruption in capture. In this recipe we will focus on this issue and what it can cause.

Getting ready

Start Wireshark and connect it on a mirrored port. The three phenomena that we want to focus on in this recipe are:

- **Previous segment lost**: This occurs when a packet arrives with a sequence number higher than the next expected sequence number on that connection, indicating that one or more packets prior to the flagged packet did not arrive

- **Out-of-order packet**: This occurs when a packet is seen with a sequence number lower than the previously received packet on that connection

- **Previous segment not captured** (Wireshark Version 1.8.x and higher): This is like the previous segment lost

How to do it...

When will it happen?

You might see these in the following events:

- **At the beginning of capture**: This event occurs when you start a capture during an open connection. In this case, you will see packets on a connection without the SYN/SYN-ACK/ACK, therefore, Wireshark thinks something went wrong.

- **Real packet losses**: In this case you will also see retransmissions of the lost packets and/or duplicate ACKs telling the sender to send the lost packets.

No.	Source	Destination	Protocol	Length	Info	SEQ	
330	62.90.90.210	10.0.0.6	TCP	1474	[TCP segment of a reassembled PDU]	312401	
331	10.0.0.6	62.90.90.210	TCP	90	[TCP Dup ACK 223#54] 57999 > http	369	
332	62.90.90.210	10.0.0.6	TCP	1474	[TCP Previous segment not captured]	319501	
333	10.0.0.6	62.90.90.210	TCP	90	[TCP Dup ACK 223#55] 57999 > http	369	1420 Bytes
334	62.90.90.210	10.0.0.6	TCP	1474	[TCP segment of a reassembled PDU]	320921	
335	10.0.0.6	62.90.90.210	TCP	90	[TCP Dup ACK 223#56] 57999 > http	369	5680 Bytes (4*1420Bytes)
336	62.90.90.210	10.0.0.6	TCP	1474	[TCP Previous segment not captured]	326601	
337	10.0.0.6	62.90.90.210	TCP	90	[TCP Dup ACK 223#57] 57999 > http	369	1420 Bytes
338	62.90.90.210	10.0.0.6	TCP	1474	[TCP segment of a reassembled PDU]	328021	
339	10.0.0.6	62.90.90.210	TCP	90	[TCP Dup ACK 223#58] 57999 > http	369	4260 Bytes (3*1420Bytes)
340	62.90.90.210	10.0.0.6	TCP	1474	[TCP Previous segment not captured]	332281	
341	10.0.0.6	62.90.90.210	TCP	90	[TCP Dup ACK 223#59] 57999 > http	369	

In the previous screenshot, we see a good example for severe packet losses. What we see here is that `10.0.0.6` is trying to browse website `62.90.90.210`. During this, the TCP segments of 1420 bytes each are sent to the web server and we see that between packets 334 and 336 three packets are missing, and between packets 338 and 340 two packets are missing. In both cases, Wireshark notices: **TCP's previous segment is not captured**.

▶ **Delay variations**: This can happen due to packets that take different routes from the source to destination. To check this use Tracert, and look for route changes between the source and destination (if it happens on the organization network) you can, for example, configure traps on the routers that will tell you when this happens.

▶ **Data capture problems**: It can be that packets are sent and received properly, but Wireshark will not have captured them. It can be because of various reasons:

    ❑ Because of very heavy traffic Wireshark might lose packets in high bit rates (over 150-180 Mbps). To avoid this problem, use other tools (mostly commercial).

    ❑ In case your laptop is not strong enough, lack of memory or CPU power will not enable Wireshark to work fast enough. This is easy to find out, and you are probably aware of it.

    ❑ When port buffers on a LAN switch are too small, packets can be dropped. Connect to the switch (as with console or telnet connection) and use the switch command line to check for the problem.

    ❑ Capturing data on a wireless network, when for some reason you don't see all packets that are sent. See *Chapter 7, Ethernet, LAN Switching, and Wireless LAN*.

How it works...

In this case, things are simple. The TCP sender sends the packets to the receiver. These packets are numbered by their bytes. When a packet does not arrive in order, it is a problem that Wireshark notices. We can have two reasons for this:

▶ **A real problem**: In this case you will see retransmissions and duplicate ACKs that are TCP's response to packets that are received out of order

▶ **A capture problem**: In this case you will see only out-of-order packets, and since you don't see any response to the suspected lost and out-of-order packets, they probably are not

TCP Zero Window, Window Full, Window Change, and other Window indicators

One of the most important mechanisms of TCP is the **Sliding Window** mechanism, and the **Flow Control** mechanism that uses it in order to control the amount of data that a TCP end node is willing to accept on the connection.

In this recipe we will focus on these types of problems, and how to discover the problem and solve it.

Getting ready

Connect Wireshark with a port mirror to the suspected link or server, and start capture. Keep track of every window message you will see in the capture window.

How to do it...

There are several types of window messages that you should be aware of:

TCP Zero Window, Zero Window Probe, and Zero Window Violation

TCP Zero Window occurs when a receiver advertises a receive window size of zero (in the window field in the TCP header). This tells the sender to stop sending data because the receiver's buffer is full. This indicates a problem on the receiver that might be:

- A weak server that cannot allocate enough memory for the process

- A problem in the application that does not receive a sufficient buffer, so the TCP has to tell the sender to stop sending data

- An application that consumes too much memory so the operating system will limit the application resources

TCP **Zero Window Probe** is a message that is sent by the sender in order to see if the receiver's Zero Window condition still exists. This message works by sending the next byte of data to the receiver. If the receiver answers with window that is still zero, the sender doubles his timer before probing again.

The sender ignores the Zero Window condition of the receiver and sends additional bytes of data. TCP Zero Window Violation can indicate a TCP error or bug in the protocol stack.

In order to check what the problem is, check if these events are coming from:

- ▶ A specific end device (server or client) that will indicate a problem in the end device.
- ▶ A problem in a specific application that will indicate a general application problem.
- ▶ A problem when you do something specific in the application, for example, open a specific table, send a file to the printer, create a report, or anything else on the application. In this case, it is of course an application problem.

TCP Window Update

TCP sends Window Update to the other side in a connection in order to indicate that it changed the buffer size, and is ready to accept higher or lower data rate (buffer size determines the throughput that the sender is allowed to send). This can happen in the case of:

- ▶ The TCP receiver recovers from the Zero Window condition, and asks the sender to start sending data again. In this case, you don't have to do anything about it, just check for the problem that caused Zero Window the first time.
- ▶ The TCP receiver changes the window's size frequently. In this case check what is disturbing the receiver. It can be an application problem, memory problem, or any other performance problems on the end devices.

If you see this kind of phenomena, there is nothing to worry about. This is how TCP works.

TCP Window Full

This message is an indication that the sent packet will completely fill the receiver buffer on the receiver. This will happen when the receiver has not sent any ACK confirming the acceptance of the previous data, and therefore, this will be the last packet of data that the sender will send before accepting an ACK from the receiver.

On the receiver side, the moment it gets this packet, it will send a Zero Window message to the sender that will stop sending the data.

This event is triggered for the same reasons that trigger Zero Window. It is simply an indication to a non-responsive server or application. A typical example is shown in the following screenshot:

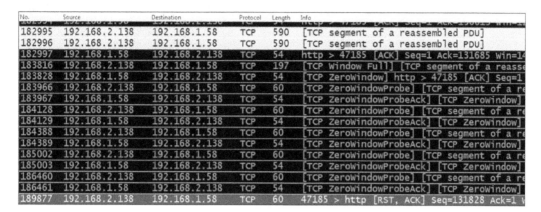

In the previous screenshot we see that:

1. Packet 183816, 192.168.2.138 tells 192.168.1.58 that the sender window is full.

2. In the next packet, 192.168.1.58 sends a signal to 192.168.2.138, telling him to stop sending data. This is a Zero Window signal.

3. Both sides continue to send Zero Window and Zero Window Probe.

4. The last packet of the connection is an RST sent by 192.168.2.138 in order to break the connection.

5. In some cases Zero Window condition will be recovered by a window-change message. In some cases it will be closed with a reset (that can be because an application does not receive any data because of Zero Window).

How it works...

The TCP Sliding Window mechanism works as follows:

1. After the connection is established, the sender sends data to the receiver, filling the receiver window.

2. After several packets, the receiver sends an ACK to the sender, confirming the acceptance of the bytes sent by it. Sending the ACK empties the receiver window.

3. This process is continuous when the sender is filling the window, and the receiving party empties it and sends confirmation of the information.

4. Increasing the receiver window size tells the sender to increase the throughput, and decreasing it tells him to decrease the throughput. It works according to the following WS/RTT rule (with some changes according to the TCP version):

$$\text{Throughput [Bytes/Sec]} = \frac{\text{Window Size [Bytes]}}{\text{RTT [Sec]}}$$

- ✔ Throughput - the effective Bytes/Sec send by an application on a TCP connection
- ✔ Window Size - the TCP receiver window size
- ✔ RTT - the Round Trip Time between the sender and the receiver

There's more...

You can also use the TCP throughput graphs and the IO graphs to view these problems. In the TCP throughput graphs, use the TCP trace graph, where the upper line indicates the window size, and its distance from the lower line indicates what is on the left-hand side of the window. No distance between them indicates a Zero Window.

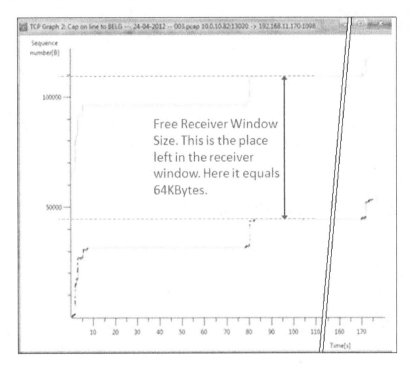

A fixed distance between the lines (as shown in the preceding screenshot) indicates a good operation on the receiving side. When the lines are getting closer, it indicates that the sender is overwhelming the receiver. As long as lines are not overlapping, TCP will continue to send data.

TCP resets and why they happen

During a normal operation, TCP will open a connection with SYN signals, and close the connection with FIN signals. One of the characters of TCP is the possibility to close a connection faster due to a problem or just for better efficiency.

In this recipe we will describe these cases, and how to understand exactly what happens, and if it is a regular condition or something went wrong.

Getting ready

Connect Wireshark with a port mirror to the suspected link or server, and start capture. Keep track of every window message you will see on the capture window. TCP resets can be sent in several cases. Some point to the proper working of the protocol, and some suggest a failure or problem. In this recipe, we will get to the reasons for it, and try to point out the problems and how to solve them.

How to do it...

Reset is a TCP signal that is sent in order to tell the receiver to break the connection. Reset is sent by setting the RST flag to a value of 1.

Cases in which reset is not a problem

The standard way of closing a connection in TCP is by FIN and FIN-ACK signals. The problem is that in order to close a connection, you need four packets: FIN/ACK and ACK from one side, and the same from the other side. It can happen, for example, when you open a standard web page, tens of connections (the main page, news bars, commercials, pictures that are updated periodically, and so on) can be opened, and in order to close all of them you will need sometime hundreds of FIN and FIN-ACK packets standard way. In order to prevent it from happening, the web server will, in many cases, send you the requested data and then break the connection with reset. This is a standard thing to do, and it depends on the application.

Cases in which reset can indicate a problem

There are some cases in which resets can indicate a problem (not necessarily a communication problem):

▸ **A reset sent by a firewall**: When you try to open a connection to a remote server, and don't get anything, you might see an RST signal coming back. This is a firewall blocking a connection. In the next screenshot, you can see that every SYN that is sent is replied to with an RST.

No.	Source	Destination	Protocol	Length	Info
54	192.168.1.123	192.168.1.141	TCP	54	ftp-data > 39542 [RST, ACK] Seq=1 Ack=
55	192.168.1.141	192.168.1.123	TCP	74	39020 > ftp [SYN] Seq=0 Win=5840 Len=0
56	192.168.1.123	192.168.1.141	TCP	54	ftp > 39020 [RST, ACK] Seq=1 Ack=1 Win
57	192.168.1.141	192.168.1.123	TCP	74	56045 > ssh [SYN] Seq=0 Win=5840 Len=0
58	192.168.1.123	192.168.1.141	TCP	54	ssh > 56045 [RST, ACK] Seq=1 Ack=1 Win
59	192.168.1.141	192.168.1.123	TCP	74	47648 > telnet [SYN] Seq=0 Win=5840 Le
60	192.168.1.123	192.168.1.141	TCP	54	telnet > 47648 [RST, ACK] Seq=1 Ack=1
61	192.168.1.141	192.168.1.123	TCP	74	44370 > 24 [SYN] Seq=0 Win=5840 Len=0
62	192.168.1.123	192.168.1.141	TCP	54	24 > 44370 [RST, ACK] Seq=1 Ack=1 Win=
63	192.168.1.141	192.168.1.123	TCP	74	48264 > smtp [SYN] Seq=0 Win=5840 Len=
64	192.168.1.123	192.168.1.141	TCP	54	smtp > 48264 [RST, ACK] Seq=1 Ack=1 Wi
65	192.168.1.141	192.168.1.123	TCP	74	49404 > 26 [SYN] Seq=0 Win=5840 Len=0
66	192.168.1.123	192.168.1.141	TCP	54	26 > 49404 [RST, ACK] Seq=1 Ack=1 Win=
67	192.168.1.141	192.168.1.123	TCP	74	46880 > nsw-fe [SYN] Seq=0 Win=5840 Le
68	192.168.1.123	192.168.1.141	TCP	54	nsw-fe > 46880 [RST, ACK] Seq=1 Ack=1
69	192.168.1.141	192.168.1.123	TCP	74	41799 > 28 [SYN] Seq=0 Win=5840 Len=0
70	192.168.1.123	192.168.1.141	TCP	54	28 > 41799 [RST, ACK] Seq=1 Ack=1 Win=

▸ **Reset sent due to a problem on one of the sides**: Here you can have many reasons. Some of them are as follows:

  ❑ One of the reasons is the five consecutive retransmissions that are not replied to by an ACK. When the sender does not get any reply for the retransmissions, it will send a reset signal to the other side, telling it to break the connection.

  ❑ Another reason is a connection without any traffic on it for a few minutes (how many minutes is the operation system default). The side that opened the connection will usually send the reset (usually but not always, it depends on the implementation).

How it works...

Here it is simple. Reset is a signal that is used in order to break a connection. It is important to remember here that everything depends on the application. If the programmer chose to send an RST on a specific case, this is what you will see on the capture file. For every reset that you see, try to figure out what caused it and you will understand it from the packets the before reset was sent.

10
HTTP and DNS

In this chapter, we will go through the following recipes:

- Filtering DNS traffic
- Analyzing regular DNS operations
- Analyzing DNS problems
- Filtering HTTP traffic
- Configuring HTTP preferences
- Analyzing HTTP problems
- Exporting HTTP objects
- HTTP flow analysis and the Follow TCP Stream window
- Analyzing HTTPS traffic – SSL/TLS basics

Introduction

Domain Name System (**DNS**) is a protocol that is used for resolving names to the IP addresses. It is used over the Internet when you browse a website, and then the DNS resolves the web server name to an IP address. It is also used in enterprise networks when looking for a server name that is translated to an IP address.

Hyper Text Transfer Protocol (**HTTP**) and **Secured HTTP** (**HTTPS**) are both used for browsing the Internet, or connecting to other software that are hosted inside your organization or in the cloud. HTTPS is used when we secure HTTP with SSL/TLS in order to hide the clear text data exchange from hacking. It is used when connecting to your bank, webmail account (for example, Gmail or Hotmail), or any other secured application.

In this chapter, we will discuss these protocols, how they work, and how to use Wireshark in order to find common errors and problems in them.

Filtering DNS traffic

DNS is a protocol responsible for resolving names to the IP addresses. In this recipe, we will learn how to filter important parameters that are related to the DNS service.

Getting ready

When suspecting a network problem, port mirror the suspected server or install Wireshark on it, then, start capturing the data.

How to do it...

There are some common filters that will assist you in troubleshooting DNS problems. The common display filters are given as follows:

- The basic filter is simply for filtering DNS traffic. The filter is dns.
    - For filtering only DNS queries we have dns.flags.response == 0
    - For filtering only DNS responses we have dns.flags.response == 1

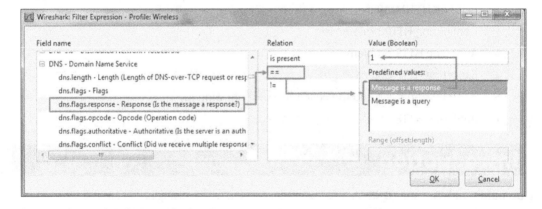

- For filtering error codes, we have the following filters:
    - No error (rcode—reply code), we have dns.flags.rcode == 0, marked in the following screenshot

❑ No such name, we have `dns.flags.rcode == 3`

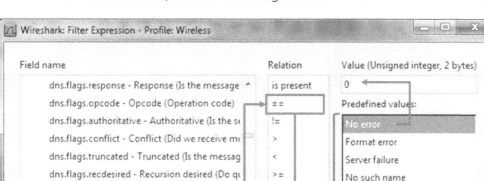

▸ For search problems, we have the following filters:

  ❑ **When looking for a specific URL**: This will be used, for example, when you are not sure whether your PC is sending the DNS query, use `dns.qry.name == "URL Name"`

  ❑ When looking for a query that contains a specific URL: For this case we have `dns.qry.name contains "URL Name"`

▸ For filtering DNS Opcodes (standard query or other requests or notifications), we have the following filters:

  ❑ For filtering only standard queries: `dns.flags.opcode == 0`

  ❑ For filtering only inverse queries: `dns.flags.opcode == 1`

  ❑ For filtering server status requests: `dns.flags.opcode == 2`

- ❑ For filtering zone change notifications: `dns.flags.opcode == 4`
- ❑ For filtering dynamic updates: `dns.flags.opcode == 5`

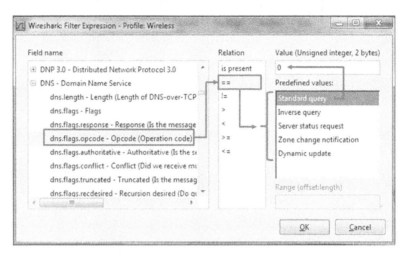

- ▶ For querying the query types (recursive/non-recursive):

  - ❑ For recursive query we have `dns.flags.recdesired == 1`
  - ❑ For non-recursive query we have `dns.flags.recdesired == 0`

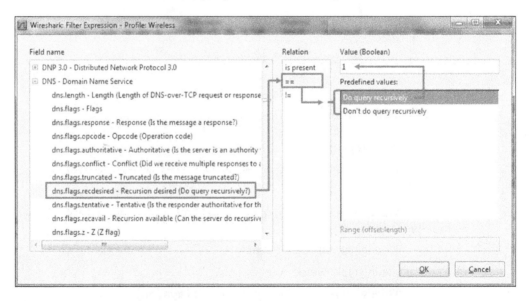

All other display filters can be found by clicking on the expression button on the right-hand side of the display filter window at the top of the Wireshark window.

How it works...

Display filters are described in depth in *Chapter 3, Using Display Filters*. As described in *Chapter 3, Using Display Filters*, you can do one of the following things to filter DNS parameters:

- ▸ Click on the expression button on the right to the display filter window, and choose the required filter from DNS

- ▸ Go to the packet details, right-click on the required field, and choose **Apply a filter** or **Prepare a filter**

- ▸ Simply write the filter string in the filter window at the top of the Wireshark window

There's more...

DNS is quite a complicated protocol, and the purpose of this chapter is to provide methods to resolve common problems with this protocol and implementation. Not all filters are mentioned here; a full list of DNS filters can be found at http://www.wireshark.org/docs/dfref/d/dns.html.

Analyzing regular DNS operations

In this recipe, we will see how to find out if DNS is working properly or not. We will see some scenarios of DNS operations, and what can go wrong.

Getting ready

Open Wireshark and start capturing data. You should mirror a device that is using DNS, or the DNS server itself.

How to do it...

Connect Wireshark to the LAN switch attached to the monitored device, and configure port mirror to the device from which you suspect the problem is coming. Go through the following steps:

1. In case of user complains, configure the port mirror for monitoring the user device.

2. In case of a general problem in the network, configure port mirror to the DNS server:

   - ❑ When the DNS server is configured on the internal server, configure port mirror on the server

   - ❑ When the DNS server is configured on external server, configure port mirror to the link that connects you to the Internet

How it works...

DNS is the major protocol used for name resolution, and it is used when browsing the Internet. It is also used for working in the organization network. The DNS standards describe three functionalities:

▶ Namespace which is what DNS names look like, and how they are allocated

▶ The name registration process, that is, how we register DNS names and how they are forwarded through the DNS servers' network

▶ The resolving process, that is, how names are resolved to the IP addresses

In this recipe we will focus on the third subject, that is, what happens when we browse the Internet, send or receive e-mails, or access internal servers in our organization. The basic DNS operation is shown in the following diagram:

DNS operation

User programs (web browser, mail client, and many others) interact with the DNS server through a resolver, which is also a part of the operating system. The resolver interacts with external name server that provide it with the required IPs (the name server can be local or remote; it is external to the resolver). The way the user queries the DNS server is OS specific. DNS queries and responses are sent and received between the resolver and the name server.

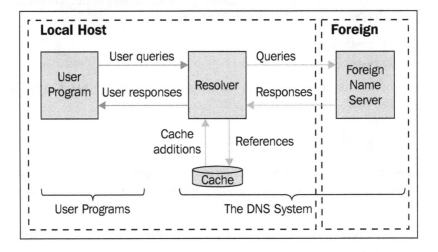

The local name server is usually located in the organization network, and interacts with the DNS server of your ISP. In the case of a home or a small office network, your DNS server can be configured on the router that connects you to the Internet, or directly to the DNS server of your ISP:

- When the DNS server is on the router, you query the DNS on the router that queries your ISP DNS
- When your DNS is located on the ISP network, you query the DNS server directly

DNS namespace

The DNS namespace is based on a hierarchical tree structure, as presented in the next diagram. The structure is as follows:

- The network of root servers (`http://www.iana.org/domains/root/servers`).
- The network of **Top Level Domain servers** (**TLDs**) (`http://www.iana.org/domains/root/db`).
- Each top-level domain has name servers similar to that of **IANA administers**. Top-level domains contain second-level domains. TLDs are the highest-level servers, for example, country servers as illustrated in the next diagram.
- **Second Level Domains** (**SLDs**) contain the domains and names for organizations and countries. The names in second-level domains are administered by the organization or country specified.

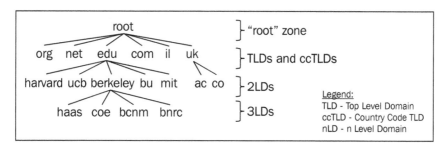

There are some important definitions, as shown in following diagram:

- **Domain**: It constitutes all branches under **ndi-com.com**, in this case a second level domain

- **Zone**: It is a contiguous portion of a DNS domain in the DNS namespace, whose database records exist and are managed in a particular DNS database file stored on one or multiple DNS servers

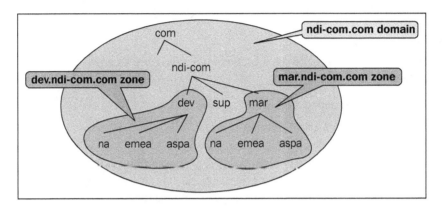

The resolving process

There are two reasons for using DNS servers:

- The first reason is that it is used for internal communication in your organization. In this case, you have a DNS server in your organization, which resolves the IP addresses to names in your organization.

- It is used for connecting to the Internet, browsing, sending mails, and so on.

When both services are used, you will send the DNS query to your organization server, which will send the query to the Internet. For example, when you want to get to a local server in your organization, you will send a DNS query to the local DNS, and you will get the server IP. When you browse a website on the Internet, your local DNS server forwards the request to the external DNS, for example, the ISP DNS.

Is it the correct DNS server you have configured? Theoretically, when you connect to the Internet, you can configure any DNS server in the world. Usually, the best DNS server to use is the nearest one. In your organization, you should configure your local DNS as first priority, and then the DNS servers of your ISP.

There are various utilities to check the DNS response. Some of them are as follows:

- ▸ **Namebench** from Google (`http://code.google.com/p/namebench/downloads/detail?name=namebench-1.3.1-Windows.exe&can=2&q=`)

- ▸ **DNS Benchmark** from GRC (`https://www.grc.com/dns/benchmark.htm`)

In the test result, you should get a good response time for your configured DNS servers. If not, change them.

There's more...

When a process on the end device is looking for the IP address of a specific name, it interacts with the local resolver that goes out to the DNS servers. When the DNS server does not find the entry you are looking for in its database, it can respond in two ways—**recursive** or **iterative**:

- ▸ **Recursive mode**: In this mode, when the application (for example, a web browser) wants to resolve the name of the website `www.packtpub.com`, it sends a DNS request to the local DNS server (marked as **1** in the following diagram). The local DNS server sends the request to a root server (marked as **2** and **3** in the following diagram), then to the TLD (marked as **3** and **4** in the following diagram), and finally to the authoritative server of `www.packtpub.com`, which gives us the required address (marked as **6** and **7** in the following diagram). Then, the local DNS server sends us the required address (marked as **8** in the following diagram). In each one of the responses, the resolver gets the DNS to query in the next step.

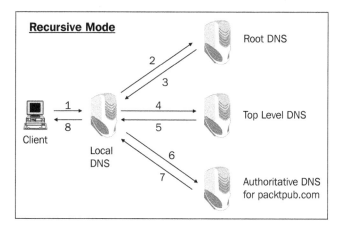

▸ **Iterative mode**: In this mode, a DNS client can receive a response from the DNS server that will tell the client where to look for the requested name. When the application (for example, a web browser) wants to browse the website `www.packtpub.com`, it sends a DNS request to the local DNS server (marked as **1** in the following diagram). The local server forwards the request to a root DNS server (marked as **2** in the following diagram). If it doesn't know the answer, it forwards the request to the TLD (marked as **3** in the following diagram) and the authoritative DNS (marked as **4** in the following diagram). Then, the answer is sent all the way back to the client (marked as **5**, **6**, **7**, and **8** in the following diagram):

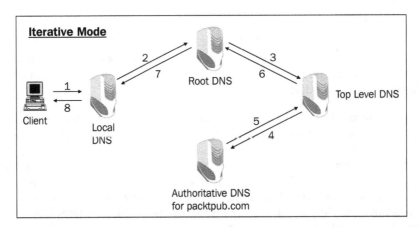

Analysing DNS problems

In the previous recipe, we saw how to identify a normal operation of DNS. In this recipe, we will learn how to discover problematic behavior of DNS, and how to figure out its source.

Getting ready

A DNS problem can result in bad performance while browsing the Internet, slow network while working inside the organization network, or any other performance issues. We will see how to isolate these problems and how to find out whether it is a DNS issue or not.

How to do it...

There are two major types of problems in DNS:

▸ DNS cannot resolve a name

▸ Slow operation of DNS

In both cases, connect your Wireshark to the network in the following order when you suspect an Internet connectivity problem:

1. First, port mirror the PC of the customer complaining about the problem. In this step, you will see specific problems on the PC.

2. Then, port mirror your DNS server. In this step, you will be able to find the general problems that are common to the entire organization (or at least to the part of it that has a problem).

DNS cannot resolve a name

How will you know that this is the problem?

1. You try but cannot browse the Internet, send e-mails, or perform any other operations on the Internet.

   Assuming your connectivity to the network is working properly, ping the website you are trying to browse (for example, issue the command: `ping www.packtpub.com`) and see if you get any response.

2. If you get a response, all is working OK.

3. If you don't get any response, it can be because of the following reasons:

   ❏ The website you are trying to ping blocks the ICMP requests

   ❏ The DNS server you are trying to get the data from is not functioning

4. To make sure that this is a DNS problem, start Wireshark and configure the DNS filter. In case of a problem, you will see one of the following:

   ❏ When a website does not exist

   ❏ Cannot reach the DNS server

 You can also use the command `nslookup` in the command line. This command checks the IP of the inserted name.

5. When the website does not exist, you will see (example in the following screenshot):

   ❏ The DNS query and response, both with code `0x971e` (the same code in query and response indicates that this is the response to the query)

   ❏ A `346 ms` delay between the DNS query and response, which means that the response came from an overseas server (for example, browsing from Europe when the DNS server is in Taiwan)

   ❏ The request was sent and was replied from `a.dns.tw` (that is, DNS server is in Taiwan), which means that the DNS system works properly and your PC queried one of the authoritative DNS servers for `.tw`

❑ The response is **No such name**, which means that there is no such server

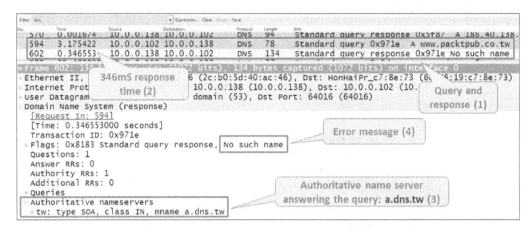

6. When the DNS server does not respond, you will see one of the following screenshots:

❑ **The DNS refused message**: In this case, your DNS server refuses the request. This is illustrated in the following screenshot (you will learn why in the *How it works...* section):

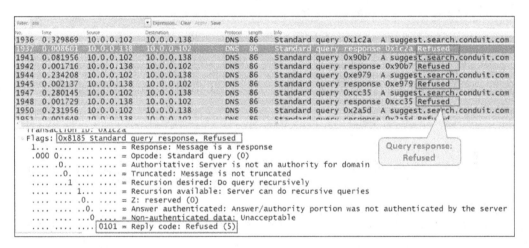

❏ **The DNS consecutive queries**: In this case, the DNS server simply does not answer. This is illustrated in the following screenshot:

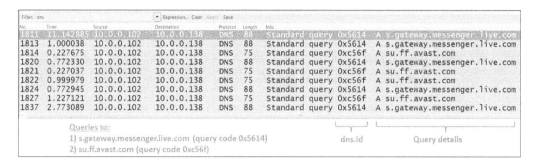

When you right-click on one of the packets in the preceding screenshot and choose **Follow UDP Stream**, you will see that the DNS resolver on your PC sends several queries (with increasing time intervals between them), and then stops. This is shown in the next screenshot:

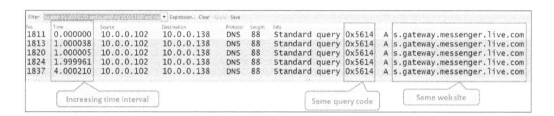

DNS slow responses

How will you know that this is the problem?

1. When you are browsing the Internet and getting very slow responses, perform the following steps:

    1. Port mirror the connection to the Internet, and check if you have any bottleneck on the way to the Internet. You can use the IO graphs for this purpose, as described in *Chapter 5, Using Advanced Statistics Tools*.

    2. Verify that you don't have a significant number of retransmissions or duplicate ACK's indicating a connection problem.

    3. Verify that you don't have any window-related problem, such as zero window or window full.

2. If answers are no for the preceding checks, it might be a DNS problem. You can have DNS problems in two cases:

    ❑ When working in your organization

    ❑ When connecting to the Internet

3. These issues can be resolved in two ways:

    ❑ When facing problems in your organization, port mirror the switch port that is connected to the DNS server

    ❑ When facing problems with the Internet, port mirror the switch port that connects your organization to the Internet

4. Watch the DNS response time that you get. There are several ways to locate the problem, and they are given as follows:

    ❑ The simplest way is to right-click on a packet from a DNS query stream, choose **Follow UDP Stream**, and then check the time between the query and response.

    ❑ Another way is to use IO graphs for this purpose. In the IO Graphs window, choose **Advanced** in the **Y Axis** configuration and configure the filter **dns. time** with **AVG(*)** in the **Graph** lines. Refer the following screenshot:

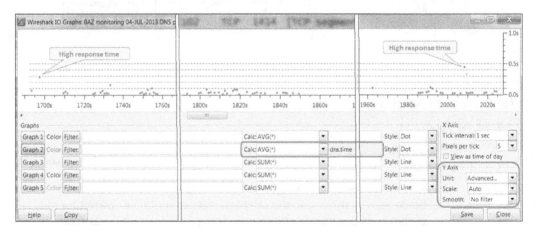

You will get a graph of the DNS response times throughout the capture time.

In this graph, you will see that most of the response times fall below 100mSec, which is quite reasonable. We have two peaks that indicate a probable problem, one at the beginning of the capture with 300 ms, and one at the end of the capture with 450 ms.

Reasonable times inside the organization (in a local site) should be not more than tens of milliseconds. When browsing the Internet, a good response time should be less than 100 ms, while up to 200 ms is still tolerant.

How it works...

There are six basic types of DNS response codes defined in `RFC 1035`. Additional error codes (up to 21) were defined in later standards (`RFC 2136`, `RFC 2671`, `RFC 2845`, and `RFC 2930`). Error codes can be found at `http://tools.ietf.org/html/rfc2929#section-2.3`.

The most common codes are shown in the following table:

Error code	Name	What is it (RFC 1035)	Why it happens	What to do
0	No error condition	No error, everything works fine.	This signifies that everything is working.	Be happy.
1	Format error	The DNS server couldn't interpret the query.	This error code is usually shown when the DNS server does not support DNS extensions, for example, EDNS0 (RFC 2671).	In most cases, there is nothing to do. The DNS request will be sent again without the extension. If the problem still exists, change the DNS server.
2	Server failure	The DNS server was not able to process the query due to a problem with the name server.	This error code signifies that there is a problem in the DNS server.	Configure another DNS server and check again.
3	Name error	This is meaningful only for responses that are coming from authoritative name servers.	This error code signifies that the domain name requested in the query does not exist.	Check the domain name.

Error code	Name	What is it (RFC 1035)	Why it happens	What to do
4	Not Implemented	The DNS server does not support the requested type of query.		
5	Refused	The DNS server refuses to perform the specified operation due to policy reasons.	A name server may not wish to provide the information to the particular requester. A name server may not wish to perform a particular operation.	This occurs due to connectivity problems, if the forward DNS is not configured, or if there is a problem in one of the DNS servers on the way.

There's more...

What DNS server should I configure? I have been asked this question many times. My answer to this is simple—a server that is physically close to you (that is, not an overseas server), and one that you know is efficient. An efficient server, that is, overseas will give slow responses due to the communication lines, and a nearby non-efficient server will also give you slow response times.

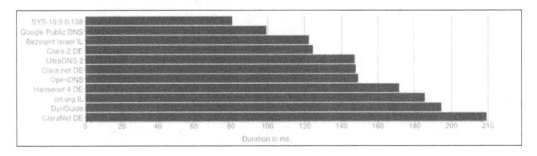

In the preceding graph, we see a measurement taken with the **Google Namebench** open software (freeware). It shows the following details:

▶ Average DNS response time of 80 ms to our local DNS server (you can see it is local from the unregistered address `10.0.0.138`)

▶ Average response time of 100 ms to the DNS server of my ISP

▶ Response times of 120 ms and above to the servers located overseas

To summarize this, it is OK to have response times of around 100 ms; and in most of the cases, 150-200 ms will also be good enough. Don't worry if there are momentary peaks—it can be that your resolver is querying authoritative servers on the other side of the globe.

When you open a web page that holds a lot of content, your browser can send even tens of DNS queries. In the following screenshot, you see what happens when I open the browser to `www.cisco.com`.

Filter: dns			▼	Expression... Clear *Apply* Save	
No.	Time	Source	Destination	Protocol	Info
2346	66.906122	10.0.0.2	10.0.0.138	DNS	Standard query 0x7444 A www.cisco.com ①
2347	67.113670	10.0.0.138	10.0.0.2	DNS	Standard query response 0x7444 CNAME www.cisco.com.akadns.n
2361	69.122842	10.0.0.2	10.0.0.138	DNS	Standard query 0x0df4 A api.webrep.avast.com
2362	69.123955	10.0.0.2	10.0.0.138	DNS	Standard query 0xd485 A ap.ff.avast.com ②
2364	69.142771	10.0.0.138	10.0.0.2	DNS	Standard query response 0x0df4 A 77.234.43.95 A 77.234.43.9
2365	69.142819	10.0.0.138	10.0.0.2	DNS	Standard query response 0xd485 A 109.123.117.68 A 77.234.44
2369	69.201093	10.0.0.2	10.0.0.138	DNS	Standard query 0x4528 A www.static-cisco.com ③
2397	69.272365	10.0.0.2	10.0.0.138	DNS	Standard query 0xdf38 A www.cisco.com
2398	69.294623	10.0.0.138	10.0.0.2	DNS	Standard query response 0xdf38 CNAME www.cisco.com.akadns.n
2501	69.388773	10.0.0.138	10.0.0.2	DNS	Standard query response 0x4528 CNAME static-cisco.cisco.com
2662	69.822286	10.0.0.2	10.0.0.138	DNS	Standard query 0x7cf8 A ciscosystemsinc.tt.omtrdc.net ④
2776	69.911815	10.0.0.138	10.0.0.2	DNS	Standard query response 0x7cf8 A 70.42.13.100 A 66.117.23.1
3056	70.547976	10.0.0.2	10.0.0.138	DNS	Standard query 0x010f A news-tags.cisco.com ⑤
3058	70.566150	10.0.0.2	10.0.0.138	DNS	Standard query 0x80ac A cisco-tags.cisco.com
3059	70.567814	10.0.0.138	10.0.0.2	DNS	Standard query response 0x010f A 72.163.10.14
3060	70.576567	10.0.0.2	10.0.0.138	DNS	Standard query 0x4468 A cisco.112.2o7.net
3066	70.584723	10.0.0.138	10.0.0.2	DNS	Standard query response 0x80ac A 72.163.10.10
3073	70.595827	10.0.0.138	10.0.0.2	DNS	Standard query response 0x4468 A 66.235.139.110 A 66.235.13
3122	71.153544	10.0.0.2	10.0.0.138	DNS	Standard query 0xfc41 A tools.cisco.com
3128	71.218031	10.0.0.2	10.0.0.138	DNS	Standard query 0x9d0c A products.mcisco.com ⑥
3129	71.218284	10.0.0.2	10.0.0.138	DNS	Standard query 0x130c A newsroom.cisco.com ⑦
3138	71.348653	10.0.0.138	10.0.0.2	DNS	Standard query response 0xfc41 A 72.163.4.38
3140	71.376504	10.0.0.2	10.0.0.138	DNS	Standard query 0xd077 A ciscocommunities.jive-mobile.com

It starts with a DNS query to the A record of `www.cisco.com` (marked as **1** in the preceding screenshot), then a query to `ap.ff.avast.com` (marked as **2** in the preceding screenshot), which is the web shield server of Avast antivirus, to `www.static-cisco.com` (marked as **3** in the preceding screenshot), `ciscosystems.tt.omtrdc.net` (marked as **4** in the preceding screenshot), news (marked as **5** in the preceding screenshot), products (marked as **6** in the preceding screenshot), and newsroom (marked as **7** in the preceding screenshot) sites.

When we look at the response time graph (shown in the next screenshot), we see that the DNS response times are up to 600 ms. This explains why it took a few seconds to open the entire web page of Cisco.

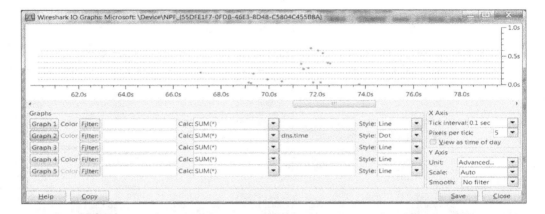

Filtering HTTP traffic

There are many filters that can be configured for HTTP. In this recipe, I will concentrate on the display filters that are mostly used in this context.

Getting ready

Configure port-mirror as described in previous recipes, and take a quick look at *Chapter 2, Using Capture Filters*.

How to do it...

To configure HTTP filters, you can write the filter expression directly in the display window bar; open the expression window and choose the HTTP parameters by right-clicking on the required parameter in the packet pane (as described in *Chapter 3, Using Display Filters*).

There are various filters that can be configured on HTTP:

- ▸ Name-based filters
  - ❑ Requests to a specific website: `http.host == "www.packtpub.com"`
  - ❑ Requests to the websites containing the word PacktPub: `http.host contains "packt.pub"`
  - ❑ Requests that were forwarded from PacktPub: `http.referer == "http://www.packtpub.com/"`

- ▸ Request methods filters
  - ❑ All GET requests: `http.request.method == GET`
  - ❑ All HTTP requests: `http.request`
  - ❑ All HTTP responses: `http.response`
  - ❑ All HTTP requests that are not GET: `http.request and not http.request.method == GET`

- ▸ Error codes filters
  - ❑ HTTP error responses (code 4xx for client errors, code 5xx for server errors): `http.response.code >= 400`
  - ❑ HTTP client error responses: `http.response.code >= 400` and `http.response.code <= 499`
  - ❑ HTTP server error responses: `http.response.code >= 500` and `http.response.code <= 599`
  - ❑ HTTP response code 404 (not found): `http.response.code == 404`

 When you configure a simple filter such as `http.host == packtpub`, you don't need to close it in the " " characters. If you need a more complex string such as `packtpub\r\n`, or a string of several words, then you will need to close it in " ", for example, `"http.host == packtpub\r\n"`.

How it works...

Let us see some details on HTTP.

HTTP methods

The main HTTP requests methods were published in RFCs 2616. There are additional HTTP methods that were standardized over the years. Additional methods were added later by updates to RFC 2616 (2817, 5785, 6266, and 6585) and additional standards (RFC 2518, 3252, 5789).

These are the basic methods as described in RFC 2612:

- ▸ **OPTIONS**: This is used for client request to determine the capabilities of a web server.
- ▸ **GET**: This is used when we request a URL.
- ▸ **HEAD**: This is like `GET`, but the server should not return a message body in the response.

- **POST**: This is used to send data to the server. For example, when using webmail, it will be used to send e-mail commands.

- **DELETE**: This is used to request the server to delete a resource identified by the `Request-URI`.

- **PUT**: This is used to request that the enclosed entity be stored under the Request-URI attached to the request.

- **TRACE**: This is used to request a remote, application-layer loopback of the request message.

- **CONNECT**: This is used to connect to a proxy device.

Status codes

These are the categories of message codes that are standardized by HTTP:

Category	Category name	What is it for
1xx	Informational	Provides general information, without any indication of failure or success
2xx	Success	Indicates that the action requested by the client was received, accepted, and processed successfully
3xx	Redirection	Indicates that further action should be taken by the user agent to fulfill the request
4xx	Client error	Indicates a client error
5xx	Server error	Indicates a server error

A full list of HTTP status codes can be found at `http://www.iana.org/assignments/http-status-codes/http-status-codes.xhtml`.

In some cases, you will see a line called **Line-based text data: text/html** under the HTTP line in the packet details pane. It is shown in the following screenshot:

You will see the **Line-based text data** right beneath to the HTTP line in the packet details pane (marked as **1** in the preceding screenshot). Below this, you will see some explanations (marked as **2** and **3** in the preceding screenshot) for what could be the reason for the error.

Configuring HTTP preferences

There are some preferences that you can change when working with HTTP. Let's see what they are.

Start Wireshark and go to the next section.

How to do it...

1. Choose **Edit | Preferences**.

2. Under **Protocols**, select **HTTP**. You will get the following window:

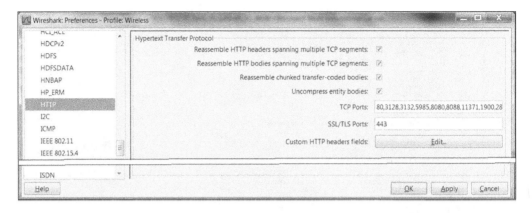

  □ By default, the upper four rows are checked. These are options that reassemble the HTTP headers and body when fragmentation is performed on the lower layers.

  □ In the **TCP Ports** field, you will get a list of the port numbers that Wireshark will dissect as HTTP. In this list, you see the default port 80, ports 8080 and 8088 that are usually used for proxies, and others. In case you have an application working with HTTP with a port that is not listed, add it here.

  □ The same with HTTPS—the default is 443 (that is for Secured HTTP, or HTTP over SSL/TLS). In case you use another port, add it here.

Custom HTTP headers fields

Custom HTTP headers fields enable us to create a new HTTP display filters under the http. header filter.

Let's look at the example in the following screenshot:

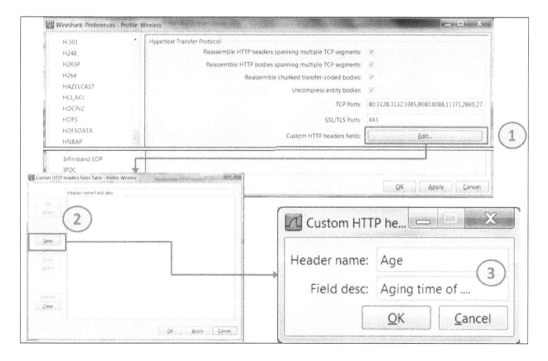

For creating a new HTTP display filter under the `http.header` filter, perform the following steps:

1. In the HTTP preferences window (marked as **1** in the following screenshot), click on the **Edit** button in **Custom HTTP headers fields**.

2. Click on **New** (marked as **2** in the preceding screenshot).

3. In **Header name**, enter the name of the filter to be used in extension to `http.header` (marked as **3** in the preceding screenshot).

   For example, if you want to configure a filter on the `Age` parameter, type the name `Age` in the **Header name** field (case sensitive!).

4. In the **Field desc** field, type any description that will remind you what you have configured.

   For example, type **Aging time of ...** (any description will do, it is just a note).

5. Click on **OK**.

6. In the **Display Filter** textbox, you will be able to use the `http.header.Age` filter.

   For example, you will be able to configure the display filter `http.header.Age` that contains `88482` that will give you all the packets with the `Age` field that contains the requested number

> This filter configuration is mostly used when you are using proprietary parameters in the HTTP header, and you want to filter accordingly.

7. You can configure many additional filters with this option.

How it works...

The reassembly feature is important because there are some cases in which IP fragmentation is used, and therefore the TCP message is also segmented. Marking the reassembly options simply tells the Wireshark to reassemble the monitored packets (what the receiver side is doing and therefore is able to understand it).

There's more...

Usually Wireshark shows dissected packets with port `80` as HTTP only if it sees a valid HTTP header. If you want to see all port `80` packets as HTTP, perform the following steps:

1. Go to **Preferences**, and choose **TCP** in **Protocols**.

2. Uncheck/disable **Allow dissector to reassemble TCP streams**.

Analyzing HTTP problems

The bottom line is, of course, how to analyze the HTTP problems. This is what this recipe is all about. HTTP problems can happen because of a slow server or client, TCP performance issues, and some other reasons that we will see in this recipe.

Getting ready

When you experience bad performance while browsing the Internet, connect the Wireshark with port mirror to the PC that experiences the problem, and when it is the whole network that suffers from bad performance, port mirror the connection to the Internet.

How to do it...

There can be various reasons for a slow browsing problem, and we'll try to figure it out step-by-step. The steps are given as follows:

1. First, check that you don't simply have loaded line to the Internet, high error rate on the communications line, or any of these obvious issues that cause most of the problems (see *Chapter 4, Using Basic Statistics Tools* and *Chapter 5, Using Advanced Statistics Tools* for further details).

2. To negate a TCP issue (as explained in detail in *Chapter 9, UDP/TCP Analysis*), check the following details:
   - In the **Expert Info** window, you don't get too many retransmissions and duplicate ACKs (up to 0.5-0.8 percent is still tolerable).
   - Make sure that you don't get resets on the HTTP connections. It might be due to firewalls or site restrictions.

3. Make sure that you don't get the following DNS problems:
   - Slow response time, as described earlier in this chapter
   - Names are not found, not correct, and so on

4. If none of these apply, well, let's dig in to HTTP.

> Don't forget to look at the network and IT environment as a whole. You cannot separate TCP from HTTP, or the DNS problems from the slow browsing of applications. It can be that you have a very slow HTTP server; and because of its slow responses, you will get TCP retransmissions. Or, because of the slow DNS server, you will get a web page that opens after many seconds. Just go step-by-step and isolate the problems.

When you open a web page for the first time, it can take a few seconds. In this case, you should check the following conditions:

1. Check if the line is not loaded.

2. Check the delay on the line (a ping to the website will do the job).

3. Look for error codes. Usually you will see the reason for the error on the browser, but not always.

4. Configure the filter `http.response >= 400` and see how many errors you get. In the following sections, we see several examples of what you should pay attention to.

Informational codes

Code	Status	Explanation	What to do
100	Continue	Request completed successfully and the session can continue.	-
101	Switching protocols	The server is changing to a different HTTP version. It will be followed by an `Upgrade` header.	-

Success codes

Code	Status	Explanation	What to do
200	OK	Standard OK response.	-
201	Created	The request has been fulfilled and a new resource has been created.	-
202	Accepted	The request was accepted and is still in process.	-
203	Non-authoritative information	The request was received with content from another server, and it was understood.	-
204	No content	The request was received and understood, and the answer that is sent back has no content.	-
205	Reset content	This is a server request to the client to reset the data that was sent to it.	-
206	Partial content	Response for a partial document request.	-

Redirect codes

Code	Status	Explanation	What to do
300	Multiple choices	The requested address refers to more than one file. It can happen, for example, when the resource has been removed, and the response provides a list of potential locations for it.	-
301	Moved permanently	The requested resource has been moved permanently. Future requests should be forwarded to the attached URI.	-
302	Moved temporarily (found)	Page has been moved temporarily, and the new URL is available. Usually, you will be automatically forwarded.	Usually, you will see a Found code, and then another GET to the URL indicated
303	See other	The response to the request can be found in a different URI. It should be retrieved using an HTTP GET to that resource.	-
304	Not modified	When a request header includes an if modified since parameter, this code will be returned if the file has not changed since that date.	-
305	Use proxy	The requested resource must be accessed through a proxy.	Check what proxy is required

Client errors

Code	Status	Explanation	What to do
400	Bad request	The request could not be understood by the server due to a syntax problem. The request should be modified by the client before resending to it.	Check the website address. This can also happen due to a site error.
401	Authorization required	The client is denied access due to the lack of authentication codes.	Check your username and password.
402	Payment required	Reserved for future use.	

Code	Status	Explanation	What to do
403	Forbidden	The client is not allowed to see a specific file. This can be due to the server access limit.	Check the credentials. Also, there are fewer chances that the server is loaded.
404	Not found	The requested resource could not be found.	This can be because the resource was deleted, or it never existed before. It can also be due to URL misspellings.
405	Method not allowed	The method you are using to access the file is not supported or not allowed by the resource.	
406	Not acceptable	Content generated by the resource is not acceptable according to the client request.	Check/update your browser.
407	Proxy authentication required	Request authentication is required before it can be performed.	The client must first authenticate itself with the proxy.
408	Request timed out	It took the server longer than the allowed time to process the request.	Check response time and load on the network.
409	Conflict	The request submitted by the client cannot be completed because it conflicts with some established rules.	Can be because you try to upload a file that is older that the existing one or similar problems. Check what the client is trying to do.
410	Gone	The URL requested by the client is no longer available from that system.	Usually this is a server problem. It can be due to a file that was deleted or location was forwarded to a new location.
411	Content length required	The request is missing its `Content-Length` header.	Compatibility issue on a website. Change/update your browser.

Code	Status	Explanation	What to do
412	Precondition failed	The client has not set up a configuration that is required for the file to be delivered.	Compatibility issue on a website. Change/update your browser.
413	Request entity too long	The requested file was too big to process.	Server limitation.
414	Request URI too long	The address you entered was overly long for the server.	Server limitation.
415	Unsupported media type	The file type of the request is not supported.	Server limitation.

A simple example for a client error is presented in the following screenshot. To get to this window, perform the following steps:

1. Right-click on the packet with the error code.

2. Choose **Follow TCP stream**. You will get the following window:

```
}
GET /poker-client/broadcast.htm HTTP/1.1  (1)
Accept: image/gif, image/jpeg, image/pjpeg, image/pjpeg, application/x-shockwave-flash, application/
x-ms-application, application/x-ms-xbap, application/vnd.ms-xpsdocument, application/xaml+xml,
application/vnd.ms-excel, application/vnd.ms-powerpoint, application/msword, */*
Referer: http://www.888poker.com/poker-client/promotions.htm  (2)
Accept-Language: en-us
Accept-Encoding: gzip, deflate
User-Agent: Mozilla/4.0 (compatible; MSIE 7.0; Windows NT 5.1; Trident/4.0; GTB7.1; Mozilla/4.0
(compatible; MSIE 6.0; Windows NT 5.1; SV1) ; .NET CLR 1.1.4322; .NET CLR 2.0.50727;
OfficeLiveConnector.1.3; OfficeLivePatch.0.0; .NET CLR 3.0.4506.2152; .NET CLR 3.5.30729;
InfoPath.1)
Host: www.888poker.com  (3)

HTTP/1.1 404 Not Found  (4)
Date: Sun, 16 Oct 2011 09:11:58 GMT
Server: Microsoft-IIS/6.0
srv: 2344432
```

3. You can see the following conditions:

   - I tried to browse the URI /poker-client/broadcast.htm (marked as **1** and **3** in the preceding screenshot)

   - The URI was forwarded by the referrer: http://www.888poker.com/ poker-client/promotions.htm (marked as **2** in the preceding screenshot)

   - The status code was **404 Not Found** (marked as **4** in the preceding screenshot)

Just to clarify things, I was not playing Poker, I was working on a networking problem.

Server errors

Code	Status	Explanation	What to do
500	Internal server error	The web server encountered an unexpected condition that prevented it from carrying out the client request for access to the requested URL.	Response that is usually caused by a problem in your Perl code when a CGI program is run.
501	Not implemented	The request cannot be executed by the server.	A server problem.
502	Bad gateway	The server you're trying to reach is sending back errors.	A server problem.
503	Service unavailable	The service or file that is being requested is not currently available.	A server problem.
504	Gateway timeout	The gateway has timed out. This message is like the 408 timeout error, but this one occurs at the gateway of the server.	Server is down or nonresponsive.
505	HTTP version not supported	The HTTP protocol version that you want to use for communicating with the server is not supported by it.	Server does not support the HTTP version.

You can get service unavailable (code 503) status due to various reasons. In the following example there is a small office that has the following complaint: they can browse Facebook, but the moment they click on a link on this site, they get the new page as blocked. In the following screenshot, you can see that the problem was simply a firewall that blocked it (obviously).

How it works...

In standard HTTP browsing, you should see a very simple pattern as follows:

1. TCP opens the connection (three-way handshake).
2. HTTP sends a `GET` command.
3. Data is downloaded to your browser.

 In most cases, opening a web page will open multiple connections—in many cases, tens of them. For example, when you open a newspage (`www.cnn.com`, `www.foxnews.com`, `www.bbc.co.uk`), it opens the main page, news bars, commercials, temperature window, connections to other sites, and more. Don't be surprised if a single page will open nearly a hundred connections, or even more.

In case of a web page that opens multiple connections (as most web pages do), each connection requires a DNS query, response, TCP SYN-SYN/ACK-ACK, and HTTP GET; only then the data will start to appear on your screen.

There's more...

When you don't see anything in the packet details pane, right-click on a packet and choose **Follow TCP stream**. This will give you a detailed window, (as in the preceding screenshot) which provides you with a lot of data for the connection.

Another tool that is widely used for HTTP is **Fiddler**. It can be found at `http://fiddler2.com/`. Fiddler is a free tool that is planned for HTTP debugging. It is not in the scope of this book.

Exporting HTTP objects

Exporting HTTP objects is a simple feature for exporting HTTP statistics—websites and files accessed by HTTP.

Getting ready

To export HTTP objects, choose **File | Export Objects | HTTP**.

How to do it...

To export HTTP objects, follow these steps:

1. You can use this feature when capture is running, or you can save the captured file. You will get the following window:

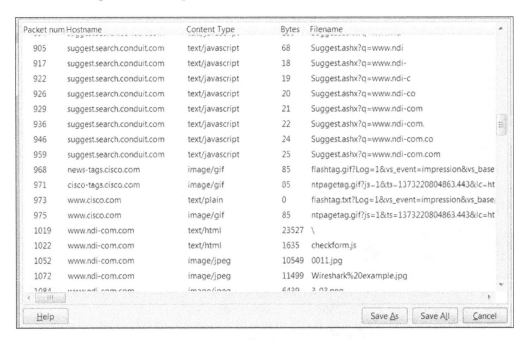

Packet num	Hostname	Content Type	Bytes	Filename
905	suggest.search.conduit.com	text/javascript	68	Suggest.ashx?q=www.ndi
917	suggest.search.conduit.com	text/javascript	18	Suggest.ashx?q=www.ndi-
922	suggest.search.conduit.com	text/javascript	19	Suggest.ashx?q=www.ndi-c
926	suggest.search.conduit.com	text/javascript	20	Suggest.ashx?q=www.ndi-co
929	suggest.search.conduit.com	text/javascript	21	Suggest.ashx?q=www.ndi-com
936	suggest.search.conduit.com	text/javascript	22	Suggest.ashx?q=www.ndi-com.
946	suggest.search.conduit.com	text/javascript	24	Suggest.ashx?q=www.ndi-com.co
959	suggest.search.conduit.com	text/javascript	25	Suggest.ashx?q=www.ndi-com.com
968	news-tags.cisco.com	image/gif	85	flashtag.gif?Log=1&vs_event=impression&vs_base
971	cisco-tags.cisco.com	image/gif	85	ntpagetag.gif?js=1&ts=1373220804863.443&lc=ht
973	www.cisco.com	text/plain	0	flashtag.txt?Log=1&vs_event=impression&vs_base
975	www.cisco.com	image/gif	85	ntpagetag.gif?js=1&ts=1373220804863.443&lc=ht
1019	www.ndi-com.com	text/html	23527	\
1022	www.ndi-com.com	text/html	1635	checkform.js
1052	www.ndi-com.com	image/jpeg	10549	0011.jpg
1072	www.ndi-com.com	image/jpeg	11499	Wireshark%20example.jpg
1094	www.ndi-com.com	image/png	6420	2_03.png

Help · Save As · Save All · Cancel

2. From here you can get a list of the websites that were accessed, including the files that were accessed in each one of them. You can see the website, file types, size, and names.

3. You can use the **Save As** or **Save All** buttons for saving the data in a file.

4. In the **Content Type** column, you will see the following contents:

   - Text: **text/plain**, **text/html**, **text/javascript**—if it's a JavaScript, check what it is, it might be a security risk
   - Images: **image/jpeg**, **image/gif**, and other types of images—you can open it with a viewer
   - Applications: **application/json**, **application/javascript**, and other types of applications
   - Any other text file discovered by Wireshark

For the export HTTP objects feature to work, first go to TCP preferences and enable TCP packets reassembly (allow subdissector to reassemble TCP streams).

You will get a directory with all the objects captured in the capture file. Objects can be pictures (for example, packet `1052` and `1057` in the preceding screenshot), text (packets `1019`, `1022`, and others in the preceding screenshot), and others.

How it works...

This feature scans HTTP streams in the currently opened capture file or the running capture, takes reassembled objects such as HTML documents, image files, executable files, and other readable formats, and lets you save them to a disk. The saved objects can then be opened with the proper viewer, or they can be executed in the case of executable files just by clicking on them. This feature can be helpful for various purposes, including eavesdropping and saving objects for backup (for example, files that were sent through e-mails).

There's more...

You have several pieces of software that perform the same things graphically, some of them are as follows:

- **Xplico** (`http://www.xplico.org/`)
- **NetworkMiner** (`http://www.netresec.com/?page=NetworkMiner`)

 When you see an unknown website with an application that you don't know, and a filename that looks suspicious—Google it; it might be a risk (we will get back to this in *Chapter 14, Understanding Network Security*).

HTTP flow analysis and the Follow TCP Stream window

The **Follow TCP Stream** feature that was discussed in brief earlier in the book is a very helpful feature that can help you with in-depth understanding of the TCP flows that are captured when you monitor the network. In this recipe, we will see some of its advantages.

Getting ready

Port mirror the device or link you want to monitor and start packet capture.

How to do it...

1. For opening the **Follow TCP Stream** window, perform the following steps:
2. Right-click on one of the packets in the stream you want to view.
3. The stream you choose is filtered by the Wireshark. You will see this in the display filter bar that will show you the number of stream in the capture. You will get the following window:

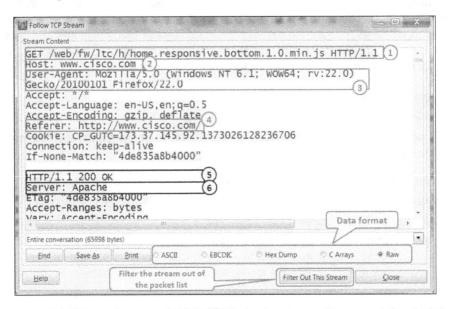

4. You can see the stream details, for example:
   - The GET method (marked as **1** in the preceding screenshot)
   - The requested HOST (marked as **2** in the preceding screenshot)
   - The client type, Mozilla Firefox in this case, (marked as **3** in the preceding screenshot)
   - The referrer, Cisco in this case, (marked as **4** in the preceding screenshot)
   - The HTTP OK response (marked as **5** in the preceding screenshot)
   - The server type (marked as **6** in the preceding screenshot)

5. These are obvious examples. When having problems, or just issues to investigate, you will be able to see many types of parameters here that will indicate the following cases:

   ❑ A user is using a Kazaa client (as shown in the following screenshot) for file sharing.

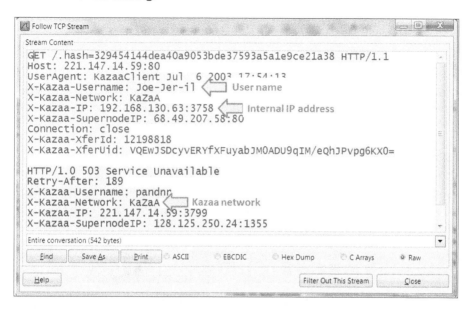

   ❑ In the following screenshot, you can see a software bug. A quick Google search shows that it is an historical one, but other bugs can be found this way.

6. You can also check for the following:

   ❑ Error and bugs messages

   ❑ Viruses and worms—names such as blast, probe, and Xprobe, especially
     when you see them with `.exe` extension should ring a big warning bell
     (more details about this issue will be provided in *Chapter 14, Understanding
     Network Security*)

How it works...

The Follow TCP Stream simply analyzes the TCP data from the first SYN-SYN/ACK/ACK
handshake to the end of the connection, which is indicated by RST of the FIN packets.
It also isolates the specific stream, helping us to follow the errors and problems in it.

There's more...

There are many problems that can be found and allocated using the Follow TCP Stream
feature, and it will be discussed further in the next chapters. Use this feature to isolate
a TCP stream.

Analyzing HTTPS traffic – SSL/TLS basics

HTTPS is a secure version of the HTTP. The "S" means that it is secured by **Secure Socket
Layer/Transport Layer Security** (**SSL/TLS**). It is used when you connect to your bank account,
webmail service, or any other service that runs over HTTP and requires security.

In this recipe, we will see how it works and what can fail when we are using HTTPS
communications.

Getting ready

Port mirror to the suspected device or link that forwards traffic from several devices, and start
capture. HTTPS works with the TCP port `443`, and this is what we should watch.

How to do it...

To monitor HTTPS sessions, perform the following steps:

1. HTTPS session establishment can be done in four or five steps. It is described in the
   How it works... section of this recipe.

2. Watch the order of the packet in the session establishment, and make sure the messages you get are according to the order shown in the following figure (in brackets you'll see what should be shown in the packet):

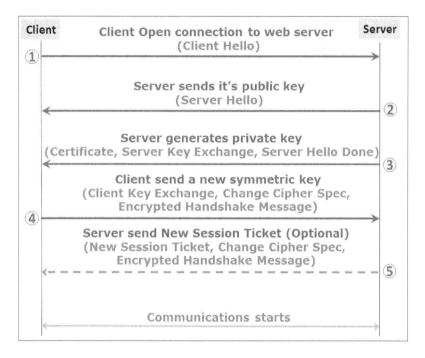

3. There are some common errors that are described in RFC 2246:

   ❏ **close_notify**: This message notifies the recipient that the sender has finished sending messages on this connection. The session can be resumed later.

   ❏ **unexpected_message**: This alert is returned if an inappropriate message was received. This is a critical error that can indicate a bad implementation on one of the sides.

   ❏ **bad_record_mac**: This alert is returned if a record is received with incorrect Message Authentication Code (MAC). This is a critical error that can indicate a bad implementation on one of the sides.

   ❏ **decryption_failed**: This alert is returned if a TLS Ciphertext was decrypted in the wrong way. This is a critical message that can indicate a bad implementation on one of the sides.

   ❏ **record_overflow**: This alert is returned if a TLS Ciphertext record was received with a length longer than the allowed length. This is a fatal error, and it usually indicates a bad implementation on one of the sides.

- **decompression_failure**: This message indicates that a decompression function received a wrong input. This is a critical error that can indicate a bad implementation on one of the sides.

- **handshake_failure**: Reception of this alert message indicates a negotiation error that occurred when the sender was unable to negotiate the set of security parameters, given the options available. This is a critical error that can indicate a bad implementation on one of the sides.

- **bad_certificate**: This is a certificate error. It occurs when a certificate is corrupt, contains signatures that were not verified correctly, or any other error.

- **unsupported_certificate**: This indicates that the received certificate was not of the supported type.

- **certificate_revoked**: This indicates that a certificate was canceled by its signer.

- **certificate_expired**: This indicates an invalid certificate or a certificate that has expired.

- **certificate_unknown**: This tells that a certificate was not accepted due to an unspecified reason.

- **illegal_parameter**: This tells that a field in the handshake process was out of range or inconsistent with other fields. This is a critical error that can indicate a bad implementation on one of the sides.

- **unknown_ca**: This indicates that a valid certificate was received, but was not accepted because it couldn't be matched with a known, trusted CA. This is a critical error, and should be checked with the certificate issuer.

- **access_denied**: This tells that a valid certificate was received, but it was not approved by the access control of the receiver, and the sender decided not to proceed with negotiation.

- **decode_error**: This tells that a message was too long and, therefore, could not be decoded. This is a critical error that can indicate a bad implementation on one of the sides.

- **decrypt_error**: This indicates that a handshake cryptographic operation failed, including the ones that failed due to signature verification, key exchange, or validation of a finished message.

- **export_restriction**: This tells that a negotiation which is not compliant with export restrictions was detected.

- ❑ **protocol_version**: This tells that the protocol version which the client has attempted to negotiate is not supported.

- ❑ **insufficient_security**: This is returned when a negotiation has failed because the server required ciphers with higher security than those supported by the client.

- ❑ **internal_error**: This is an internal error not related to the peer of the connection.

- ❑ **user_canceled**: This tells that the handshake was canceled for a reason other than a protocol failure.

- ❑ **no_renegotiation**: This is sent by the client or the server in response to a hello request after the initial handshaking.

In each one of the failures mentioned, the connection will not be established.

How it works...

SSL and **TLS** are protocols that secure a specific application, for example, HTTP, SMTP, Telnet, and others. SSL Versions 1, 2, and 3 were developed by Netscape in the mid 90s for their Navigator browser, while TLS is a standard from the IETF (RFC 2246, RFC 4492, RFC 5246, RFC 6176, and others). TLS 1.0 was first introduced in RFC 2246 in January 1999 as an upgrade of the SSL Version 3.0 (third paragraph at http://tools.ietf.org/html/rfc2246).

The TLS handshake protocol involves the following procedures for establishing a TLS connection:

1. Exchange hello messages to agree on the algorithms to work with, and exchange random values for the key generation.

2. Exchange the necessary cryptographic parameters to allow the client and the server to agree on a premaster secret key.

3. Exchange certificates and cryptographic information to allow the client and server to authenticate each other.

4. Generate a master secret key from the premaster secret and exchanged random values.

5. Allow the client and server to verify that their peer has calculated the same security parameters and that the handshake occurred without being tampered with by an attacker.

These procedures are performed in the following order:

1. Select cryptographic algorithms:

   ❑ The **Client Hello** message (marked as **1** in the following screenshot)

   ❑ The **Server Hello** message (marked as **2** in the following screenshot)

2. Authenticate the server and exchange key (marked as **3** in the following screenshot).

3. Authenticate the client and exchange key (marked as **4** in the following screenshot).

4. Complete the handshake (marked as **5** in the following screenshot).

Filter: (tcp.stream eq 14)				▾ Expression... Clear Apply Save	
No.	Time	Source	Destination	Protocol	Info
157	16.866912	10.0.0.3	173.194.34.86	TCP	62900 > https [SYN] Seq=0 Win=8192 Len=0 MSS=14(
158	16.953453	173.194.34.86	10.0.0.3	TCP	https > 62900 [SYN, ACK] Seq=0 Ack=1 Win=62920
159	16.953528	10.0.0.3	173.194.34.86	TCP	62900 > https [ACK] Seq=1 Ack=1 Win=66792 Len=0
160	16.954763	10.0.0.3	173.194.34.8①	TLSv1	Client Hello
161	17.040545	173.194.34.86	10.0.0.3	TCP	https > 62900 [ACK] Seq=1 Ack=173 Win=64000 Len
162	17.043587	173.194.34.86	10.0.0.3 ②	TLSv1	Server Hello
163	17.043715	173.194.34.86	10.0.0.3 ③	TLSv1	Certificate, Server Key Exchange, Server Hello
164	17.043790	10.0.0.3	173.194.34.86	TCP	62900 > https [ACK] Seq=173 Ack=1936 Win=66792
165	17.066539	10.0.0.3	173.194.34.8④	TLSv1	Client Key Exchange, Change Cipher Spec, Encryp
166	17.152661	173.194.34.86	10.0.0.3 ⑤	TLSv1	New Session Ticket, Change Cipher Spec, Encrypt
167	17.154064	10.0.0.3	173.194.34.86	TLSv1	Application Data
168	17.154412	10.0.0.3	173.194.34.86	TCP	[TCP segment of a reassembled PDU]
169	17.154416	10.0.0.3	173.194.34.86	TLSv1	Application Data
170	17.154515	173.194.34.86	10.0.0.3	TLSv1	Application Data

Let's see how it works. In the preceding screenshot, we see how TCP SSL/TLS establishes a connection (packets 157-158-159) and packet 160 starts the TLS handshake. Let us see the details:

1. In packet 160, the client sends a **Client Hello** message that starts the negotiation.

2. The server answers with a **Server Hello** message.

3. The server sends a certificate to the client.

4. The client takes the certificate and generates a premaster key.

5. The server creates the master key, and the conversation begins. This is an optional message.

This refers to a mechanism (defined in RFC 4507) that enables the TLS server to resume sessions and avoid keeping the per-client session state. The TLS server encapsulates the session state into a ticket and forwards it to the client. The client can subsequently resume a session using the obtained ticket. This happens, for example, when you re-open a connection to your webmail account (Gmail, Hotmail, and so on) and is common to these scenarios.

Communication between the client and the server will start after step 4 or 5.

Let's look at each one of them:

In step 1, packet `160` is a **Client Hello** message which is the first packet in the TLS handshake. Some of the parameters that we can see are shown in the following screenshot:

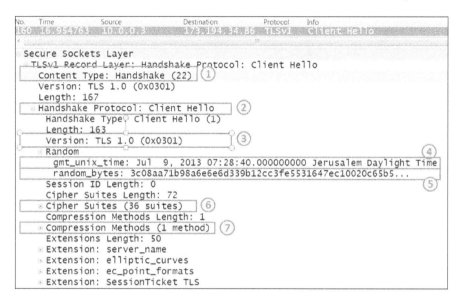

- ▸ The area highlighted as **1** shows that the content of the packet is a handshake (`ssl.record.content_type == 22`).

- ▸ The area highlighted as **2** shows that the packet is a **Client Hello** message sent from the client to the web server. This message starts the handshake.

- ▸ The area highlighted as **3** shows the highest SSL and TLS version supported by the client.

- ▸ The area highlighted as **4** shows the client time that will be used in the key generation process.

- ▸ The area highlighted as **5** shows the random data that is generated by the client for use in the key generation process.

- ▸ The area highlighted as **6** shows the ciphers supported by the client. The ciphers are listed in order of preference.

- ▸ The area highlighted as **7** shows the data compression methods that are supported by the client.

As shown in the following screenshot, Packet `162` is a **Server Hello** message, which includes the following details:

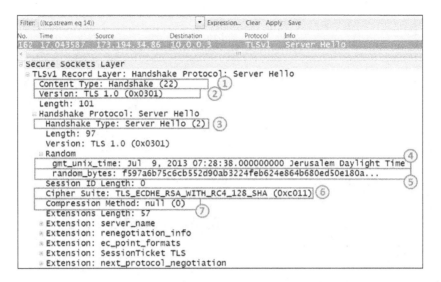

- ▸ The area highlighted as **1** shows that the content of the packet is a handshake (`ssl.record.content_type == 22`).

- ▸ The area highlighted as **2** shows the TLS version that will be used in this session.

- ▸ The area highlighted as **3** shows that the packet is a **Server Hello** message sent from the server to the client.

- ▸ The area highlighted as **4** shows the server time used in the key generation process.

- ▸ The area highlighted as **5** shows the random data that is generated by the server for use in the key generation process.

- ▸ The area highlighted as **6** shows the cipher suite to be used in this conversation. It is chosen from the list of ciphers sent by the client.

- ▸ The area highlighted as **7** shows the data compression method that will be used for the session.

The next packet is the response from the server issuing a certificate:

```
Filter: ((tcp.stream eq 14))                    ▼ Expression.. Clear Apply Save
No.   Time          Source          Destination       Protocol   Info
163   17.043715   173.194.34.86   10.0.0.3          TLSv1   Certificate, Server Key Exchange, Server Hello Done
◀                                                        Ⅲ                                                      ▶
⊕ Frame 163: 559 bytes on wire (4472 bits), 559 bytes captured (4472 bits) on interface 0
⊕ Ethernet II, Src: D-LinkIn_f4:7b:a2 (14:d6:4d:f4:7b:a2), Dst: HonHaiPr_c7:8e:73 (60:d8:19:c7:8e:73)
⊕ Internet Protocol Version 4, Src: 173.194.34.86 (173.194.34.86), Dst: 10.0.0.3 (10.0.0.3)
⊕ Transmission Control Protocol, Src Port: https (443), Dst Port: 62900 (62900), Seq: 1431, Ack: 173, Len: 505
⊕ [2 Reassembled TCP Segments (1829 bytes): #162(1324), #163(505)]
⊖ Secure Sockets Layer
  ⊞ TLSv1 Record Layer: Handshake Protocol: Certificate          1
  ⊞ TLSv1 Record Layer: Handshake Protocol: Server Key Exchange   2
  ⊞ TLSv1 Record Layer: Handshake Protocol: Server Hello Done     3
```

- The area highlighted as **1** shows that the server sends the **Certificate** command, which includes the server's certificate. By clicking on the (**+**) sign on the left of this line and digging into the details, you will see the certificate issuer, validity time, algorithm, and other data.

- The area highlighted as **2** shows that the server sends the **Server Key Exchange** command (usually Diffie-Hellman), including the required parameters (public key, signature, and so on).

- The area highlighted as **3** shows that the server sends the **Server Hello Done** command. This command indicates that the server has completed this phase of the SSL handshake. The next step is the client authentication.

The next packet (packet `165` in this example) is the response from the server, issuing a certificate.

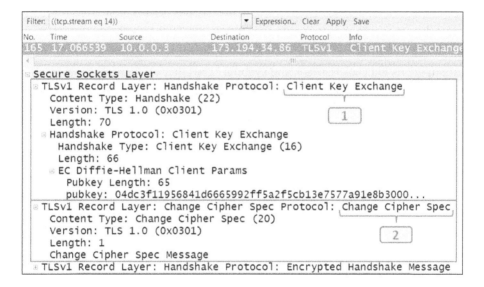

- The area marked as **1** shows that the client sends the **Client Key Exchange** command. This command contains the premaster secret that was created by the client and was then encrypted using the server's public key. The symmetric encryption keys are generated by the client and the server, based on the data exchanged in the client and server hello messages.

- The area marked as **2** shows that the client sends the **Change Cipher Spec** notification to the server. This is done in order to indicate that the client will start using the new session keys for hashing and encryption.

The last step is when the server sends a **New Session Ticket** to the client, and it will look like the example in the following screenshot:

```
Filter: ((tcp.stream eq 14))                    ▼ Expression... Clear Apply Save
No.   Time        Source          Destination       Protocol    Info
166   17.152661   173.194.34.86   10.0.0.3          TLSv1       New Session Ticket, Change Cipher Spec, Encrypted Handsha
                                        III
⊞ Frame 166: 280 bytes on wire (2240 bits), 280 bytes captured (2240 bits) on interface 0
⊞ Ethernet II, Src: D-LinkIn_f4:7b:a2 (14:d6:4d:f4:7b:a2), Dst: HonHaiPr_c7:8e:73 (60:d8:19:c7:8e:73)
⊞ Internet Protocol Version 4, Src: 173.194.34.86 (173.194.34.86), Dst: 10.0.0.3 (10.0.0.3)
⊞ Transmission Control Protocol, Src Port: https (443), Dst Port: 62900 (62900), Seq: 1936, Ack: 331, Len: 226
⊟ Secure Sockets Layer
  ⊞ TLSv1 Record Layer: Handshake Protocol: New Session Ticket
  ⊞ TLSv1 Record Layer: Change Cipher Spec Protocol: Change Cipher Spec
  ⊞ TLSv1 Record Layer: Handshake Protocol: Encrypted Handshake Message
```

There's more...

I've been asked several times if it is possible to decrypt sessions that are encrypted with SSL/TLS. Well it's possible if you have the private key, which is provided to you by the server you connect to; and to get it is not an easy thing to do.

There are methods to hijack this key, and in some cases they will work. It is not an obvious thing to do, and in any case it is not in the goal of this book. If you get the private key, you simply add it in the protocol list in the preferences window and continue from there. Additional details about this feature can be obtained from `http://wiki.wireshark.org/SSL`, as well as from many other websites and blogs.

11
Analyzing Enterprise Applications' Behavior

In this chapter, we will cover the following topics:

- ▶ Finding out what is running over your network
- ▶ Analyzing FTP problems
- ▶ Analyzing e-mail traffic and troubleshooting e-mail problems – POP, IMAP, and SMTP
- ▶ Analyzing MS-TS and Citrix communication problems
- ▶ Analyzing problems in the NetBIOS protocols
- ▶ Analyzing database traffic and common problems

Introduction

One of the important things that you can use Wireshark for is application analysis and troubleshooting. When the application slows down, it can be because of the LAN (quite uncommon in wired LAN), the WAN service (common due to insufficient bandwidth or high delay), or slow servers or clients (we will see this in TCP window problems). It can also be due to slow or problematic applications.

The purpose of this chapter is to get in to the details of how applications work, and provide some guidelines and recipes for isolating and solving these problems. In the first recipe, we will learn how to find out and categorize applications that work over our network. Then, we will go through various types of applications, see how they work, how networks influence their behavior, and what can go wrong.

In this chapter, we will learn how to use Wireshark in order to resolve and troubleshoot common applications that are used in an enterprise network. These are FTP, various e-mail protocols, Microsoft Terminal Server and Citrix, databases, NetBIOS protocols, and others.

Finding out what is running over your network

The first thing to do when monitoring a new network is to find out what is running over it. There are various types of applications and network protocols, and they can influence and interfere with each other when all of them are running over the network.

In some cases, you will have different VLANs, different **Virtual Routing and Forwarding** (**VRFs**), or servers that are connected to virtual ports in a **Bladeserver**. Eventually everything is running on the same infrastructure, and they can influence each other.

 There is a common confusion between VRFs and VLANs. Even though their purpose is quite the same, they are configured in different places. While VLANs are configured in the LAN in order to provide network separation in the OSI layers 1 and 2, VRFs are multiple instances of routing tables to make them co-exist in the same router. This is a layer 3 operation that separates between different customer's networks. VRFs are used in **Multi Protocol Label Switching** (**MPLS**) to provide layer 3 connectivity to different customers over the same router's network, in such a way that no customer can see any other customer's network.

In this recipe, we will see how to get to the details of what is running over the network, and the applications that can slow it down.

 The term **Bladeserver** refers to a server enclosure, which is a chassis of server shelves on the front and LAN switches on the back. There are several different acronyms for it; for example, IBM calls them **Bladecenter** and HP calls them **Bladesystem.**

Getting ready

When you get into a new network, the first thing to do is to connect Wireshark to sniff what is running over the network. Make sure you follow these points:

- When you are required to monitor a server, port mirror it and see what is running on its connection to the network.

- When you are required to monitor a remote office, port mirror the router port that connects you to the WAN connection. Then, check what is running over it.

- When you are required to monitor a slow connection to the Internet, port mirror it to see what is going on there.

In this recipe, we will see how to use the Wireshark tools for analyzing what is running and what can cause the problems.

How to do it...

For analyzing who is talking, follow these steps:

1. Connect Wireshark using one of the options mentioned in the previous section.

2. You can use the following tools:

   ❏ Navigate to **Statistics | Protocol Hierarchy** for viewing the protocols that run over the network and their percentage of the total traffic

   ❏ Navigate to **Statistics | Conversations** to see who is talking and what protocols are used

3. In the **Protocol Hierarchy** feature, you will get a window that will help you analyze who is talking over the network. It is shown in the following screenshot:

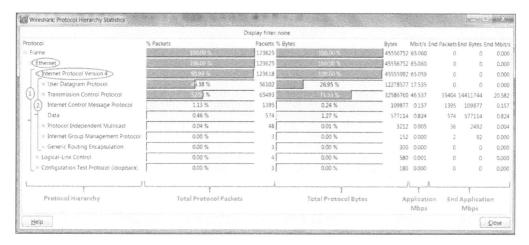

4. In the screenshot you can see the protocol distribution:

   1. **Ethernet**: IP, Logical-Link Control (LLC) and Configuration Test Protocol (loopback)

   2. **Internet Protocol Version 4**: User Datagram Protocol (UDP), Transport Control Protocol (TCP), Protocol Independent Multicast (PIM), Internet Group Management Protocol (IGMP), and Generic Routing Encapsulation Protocol (GRE)

5. If you click on the **+** sign, all underlying protocols will be shown.

6. To see a specific protocol throughput, click down to the protocols as shown in the following screenshot. You will see the application average throughput during the capture (HTTP in this example):

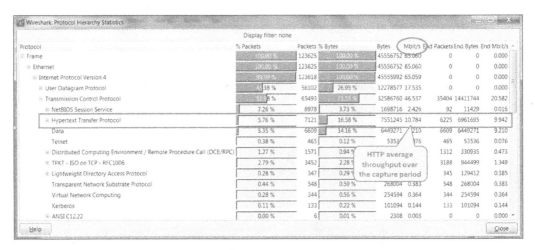

7. Clicking on the **+** sign to the left of HTTP will open a list of protocols that run over HTTP (XML, MIME, JavaScripts, and more) and their average throughput during the capture period.

There's more...

In some cases (especially when you need to prepare management reports), you are required to provide a graphical picture of the network statistics. There are various sources available for this, for example:

▶ **Etherape (for Linux)**: `http://etherape.sourceforge.net/`

▶ **Compass (for Windows)**: `http://download.cnet.com/Compass-Free/3000-2085_4-75447541.html?tag=mncol;1` (from Wildpackets)

Analyzing FTP problems

File Transfer Protocol (**FTP**) is a protocol created for transferring files over TCP/IP across a network. FTP is a protocol that runs over TCP ports `20` and `21` for the data and control connections (FTP commands) respectively.

FTP has two modes of operation:

- **Active mode** (**ACTV**): In this mode, the client initiates a control connection to the server, and the server initiates a data connection to the client
- **Passive mode** (**PASV**): In this mode, the client initiates the control and data connections to the server

Both types of connections can be implemented, and they will be explained later in this recipe in the *How it works...* section.

Getting ready

When working with FTP, if you suspect any connectivity or slow response problems, configure port mirror to one of the following:

- The FTP server port
- The client port
- A link that the traffic crosses

If required, configure a capture or display filter.

How to do it...

To check FTP performance problems, follow these steps:

1. First, check for any Ethernet, IP, or TCP problems, as described in previous chapters. In many cases, slow responses happen due to networking problems and not necessarily due to application problems.

2. Check for TCP retransmissions and duplicate ACKs. Check if they are on the entire traffic or only on the FTP connection.

   If you get it on various connections, it is probably due to a slow network that influences the entire traffic.

   If you get it only on FTP connections to the same server or client, it can be due to a slow server or client.

3. When you are copying a single file in an FTP file transfer, you should get a straight line in the IO graph and a straight gradient in the TCP stream graph (time-sequence).

4. In the following screenshot, we can see what a bad FTP looks like in the TCP stream graph (time-sequence):

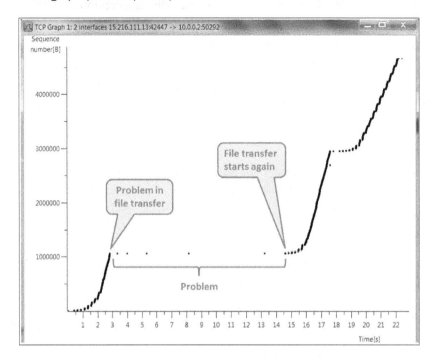

5. In the following screenshot, we can see how it looks in the IO graph (configured with filters):

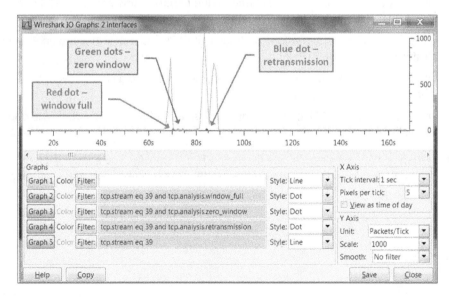

6. In the capture file shown in the following screenshot, we can see TCP window problems. These are listed as follows:

    1. The server `15.216.111.13` sends a **TCP Window Full** message to the client, indicating that the server send window is full (packet `5763`).

    2. The client `10.0.0.2` sends a **TCP Zero Window** message to the server, telling the server to stop sending data (packet `5778`).

    3. The server keeps sending **TCP Zero Window Probe** messages to the client, asking the client if the condition is still zero window (that tells the server not to send any more data). The client answers these messages with **TCP Zero Window Probe Ack**, indicating that this is still the case (packets `5793` to `5931`).

    4. After a while, the client sends the message **TCP Window Update** to the server, telling it to start increasing the FTP throughput (packet `5939`).

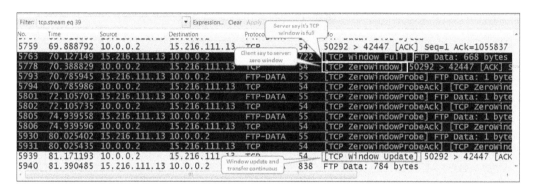

7. In the preceding case, it was simply a slow client. We solved the problem by working over it and deleting some unnecessary processes.

If you are facing connectivity problems, it can be due to a non-functioning server, firewall that blocks the connection on the way, or software installed on the server or client that blocks it. In this case, go through the following steps:

1. Was the TCP connection opened properly with the `SYN/SYN-ACK/ACK` packets? If not, it can be due to:

    ❑ The firewall that blocks communications. Check with the system administrator.

    ❑ The server that is not running. Check this on the server— in the process table, FTP server management, and so on.

- ❑ A software of the server blocks connectivity. It can be an antivirus that has an additional firewall that blocks connections, VPN client, or any other security or protection software.

- ❑ Check the connectivity on the client, too. It can be that it is blocked by a VPN client, a firewall on the client, and so on.

2. In the active mode, the client opens connection to the server that opens another connection. Make sure that the firewalls on the way support it, or use passive mode.

How it works...

There are two modes of FTP: active and passive. In the active mode, the server opens another connection to the client, while in passive mode, it is the client that opens the second connection to the server. Let's see how it works.

In passive mode, the operations are as shown in the following screenshot:

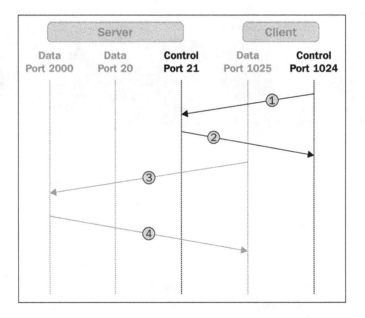

1. The client opens a control connection from a random port *P* (1024 in the example) to the server port 21.

2. The server answers back from port 21 to the client port 1024.

3. Now, the client opens a data connection from the port *P+1* (1025 in the example) to a data port that the server has opened and notified the client about (port 2000 in the example).

4. The server answers from the data port (2000 in the example) to the client port that initiated the connection, that is, the data port *P+1* (1025 in the example).

In the active mode, the operation is slightly different:

1. The client opens a control connection from a random port *P* (1024 in the example) to the server port 21.

2. The server answers from port 21 to the client port 1024.

3. The server opens the data connection from port 20 to the client port *P+1* (1025 in the example).

4. The client answers from the data port *P+1* (1025 in the example) to the server port 20.

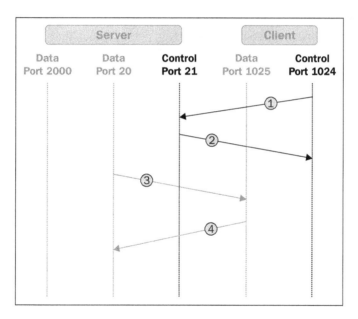

There's more...

FTP is a very simple application; and in most cases, FTP problems have very simple solutions. Some examples are as follows:

▶ **Problem 1**: I've monitored an international connection with FTP clients on one side of the network and an FTP server on the other side. The customer complained about slow performance and blamed the international service provider. After checking with the service provider, they said the connection is nearly not loaded (20 percent of a 10 Mbps line), a fact that I confirmed when I checked the line. When I looked at the TCP issues (retransmissions, window problems, and so on), there were none. Just to check, I removed the FTP server and installed another one (there are many free ones), and it started to work. It was a simple problem of an inefficient FTP server.

▶ **Problem 2**: A customer complained that when connecting to an FTP server, the connection was refused after every 5 or 6 trials. When I checked it with Wireshark, I saw that the FTP connection refused messages (and I already knew about this from the customer's complaint), so it looked like a dead end. Just to check, I started to stop the services running on the server, and the problem came out. It was an antivirus software that was interfering with this specific FTP server.

The bottom line is: even with Wireshark (and other software), sometimes common sense will help you more.

Analyzing e-mail traffic and troubleshooting e-mail problems – POP, IMAP, and SMTP

The common mail protocols for mail client to server and server to server communications are **Post Office Protocol version 3** (**POP3**), **Simple Mail Transfer Protocol** (**SMTP**) and **Internet Message Access Protocol version 4** (**IMAP4**).

Another common method for accessing e-mails is web access to mail, in which you have common mail servers such as Gmail, Yahoo!, and Hotmail. Some examples include **Outlook Web Access** (**OWA**) and **RPC over HTTPS** for the Outlook web client from Microsoft and others.

In this recipe, we will talk about the most common client-server and server-server protocols: POP3 and SMTP. We will also look at some typical problems by using the other methods.

Getting ready

When users are complaining about mail problems, first check if there are any obvious problems such as wrong username, bad password, and authentication protocols that are not configured. If none, connect Wireshark with port mirror to the complaining client; and if there are many of them, configure port mirror to the common server or the communications line connecting to it (when there is a remote server).

How to do it...

POP3 will usually be used for client to server communications, while SMTP will usually be used for server to server communications.

POP3 communications

POP3 is usually used for mail client to mail server communications. When a client cannot access the mail server, perform the following checks:

1. First, check if the correct username and password have been configured.

2. Then, check if the authentication has passed correctly. In the following screenshot, you can see a session opened with a username that starts with `doronn@` (all IDs were deleted) and a password that starts with `u6F`.

3. To see the TCP stream shown in the following screenshot, right-click on one of the packets in the stream and choose **Follow TCP Stream** from the dropdown menu:

4. Any error messages in the authentication stage will prevent the communications from being established. You can see an example of this in the following screenshot where user authentication failed. In this case, we see that when the client gets the **Logon failure**, it closes the TCP connection.

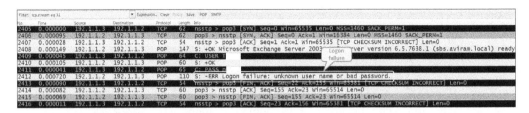

5. During the mail transfer, be aware that mail clients can easily fill a narrow-band communications line. You can check this by simply configuring the IO graphs with a filter on POP.

6. Always check for common TCP indications: retransmissions, zero-window, window-full, and others. They can indicate a busy communication line, slow server, and other problems coming from the communications lines or end nodes and servers. These problems will mostly cause slow connectivity.

SMTP communications

SMTP is commonly used for the following purposes:

▶ Server to server communications, in which SMTP is the mail protocol that runs between the servers

▶ In some clients, POP3 or IMAP4 are configured for incoming messages (messages from the server to the client); while SMTP is configured for outgoing messages (messages from the client to the server)

When you suspect slow server-to-server communications, follow these steps to resolve the problems.

1. Check if the servers are located on the same site:

   ❑ If they are located on the same site, you probably have slow servers or another application problem. In most of the cases, the LAN will not cause any problems—especially when both servers are in the same data centre.

   ❑ If they are not located on the same site (when the servers are located in a remote site through WAN connections), check the load on the WAN connections. When sending large mails, they can easily block these lines—especially when they are narrow band (several Mbps).

2. First, look for TCP problems; and check if you see them only on SMTP or on all other applications. For example, in the following screenshot, you can see many TCP retransmissions:

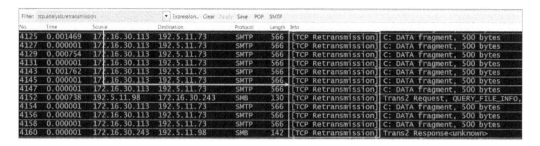

3. Check if they are because of a slow SMTP server. Is it a mail problem? When you look at the following screenshot, you see that I've used the **TCP Conversation** statistics. After checking the **Limit to display filter** checkbox and clicking on **Packets** at the top of the window (to get the list from the higher amount of packets), we can see that only 793 packets are SMTP from the retransmitted packets. There are 9014 packets retransmitted between 172.16.30.247 and 172.16.30.2 on port 445 (Microsoft DS), 2319 packets are retransmitted between 172.16.30.180 and 192.5.11.198 on port 80 (HTTP), and so on.

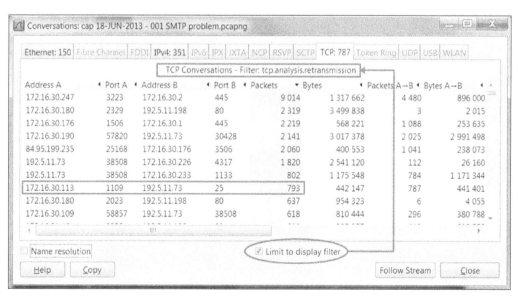

4. In this case, SMTP is influenced only by bad communications. It is not an SMTP problem.

5. Check for SMTP errors. In the following screenshot, you see an error code `451`, which is also called the `local error in processing` server error. Also, a list of errors is listed.

 When something goes wrong, in most cases the server or the client will tell you about it. You just have to look at the messages and Google them. We will see many examples of this later.

You can also find a list of SMTP status codes in RFC 1893 (http://www.ietf.org/rfc/rfc1893.txt).

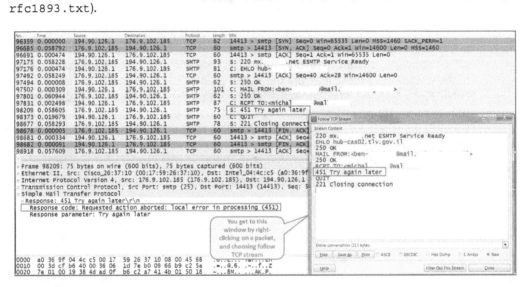

1. When you want to know which errors have been sent by the two sides, configure a filter as shown in the following screenshot:

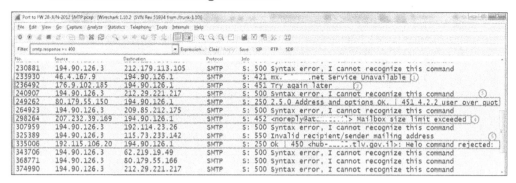

2. Here you can see various events:

   ❑ **Code 421**: This indicates that the mail service is probably unavailable (**1**).

   ❑ **Code 452**: This indicates that the server cannot respond, and tells you to try again later. This happens due to load on the server or a server problem (**2**).

   ❑ **Code 451**: (code 250 is shown in the screenshot, see the following note) This indicates the user over quota (**3**).

   ❑ **Code 452**: This indicates that the mailbox size limit has been exceeded (**4**).

   ❑ **Code 450**: (code 250 is shown in the screenshot, see the following note) This indicates that the host was not found (**5**).

In SMTP (like in many other protocols), you can get several error codes in the same message. What you see in the packet list in Wireshark can be the first one, or a partial list of it. To see the full list of errors in the SMTP message, go to the packet details and open the specific packet, as in the following screenshot.

When you see too many codes, it indicates unavailability of the server. check with the server administrator.

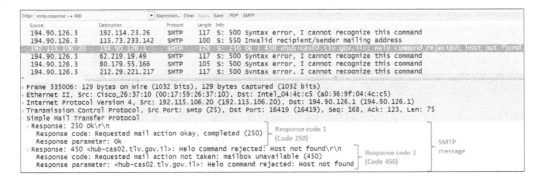

Some other methods and problems

Some other common methods that I mentioned earlier are web mail and RPC over HTTP:

▶ In web mail, we connect to the server with HTTPS; therefore this is exactly like working with HTTPS, as described in *Chapter 10, HTTP and DNS*. After logging in to the server, if any problems occur, they will be HTTPS problems.

▶ RPC over HTTPS will be same. Since RPC is a protocol which usually loads the network, it is considered to be sensitive to high delays and jitter. Microsoft came up with a solution to work with their Outlook client over HTTPS and not with the standard RPC. Again, since communication runs over HTTPS, problems will be HTTPS problems.

How it works...

Mail clients will mostly use POP3 for communications with the server. In some cases, they will use SMTP as well. IMAP4 is used when server manipulation is required, for example, when you need to see messages that exist on a remote server without downloading them to the client. Server to server communications are usually implemented by SMTP.

> The difference between IMAP and POP is that in IMAP the mail is always stored on the server. If you delete it, it will be unavailable from any other machine. In POP, deleting a downloaded email may or may not delete that e-mail on the server.

In general, SMTP status codes are divided into three categories, which are structured in a way that helps you understand what exactly went wrong. The method and details of SMTP status codes is discussed in the following section.

POP3

POP3 is an application layer protocol used by mail clients to retrieve e-mail messages from the server. A typical POP3 session will look like the following screenshot:

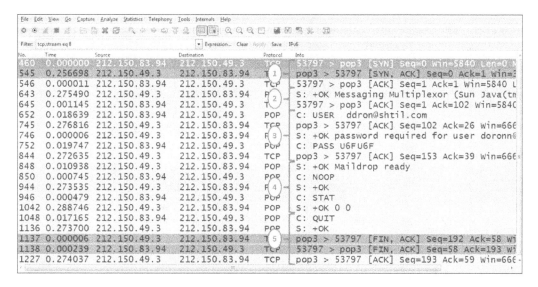

1. The client opens a TCP connection to the server.

2. The server sends an OK message to the client (**OK Messaging Multiplexor**).

3. The user sends the username and password.

4. The protocol operations begin. **NOOP** (no operation) is a message sent to keep the connection open, **STAT** (status) is sent from the client to the server to query the message status. The server answers with the number of messages and their total size (in packet 1042, **OK 0 0** means no messages and it has total size zero).

5. When there are no mail messages on the server, the client sends a **QUIT** message (1048), the server confirms it (packet 1136) and the TCP connection is closed (packets 1137, 1138, and 1227).

In the case of encrypted connection, it will look nearly the same (see the following screenshot). After the connection establishment (**1**), there are several POP messages (**2**), TLS connection establishment (**3**), and then the encrypted application data.

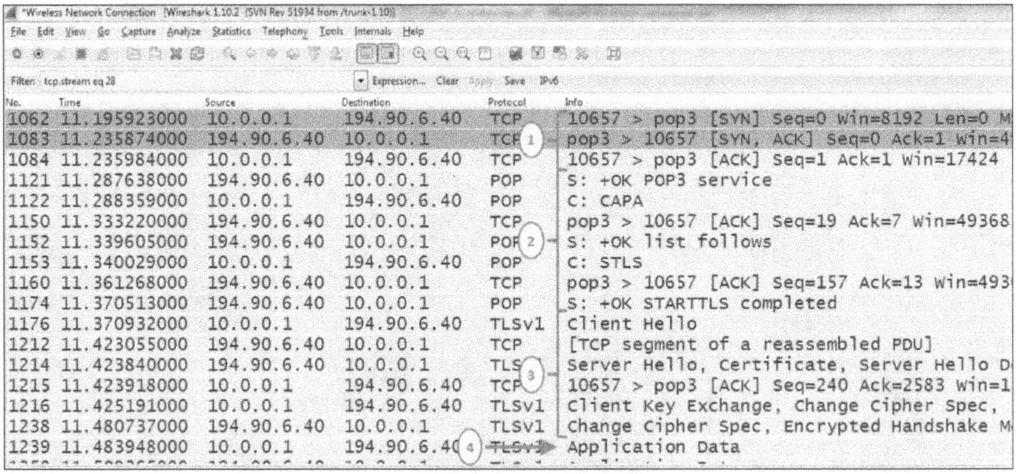

SMTP and SMTP error codes (RFC3463)

The structure of SMTP status codes is as follows:

```
class . subject . detail
```

For example, when you see status code 450, it means the following:

> ▶ **Class 4** indicates that it is a temporary problem
> ▶ **Subject 5** indicates that it is a mail delivery status
> ▶ **Detail 0** indicates an undefined error (RFC 3463, Paragraph 3.6)

The following table lists the various classes:

Status code	Meaning	Reason
2.x.xxx	Success	Operation succeeded
4.x.xxx	Persistent transient failure	A temporary condition has prevented the server from sending the message. It can be due to server load or network bottleneck. Usually, sending the message again will succeed.
5.x.xxx	Permanent failure	A permanent problem prevented the server from sending the message. Usually server or compatibility errors.

The following table lists the various subjects:

Status code	What is it	What can be the reason
x.0.xxx	Other or undefined status	-
x.1.xxx	Addressing status	-
x.2.xxx	Mailbox status	-
x.3.xxx	Mail system status	-
x.4.xxx	Network and routing status	-
x.5.xxx	Mail delivery protocol status	-
x.6.xxx	Message content or media status	-
x.7.xxx	Security or policy status	-

The list of status details are too long to be listed here. A full list can be found in the standard pages at `http://tools.ietf.org/html/rfc3463`.

Some common status codes are listed in the following table:

Status code	What is it	What can be the reason
220	Service is ready	Service is running and ready to perform mail operations.
221	Service closing transmission channel	Usually OK. This is how the server closes the service when it is not required.
250	Requested mail action is OK	Message is delivered successfully.
251	Not a local user, mail will be forwarded	Everything is OK.
252	Cannot verify the user	The user couldn't be verified by the server. The mail will be delivered.
421	Service not available	The mail transfer service is not available and cannot serve incoming mail due to a transient event. This can be due to a server problem (service that is not running) or server limitation.
422	Mail size problem	The recipient mailbox has passed its quota or has a limitation on incoming mail.
431	Out of memory or disk full	Server disk is either full, or out of memory. Check the server.
432	Incoming mail queue has been stopped	It can be due to a server error (a service that stopped).
441	The receiving server is not responding	The server that sends the message indicates that the destination server does not respond.
442	Bad connection	There is a problem with the connection to the destination server.
444	Unable to route	The server was unable to determine the next hop for the message.
445	Mail system congestion	The mail server is temporarily congested.
447	Delivery time has expired	The message was considered too old by the rejecting system. This is usually due to queuing or transmission problems.
450	Requested action not taken	Message could not be transmitted. This is usually due to a problem with the mail service on the remote server.

Status code	What is it	What can be the reason
451	Invalid command	This indicates an unsupported or out of sequence command. The action was aborted by the receiving server. This was mostly due to load on the sending or the receiving server.
452	Requested action was not taken	Insufficient storage on the receiving server.
500	Syntax error	The command sent by the server was not recognized as a valid SMTP or ESMTP command.
512	DNS error	The host server, which is the destination for the mail that was sent, could not be located.
530	Authentication problem	Authentication is required from the receiving server, or your server has been added to a black list by the receiving server.
542	Recipient address was rejected	A message indicating that your server address was rejected by the receiving server. This is usually due to Anti-spam, IDS/IPS systems, smart firewalls or other security system.

There's more...

E-mails are sometimes referred to as one of the "silent killers" of networks, especially in small enterprises that use asymmetric lines to the Internet. When sending text messages, they will not consume anything from the network; but when you send a large file of several megabytes or even tens of megabytes over a narrow-band uplink to the ISP, the rest of the users in your office will suffer from network slowdown for many seconds, even minutes. I've seen this problem in many small offices.

Another issue with mail clients is that in some cases (configurable), mail clients are configured to download all new data from the server when they start to work. If you have a customer that complains of a network slowdown at the time when all employees start their day in the office, it might be due to the tens or hundreds of clients who opened their mail clients simultaneously and the mail server is located over a WAN.

Analyzing MS-TS and Citrix communications problems

Microsoft Terminal Server (**MS-TS**) that uses **Remote Desktop Protocol** (**RDP**) and **Citrix Metaframe Independent Computing Architecture** (**ICA**) protocols are widely used for local and remote connectivity for PCs and thin clients. The important thing to remember about these types of applications is that they are transferring screen changes over the network. If there are only a few changes, they will require low bandwidth. If there are many changes, they will require high bandwidth.

Another thing is that the traffic in these applications is entirely asymmetric. Downstream traffic takes from tens of Kbps up to several Mbps, while the upstream traffic will be at most several Kbps. When working with these applications, don't forget to design your network according to this.

In this recipe, we will see some typical problems of these applications and how to locate them. For the convenience of writing, we will refer to Microsoft TS; and every time we will write MS-TS, we will refer to all applications in this category, for example, Citrix Metaframe.

Getting ready

When suspecting a slow performance with MS-TS, first check with the user what the problem is. Then, connect the Wireshark to the network, with port mirror to the complaining client or to the server.

How to do it...

For locating a problem when MS-TS is involved, start with going to the users and asking questions. Follow these steps:

1. When users complain about a slow network, ask them a simple question: Do they see the slowness in the data presented on the screen, or when they switch between windows?

2. If they say that the switch between windows is very fast, it is not an MS-TS problem. MS-TS problems will cause slow window changes, picture freezes, slow scrolling of graphical documents, and so on.

3. If they say that they are trying to generate a report (when the software is running over MS-TS) but the report is generated after a long period of time, this is a database problem and not MS-TS or Citrix.

4. When a user works with MS-TS over a high-delay communication line and types very quickly, they might experience delays with the characters. This is because MS-TS is transferring window changes, and with high delays these windows changes will be transferred slowly.

5. When measuring the communication line with Wireshark:

   ❑ Use IO graphs for monitoring the line

   ❑ Use filters to monitor the upstream and the downstream directions

   ❑ Configure bits per second on the y-axis

6. You will get the following screenshot:

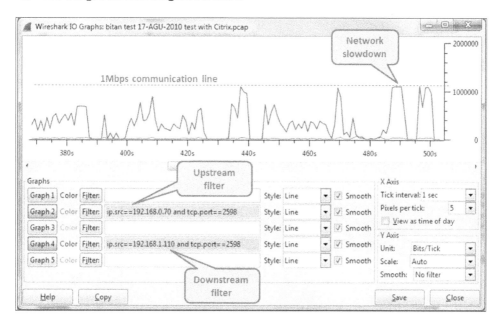

7. In the preceding screenshot, you can see a typical traffic pattern with high downstream and very low upstream traffic. Notice that the **Y-Axis** is configured to **Bits/Tick**. In the time between 485 s and 500 s, you see that the throughput got to the maximum. This is when applications will slowdown and users will start to feel screen freezes, menus that move very slowly, and so on.

> When a Citrix ICA client connects to a presentation server, it uses TCP ports 2598 or 1494.

8. When monitoring MS-TS servers, don't forget that the clients access the server with MS-TS and the servers access the application with another client that is installed on the server. The performance problem can come from the MS-TS or from the application.

9. If the problem is an MS-TS problem, it is necessary to figure out if it is a network problem or a system problem:

   ❏ Check the network with Wireshark to see if there are any loads. Loads such as the one shown in the previous screenshot can be solved by simply increasing the communication lines.

   ❏ Check the server's performance. Applications like MS-TS are mostly memory consuming, so check mostly for memory (RAM) issues.

How it works...

MS-TS, Citrix Metaframe, and applications simply transfer window changes over the network. From your client (PC with software client or thin client), you connect to the terminal server; and the terminal server runs various clients that are used to connect from it to other servers. In the following screenshot, you can see the principle of terminal server operation:

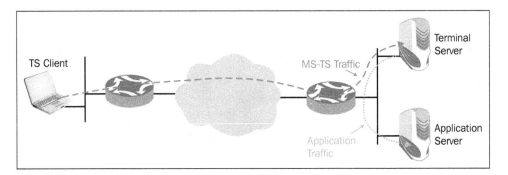

There's more...

From the terminal server vendors, you will hear that their applications improve two things. They will say that it improves manageability of clients because you don't have to manage PCs and software for every user—you simply install everything on the server, and if something fails you fix it on the server. They will also say that traffic over the network will be reduced.

Well, I will not get into the first argument. This is not our subject, but I strongly reject the second one. When working with a terminal client, your traffic entirely depends on what you are doing:

1. When working with text/characters-based applications, for example, some **Enterprise Resource Planning (ERP)** screens, you type in and read data. When working with the terminal client, you will connect to the terminal server that will connect to the database server. Depending on the database application you are working with, the terminal server can improve performance significantly or does not improve it at all. We will discuss this in the database section. Here, you can expect a load of tens to hundreds Kbps.

2. In cases where you are working with regular office documents such as Word, PowerPoint, and so on, it entirely depends on what you are doing. Working with a simple Word document will require tens to hundreds of Kbps. Working with PowerPoint will require hundreds Kbps to several Mbps, and when you present the PowerPoint file with full screen (function **F5**) the throughput can jump up to 8 to 10 Mbps.

3. Browsing the Internet will take between hundreds of Kbps to several Mbps, depending on what you are doing. High resolution movies over terminal server to the Internet—well, just don't do it.

Before implementing any terminal environment, test it. I once had a software house that wanted their logo (at the top-right corner of the user window) to be very clear and striking. They refreshed it 10 times a second, which caused the 2 Mbps communication line to be blocked. You never know what you don't test.

Analyzing problems in the NetBIOS protocols

Network Basic Input/Output System (**NetBIOS**) is a set of protocols developed in the early 1980s for LAN communications. A few years later, it was adopted by Microsoft for their networking over the LAN, and then it was migrated for working over TCP/IP (NetBIOS over TCP/IP, RFCs 1001, and 1002).

In today's networks, NetBIOS provides three services:

▸ **Name service** (port 137) for name registration and name to IP address resolution.

▸ **Datagram distribution service** (port 138) for service announcements by clients and servers.

▸ **Session service** (port 139) for session negotiation between hosts. This is used for accessing files, open directories and so on.

In this chapter, we will get into some common problems with the NetBIOS suite of protocols, and we will learn how to try and solve them. Since the NetBIOS set of protocols is quite complicated, and there are hundreds of scenarios of things that might go wrong, we will try to provide some guidelines for how to look for common problems and what might go wrong.

Getting ready

NetBIOS protocols work in the Windows environments, along with MAC and Linux machines communicating with Windows. When facing problems such as instability, slow response times, disconnections, and so on in these environments NetBIOS issues can be one of the reasons for it. When facing these problems, the tool for solving them is Wireshark. It will show you what runs over the network, and Windows tools will show you what runs in the clients and servers.

How to do it...

To try and find out what a problem could be, connect your laptop with the Wireshark to the network, and port mirror the suspected clients or server as described below. In the following sections, we will see several scenarios for several problems.

There are many predefined filters that are used with NetBIOS. You can find them by clicking on the **Expression** button, which is on the right-hand side of the **Display Filters** window.

1. For general NetBIOS commands, they start with `netbios`.
2. For NetBIOS name service, they start with `nbns`.
3. For NetBIOS datagram service, they start with `nbds`.
4. For NetBIOS session service, they start with `nbss`.
5. For SMB, they start with `smb`.

General tests

First, take a general look at the network. Then, look for suspicious patterns:

1. Connect Wireshark to the network. Each one of the ports will do fine, as long as you are on the same broadcast domain with the clients that are having the problems.
2. Configure the display filter `nbns.flags.response == 0`. It will give you the NBNS requests. You will see many broadcasts, as shown in the following screenshot:

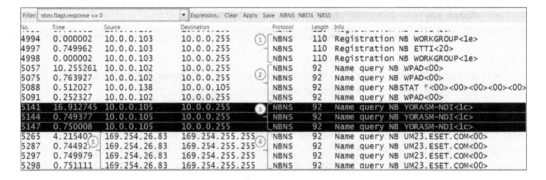

3. As you saw in the previous screenshot, in the capture file you will see the following:

   ❏ **NBNS registration packets (1)**: In the examples, there are registrations with the names `WORKGROUP` and `ETTI`. NBNS server will accept or reject the name registration by issuing a positive or negative Name Registration Response to the requesting node. If none are received, the requesting node will assume it is OK.

❑ **NBNS Queries (2, 3 and 4)**: Queries are sent for the name specified. If there is an NBNS server (this is the domain controller), you will see one of the following responses:

❑ requested name does not exist (code 3)

❑ no error (code 0)

4. Make sure there is no registration or any other requests coming from addresses that start with `169.254` (**5**). These are **Automatic Private IP Addressing** (**APIPA**) addresses. This actually means that the PC is configured to accept addresses automatically (by DHCP) and it has not received one.

5. There are many announcement packets as well. These will be broadcast on UDP port `138`. Here, you will see that every station announces its capabilities: workstation, server, print server, and so on. For example, you can see here that:

❑ `172.16.100.10` name is `FILE-SRV`, and it functions like workstation, server, and SQL server (**1**)

❑ `172.16.100.204` name is `GOLF`, and it functions like workstation, server, and a print queue server (**2**)

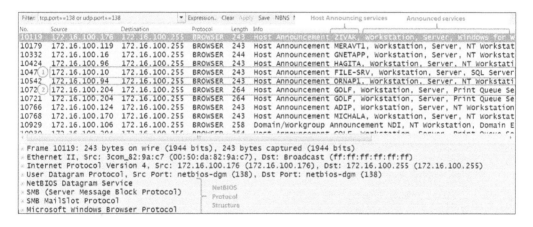

6. There are some worms and viruses that are using the NetBIOS name service to scan the network. Look for unusual patterns like massive scanning, high broadcast rate, and so on.

7. Verify that you don't have too many broadcasts. Five to 10 broadcast/minute/device are reasonable. More than this usually means problems.

 There are hundreds of message scenarios you can see here. Use the Wireshark Expert system, Google, and common sense to discover the problem.

Specific issues

Here are some issues and problems you might see during usual operation:

1. Using **Server Message Block** (**SMB**), which is the protocol that is used for browsing directories, copying files, and other operations over the network, you might see some error codes. The full list of error codes is listed in Microsoft MSDN: `http://msdn.microsoft.com/en-us/library/ee441884.aspx`.

2. Code 0 means STATUS_OK, when everything works fine and there is no problem. Any other code should be examined.

3. In the following example, you can see a message STATUS_ACCESS_DENIED. This is one of many error codes you should look for. In the example, access to \\NAS01\ HOMEDIR on a server with an IP address that starts with 203 (full address hidden due to security reasons) was denied.

4. When you try to see the home directory by browsing it, Windows will usually show you an **ACCESS DENIED** message or something similar. The problem can happen when an application is trying to access a directory, and cannot get access to it. In this case, you can see an **ACCESS DENIED** message, a software message of communication problem, or any other message the programmers have made for you. Using Wireshark in this case will get you to the exact error and Google will show you the reason for it.

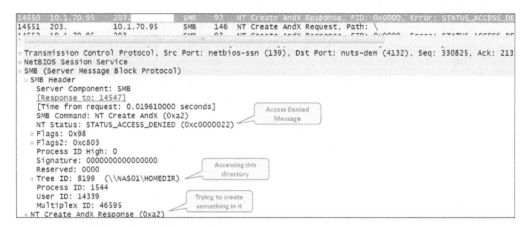

5. In the next example, we see a status STATUS_MORE_PROCESSING_REQUIRED (**2**) that happened during session setup (**1**) on \\NAS01\SAMIM (**3**).

    ❑   Looking at the link mentioned earlier, we see that this is because on the designated named pipe, there is more data available to read.

❑ A short Google lookup tells us that it might indicate a credentials problem. Check with your system administrator.

6. To see all SMB error messages, type the filter `smb.nt_status != 0x0`. You will get all error responses, as shown in the following screenshot:

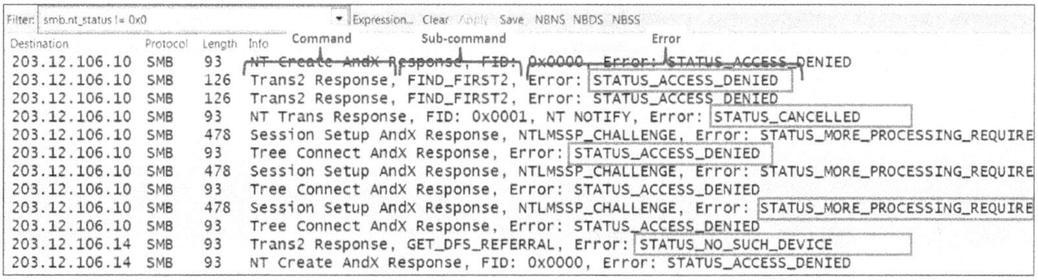

How it works...

As we saw in the introduction to this section, NetBIOS provides three services: **Net BIOS Name Service** (**NBNS**), **NetBIOS Datagram Distribution Service** (**NBDS**), and **NetBIOS Session Service** (**NBSS**).

NBNS is the service that registers and translates names to IP addresses. Registration happens when a client registers its name in the domain controller. The client sends a registration request, and then gets a response whether the registration is OK or the name is registered with another device. Microsoft environment was implemented with WINS when most networks did not use it, and later it was replaced by DNS. It works over UDP port `137`.

NBDS is used for service announcements by clients and servers. With this service, devices on the network announce their names, services that they can provide to other devices on the networks, and how to connect to these services. It works over UDP port 138.

NBSS is used to establish sessions between hosts, open or save files, and execute remote files and other sessions over the network. It works over TCP port 139.

There are additional protocols such as **Server Message Block** (**SMB**) that run over NBSS for transaction operations and over NBDS for service announcement, **SPOOLS** for printer requests, and several others. To get to the details of NetBIOS is beyond the scope of this book. In the case that you are required to troubleshoot NetBIOS protocols, follow the instructions in this section—pay special attention to error messages and notes.

There's more...

In this section, I would like to show some examples to get a better understanding of the NetBIOS protocols.

Example 1 – application freezing

In the following screenshot, we see the reason for an application freeze:

No.	Time	Source	Destination	Protocol	Info
26562	362.699257	203.	10.1.70.95	SMB	Tree Connect AndX Request, Path: \\NAS01\SAMIM
26563	362.717483	10.1.70.95	203	SMB	Tree Connect AndX Response, Error: STATUS_ACCESS_DENIED
26564	362.717635	203.	10.1.70.95	SMB	Logoff AndX Request
26565	362.734572	10.1.70.95	203.	SMB	Logoff AndX Response
26572	362.853441	203.	10.1.70.95	TCP	nuts-dem > netbios-ssn [ACK] Seq=226260 Ack=359968 Win=
36000	482.813425	10.1.70.95	203.	TCP	netbios-ssn > nuts-dem [ACK] Seq=339967 Ack=226260 Win=
36001	482.813508	203.	10.1.70.95	TCP	[TCP Dup ACK 26572#1] nuts-dem > netbios-ssn [ACK] Seq=
44869	602.799670	10.1.70.95	203.	TCP	[TCP Keep-Alive] netbios-ssn > nuts-dem [ACK] Seq=35996
44872	602.800321	203.	10.1.70.95	TCP	[TCP Keep-Alive ACK] nuts-dem > netbios-ssn [ACK] Seq=2
55372	722.786747	10.1.70.95	203.	TCP	[TCP Keep-Alive] netbios-ssn > nuts-dem [ACK] Seq=35996
55375	722.787380	203.	10.1.70.95	TCP	[TCP Keep-Alive ACK] nuts-dem > netbios-ssn [ACK] Seq=2
59751	798.181386	10.1.70.95	203.	NBSS	Session keep-alive
59758	798.390573	203.	10.1.70.95	TCP	nuts-dem > netbios-ssn [ACK] Seq=226260 Ack=359972 Win=
60622	816.812860	203.	10.1.70.95	SMB	Tree Disconnect Request
60623	816.829093	10.1.70.95	203.	SMB	Tree Disconnect Response
60627	816.984481	203.	10.1.70.95	TCP	nuts-dem > netbios-ssn [ACK] Seq=226299 Ack=360011 Win=
64565	936.948575	10.1.70.95	203.	TCP	[TCP Keep-Alive] netbios-ssn > nuts-dem [ACK] Seq=36001
64568	936.949116	203.	10.1.70.95	TCP	[TCP Keep-Alive ACK] nuts-dem > netbios-ssn [ACK] Seq=2
75087	1056.936316	10.1.70.95	203.	TCP	[TCP Keep-Alive] netbios-ssn > nuts-dem [ACK] Seq=36001
75088	1056.936568	203.	10.1.70.95	TCP	[TCP Keep-Alive ACK] nuts-dem > netbios-ssn [ACK] Seq=2
84066	1142.229579	10.1.70.95	203.	TCP	netbios-ssn > nuts-dem [RST, ACK] Seq=360011 Ack=226299

In the example, we make the following observations:

1. A client with IP address that starts with 203 is trying to connect to \\NAS01\SAMIM on a server with an IP address 10.1.70.95, and gets back a STATUS_ACCESS_DENIED error.

2. The client logs off and the server confirms it.

3. Since the applications waits, TCP is holding the connection with keep-alive messages.

4. After a while, the client sends disconnect requested that is approved by the server.

5. The application waits and TCP maintains the connection with keep-alives.

6. TCP closes the connection with `RST` (Reset).

What the customer saw here was an application freeze.

Example 2 – broadcast storm caused by SMB

In one of my client's networks, I got an urgent call that a remote office was disconnected from the HQ. Some network details are as follows:

▶ The remote office addresses are on subnet `172.30.121.0/24`, with a default gateway `172.30.121.254`.

▶ The HQ addresses are on subnet `172.30.0.0/24`. The connections between the remote offices and the centre are with L3 IP-VPNs over MPLS network.

To solve the problem, I did the following:

1. I tried to ping the servers in the HQ. I got no response.

2. I called the service provider that provides the lines to the centre, and they said that on their monitoring system they don't see any load on the line.

3. I pinged the local router, `172.30.121.254`, and got no response. The meaning is that PCs on the LAN couldn't get to their local router, which is the default gateway.

4. I connected a Wireshark with port mirror to the router port, and I saw something like the following screenshot:

No.	Time	Source	Destination	Protocol	Info
22	0.000002	172.30.121.1	172.30.121.255	SMB Mailslot	Write Mail Slot
23	0.000001	172.30.121.1	172.30.121.255	SMB Mailslot	Write Mail Slot
24	0.000001	172.30.121.1	172.30.121.255	SMB Mailslot	Write Mail Slot
25	0.000001	172.30.121.1	172.30.121.255	SMB Mailslot	Write Mail Slot
26	0.000002	172.30.121.1	172.30.121.255	SMB Mailslot	Write Mail Slot
27	0.000910	172.30.121.1	172.30.121.255	SMB Mailslot	Write Mail Slot
28	0.000002	172.30.121.1	172.30.121.255	SMB Mailslot	Write Mail Slot
29	0.000001	172.30.121.1	172.30.121.255	SMB Mailslot	Write Mail Slot
30	0.000001	172.30.121.1	172.30.121.255	SMB Mailslot	Write Mail Slot
31	0.000857	172.30.121.1	172.30.121.255	SMB Mailslot	Write Mail Slot

```
Frame 1: 277 bytes on wire (2216 bits), 277 bytes captured (2216 bits) on interface 1
Ethernet II, Src: Hewlett-_2b:5d:e3 (f4:ce:46:2b:5d:e3), Dst: Broadcast (ff:ff:ff:ff:ff:ff)
Internet Protocol Version 4, Src: 172.30.121.1 (172.30.121.1), Dst: 172.30.121.255 (172.30.121.255)
User Datagram Protocol, Src Port: netbios-dgm (138), Dst Port: netbios-dgm (138)
NetBIOS Datagram Service                     SMB
SMB (Server Message Block Protocol)       Mailslot
SMB MailSlot Protocol                      Protocol
Data (65 bytes)
```

5. I saw that a huge amount of packets are generated within microseconds (1) by a host with IP address `172.30.121.1`. The packets are broadcast (3), and the service that generated them is Write Mail Slot (5), which is sent by the SMB Mailslot protocol (4).

6. To get the picture of the number of packets, I used the IO Graphs feature. I got 5000 packets per second, that generated 10 Mbps that block the poor old router port (changing the router port to 100 Mbps or 1 Gbps wouldn't help. It would have been blocked too).

7. When I didn't find anything about it on Google or Microsoft, I started to stop services that I don't know, keeping track of what happened with the broadcast. Eventually, the service that caused the problem was called `LS3Bcast.exe`. I stopped it, made sure it didn't come back and that was it.

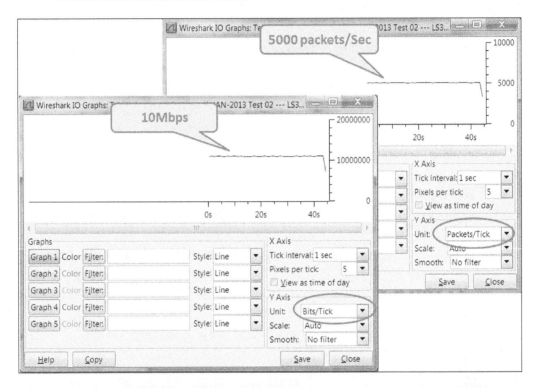

Analyzing database traffic and common problems

Some of you may wonder why I have added this section here. After all, databases are considered to be a completely different branch in the IT environment. There are databases and applications on one side and the network and infrastructure on the other side. It is correct since we are not supposed to debug databases; there are DBAs for this. But through the information that runs over the network, we can see some issues that can help the DBAs with solving the problem.

In most cases, the IT staff will come to us first because people blame the network for everything. We will have to make sure that the problems are not coming from the network and that's it. In a minority of the cases, we will see some details on the capture file that can help the DBAs with what they are doing.

Getting ready

When the IT team come to us complaining about the "slow network", there are some things to do just to verify that it is not the case. Follow the instructions in the following section to make sure we avoid the "slow network" issue.

How to do it...

In the case of database problems, follow these steps:

1. When you get complaints about the "slow network responses" start asking these questions:

    □ Is the problem local or global? Does it occur only in the remote offices, or also in the center? When the problem occurs in the entire network, it is not a WAN bandwidth issue.

    □ Does it happen the same for all clients? If not, there might be a specific problem that happens only with some users because only these users are running a specific application that causes the problem.

    □ Is the communication line between the clients and the server loaded? What is the application that loads them?

    □ Do all applications work slowly, or is it only the application that works with the specific database? Maybe some PCs are old and tired, or is it a server that runs out of resources?

2. When we are done with the questionnaire, let's start our work:

    1. Open Wireshark and start capturing packets. You can configure port mirror to a specific PC, to the server, to a VLAN, or to a router that connects to a remote office in which you have the clients.

    2. Look at TCP events (expert info). Do they happen on the entire communication link, on specific IP address/addresses, or on specific TCP port number/numbers? This will help you isolate the problem and verify whether it is on a specific link, server, or application.

> When measuring traffic on a connection to the Internet, you will get many retransmissions and duplicate ACKs to websites, mail servers, and so on. This is the Internet. In an organization, you should expect 0.1 to 0.5 percent retransmissions. When connecting to the Internet, you can expect much higher numbers.

3. If you see problems in the network, solve them as we learned in previous chapters. But, there are some network issues that can influence database behavior. In the following example, we see the behavior of a client that works with the server over a communication line with a roundtrip delay of 35 to 40 ms.

    1. We are looking at the TCP stream number 8 (**1**), and the connection started with TCP SYN/SYN-ACK/ACK. I've set this as a reference (**2**). We can see that the entire connection took 371 packets (**3**).

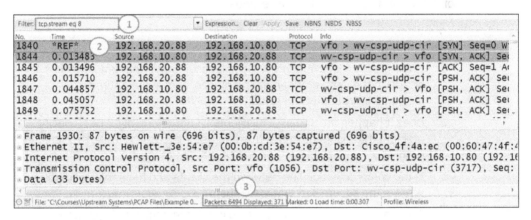

    2. The connection continues, and we see time intervals of around 35 ms between DB requests and responses.

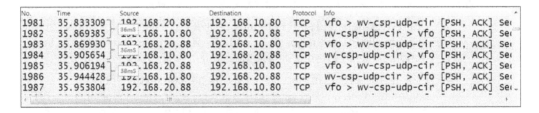

    3. Since we have 371 packets travelling back and forth, 371*35 ms gives us around 13 seconds. Add to this some retransmissions that might happen and some inefficiencies, and this leads to a user waiting for 10 to 15 seconds and more for a database query.

4. In this case, you should consult with the DBA on how to significantly reduce the number of packets that run over the network; or you can move to another way of access, for example, terminal server or web access.

4. Another problem that can happen is that you will have a software issue that will reflect in the capture file. If you have a look at the following screenshot, you will see that there are five retransmissions (**1**), and then a new connection is opened from the client side (**3**). It looks like a TCP problem but it occurs only in a specific window in the software. It is simply a software procedure that stopped processing, and this stopped the TCP from responding to the client (**2**).

No.	Time	Source	Destination	Protocol	Info
274	0.078889	192.168.3.50	192.168.200.227	TCP	http > vrtp [ACK] Seq=1 Ack=59884 Wir
275	0.380166	192.168.200.227	192.168.3.50	TCP	[TCP Retransmission] [TCP segment of
276	0.983678	192.168.200.227	192.168.3.50	TCP	[TCP Retransmission] [TCP segment of
277	2.195589	192.168.200.227	192.168.3.50	TCP	[TCP Retransmission] [TCP segment of
278	4.604757	192.168.200.227	192.168.3.50	TCP	[TCP Retransmission] [TCP segment of
279	9.432867	192.168.200.227	192.168.3.50	TCP	[TCP Retransmission] [TCP segment of
280	18.989050	192.168.200.227	192.168.3.50	TCP	rcts > http [SYN] Seq=0 Win=65535 Ler
281	18.994054	192.168.3.50	192.168.200.227	TCP	http > rcts [SYN, ACK] Seq=0 Ack=1 Wi
282	18.994085	192.168.200.227	192.168.3.50	TCP	rcts > http [ACK] Seq=1 Ack=1 Win=655
283	18.994264	192.168.200.227	192.168.3.50	TCP	[TCP segment of a reassembled PDU]
284	18.994280	192.168.200.227	192.168.3.50	TCP	[TCP segment of a reassembled PDU]
285	19.000271	192.168.3.50	192.168.200.227	TCP	http > rcts [ACK] Seq=1 Ack=537 Win=6

How it works...

Well, how databases work was always a miracle to me. Our task is to find how they influence the network, and this is what we've learned in this section.

There's more...

When you right-click on one of the packets in the database client to the server session, a window with the conversation will open. It can be helpful to the DBA to see what is running over the network.

When you are facing delay problems, for example, when working over cellular lines over the Internet or over international connections, the database client to the server will not always be efficient enough. You might need to move to web or terminal access to the database.

An important issue is how the database works. If the client is accessing the database server, and the database server is using files shared from another server, it can be that the client-server works great; but the problems come from the database server to the shared files on the file server. Make sure you that know all these dependencies before starting with your tests.

And most importantly, make sure you have very professional DBAs in your friends. One day you will need them.

12

SIP, Multimedia, and IP Telephony

In this chapter, we will learn how to use Wireshark in order to resolve and troubleshoot IP telephony, voice and video calls, video streams, and other types of multimedia sessions. In this chapter we have the following recipes:

- ▸ Using Wireshark's features for telephony and multimedia analysis
- ▸ Analyzing SIP connectivity
- ▸ Analyzing RTP/RTCP connectivity
- ▸ Troubleshooting scenarios for video and surveillance applications
- ▸ Troubleshooting scenarios for IPTV applications
- ▸ Troubleshooting scenarios for video-conferencing applications
- ▸ Troubleshooting RTSP

Introduction

Various types of multimedia applications take up a significant part of modern communication networks. Among these applications, we have telephony, video conferencing, surveillance systems, distance-learning systems, and many more.

In multimedia applications, the requirements from the network are different from the requirements in other enterprise applications. While applications such as HTTP, e-mail, and file sharing require high bandwidth, a telephone call, for example, requires less than 100 Kbps, but is sensitive to delays, and very sensitive to jitter (delay variations). While most applications require high downstream to clients in remote offices, surveillance systems require the upstream direction as they are watched from monitors in the HQ, so the monitors actually download the video from the remote site.

In this chapter, we will focus on these voice, video, and multimedia applications, how they behave over network connections, and how to use Wireshark to troubleshoot problems when they don't work properly.

In this chapter, we will focus on **Session Initiation Protocol (SIP)**, **Real Time Protocol / Real-time Transport Control Protocol (RTP/RTCP)**, **Real Time Streaming Protocol (RTSP)**, and other common multimedia protocols.

We will start this chapter by presenting the available tools that Wireshark provides us for troubleshooting voice and multimedia sessions. We will focus on how to resolve SIP problems and how to troubleshoot RTP/RTCP sessions, then we will learn how to troubleshoot video systems, including video conferencing and surveillance systems.

Using Wireshark's features for telephony and multimedia analysis

First, let's see what tools are provided by Wireshark for monitoring voice, video, and multimedia.

Getting ready

While facing problems with voice calls, video-conference calls, or other multimedia sessions, connect your laptop with Wireshark and port mirror one of the following devices as shown in the following diagram:

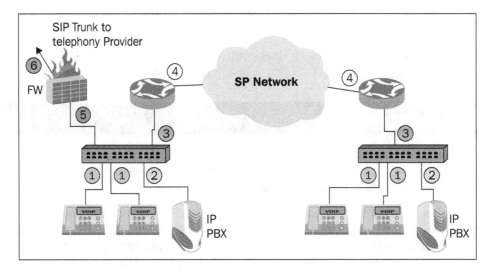

Follow these steps to use Wireshark's features for telephony and multimedia analysis:

1. Monitor the local or remote clients (**1**) in cases where you suspect a specific client problem.

2. Monitor the local or remote **IP PBX** system (**2**) when you suspect a central problem that influences the entire IP Telephony network.

3. Monitor the connections to the router (**3** and **4**) while suspecting an interoffice connectivity problem.

4. Monitor the firewall on the LAN port (**5**) or on the connection to the service provider (**6**). This connection will usually be over the Internet, but can also be on a direct line to the provider.

How to do it...

In the Wireshark window, open the **Telephony** menu, as shown in the following screenshot:

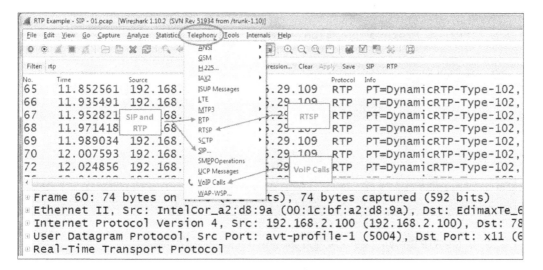

For telephony networks, use the following menus:

1. To view RTP information, navigate to **RTP | Show All Streams** as shown in the following screenshot:

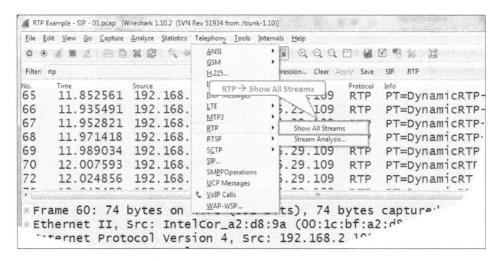

2. The following window will open:

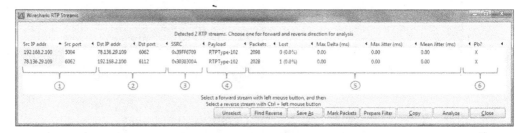

3. In the RTP Streams window, you will see the following details:

   ❑ The source IP address and UDP port

   ❑ The destination IP address and UDP port

   ❑ Synchronization Source (**SSRC**), which is an RTP stream identifier

   ❑ RTP payload type (usually codec type)

   ❑ Stream data, which is the total amount of captured packets, packet loss, maximum time between packets, maximum, and mean jitter

   ❑ **Pb?** that indicates a general problem in the stream

In the lower part of the window, you have the following buttons:

- **Unselect**: When you select a stream by clicking on its line, the **Unselect** button will cancel the selection.

- **Find reverse**: On a voice or multimedia call, a reverse stream is the stream in the opposite direction (which will be highlighted in light gray).

- **Save as**: This button can be used to save a stream in the `rtpdump` format. For information about the format, go to `http://www.cs.columbia.edu/irt/software/rtptools/`.

- **Mark packets**: not functioning.

- **Prepare filter**: This prepares a display filter in the display filter window.

- **Copy**: This option copies the RTP streams to a text file. For doing so, click on **Copy**, open a text editor, and paste the content to the text file.

- **Analyze**: When you click on a stream, and then click on the **Analyze** button, it opens the **RTP Stream Analyze** window. The same window can be opened by clicking on an RTP packet and navigating to **Telephony | RTP | Stream Analysis** from the menu.

- **Close**: Clicking on this button closes the window.

4. To view SIP information, navigate to **Telephony | SIP**. Enter `ip` (or `udp` or `sip`) in the **SIP Packet Counter** window that opens, and the window **SIP statistics with filter: ip** will open as shown in the following screenshot:

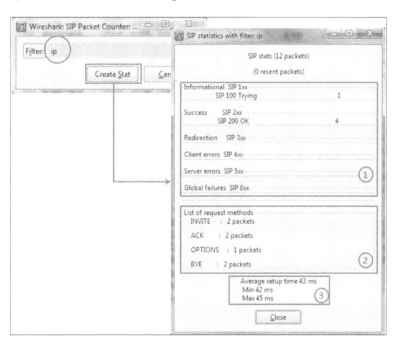

1. In the window, you will get the following SIP statistics:

    ❑ Number of packets sent with SIP response codes (numbered as **1** in the preceding screenshot)

    ❑ Total number of each one of the SIP methods (these are SIP commands) that were sent (numbered as **2** in the preceding screenshot)

    ❑ Minimum, maximum, and average session setup times (numbered as **3** in the preceding screenshot)

2. For RTSP statistics, navigate to **Telephony | RTSP | Packet Counter**, write ip, rtsp, or just leave it blank in the pop up that comes up, and then click on **Create Stat** that opens a window as shown in the following screenshot:

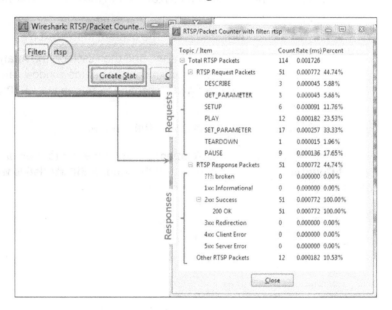

3. For watching which telephone calls were captured, navigate to **Telephony | VoIP Calls**. A window as shown in the following screenshot will open:

4. In the VoIP calls, you see the following parameters:

    ❑   The start and end time that give the duration of the call (numbered as **1** in the preceding screenshot)

    ❑   The IP address from where the session had started (numbered as **2** in the preceding screenshot)

    ❑   The SIP address from where the session started (numbered as **3** in the preceding screenshot)

    ❑   The SIP address for whom the session was intended (numbered as **4** in the preceding screenshot)

    ❑   The protocol of the session (usually SIP), the number of protocol packets, and the session status (numbered as **5** in the preceding screenshot)

How it works...

For transferring voice, video, or multimedia, we need two functions to be performed. The first one is to carry the media stream, which is mostly voice or video, and the second one is the signaling, which is to establish and terminate the call, to invite participants to the call, and so on. Two protocol suites were proposed over the years for the signaling:

▸   The **ITU-T** suite of protocols, including **H.323** as an umbrella protocol for the suite, **H.225** for registration and address resolution, **H.245** for control, and some others.

▸   The **IETF** suite of protocols including SIP as a signaling protocol (RFC 3261 with later updates) and **Session Description Protocol** (**SDP**) that describes the session parameters (RFC 4566).

The ITU-T set of protocols phased out in the last few years, and the majority of the applications today are using the IETF set of protocols, on which we will focus in this chapter. In the following diagram you see the structure of the IETF protocol suite.

For the stream transfer, both suites use RTP and RTCP (RFC 3550 with later updates). RTP is used for the media transfer, and RTCP for controlling the quality of the stream.

There are several protocols for transferring multimedia sessions over an IP-based network, as shown in the following diagram:

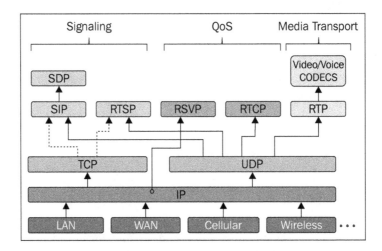

SIP is used for signaling the structured packets that are sent between end clients. **SDP** data is carried by SIP messages for the description of the session. RTSP is used for controlling streams, usually video transmissions (typically IPTV streams).

RTP is used for carrying the media. Above **RTP**, we have various types of codec for voice and video compression.

RTCP is used for controlling the quality of the stream, and RSVP is a protocol for establishing the quality of service through the network.

All these protocols are carried by the TCP/IP protocol suite, as shown in the preceding diagram. Later, you will find in this chapter a detailed description for most of them.

There's more...

SIP uses fixed port numbers; therefore, Wireshark will always refer to these ports as an SIP session—port 5060 for SIP and port 5061 for SIP over TLS (which is SIP secured with TLS). The standard allows using SIP over TCP or UDP, but in the majority of the cases, it will be used over UDP.

RTP and RTCP, on the other hand, do not use standard fixed ports. RTP uses even port numbers, and the corresponding RTCP stream uses the next higher odd port numbers. For example, if RTP uses port 5004 on one end, and port 2006 on the other, RTCP will use ports 5005 and 2007 respectively. This is why Wireshark, by default, will not resolve RTP, RTCP, and such others, but it will show you UDP traffic instead.

To resolve it, you can do the following:

1. Right-click on a packet in the RTP stream (which currently looks like UDP) and click on **Decode as**. In the window that opens, select **RTP**.

2. You can go to **Edit | Preferences**, and from the protocol list, choose **RTP**. In the RTP window, select **Try to decode RTP outside of conversations**, and in most cases, RTP will be decoded automatically in this manner. You can do the same for RTCP.

Analyzing SIP connectivity

As we learned in the previous recipe, **SIP** (RFC 3261 and various extensions) is a signaling protocol that is used for creating, modifying, and terminating user sessions between one or more participants. While sending SIP requests, the session parameters are sent via **SDP** (**SDP**, RFC 4566) which enable users to agree on a set of compatible media types between them. When sessions are created, the voice or video is carried by RTP and optionally controlled by **RTCP** (RTCP is optional, and can be used by multimedia applications, but it is not a mandatory protocol).

SIP defines endpoints as **User Agents** (**UAs**), and the process of creating a session involves UA negotiation in order to agree on a characterization of a session that they would like to create. For additional services such as locating session participants, registration, call forwarding, and others, SIP defines network hosts called **servers** to which UAs can send registrations, invitations to sessions, and other requests.

In this recipe, we will discuss the signaling part of the protocol suite, which is SIP, and how to use Wireshark in order to troubleshoot signaling problems, while in the next recipe, we will learn about **RTP** and **RTCP**.

Problems in voice and video over IP can be categorized in to two groups:

▶ **Problems of call establishment, modification, and termination**: These will be problems such as instances when you pick up the phone and you don't hear a dial tone, you hear the dial tone but cannot dial a number, you dial a number but the other side doesn't get the call, and so on. These types of problems are usually caused by signaling issues.

▶ **Problems of quality:** These are problems related to quality, such as voice quality, disturbances (like noise) during the call, video freezes, and so on, which are usually caused by networking problems, RTP problems, or various types of media issues.

In this recipe, we will discuss the first type, and in the next recipe the second type.

 It is important to note that not all problems in this area are networking problems, and in many cases, they will be a result of bad configuration of the equipment (for example, telephony switches or end devices).

Getting ready

While facing problems of the first type, in most of the cases you are having signaling problems. Connect the Wireshark to the network, and follow the steps in this recipe in order to solve it.

We have two major types of messages in SIP: **methods** and **responses**. Methods are commands initiated by one side of the session, and responses are generated as a reply.

While troubleshooting an SIP session, keep track of the responses and what they say. Only the major types are brought here.

How to do it...

After you've connected Wireshark to the network, follow these steps:

1. When a UA desires to establish a multimedia session, it sends an **INVITE** method to the remote UA. In the following diagram, you can see an example for a basic call flow.

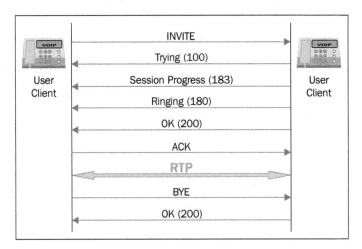

An end device in SIP is called **User Agent** (**UA**). A user agent can initiate or receive a call. A UA can be an IP phone, video camera, software client, or any device or software that participates in an SIP session.

2. In the following screenshot, you see an example for a telephone call flow:

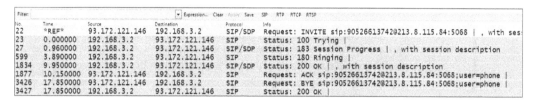

3. To see the detailed call flow, navigate to **Statistics | Flow Graph**, and mark the following:

- ❏ Displayed packets
- ❏ General flow
- ❏ Standard source/destination addresses

The **Graph Analysis** window is shown for reference as follows:

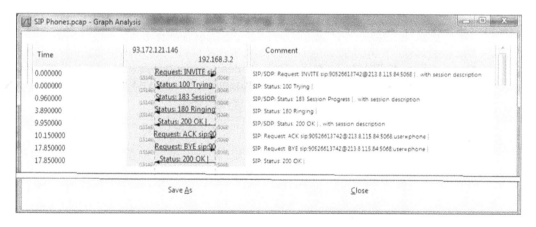

4. After **INVITE**, you should see **Trying, Session Progress, Ringing**, or a combination of them coming from the other side.

5. We can see here how the session progresses between the initiator on **93.172.121.146** to the responder on **192.168.3.2**:

1. The **INVITE** method is sent from the session initiator; this will always be the first packet that starts the conversation.

2. The responder answers with **Trying** (code **100**), **Session progress** (code **183**), and after three seconds with **Ringing** (code **180**). Then it answers with **OK** (code **200**), meaning that the handset was picked up.

> Not all these messages should be there, and in some cases, you will see only some of them, and it is still okay. Later in this chapter, we will see how to find out whether it is a problem or just standard protocol behavior.

3. The initiator sends ACK, and the session is established.

6. If an error message is received at this stage, the connection will not be established.

> Don't forget that SIP works over UDP, and since UDP does not open any connection to the other side before sending the request, it can be possible that a request will not arrive to the destination simply because of a network-reachability problem. For this reason, when you don't get a response, it can be that **INVITE** simply didn't get to the destination because of a network problem.

7. When there is a telephone switch between the user clients, the session will look like the one shown in the following screenshot. You will hear the term IP telephone switch, Call manager, IP PBX, and others. They all mean a telephony switch that handles the signaling between devices. The SIP terms together make up a Proxy that we will talk about in the *How it works...* section of this recipe.

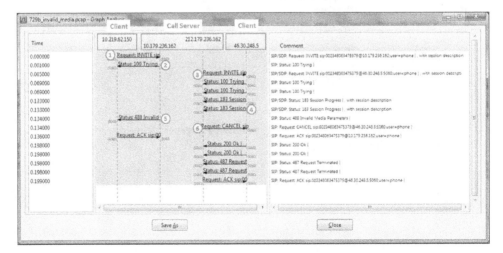

8. Here you see that the switch has two interfaces—the first one on the internal network (**10.179.236.162**), and the second one on the external network (**212.179.236.162**):

    1. The client on the left, **10.219.62.150**, sends an **INVITE** request to the switch (numbered as **1** in the preceding screenshot).

    2. The switch replies by saying that it is **Trying** (numbered as **2** in the preceding screenshot).

    3. The switch sends **INVITE** to the client on the right (numbered as **3** in the preceding screenshot).

    4. The client sends **Trying** (code **100**), and then the session progresses (code **183**) to the switch (numbered as **4** in the preceding screenshot).

    5. After a while, the switch sees that the client has not responded, and to notify the initiator, it sends them code **488**, which means invalid or not acceptable, with an explanation as to why it was not accepted (numbered as **5** in the preceding screenshot).

    6. The switch sends a **Cancel** message to the client on the right (numbered as **6** in the preceding screenshot).

9. To allocate problems in SIP, do the following:

    1. Draw the network with all of its components.

    2. Check for the error codes.

    3. Figure out the reason for the errors.

10. SIP error codes are listed in the following table, along with their possible reasons. Unless mentioned otherwise, codes are defined in RFC 3261.

1xx codes – provisional/informational

The 1xx codes or provisional/informational codes are those where the received request is still in process, and the receiver notifies the sender about it. They are described in detail in the following table:

Code	Event Name	Reason
100	Trying	The request has been received and accepted by the server, and an action is being taken for this call.
180	Ringing	The UA that received the call is alerting the end user. This is the message that is sent back to the client while doing so.
181	Call forward	The call is being forwarded to another destination.

Code	Event Name	Reason
182	Queued	The called party is temporarily unavailable, and the server saves the message for later delivery.
183	Session progress	The session is being handled by the receiving server. Additional details on the call progress can be conveyed in the message header.

2xx codes – success

The 2xx codes or the success codes indicate that the action was successfully received, understood, and accepted. They are described in detail in the following table:

Code	Event Name	Reason
200	Ok	The request has been accepted, processed, and it succeeded.
202	Accepted	The request has been accepted for processing, but the processing of it has not been completed (RFC 3265).

3xx codes – redirection

The 3xx codes indicate that a redirection action needs to be taken in order to complete the request. They are described in detail in the following table:

Code	Event Name	Reason
300	Multiple choices	The address in the request was resolved to several choices, and the accepting server can forward it to one of them. The UA can use the addresses in the contact header field for automatic redirection, or confirm it with the sender before redirecting the message.
301	Moved permanently	The user could not be located at the address in the Request-URI, and the requesting client should try at the address provided in the contact header field. The sender should update its local directories with the change.
302	Moved temporarily	The requesting client should retry the request at the new address/ addresses provided in the contact header field.
305	Use proxy	The requested resource must be accessed through the proxy, whose address is given by the contact field.
380	Alternative service	The call was not successful, so the recipient sends this response for alternative services to be made available on the receiver. These services are described in the message body.

4xx codes – client error

The 4xx codes or client error indicate that the request contains bad syntax or cannot be fulfilled in this server. They are described in detail in the following table:

Code	Event Name	Reason
400	Bad request	The request couldn't be processed due to syntax error.
401	Unauthorized	The request that was received requires user authentication. Usually the client will ask the user for it.
402	Payment required	This is reserved for future use.
403	Forbidden	The server has understood the request, but is refusing to perform it. The client should not try it again.
404	Not found	The server notifies the client that the user does not exist in the domain specified in the Request URI.
405	Method not allowed	A method sent by the client is not allowed to be used by it. The response will include an `allow` header field to notify the sender which methods he is allowed to use.
406	Not acceptable	The resource identified by the request is only capable of generating response entities that have content characteristics not acceptable according to the `accept` header field sent in the request.
407	Proxy authentication required	The client must authenticate with a proxy server.
408	Request timeout	The server couldn't respond during the expected time. The client may send the request again after a while.
410	Gone	The requested resource is no longer available at the server, and the forwarding address is not known. This condition is considered to be permanent.
413	Request entity too large	The server is refusing to process a request because the request entity's body is larger than what the server is able or willing to process.
414	Request-URI too long	The server is refusing to service the request because the Request URI is longer than what the server is able or willing to interpret.
415	Unsupported media type	The server is refusing to process the request because the message body of the request is in a format that is not supported by the server.
416	Unsupported URI scheme	Request URI is unknown to the server, and therefore, the server cannot process the request.

Code	Event Name	Reason
420	Bad extension	The server did not understand the protocol extension received from the client.
421	Extension required	The UA that received the request requires a particular extension in order to process it, but this extension is not listed in the supported header field of the request.
423	Interval too brief	The server is rejecting the request because the expiration time of the resource refreshed by the request is too short.
424	Bad location information	This response code indicates a rejection of the request due to its location contents. This indicates malformed or not satisfactory location information (RFC6442).
428	Use Identity header	It is sent when a verifier receives an SIP request that lacks an Identity header in order to indicate that the request should be re-sent with an Identity header (RFC4474).
429	Provide referrer identity	This provides referrer identity (RFC3892).
433	Anonymity disallowed	This indicates that the server refused to satisfy the request because the requestor was anonymous (RFC5079).
436	Bad identity info	This response is used when there is bad information in the Identity-Info header (RFC4474).
437	Unsupported certificate	This is used when the verifier cannot validate the certificate referenced by the URI in the Identity-Info header (RFC4474).
438	Invalid identity header	This is used when the verifier (the receiver UA) receives a message with an Identity signature that does not correspond to the digest-string calculated by the verifier (RFC4474).
470	Consent needed	This is the response to a request that contained a URI list in which at least one URI was such that the relay had no access permissions (RFC5360).
480	Temporarily unavailable	The callee's end system was contacted successfully, but the callee is currently unavailable.
481	Call/ transaction does not exist	The receiving UA received a request that does not match any existing transaction or dialog.
482	Loop detected	The server has detected a loop.
483	Too many hops	The server received a request that contains a Max-Forwards header field that equals zero.
484	Address incomplete	The server received a request with an incomplete Request-URI.

Code	Event Name	Reason
485	Ambiguous	The Request-URI was unclear. The response may contain a listing of possible addresses in the Contact header fields.
486	Busy here	The callee's end system was contacted successfully, but the callee is currently unable or unwilling to take additional calls by this end system.
487	Request terminated	The request was terminated by a BYE or CANCEL request.
488	Not acceptable here	Specific resources addressed by the Request-URI are not accepted.
491	Request pending	The receiving UA had a pending request.
493	Undecipherable	The request contains an encrypted MIME body, which cannot be decrypted by the recipient.

5xx codes – server error

The 5xx codes or server error codes indicate that the server failed to fulfill an apparently valid request. They are described in detail in the following table:

Code	Event Name	Reason
500	Server internal error	An unexpected condition prevented the server from fulfilling the request.
501	Not implemented	The functionality that requested to fulfill the request is not supported by the server.
502	Bad gateway	A gateway or proxy received an invalid response from the downstream server it accessed while attempting to fulfill the request.
503	Service unavailable	The server is temporarily unable to process the request due to temporary overloading or maintenance of the server.
504	Server time out	The server processing the request has sent the request to another server in order to process it, and the response did not arrive on time.
505	Version not supported	The server does not support the SIP protocol version that is used in the request.
513	Message too large	The server was unable to process the request since the message length is too long.

6xx codes – global failure

The 6xx codes or global failure codes indicate that the request cannot be fulfilled at any server. They are described in detail in the following table:

Code	Event Name	Reason
600	Busy everywhere	The recipient's end system was contacted successfully, but the user is busy and does not wish to take the call at this moment.
603	Decline	The receiving UA was successfully contacted, but the user explicitly does not wish to or cannot participate.
604	Does not exist anywhere	The server has authoritative information that the user indicated in the Request URI, which does not exist anywhere.
606	Not acceptable	The US was contacted successfully, but some aspects of the session description described by SDP were not acceptable.

How it works...

SIP is an application-layer control protocol that is used to establish, maintain, and terminate calls between two or more end nodes.

SIP defines two basic classes of network entities—clients and servers:

- ▶ A client is an entity (or application) that sends SIP requests
- ▶ A server is an entity (or application) that responds to those requests

For connectivity to other network types, we have gateways. A gateway connects between SIP and **Public Switched Telephone Networks** (**PSTN**), or SIP and H.323.

As illustrated in the following diagram, a client is made of **User Agent Client** (**UAC**) and **User Agent Server** (**UAS**), and each client can initiate or respond to requests.

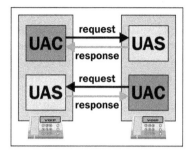

SIP servers can be of various types:

▸ **Proxy Server**: This receives SIP requests from a user agent or another proxy and forwards or proxies the request to another location

▸ **Redirect Server**: This receives requests from a user agent or proxy, and returns a redirection response (3xx), indicating where the request should be present

▸ **Registrar**: This receives SIP registration requests and updates the user agent information to a location service or other database

In the following diagram, you see how they all fit together:

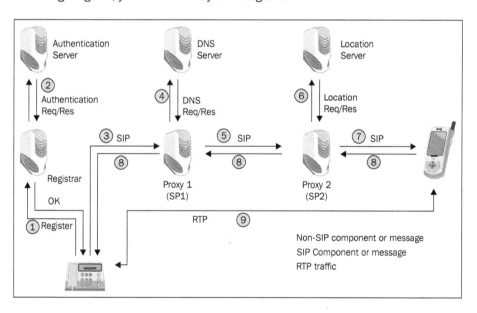

An IP phone registers to the registrar (**1**). The registrar checks with the organization server (**2**), and if it's all OK, it sends an SIP request to the provider's proxy (**3**). The provider's proxy checks with the DNS server for the IP address of the requested client's domain (**4**), and then it forwards the requests to the destination proxy (**5**). The destination proxy sees that the client is not in its place and checks with the location server for its location (**6**). When found, the SIP request is forwarded to the destination client (**7**). The destination client confirms the acceptance of the request to the sender (**8**). When all is okay, an RTP session is opened on the UDP ports described in SDP when opening the session (**9**).

The SIP message is built as you see in the following diagram:

```
1    0.000000   10.219.62.200   10.179.236.114   SIP/SDP   Request: INVITE sip:9714352409910.179.236.114;user=phone
2    0.000010   10.219.62.200   10.179.236.114   SIP/SDP   Request: INVITE sip:9714352409910.179.236.114;user=phone
3    0.000449   10.179.236.114  10.219.62.200    SIP       Status: 100 Trying |

Frame 1: 807 bytes on wire (6456 bits), 807 bytes captured (6456 bits)
Ethernet II, Src: Cisco_e4:4b:ff (00:0d:bc:e4:4b:ff), Dst: AcmePack_fa:68:c1 (00:08:25:fa:68:c1)
Internet Protocol Version 4, Src: 10.219.62.200 (10.219.62.200), Dst: 10.179.236.114 (10.179.236.114)
User Datagram Protocol, Src Port: sip (5060), Dst Port: sip (5060)
Session Initiation Protocol (INVITE)
  Request-Line: INVITE sip:9714352409910.179.236.114;user=phone SIP/2.0              ┐
    Method: INVITE                                                                   ├─ Request
    Request-URI: sip:9714352409910.179.236.114;user=phone                           │
    [Resent Packet: False]                                                           ┘
  Message Header                                                                     ┐
    Call-ID: 6998686179937202994-1341127643-24746                                    │
    From: <sip:01010@sipgw49.com;user=phone>;tag=6998686179937202994                 │
    To: <sip:9714352409910.179.236.114;user=phone>                                   │
    Content-Type: application/sdp                                                    │
    CSeq: 1 INVITE                                                                   │
    Via: SIP/2.0/UDP 10.219.62.200:5060;branch=z9hG4bK-612054000197b332-c072451b-1   ├─ Message header
    Contact: <sip:01010@10.219.62.200:5060;user=phone>                               │
    Allow: INVITE,CANCEL,BYE,ACK,REFER,UPDATE,INFO,PRACK                             │
    Supported: timer,100rel                                                          │
    Max-Forwards: 8                                                                  │
    Content-Length: 246                                                              ┘
  Message Body                                                                       ┐
    Session Description Protocol                                                     │
      Session Description Protocol Version (v): 0                                    │
      Owner/Creator, Session Id (o): - 1341127643 1341127643 IN IP4 192.115.185.144 │
      Session Name (s): -                                                           │
      Connection Information (c): IN IP4 192.115.185.144                            │
      Time Description, active time (t): 0 0                                        ├─ Message body (SDP)
      Media Description, name and address (m): audio 44714 RTP/AVP 18 8 0 101       │
      Media Attribute (a): rtpmap:18 G729/8000                                      │
      Media Attribute (a): rtpmap:8 PCMA/8000                                       │
      Media Attribute (a): rtpmap:0 PCMU/8000                                       │
      Media Attribute (a): rtpmap:101 telephone-event/8000                          │
      Media Attribute (a): fmtp:101 0-15                                            ┘
```

The first part is the **Request** line in which we have:

- The method; **INVITE** in this case
- The requested URI

The second part is **Message Header**, in which we have:

- **Call-ID**: This provides a unique ID for the call
- **From**: This indicates the initiator of the call
- **To**: This indicates the destination of the call

- ▶ **CSeq**: This contains the sequence number, which contains an integer followed by the request method. Each successive request during the call will have a higher CSeq number, and the caller and called parties each maintain their own separate CSeq counts.

- ▶ **Via**: This indicates the path taken by the request so far and indicates the path that should be followed in routing responses.

- ▶ **Contact**: This contains one or more SIP URIs that provide the other party in the session with information for contacting the initiating user

- ▶ **Allow**: This indicates which methods are allowed

- ▶ **Supported**: This indicates whether parameters such as timers are supported

- ▶ **Max-Forwards**: This is the maximum number of hops to pass to the destination

- ▶ **Content-Length**: This is the byte count of the message body

- ▶ **Message Body**: This contains information on the codecs that are supported by the sender; for example, timers supported

There's more...

When debugging a phone call, first filter the call with the **Call-ID** parameter. To do so, you can do one of the following:

- ▶ Look for the **Call-ID** parameter in the **Message Header** field in the SIP header, right-click on it, and select **Apply as Filter**, as illustrated in the following screenshot

- ▶ Use the **VoIP Calls** feature from the Wireshark menu

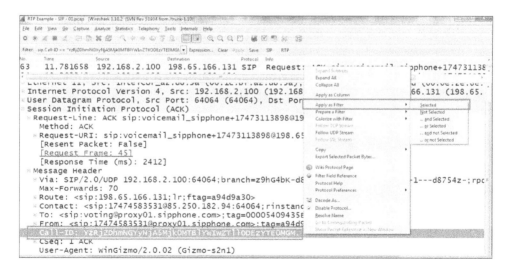

When debugging an SIP trunk that is signaling between IP PBXs, try to figure out whether there is there a specific call that doesn't work or whether all calls have the same problem.

To troubleshoot VoIP calls, the best way is to read the SIP messages. They will tell you what to do.

Analyzing RTP/RTCP connectivity

In the previous recipe, we talked about signaling, that is, SIP and RDP. In this recipe, we will see how to use the voice or video call itself and see what might go wrong with it.

It will always start with a user complaining about voice or video quality, low speech quality, noises, and so on.

Also, don't forget that it might look like everything works fine in Wireshark, but further tuning of the IP PBX should be done say to increase the transmit volume.

Getting ready

When facing problems on a specific client, connect Wireshark to the client port with a port mirror. When facing problems with all clients connected to the same link, connect Wireshark to the link with a port mirror.

How to do it...

To locate performance problems, follow these steps:

1. After you connect Wireshark with a port mirror, start the capture.

2. Make sure there are calls running.

3. From the **Telephony** menu, navigate to **RTP | Show All Streams**. This will show you all RTP streams running on the port that you are monitoring.

4. The following window will open:

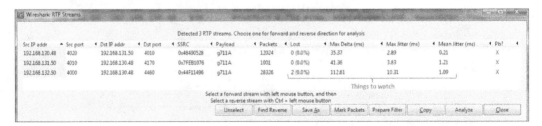

5. Parameters that are important to watch are the packets lost, **Max Delta (ms)**, **Max Jitter (ms)**, and **Mean Jitter (ms)**.

Delay values higher than 300 ms (RTT) and Jitter values higher than 50 ms are considered to be problematic for interactive voice and video over IP. Further discussion on this subject is in the *How it works...* section in this recipe.

In the case of delay, follow these steps to locate the problem:

1. Use a simple ping test to check the delay between the two ends of the network:

    1. When you see a high delay, check if it is typical to the communications line that you are measuring (see a list of typical delays in the *There's more...* section in this recipe).

    2. If it is a typical delay, you don't have anything to do here. Check with the phone and switch providers for tuning solutions for their equipment.

    3. If you have a longer delay than expected, ping the two phones from your laptop and check where the delay came from.

    4. When you locate the link with the higher delay, ping in a step-by-step manner along the link to see where the delay came from.

    5. In parallel, use Wireshark to check the load on the line. The delay can come from there, and in most of these cases, you will have Jitter coming with it.

2. Delay can come from the following sources as well:

    ❑ **Congested link**: Check the case using Wireshark.

    ❑ **Load on a router**: Use provider tools, SNMP tools, or router CLI to measure load on these devices (use the provider manuals). It can be CPU load, memory load, and so on.

    ❑ **Queuing delay on routers buffers**: Check the vendor manuals.

In the case of Jitter, follow these steps to locate the problem:

1. Use the same methodology as in the delay measurement and try to figure out where the Jitter comes from.

2. Jitter can come from several sources:

    ❑ **Congested line**: Check the line with a `ping` command to see if you have any problems here

    ❑ **Load on a router (CPU/memory)**: Check the vendor manuals to see how you can monitor these parameters

In the case of packet loss, follow these steps to locate the problem:

1. Check using the `ping` command to see if there is a packet loss across the link.

2. If so, check the equipment along the way to see for packet losses.

3. You can also click on a specific RTP packet in the packet list window and then navigate to **RTP | Stream Analysis**. It will show you the parameters on the stream that the packet is a part of. The following window will open:

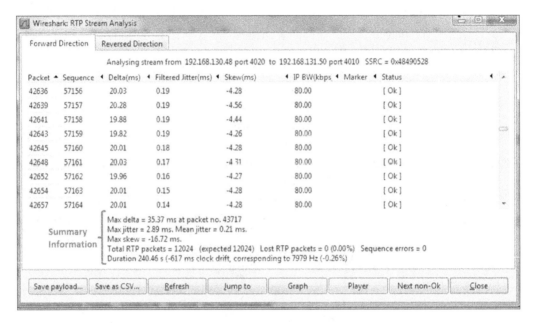

4. In the window, you will see the following parameters on the stream that you've opened:

   - **Packet**: This parameter denotes the number of packets in the captured file.

   - **Sequence**: This parameter denotes the RTP sequence number.

   - **Delta (ms)**: This is the time difference between the current and previous packet in the stream.

   - **Filtered Jitter (ms)**: This parameter refers to the difference between the real arrival time and the RTP timestamp parameter. It should be as low as possible and preferably zero.

- ❏ **Skew (ms)**: This parameter denotes how early (or late) the packet is in relation to where it was supposed to be. For example, if we have a packet rate of 20 packets per second, we should have 50 ms between packets, and if a packet arrives 49 ms after the previous one, it will be a skew of -1 ms.

- ❏ **IP BW (kbps)**: This parameter refers to the bandwidth consumption at the IP level that is with all headers down to layer 3.

- ❏ **Marker**: This parameter denotes whether the marker is SET (SET=1, UNSET=0). A marker indicates various phenomena such as end of silence period and end of video frame, and is added by the application.

- ❏ **Status**: This parameter lets you check whether the status is **OK**.

5. From the **Summary Information** window, we can see a maximum Jitter of **2.89 ms**; this is very low, so we should not expect any problems here.

6. Clicking on the **Graph** button in the middle of the lower part of the **RTP Stream Analysis** window will open the following IO Graph:

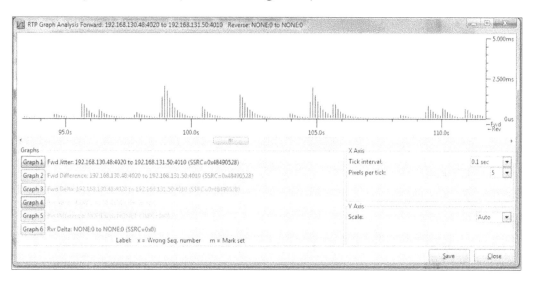

7. In this case, we see that the network looks great—the Jitter is less than **2.500 ms**.

8. When we use Wireshark and it looks like all the parameters measured in the previous points are OK, the problem in connectivity is a probably configuration problem in the equipment itself.

9. You might see some problems such as wrong sequences and timestamps (see the following screenshot). These errors usually occur due to Jitter and delay problems.

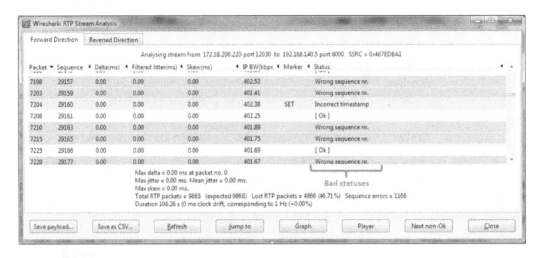

How it works...

RTP is used in conjunction with RTCP (both were first standardized in RFC 3550). RTP is used to carry the media streams (audio and video), and RTCP is used to monitor transmission statistics and quality of service. While establishing a session, RTP uses even port numbers, whereas RTCP uses the next corresponding odd port number (higher by one).

RTP provides mechanisms for timing recovery, loss detection and correction, payload and source identification, and media synchronization.

RTCP specifies reports that are exchanged between the source and destination of the session. Reports contain statistics such as the number of RTP-PDUs sent, the number of RTP-PDUs lost, inter-arrival Jitter, and so on. These reports can be used by applications to modify the sender's transmission rates and for diagnostic purposes.

RTP principles of operation

RTP lies over UDP, which lies over IP. In the following diagram, you see the RTP packet structure:

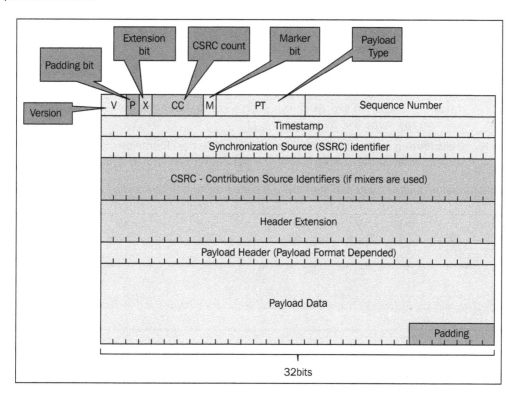

The fields in the header are as follows:

- **Version (V)**: This field indicates the RTP version

- **Padding (P)**: This field indicates that the packet contains one or more additional padding bytes at the end that are not part of the payload

- **Extension bit (X)**: This field indicates a fixed header that follows the standard header

- **CSRC count (CC)**: This field contains the number of CSRC fields that follow the fixed header

- ▸ **Marker (M)**: This field is used to indicate application events, for example video frame boundaries

- ▸ **Payload type**: This field identifies the format of the RTP payload to be interpreted by the receiving application

- ▸ **Sequence number**: This field is incremented by one for each RTP packet sent. Used by the receiver to detect packet losses

- ▸ **Timestamp**: This field reflects the sampling rate of octets in the RTP data stream

- ▸ **Synchronization source (SSRC)**: This field is the stream identifier that is chosen randomly, so that no two synchronization sources within the same RTP session will have the same SSRC identifier

- ▸ **Contributing source identifiers list (CSRC)**: This field identifies the contributing sources (that is, the stream source) for the payload contained in this packet

In the following diagram, you can see how the sequence and timestamps mechanisms work:

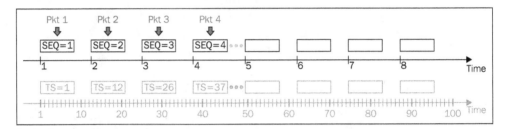

As we can see in the diagram, the sequence numbers are increased by one for each RTP packet transmitted, while timestamps increase by the time covered by a packet. Packet number 1, for example, will have both set to 1; packet 2 will have a sequence number of 2 and a timestamp of 12; it goes on in this manner for the other packets. The receiver will receive the sequence numbers that tell him the order of the packets, and timestamps that tell him the time at which they left the receiver. The receiver will use both to play back the received data.

The RTCP principle of operation

RTCP has several report types, in which the sender and receiver update each other on the data that was sent and received. In the following diagram, you can see an example of this, in which we see a sender report that tells the receiver how many packets and octets were sent, timestamp information, and other parameters that can be used by the receiver.

```
File Edit View Go Capture Analyze Statistics Telephony Tools Internals Help

Filter:                                          ▼ Expression... Clear Apply Save  SIP  RTP
No.          Time          Source              Destination          Protocol  Info
13014        89.845598     212.179.237.161     37.26.146.90         RTCP      Sender Report     Source
```
```
 Frame 13014: 138 bytes on wire (1104 bits), 138 bytes captured (1104 bits)
 Ethernet II, Src: AcmePack_fa:60:80 (00:08:25:fa:60:80), Dst: All-HSRP-routers_1f
 Internet Protocol Version 4, Src: 212.179.237.161 (212.179.237.161), Dst: 37.26.14
 User Datagram Protocol, Src Port: 60131 (60131), Dst Port: 43555 (43555)
 Real-time Transport Control Protocol (Sender Report)
   [Stream setup by SDP (frame 12022)]
   10.. .... = Version: RFC 1889 Version (2)
   ..0. .... = Padding: False
   ...0 0001 = Reception report count: 1
   Packet type: Sender Report (200)
   Length: 12 (52 bytes)
   Sender SSRC: 0x49424f58 (1229082456)
   Timestamp, MSW: 3550373021 (0xd39e649d)  ⎤
   Timestamp, LSW: 1766374618 (0x6948bcda)  ⎬ Timestamp information
   [MSW and LSW as NTP timestamp: Jul  4, 2012 06:43:41.411266000 UTC]
   RTP timestamp: 87538356
   Sender's packet count: 246   ⎤
   Sender's octet count: 4920   ⎦ Packets/Octets information
 ▸ Source 1
 Real-time Transport Control Protocol (Source description)
 Real-time Transport Control Protocol (Goodbye)
```

There's more...

Delay can come from several sources:

▸ **Coding delay**: This is the delay that comes from the digital processing of the voice signals.

▸ **Handling delay (packetization)**: This delay is the time that it takes to build packets and insert voice information into them.

▸ **Serialization delay**: This is the fixed delay that occurs when sending packets over the communication line. This delay depends on packet size and line speed.

▶ **Typical delays (round trip)**: This is the delay that you can expect when pinging over a communication line (all the following points refer to unloaded lines):

  ❑ **Over a LAN**: The delay is less than 1 ms.

  ❑ **Over a WAN connection**: The delay is 1-2 ms in a short-range connection (up to 250-300 km / 150-190 miles) and about 15-20 ms in long range connections (for example, US coast to coast). In older networks you can add several tens of milliseconds to these numbers.

  ❑ **For home connections, usually xDSL or CaTV**: The delay is somewhere between 10 and 25 ms.

  ❑ **For inter-continent connections**: The delay is somewhere between 100 and 200 ms.

  ❑ **For cellular connections**: The delay ranges from 300 ms to 600 ms for old 2.5G networks (GPRS or CDMA 1X), 120 to 150 ms for 3.0G (UMTS or EVDO), 60 to 100 ms for HSDPA, HSUPA, and HSPA+, and goes down to 20 to 50 ms for LTE networks.

  ❑ **For satellite communications**: The delay is 500 to 600 ms.

The delay over a communication line is the sum of the time that it takes the light signal to cross the distance and time consumed by switching or routing delays on the service provider network. While technologies since the early 2000s (for example, MPLS or Carrier Ethernet) are implemented fast switches and routers, technologies older than 2000 (such as Frame Relay or ATM) have slower switching times and therefore will have higher delays.

Troubleshooting scenarios for video and surveillance applications

In the last 10 to 12 years, security and surveillance systems have taken on a larger and more important role in communications networks. The problems we might see in these types of networks will usually start from video freezes due to lack of bandwidth but can also be much more complicated as will be discussed in this recipe. In this recipe we will discuss some of the problems with these systems and how to approach and solve them.

Getting ready

Usually, you will be called to solve problems that users experience when watching security cameras. In this case, you can port mirror the specific camera (**1**), the communication line in the remote site (**2**), and a camera server (**3**), or you can monitor the central line with a filter to the remote network (**4**).

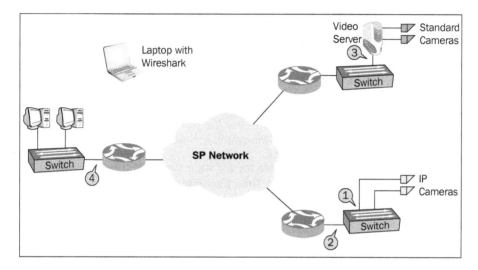

How to do it...

To identify problems in this network, follow these steps:

1. First, if possible, port mirror a connection between the viewer and a locally connected camera (over the LAN). When doing so, you will be able to note the required bandwidth for every picture resolution you try.

> When watching a video, the bandwidth can start at 128 Kbps for a very basic black-and-white movie at a low resolution, average around 0.5 to 1.0 mbps for a black-and-white or colored video stream at a reasonable resolution, and go up to several megabits per second for high definition streaming (usually at 6 to 8 mbps).

2. As a basic—make sure your bandwidth is sufficient.

   ❏ When viewing freezes, use IO graphs to monitor the bandwidth. Make sure you have enough bandwidth and the line is not completely loaded.

   ❏ To make sure you are watching only the bandwidth consumed by the camera or camera server, configure a filter to its IP address.

[Video streaming can be transferred over UDP and RTP or over TCP. UDP is mostly used for interactive applications, while TCP is mostly used for watching remote cameras.]

3. Make sure you don't have any packet losses or significant delays or Jitter.

   ❏ For packet losses, log in to the communications equipment or use SNMP

   ❏ For delay and Jitter, you can use the `ping` command or graphical utilities (many of them are free, for example, from Colasoft)

4. While monitoring a remote camera feed, if you have short freezes, navigate to **Statistics | TCP Stream Graph | Time Sequence (Stevens)**. Make sure all I and P frames are received at constant intervals.

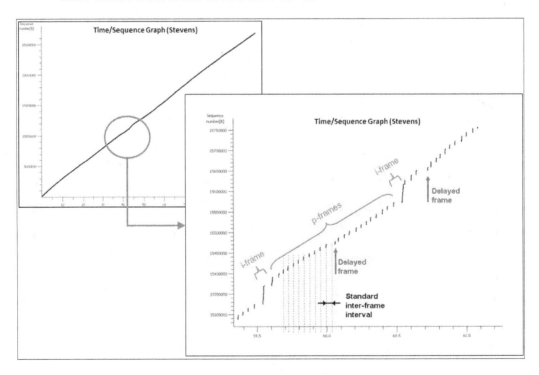

5. The problem here is that there were cameras in the customer sites that transmitted the video to a central server and the central server transmits it to the monitors. What we see in the preceding graph is the server delayed some of the **p-frames** and that was the reason for the short freezes in that case. It turned out to be a software problem on the server.

6. When trying to log in to a camera server, several ports may be in use and you may not get the picture; or it may so happen that you get the picture but something else does not appear. To verify that all TCP port numbers are open, you can do this:

   ❏ Look at the firewall (if there is one between you and the camera server) if connections were blocked

   ❏ In Wireshark, make sure you don't get any **triple SYN**, which indicates that something is blocking your access to the server

7. In the following screenshot, you see how the HTTP session (**1**) is running between the internal office address **10.0.0.3** and the external address of the web camera **82.82.182.182** (don't use these; they are just sample values). In the line **2614**, you see a **SYN** packet is sent from **10.0.0.3** to **82.82.182.182**; this packet is blocked in packet **2615** via the **TCP RST** (reset) PDU (**2**). The same event occurs twice more (**3** and **4**). The fact that you see one established connection does not mean that there are no other connections being attempted.

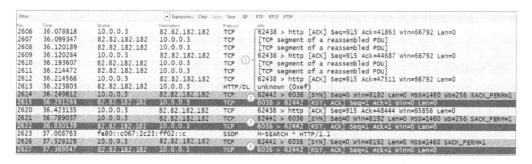

8. In this case, the HTTP connection had connectivity to the web server. To log in, another connection was opened. Since the log in connection was blocked, it was possible to see the camera server but not to log in to it and watch the video.

How it works...

Video streams are made of **I-frames** (Intra-coded frames), **P-frames** (Predicted frames), and **B-frames** (Bi-predictive frames). I-frames are frames that contain the full picture, while P-frames contain changes from the previous one. There are also B-frames, which also use prediction mechanism for the next frame.

In TCP, each video frame, I, P, or B, is divided between several TCP packets; therefore, when you have TCP problems (retransmissions and others) it can directly influence the video stream.

There's more...

The quality of video transmission depends on the codec that you are using, number of frames per second that are transmitted, time interval between frames, and more parameters that can be configured in the camera or on the camera server. Make sure you've set all parameters correctly to get a good picture.

Troubleshooting scenarios for IPTV applications

IPTV applications have become more and more popular over the last few years, while more and more TV stations are moving to the Internet. E-learning applications are also more popular along with various types of other applications.

Basically, IPTV applications use TCP, and the problems you will face are mostly TCP problems, such as retransmissions. In this recipe we will see some examples.

Getting ready

When getting complaints about quality of video, freezes, and so on, connect the instance of Wireshark that has a port mirror to the device or the link that connects you to the network.

How to do it...

Start the capture and go through these steps:

1. Open the IO graph and verify that you have buffering type of traffic, as illustrated in the following screenshot:

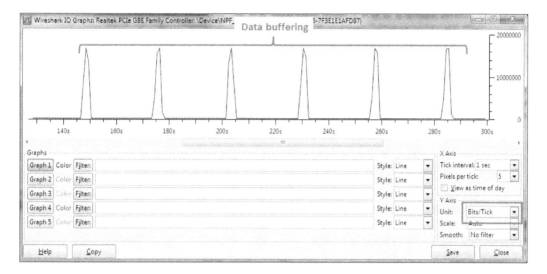

2. If you see that the line is blocked at the top, check your bandwidth to the Internet and tune the viewer accordingly (it's usually done automatically).

3. Check for TCP retransmissions, duplicate ACKs, and TCP window problems, and if you find any, go through it to find what is disturbing the transmission.

How it works...

From the network point of view, IPTV is not more than a simple application that runs over a TCP connection.

There's more...

When troubleshooting problems on it, go through the regular TCP troubleshooting procedures described in *Chapter 9, UDP/TCP Analysis*.

Troubleshooting scenarios for video conferencing applications

Video conferencing uses the same protocols as standard telephony, but there is a difference: while in telephony we have one stream of data in each direction, we have a stream of data and a stream of video in video conferencing. When you capture data on the end device, you will see four streams of data: two streams that you send to the other side and two streams of data that are sent back to you.

Another difference is that some video conference applications are still using the H.323 protocol suite, so instead of troubleshooting SIP problems, you will have to troubleshoot H.225 and H.245 connectivity issues. Due to the fact that most applications use SIP and the IETF protocol stack, we will focus on them only.

Getting ready

To troubleshoot a problem in your video conference system, connect the instance of Wireshark with port mirror to the device or to the link to the devices that are functioning badly.

How to do it...

What you will get for every conference will be as in the following screenshot:

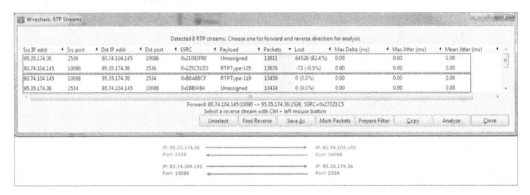

1. As you can see in the screenshot, there are two streams of data in each direction.

2. On one of them (the first one), we see massive degradation in performance.

3. To focus on it, click on the stream, and then click on **Analyze**.

4. The following window will open:

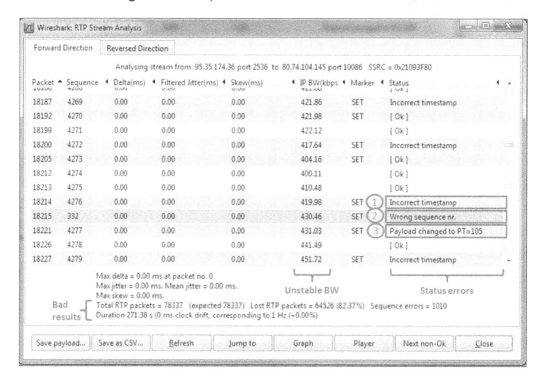

5. In the preceding screenshot, you see that there are many errors, the bandwidth is unstable, and there are many error statuses:

    ❑ Incorrect timestamp (**1**) and wrong sequence number (**2**) are caused by a communication line with high Jitter

    ❑ Payload change (**3**) occurs when the system on the sender's side changes the codec to a better one to fit into the channel

6. There was a problem here simply because this was a video conference call over an unstable cellular connection.

Troubleshooting RTSP

RTSP is an application-layer control protocol that is used for the control of a single or multiple time-synchronized streams of continuous media such as audio and video. The purpose of RTSP is to provide control over remote media servers. It is used when we click on **Play**, **Pause**, and so on, and can be used also to invite a new media server for viewing on the screen, for example, for a conference. While RTSP is the control protocol, the streaming itself is usually carried out by RTP—which carries the data—and RTCP —used for the monitoring of the data transfer.

The RTSP standard (RFC2326) does not define any transport protocol, but most implementations use TCP. RTSP is commonly used while watching IPTV. In this recipe we will learn how to monitor and troubleshoot these streams.

Getting ready

RTSP monitoring should be used in cases in which you experience transmission disturbances; for example, problems with the media player control or cases with connectivity problems to a server. RTSP works as illustrated in the following diagram:

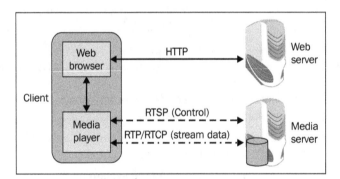

When monitoring a stream, we can have problems with RTP/RTCP (discussed earlier in the chapter), HTTP (discussed in *Chapter 10, HTTP and DNS*), or even TCP problems (discussed in *Chapter 9, UDP/TCP Analysis*). In this recipe we will talk about RTSP (the center line with long dashes in the preceding diagram).

The web server and the media servers can be on single or multiple physical servers, or on different virtual machines. The functionality in any case is as presented.

How to do it...

To find problems with RTSP, connect the instance of Wireshark with port mirror to the client experiencing the problems, and in the case of multiple clients, connect it to a mutual link or to the server.

1. To view all RTSP traffic, filter the packets with TCP port 554; the filter for this is `tcp.port==554`.

    The filter `tcp.port == 554` gives us all traffic over this port, while filter `rtsp` only gives us packets in which Wireshark is recognized as an RTSP header.

2. To view RTSP requests and responses, navigate to **RTSP | Packet Counter** from the **Statistics** menu as described earlier in this chapter. Error responses are those with code values that are higher than 400.

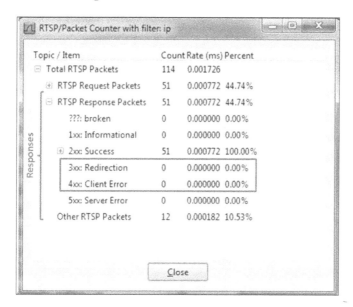

3. Look for RTSP response codes that are 4xx or higher. To do so, you can configure the display filter `rtsp.status >= 400`.

How it works...

As with SIP (which is used for signaling, while RTP is used for the transport of the media), the streams controlled by RTSP may use any transport protocol; in many cases, they also use RTP. The protocol is intentionally similar in syntax and operation to HTTP and uses the same syntax.

The most common RTSP methods (commands) are (C-Client, S-Server):

Command	Direction	Function
OPTIONS	C to S or S to C	Determines capabilities of server/client
DESCRIBE	C to S	Gets description of media stream
ANNOUNCE	C to S or S to C	Announces a new session's description
SETUP	C to S	Creates a media session
PLAY	C to S	Starts media delivery
RECORD	C to S	Starts media recording
PAUSE	C to S	Pauses media delivery
REDIRECT	S to C	Redirects to another server
TEARDOWN	S to C	Performs immediate teardown

The response categories are:

Code series	Type	Meaning
1xx	Informational	Request received, continue with processing
2xx	Success	The action was successfully received, understood, and accepted
3xx	Redirection	Further action must be taken in order to complete the request
4xx	Client error	The request contains bad syntax or cannot be fulfilled
5xx	Server error	The server failed to fulfill an apparently valid request

There's more...

In the following screenshot you see a typical RTSP stream:

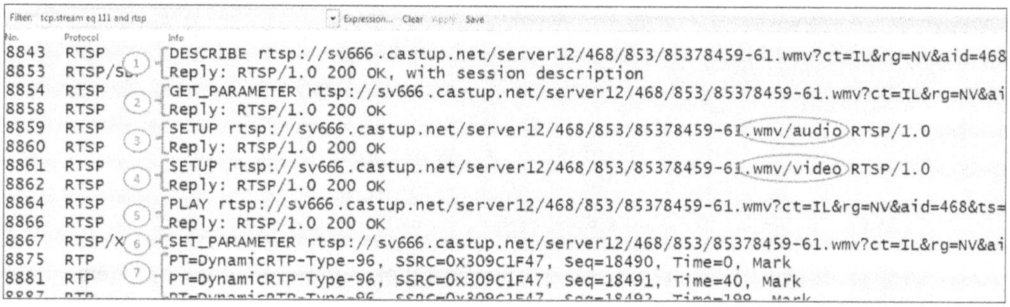

The typical RTSP stream is processed in the following order:

1. A **DESCRIBE** request is sent to the server, asking to retrieve the description of a presentation or media object identified by the request URL from that server, and the server replies with **200 OK**.

2. A **GET_PARAMETER** request retrieves the parameter value of a presentation or stream specified in the URI.

3. A **SETUP** request is sent to open the audio stream and is confirmed with **200 OK**.

4. A **SETUP** request is sent to open the audio stream and is confirmed with **200 OK**.

5. A **PLAY** request is sent to the server to start playing the stream.

6. A **SET_PARAMETER** request is sent to the server to set a parameter value for a presentation or stream specified by the URI.

7. The stream starts to play with RTP.

In the following screenshot, we see how the stream is broken down:

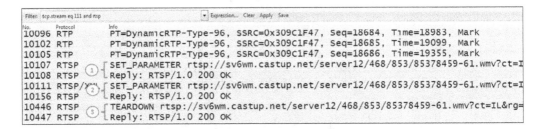

The process for the breakdown of the stream is as follows:

1. **SET_PARAMETER** is sent to the server to set a parameter value for a presentation or stream specified by the URI.

2. A second **SET_PARAMETER** request is sent to the server.

3. The **TEARDOWN** command is sent to close the connection.

13
Troubleshooting Bandwidth and Delay Problems

In this chapter we have the following recipes:

- ▸ Measuring total bandwidth on a communication link
- ▸ Measuring bandwidth and throughput per user and per application over a network connection
- ▸ Monitoring jitter and delay using Wireshark
- ▸ Discovering delay/jitter-related application problems

Introduction

When measuring communication lines, there are four major parameters that we should be aware of: **bandwidth**, **delay**, **jitter**, and **packet loss**. While there are applications that require high bandwidth, there are other applications that are more sensitive to delay and jitter. Packet loss can influence all types of applications, but there are applications that are more sensitive to it and some that are less.

In this chapter we will learn how to measure these parameters, how to check for network problems caused by it, and how to solve them when possible.

Measuring total bandwidth on a communication link

In this recipe, we will see how to measure the total bandwidth over a communication line. The first thing of course is to verify the communication line with the service provider. Check whether it is a symmetric or an asymmetric line, and if it is asymmetric, check what the bandwidth is in both directions.

Getting ready

There are two cases that you might need to test:

▶ When you measure a communication line between two offices: in this case connect your laptop (or any PC on the network) to the LAN, and verify whether you have a server or another PC on the other side of the line

▶ When you measure a communication line to the Internet, make sure you have a testing server on the **Service Provider** (**SP**) side or on the **Internet Service Provider** (**ISP**) side

How to do it...

To check the bandwidth on a communication line, follow these steps:

1. Ask for the following details:

    1. Ask the SP what the line bandwidth is.

    2. If it is a line to the Internet, in addition to the preceding step ask the ISP what is the bandwidth to the Internet.

2. Locate a server, a PC, or a laptop on the remote location.

When using a PC or laptop for the test, don't forget that the PC itself should be strong enough to generate the traffic. A standard Windows 7 is able to generate around 200 Mbps per TCP connection, and when opening several connections, you can get into other limitations such as disk performance and so on. Therefore, it is recommended to try the transfer first on a LAN, where there are no bandwidth limits (practically), and only then to test the SP or the ISP lines. If you are using FTP, use an efficient one (FileZilla, for example). The best way of course is to use test equipment, if it's available. Dedicated test equipments are available from many vendors such as VeEX, Fluke Networks, and IXIA.

❑ In case you want to test the bandwidth between two sites, download and then upload a big file between nodes numbered as **1** and **2** or between nodes numbered as **1** and **3**. A file big enough should load the line for a significant amount of time, that is, a minute or more. For example, if you want to test a 10 Mbps (Megabits per second) line, use a file of at least 10/8 = 1.25 MB (Megabytes).

❑ In case you want to test your connection to the Internet, usually you can perform the test on your service provider (numbered as **1** to **4** in the following diagram), and then to your Internet service provider (numbered as **1** to **5** in the following diagram).

> If possible, it is better to use the IP or UDP test, since when you copy a file, it is done over TCP, so you can get into TCP issues that influence the test. For this purpose, use **Iperf** or another testing tool that can generate IP or UDP traffic.

In the following illustration, you can see two local networks connected via a **Service Provider** (**SP**) line. The site on the left is connected to the Internet through a firewall. The connection to the Internet goes through the Service Provider (**SP**, **Server 4**) to the **Internet Service Provider** (**ISP**, **Server 5**).

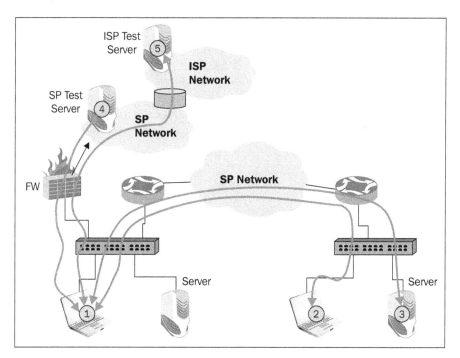

Follow these steps to measure the bandwidth over the communication lines:

1. Use Wireshark **Statistics | IO Graphs** for the test.

 Don't forget that Wireshark has its own limitations when working with high bandwidth lines. In this case, you can configure it to use multiples files. Personally, I prefer to use other tools (**Omnipeek**, for example) when monitoring lines of 200-300 Mbps and higher.

2. When testing your enterprise network, you can use software tools such as Iperf (`http://sourceforge.net/projects/iperf/`).

Following are the steps to measure network bandwidth with IPerf:

1. Install Iperf on both ends of the connection.

2. Configure one side as a client, and the other side as a server.

3. Start the test and use I/O Graphs to verify that you have a stable bandwidth.

 When downloading or uploading a file, do it with a single large file and not a directory of multiple files. When transferring many small-sized files, it will take time to open and transfer each one of them, so the test will not give good results.

When getting less bandwidth than expected, perform the following steps:

1. When getting a value up to around 5% more or less than expected, it can be due to the reasons mentioned in the *There's more...* section in this recipe. Check the configurations and the technology that the line is running on (**SDH/SONet, Carrier Ethernet**, and so on)

2. If you test the line with file copy, and in the IO graphs see sawtooth, there might be errors on the line. Check TCP retransmissions, and then check for errors in the switch/router port connected to the service provider.

 To check switch or router port statistics, you can use console or telnet to connect to it and use the switch or router commands (for example, **show interface** commands in Cisco). You can also use SNMP management software or any MIB browser and browse the `IfInErrors` and `InOutErrors` objects.

3. If you see a degradation of 80 to 90 percent of what you had expected (for example, you test a line of 100 Mbps and get 10 to 20 Mbps); in most of the cases, it is a **duplex-mismatch** problem. As shown in the *How it works...* section of this recipe.

   It isn't common, but it can also be that your service provider has a configuration problem. Check it with them. If none of the preceding cases are true, it can be that this is the reason.

How it works...

First, there are two different definitions; it is important to distinguish between:

▸ **Bandwidth**: This is the total bits per second that can be transferred over a communications line

▸ **Throughput**: This is the effective application bytes per second that is transferred between the two ends of a connection

To check the bandwidth of a communication line, you can ask the service provider for the line details, or you can simply transfer some traffic over it, use Wireshark or SNMP tool, and see what you get.

Most of the cases in which a duplex mismatch problem occurs is when you connect using Ethernet on one side with 100 Mbps full duplex, and the other side configured to auto-negotiate.

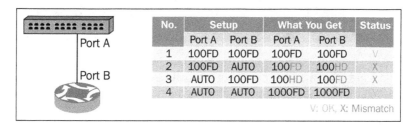

No.	Setup		What You Get		Status
	Port A	Port B	Port A	Port B	
1	100FD	100FD	100FD	100FD	V
2	100FD	AUTO	100FD	100HD	X
3	AUTO	100FD	100HD	100FD	X
4	AUTO	AUTO	1000FD	1000FD	V

V: OK, X: Mismatch

As you see in the diagram, when you connect a device (a router in this example) to a switch, when both sides are manually configured, for example, to 100 Mbps **Full Duplex** (**FDX**), the intended configuration will take place (numbered **1** in the preceding diagram).

When you configure both sides to auto-negotiation (numbered **4** in the preceding diagram), it will also be fine, and will be automatically set to 1 Gbps (in the case of gigabit adapters).

In the case when one side is configured to 100 FDX and the other side to auto negotiate, the auto negotiate will be automatically set to 100 Mbps **Half-Duplex** (**HDX**). In this case, when one side is set to HD and the other to FD, many packets will be lost, and you will experience significant degradation in performance (numbered **2** and **3** in the preceding diagram).

There's more...

When we buy a line at a certain bandwidth, it can be that we'll get a little bit more or less of what we've bought. For example, when we buy 10 Mbps line, and the line runs over the **Synchronous Digital Hierarchy** (**SDH**) or **Synchronous Optical Network** (**SONet**) line; the 10 Mbps is made of 5 VC-12s, which is 5*2.176 Mbps, so the total bandwidth will be 10.88 Mbps.

On the other hand if, for example, we use site-to-site VPN over the Internet, and the line is 10 Mbps, even if we have a very good Internet connection (for example, when the two ends are connected to the same ISP), the encryption mechanisms of the VPN itself can take 5 to 10 percent of the line, and when measuring it, you will get somewhere between 9.0 to 9.5 Mbps. In this case, for example, when you transfer a file over the line, you will see that the line is loaded with 10 Mbps (that is, the bandwidth), while what is left for the file copy is usually between 9.0 to 9.5 Mbps (that is, the throughput).

Measuring bandwidth and throughput per user and per application over a network connection

In many cases, we need to know not only the total bandwidth of a connection, (communication line or on a server port), but also who exactly are the consumers, that is from which IP addresses and port numbers the traffic is coming. In this recipe, we will see how to measure it.

In order to see this, you can use proprietary tools that collect the data from the switch (**RMON1**, **RMON2**, **sFlow**) or router (**Cisco Netflow** or **Juniper Jflow**), or to use Wireshark with port mirror to the communication link, and this is what we'll learn in this recipe.

Getting ready

For using Wireshark to get traffic distribution, connect a laptop with a port mirror to the link you wish to monitor and start packet capture. You can also use the Tshark command from the CLI.

How to do it...

For basic statistics on users and applications that are using the communications link, perform the following steps:

- For general statistics:

  1. From the **Statistics** menu, choose **Conversations**.

  2. In the **Conversations** window, you see the statistics on the total number of packets captured until now.

  3. You can also use graphical tools such as **Compass** (*Chapter 11, Analyzing Enterprise Applications, Behavior*).

- For flow analysis, use IO graphs with filters on IP addresses and/or port numbers:

  1. From the **Statistics** menu, select **IO Graphs**.

  2. In the **IO graphs** window (*Chapter 5, Using Advanced Statistics Tools*), configure IP and port numbers and display filters for the applications that you wish to monitor.

- For continuous monitoring, use Wireshark with multiple files with ring buffer, or use tools such as Netflow or Jflow for router monitoring.

How it works...

With Wireshark, like we learned in *Chapter 1, Introducing Wireshark*, we capture data and analyze it.

In Netflow, Jflow, and applications that collect data from the router, the router periodically sends the collected data to the management console that analyzes it.

In **Remote Monitoring 1** (**RMON1**) and **Remote Monitoring 2** (**RMON2**), when the end switch supports it, you access the data with the SNMP software that reads from the RMON1/RMON2 MIB. While RMON1 provides you layer 1 to 2 statistics, RMON2, when implemented provides you layer 3 to 4 statistics. The main standards of RMON were published in RFCs 2613, 2819, 3577, and 4502. In various applications and devices such as firewalls, **Intrusion Detection Systems** (**IDS**), **Deep Packet Inspection** (**DPI**) devices, and WAN Accelerators, you will get the data from the monitored device.

See also

Additional data on these applications can be found at:

Cisco Netflow: `http://www.cisco.com/en/US/products/ps6601/products_ios_protocol_group_home.html`

`http://www.ietf.org/rfc/rfc3954.txt`

For Juniper Jflow:

`http://www.juniper.net/techpubs/software/erx/junose82/swconfig-ip-services/html/ip-jflow-stats-config2.html`

sFlow:

`http://www.ietf.org/rfc/rfc3176.txt`

Various applications can be located in:

For switch monitoring:

`http://www.sflow.org/index.php`

`http://tools.ietf.org/html/rfc3176`

Monitoring jitter and delay using Wireshark

Jitter and delay are characteristics that can significantly influence various network applications. For monitoring jitter and delay on a communication line, you can use simple or graphical Ping tools that will show you the line characteristics. Wireshark on the other hand does not measure the end-to-end delay but the influence that it has on the network traffic, that is inter-frame delay and how it influences applications.

In this recipe, we will see how to use Wireshark tools for monitoring these parameters, and in the next recipe we will see how to discover problems caused by them.

Getting ready

For monitoring delay on a communication line, first use the `ping` command to get the feeling of the line, and then configure port mirror to the port you want to monitor.

How to do it...

To monitor inter-frame delay:

1. From **Statistics**, select **IO Graph**.

2. For monitoring time between frames in a specific stream of data:

    1. Click on a packet in the TCP or UDP stream.

    2. Click on **Follow TCP Stream** or **Follow UDP stream**.

    3. Copy the displayed filter string that showed up (numbered **1** in the next screenshot).

3. From statistics open **IO Graph**.

4. In **IO Graph**, in the **Y Axis** part (bottom-right side of the window), select **Advanced...** (numbered **2** in the following diagram).

5. Copy the **TCP stream number** (numbered **1** in the following diagram) to the **Filter** field in the IO Graph (numbered **3** in the following diagram).

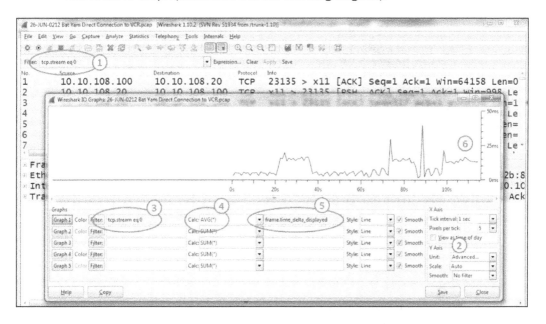

6. Select **AVG(*)** (numbered **4** in the preceding diagram).

7. Configure the filter `frame.time_delta_displayed` (numbered **5** in the preceding diagram).

8. In the graph (numbered **6** in the preceding diagram), you see the time between frames in milliseconds.

9. By navigating to **Statistics | TCP Stream Graph | Round Trip Time Graph**, you will get the same results as shown in the following diagram:

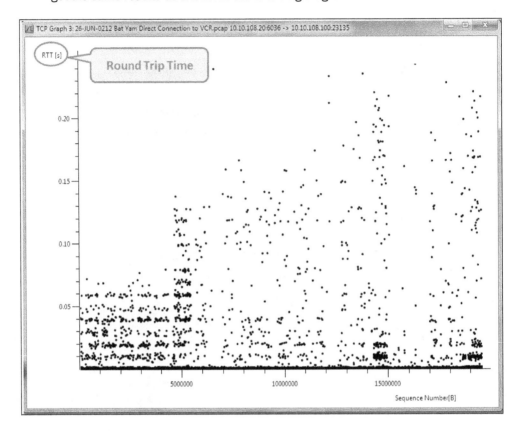

10. In the diagram, we see that the **Round Trip Time** (**RTT**) varies between values that are lower than 10 ms and up to 200-300 ms.

11. To measure delays in layer 4, use the TCP filter `tcp.analysis.ack_rtt` that will give you the time that it takes to acknowledge every received packet.

How it works...

The software simply captures packets over the line, and shows you the time difference between them. It is important to notice that there is a delay or jitter, but we will not see where it is coming from.

Delay is the time that it takes a packet to get from one end of the network to the other. It is usually referred to as RTT. Delay can be measured with simple Ping or graphical Ping tools. Delay is measured in seconds – milliseconds (ms), microseconds (μs), and so on.

Jitter in IP networks measure the variations in delay. For example, if we have an average delay of 100 ms, and it varies between 80 ms and 120 ms, the jitter is 20 percent.

There's more...

Graphical Ping tools are available for free on many websites. You can use, for example, `http://www.colasoft.com/download/products/download_ping_tool.php`.

Discovering delay/jitter-related application problems

Jitter and delay can influence various types of applications. In applications that run over TCP, high delay reduces the effective throughput that can be sent and high jitter can cause packet losses and retransmissions. In multimedia applications that run over RTP, which runs over UDP, high jitter and delay can cause severe disturbances in the voice and video quality.

In this recipe, we will get into the details: the influence of behavior on TCP, and how it can influence the application behavior. RTP over UDP behavior was discussed in *Chapter 12, SIP, Multimedia, and IP Telephony*.

Getting ready

When you ping a remote site and get high delays, and in the Wireshark you see many retransmissions, it can be because of high network or applications delay. Connect the Wireshark to the network and configure port mirror to the link that you test.

The purpose of this recipe is to check whether the TCP retransmissions and duplicate ACKs are due to delay and jitter or other problems.

How to do it...

When experiencing many TCP retransmissions, perform the following tests:

1. Check whether retransmissions are coming from the same application or from the same IP address. In this case, it is a slow application or a slow device and probably not a network delay issue.

   If retransmissions are distributed between various applications and devices, it can be because of unstable line that causes network delays.

2. Configure a display filter `tcp.analysis.retransmissions` (numbered **1** in the following diagram). A list of all retransmissions in the packet list will appear.

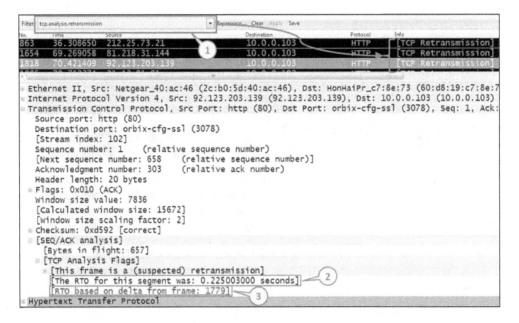

3. Down the packet details pane, expand the **TCP Analysis Flags**, and you will get:

   ❑ The time since the original packet is retransmitted (numbered **2** in the preceding diagram). In this case, **0.225003000** seconds.

   ❑ The packet that is retransmitted (numbered **3** in the preceding diagram). In this case, packet number **1779**.

4. Usually the **Retransmission Time Out** (**RTO**) timer will be around 0.2 seconds for local connections, and up to 0.3 to 0.4 seconds for international connections. Start with assuming 0.2 seconds. Refer to the *How it works...* section in this recipe for explanation about the RTO mechanism.

5. To check TCP delay over a connection, use **IO Graphs** with the following filters, as presented in the next diagram:

   ❑ `tcp.stream eq <the stream number>` to get to the stream number right-click on a packet and select **Follow TCP stream**.

   ❑ `frame.time_delta` to see the time difference between frames in the TCP stream. This parameter actually shows inter-frame delta in layer 2, but since it is shown only for the stream, it will show us inter-frame deltas in a specific TCP stream.

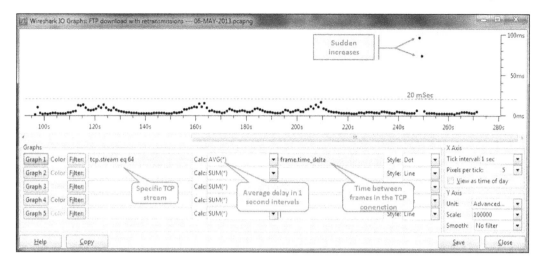

You get a graph that shows a very stable connection, with delays that are lower than 20 ms, except for the two increases in delay in time **250s** (250 seconds since the beginning of the capture), that causes retransmissions.

6. When we add the `tcp.analysis.ack_rtt` filter on the same connection, we see the delays between TCP packets and ACKs.

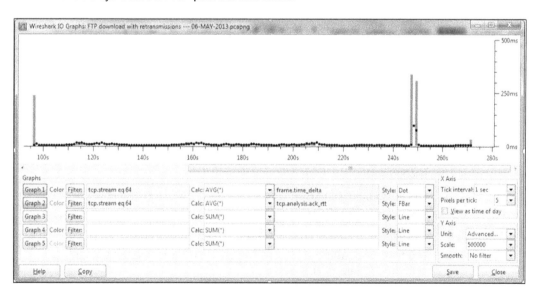

In the following diagram, you see a graph which is an example for delays not due to line delay issues:

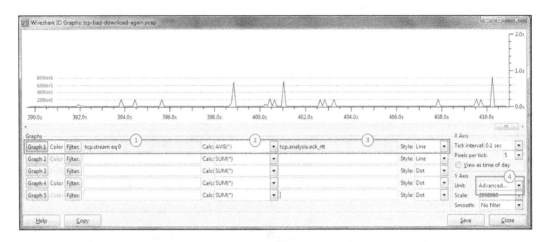

7. You can see here that I've configured:

   ❑ The **Advance** option in the **Y Axis**

   ❑ The **Filter** field: **tcp.stream eq 0** (numbered **1** in the preceding diagram) to present a single stream

   ❑ The calculation **AVG(*)** to see the average (**2**)

   ❑ You can also configure **MAX(*)** and the filter tcp.analysis.ack_rtt to see the time to acknowledge every TCP sequence

   What we've got is the time that it took to acknowledge every TCP packet.

8. Now, let's configure **IO Graphs** to see if there are TCP retransmissions, and why they happen:

   ❑ Use the same IO Graph with **Advance** in **Y Axis,** and configure the second line.

   ❑ The **Filter** field: **tcp.stream eq 0** (numbered **1** in the preceding diagram) to present a single stream.

   ❑ The calculation **COUNT FRAMES(*)** to see the average.

   ❑ The filter tcp.analysis.retransmissions to see the time to acknowledge every TCP packet.

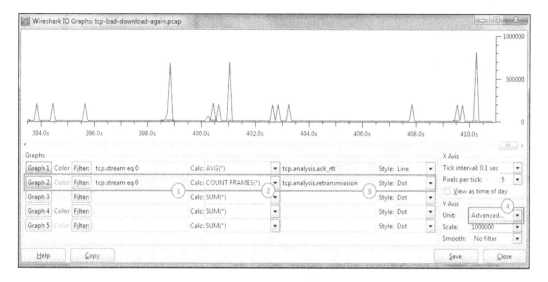

9. We can see from here that all retransmissions happened when there was a significant increase in the delay, so it is a delay problem. We cannot say from here if the delay is from the network, from the end device or from the application, so for isolating the problem check how retransmissions are distributed (see *Chapter 9, UDP/TCP Analysis*).

10. Retransmissions that are not due to increase in RTT are probably due to packet losses.

How it works...

TCP uses the retransmission mechanism to ensure data delivery in the absence of any feedback from the remote data receiver. The duration of this timer is referred to as **Retransmission Time Out** (**RTO**). This mechanism was first standardized in RFC1122 that specified that the RTO should be calculated as outlined in the *Jacobson V. and M. Karels, Congestion Avoidance and Control*, article from 1988. An update to this RFC came out in RFC 2988 in November 2000, and later in RFC 6298 *Computing TCP's Retransmission Timer*, June 2011.

There's more...

For delay variations, you can also navigate to **Statistics | TCP Stream Graph | Round Trip Time Graph**.

When experiencing high delays, it also influences the throughput you can get from the network. This is what is called as the bandwidth delay product as shown in the following figure:

$$\text{Throughput [Bytes/Sec]} = \frac{\text{Window Size [Bytes]}}{\text{RTT [Sec]}}$$

From here we can see that the higher the delay is, the lower the throughput becomes. In networks with high delays, for example, old cellular networks, satellite lines, and long distance international lines, we have several methods to improve the application's throughput. Among these methods are applications that use multiple connections per application, usage of the TCP increases the window size (comes as default in Window Vista and the higher versions, along with various Linux versions).

14
Understanding Network Security

In this chapter, we will cover the following recipes:

- ▶ Discovering unusual traffic patterns
- ▶ Discovering MAC- and ARP-based attacks
- ▶ Discovering ICMP and TCP SYN/Port scans
- ▶ Discovering DoS and DDoS attacks
- ▶ Locating smart TCP attacks
- ▶ Discovering brute-force and application attacks

Introduction

Information security is one of the fascinating areas in information systems, and its purpose is to secure the organization's systems against internal and external attacks that can come in various patterns. These attacks can come from the Internet or from the internal network, and as such, they all come through the network and therefore, can be monitored with Wireshark (and other tools that will be mentioned later).

For monitoring the network against malicious traffic, we must first understand what constitutes normal traffic. We can then try to find out how malicious traffic is short of being normal traffic. Among unusual traffic, we might see an ARP, IP, or TCP scanning, DNS responses without queries, unusual TCP flags, unknown IP addresses or port numbers whose purpose is not known to us, and so on.

It is also important to understand the difference between security problems and networking problems, and distinguish between them. For example, ICMP scan can be a malicious software scanning the network but also a management software that discovers the network, while TCP SYN scan can be a worm but also a software bug. We will elaborate on these in each of the recipes.

In this chapter, we will start by differentiating between normal and unusual network traffic and then understand the various types of attacks, where they come from and how to isolate and solve them.

Discovering unusual traffic patterns

In this recipe, we will learn what are usual and unusual traffic patterns and how to distinguish between them.

Getting ready

The first thing is to locate Wireshark. There are several options for this
(see the following diagram):

1. When you suspect an attack that comes from the Internet, locate Wireshark after the firewall (**1**), and when you suspect that it crosses the firewall, locate it before (**2**).

2. When you suspect malicious traffic coming from a remote office, port mirror the traffic coming on the central line before (**3**) or after (**4**) the router. In this case, you can filter the suspicious traffic with IP networks to see patterns from different offices in order to isolate the problematic office.

3. You can also port mirror the traffic in the remote office before (**7**) or after (**6**) the routers.

4. When a PC or a server is the suspect, port mirror its port on the switch (**5**) or (**8**).

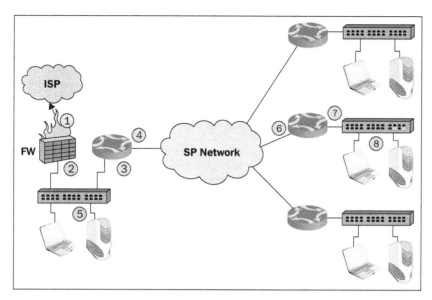

Now, we will try to see what are the types of traffic that we should look out for, what are the types of traffic that are normal, and what traffic should be followed.

Before starting with the tests, make sure that you have an updated topology of the network that includes:

- Servers' IP addresses and LANs' IP address ranges
- Routers, switches, and other communications equipments' IP addresses and topology
- Security devices—firewalls, **Intrusion Detection Systems / Intrusion Prevention Systems (IDSs/IPSs)**, **Web Application Firewalls (WAF)**, database and application firewalls, antivirus systems, and any other device that has an IP address and generates, filters, or forwards network traffic
- What are the applications that work over the network including TCP/UDP port numbers and IP addresses of software

How to do it...

When you monitor internal traffic in your organization, the following things should be checked:

1. Traffic that is generated from known addresses (in the organization):

   ❑ **Normal**: This is the traffic from known addresses and address ranges

   ❑ **Suspicious**: This is the traffic from/to addresses that you don't know

2. Applications and port numbers:

   ❑ **Normal**: This includes standard port numbers, 80 (HTTP), 137/8/9 (NetBIOS), 3389 (RDP), 20/21 (FTP), 25,110 (Mail), 53 (DNS), and so on. Be sure of the applications that run over the network, and verify that these are the only port numbers that you see.

   ❑ **Suspicious**: This includes unusual port numbers, that is, port numbers that do not belong to applications that run on server (for example, RDP packets to web server).

3. TCP patterns:

   ❑ **Normal**: TCP SYN/SYN-ACK/ACK that indicates a connection establishment, single reset (RST) that indicates a fast connection tear-down, FIN/FIN-ACK packets that indicate a regular tear-down of a connection, standard packets, and acknowledgments

   ❑ **Suspicious**: Large amount of SYN packets that go to a single or multiple destinations or coming from multiple sources (usually in a scan pattern that will be described later in this chapter), unusual flags combination (RST/FIN, URG), and so on

4. Massive traffic to a single or multiple sites that you don't know about:

   ❑ **Normal**: Traffic patterns are usually not of fixed bandwidth. When you save or open files, browse the Internet, send or receive mails, or access a server with RDP, you see ups and downs.

   ❑ **Suspicious** (in some cases): Fixed bandwidth patterns can indicate that someone is connected to your device, but it can also indicate that someone is listening to the radio over the Internet (100-150 Kbps), watching video (in some cases), and so on. When you see a fixed bandwidth pattern of traffic, check what it is. A fixed bandwidth pattern is illustrated in the following screenshot:

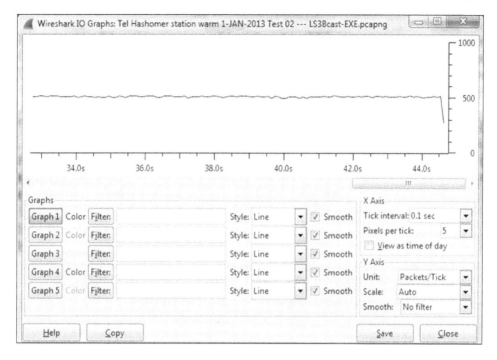

5. Broadcasts:

   - **Normal**: NetBIOS broadcasts, ARP broadcasts (not too many), DHCP (not too many), application broadcasts (usually once every several seconds and more), and so on

   - **Suspicious**: Tens, hundreds, or thousands and more broadcasts per seconds per device

6. DNS queries and responses:

   - **Normal**: A standard query-response pattern up to several tens per second per client, occasionally

   - **Suspicious**: Massive amount of DNS queries and/or responses, responses without queries, and so on

How it works...

Network forensics is quite similar to what you see in police dramas on television. Something is going wrong; so, you go to the crime scene (this is your network) and look for evidence (these are the traces that are left in the network).

What you look for are the things that do not match the crime scene (your network), things that are left behind (unusual traffic patterns), fingerprints, and DNA (patterns that can identify the attacker).

In the following recipes, we will get to the details of various types of attacks and abnormalities that can indicate that a crime was committed, and we will see how to isolate the problems and solve them.

Some common attacks that can come from the network are:

▶ **Viruses**: These are small programs that attack your computer and try to cause damage. Viruses should be discovered and fixed by antivirus software.

▶ **Worms**: These are usually programs that attempt to replicate themselves across the network. There is a major impact on resource consumption, for example, bandwidth consumption and CPU load. The important thing is that the moment you fix the problem, everything will go back to normal.

▶ **Denial of Service (DoS) and Distributed DoS (DDoS)**: These are attacks that deny access to network resources. These types of attacks are usually very easy to discover since they have a distinct behavior that can be located easily.

▶ **Man-in-the-middle attacks**: These are attacks in which the attacker intercepts messages and then retransmits them. In this way, the attacker can eavesdrop on the traffic or change it before it gets to the destination.

▶ **Scanning**: There are various types of scans ranging from simple ICMP scans that usually are a form of DDoS, TCP scans that send, for example, SYN requests on various port numbers in order to try and open connections to services running on a server, and also application scans that try to connect to applications running on your servers.

▶ **Application-layer attacks**: These are attacks that target applications on your servers by intentionally causing a fault in a server's operating system or applications.

In the following recipes, we will see each of them (and some more).

There's more...

An important indication that something went wrong is when a server, a PC, a communication link, or any other entity on the network becomes slow without any logical reason. For example:

► When a server becomes slow, check for hardware and software issues, check for network problems, but also check if someone is attacking it

► When a link from a remote office to the center becomes slow, it can be because of the load (constant or sudden), but it can also be because of an attack that blocks it (usually DOS/DDoS)

► When a PC becomes slow, it can be because it is doing something that you know about, but there is not just one possibility, check for the things you don't know

It is important to mention here that there are various systems that can protect us from attacks; a few of them are listed as follows:

► **Firewalls**: They protect unauthorized traffic from getting into specific areas. Firewalls can be located on the connection to the Internet, before the organization servers, between organization areas, and even as personal firewalls on every PC.

► **Network Access Control** (**NAC**): These systems allow only authorized users to connect to the network. When connecting an unauthorized device to the network, you will see that the link on the device will be turned on and immediately off, and the unauthorized device will be blocked on the MAC layer.

► **IDS/IPS**: These systems can identify intrusion patterns and block them. There are usually two lines of defense here—one at the ISP network and one at the customer premises. IDS/IPS can be a dedicated device located between the firewall and the Internet or an additional software on the firewall.

► **Web Application Firewalls** (**WAF**), **Application Firewalls**, **Database Firewalls, and other application protection devices**: This group of products are layer-7 protection devices that look inside the applications and forward or block application layer attacks.

► **Web Filters and Mail Filters**: These are devices that scan mail and/or web content and forward only those messages and traffic that are allowed.

The features mentioned above can come as different devices, software on Virtual Machines (VMs), or features on the same device.

See also

In this recipe, we talked about some security components. Some examples are:

- **Firewalls**: Checkpoint (`www.checkpoint.com`), Juniper SSG series (`http://www.juniper.net/us/en/products-services/security/ssg-series/`), Cisco ASA series (`http://www.cisco.com/en/US/products/ps5708/Products_Sub_Category_Home.html`), and many others.

- **NAC**: In this category, you have, for example, Forescout (`http://www.forescout.com/solutions/network-access-control/`) and Enterasys (`http://www.enterasys.com/company/literature/nac-ds.pdf`).

- **IDS/IPS**: In this category, we have, for example, the Juniper IDP device series (`http://www.juniper.net/us/en/products-services/security/idp-series/`) and the Check Point software blade for the firewall (`http://www.checkpoint.com/products/ips-software-blade/`).

- **WAF**: Here we have, for example, Imperva (`http://www.imperva.com/products/wsc_web-application-firewall.html`) and F5 (`http://www.f5.com/glossary/web-application-firewall/`). Database firewalls are available, for example, from Imperva (`http://www.imperva.com/products/dsc_database-firewall.html`) and Oracle (`http://www.oracle.com/us/products/database/security/audit-vault-database-firewall/overview/index.html`).

- **Web and mail filters**: Here we have, for example, McAfee (`http://www.mcafee.com/au/products/email-and-web-security/index.aspx`), Blue Coat (`http://www.bluecoat.com/security-policy-enforcement-center`), and Websense (`http://www.websense.com/content/Home.aspx`).

Discovering MAC- and ARP-based attacks

There are various types of layer-2 MAC-based attacks and layer-2/3 ARP attacks that can be easily discovered by Wireshark. These attacks are usually caused by scanners (described in the next recipe) and man-in-the-middle attacks (described in the *Analyzing connectivity problems with ARP recipe in Chapter 8, ARP and IP Analysis*). In this recipe, we will see some typical attack patterns and their meanings.

Getting ready

When viewing too many ARP requests on a network or when seeing non-standard MAC addresses in the network, connect Wireshark with port mirror to their source and start the capture.

How to do it...

To look for ARP/MAC-based attacks, follow these steps:

1. Connect Wireshark to any port on the network.

2. Look for massive ARP broadcasts. Since ARP requests are broadcasts, they will be distributed in the entire layer-2 network (that is, on a single VLAN). In the following screenshot, you can see a typical ARP-scan pattern. It's important to note that this ARP scan can be an application that works this way, for example, SNMP software that discovers the network and router that uses gratuitous ARP. It is a problem only if it comes from an unidentified source.

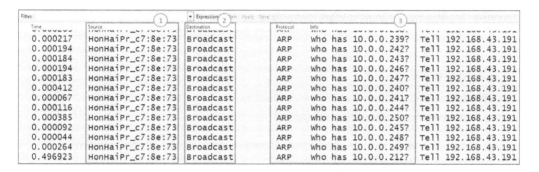

Time	Source	Destination	Protocol	Info		
0.000217	HonHaiPr_c7:8e:73	Broadcast	ARP	who has 10.0.0.239?	Tell	192.168.43.191
0.000194	HonHaiPr_c7:8e:73	Broadcast	ARP	who has 10.0.0.242?	Tell	192.168.43.191
0.000184	HonHaiPr_c7:8e:73	Broadcast	ARP	who has 10.0.0.243?	Tell	192.168.43.191
0.000194	HonHaiPr_c7:8e:73	Broadcast	ARP	who has 10.0.0.246?	Tell	192.168.43.191
0.000183	HonHaiPr_c7:8e:73	Broadcast	ARP	who has 10.0.0.247?	Tell	192.168.43.191
0.000412	HonHaiPr_c7:8e:73	Broadcast	ARP	who has 10.0.0.240?	Tell	192.168.43.191
0.000067	HonHaiPr_c7:8e:73	Broadcast	ARP	who has 10.0.0.241?	Tell	192.168.43.191
0.000116	HonHaiPr_c7:8e:73	Broadcast	ARP	who has 10.0.0.244?	Tell	192.168.43.191
0.000385	HonHaiPr_c7:8e:73	Broadcast	ARP	who has 10.0.0.250?	Tell	192.168.43.191
0.000092	HonHaiPr_c7:8e:73	Broadcast	ARP	who has 10.0.0.245?	Tell	192.168.43.191
0.000044	HonHaiPr_c7:8e:73	Broadcast	ARP	who has 10.0.0.248?	Tell	192.168.43.191
0.000264	HonHaiPr_c7:8e:73	Broadcast	ARP	who has 10.0.0.249?	Tell	192.168.43.191
0.496923	HonHaiPr_c7:8e:73	Broadcast	ARP	who has 10.0.0.212?	Tell	192.168.43.191

3. There are also some suspicious MAC patterns. You can identify them when you see:

   ❑ Two identical MAC addresses with different IP addresses. It can be two IP addresses configured on the same network adapter, which is OK, but it can also be an attack pattern in which someone has changed its MAC address to the MAC address of a server (can be performed in every adapter).

   ❑ The case mentioned above can also indicate a man-in-the-middle attack as mentioned in the *ARP poisoning and man-in-the-middle attacks* section in *Chapter 8, ARP and IP Analysis*.

How it works...

ARP sends broadcasts to the network asking for the MAC address of a specific IP destination. Anything that is not according to this pattern should be considered malicious.

There's more...

ARP requests can also come from the SNMP software that discovers the network (auto-discovery feature), the DHCP server that sends gratuitous ARP, and so on. Whenever you see ARP scanning something, it is not necessarily a problem; the question is who sends them. You can find more information on the ARP process in *Chapter 8, ARP and IP Analysis*.

Discovering ICMP and TCP SYN/Port scans

Scanning is the process of sending packets to network devices in order to see who is answering the ping requests, to look for listening TCP/UDP ports, and to find which types of resources are shared on the network including system and application resources.

Getting ready

A scanning attack is usually detected by users complaining about slow network responses, management systems that discover unusual load on servers or communication lines, and when the attack is implemented also by **Security Information and Event Management Systems (SIEM)** that identifies suspicious usage patterns. In these cases, locate the Wireshark with port mirror as close as possible to the area that you suspect is infected, and start capture.

How to do it...

To discover the problem, follow these steps:

1. Start Wireshark with capture on the interface that is close to the problem:

    ❑ If the line to the Internet becomes slow, port mirror the line

    ❑ If a server becomes slow, port mirror the server

    ❑ If remote offices become slow, port mirror the lines to them

2. If you see that Wireshark does not respond, it is probably because you have a very strong attack that generates thousands or more packets per second; so, Wireshark (or your laptop) cannot process them. In this case, stop Wireshark (with *Ctrl+Alt+Del* in Windows or with the `kill` command in Unix if necessary) and configure it to capture multiple files (described in the *Starting the capture of data* recipe in *Chapter 1, Introducing Wireshark*)

3. There are various patterns that you might see, all of them with the same behavior— massive scanning, ICMP or TCP in most of the cases, but also other types. The best way to understand all is to see them with some examples.

4. In the following diagram, you see a network that was under attack. Users from all the remote sites complained about a very slow network. They were all accessing servers on the center on the left-hand side of the diagram.

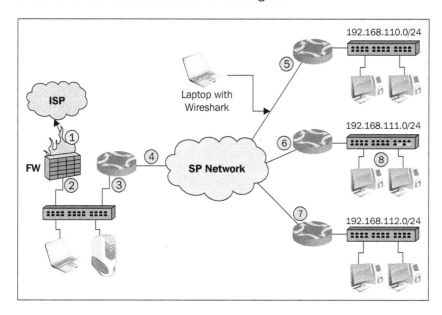

□ What I got when I connected Wireshark to a remote site (as illustrated below) was many ICMP requests (3), coming from the LAN 192.168.110.0 (1) to random destinations (2). Was it random?

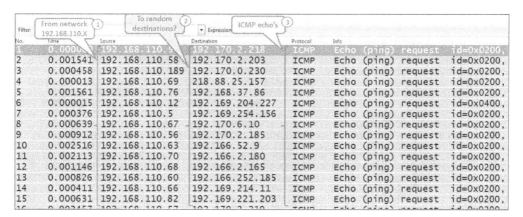

- Also, look at the time between packets. If scanned, it will usually be very short.

- When you go to **Statistics | Conversations**, you will see something interesting:

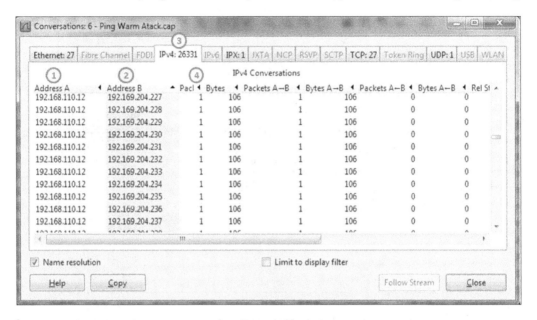

- When we sort the table by address A (**1**), we see a pattern of ICMP requests coming from various addresses on the network 192.168.110.0 (here, we see a very small part of it, that is, 192.168.110.12 scans the network).

- This worm simply scans the network with ICMP requests. The moment someone answers, the worm infects him/her also, and after a few minutes, all communication lines are blocked with ICMP requests going out of the remote offices.

Conclusion

When you see a massive number of pings scanning on a communication channel or link, that is, thousands and more pings, check for the problem. It can be the SNMP software discovering the network, but it can also be a worm that will flood your communications line or server links (or both).

5. Another common type of scan is the TCP-SYN scan. In this case, the attacker scans random TCP ports with TCP-SYN packets waiting for someone to answer with SYN-ACK. The moment it happens, there are two options:

   ❑ The attacker will continue to send SYN packets and receive the SYN-ACKs, thus leaving many half-open connections on the device under attack

   ❑ The attacker will answer with ACK, thus initiating the connection, and leave it open as in DoS/DDoS attacks or try to harm the device under attack with this connection

6. The TCP-SYN scan will look like one of the patterns in the following screenshots:

   ❑ You will see many SYN packets without any response from the node under attack.

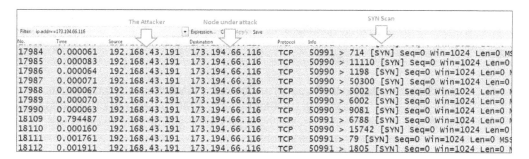

   ❑ You will see many SYN packets when a TCP RST packet is sent as a response to each one of them. This is usually when you have a firewall on the device that is under attack or will be attacked.

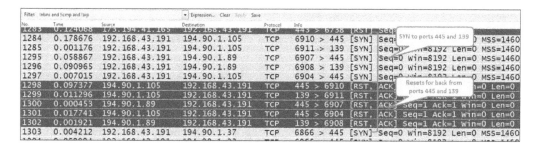

- ❑ You can also have consecutive SYN and RST packets. When there is a port number that is opened, you will see the complete SYN/SYN-ACK/ACK when the scanner opens connection to the victim. This is illustrated in the following screenshot:

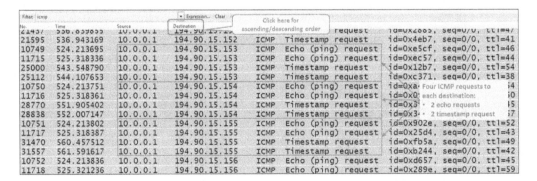

No.	Time	Source	Destination	Protocol	Info
186	0.0011/1	192.168.1.101	192.168.1.103	TCP	1416 > 111 [SYN] Seq=0 Win=16384 Len=0 MSS=1460
187	0.000153	192.168.1.103	192.168.1.101	TCP	111 > 1416 [RST, ACK] Seq=1 Ack=1 Win=0 Len=0
188	0.000486	192.168.1.101	192.168.1.103	TCP	1417 > 113 [SYN] Seq=0 Win=16384 Len=0 MSS=1460
189	0.000141	192.168.1.103	192.168.1.101	TCP	113 > 1417 [RST, ACK] Seq Blocked ports Win=0 Len=0
190	0.001459	192.168.1.101	192.168.1.103	TCP	1418 > 118 [SYN] Seq=0 Win=16384 Len=0 MSS=1460
191	0.000161	192.168.1.103	192.168.1.101	TCP	118 > 1418 [RST, ACK] Seq=1 Ack=1 Win=0 Len=0
192	0.001194	192.168.1.101	192.168.1.103	TCP	1419 > 135 [SYN] Seq=0 Win=16384 Len=0 MSS=1460
193	0.000179	192.168.1.103	192.168.1.101	TCP	135 > 1419 [SYN, ACK] Se Open port (135) n=17520 Len=
194	0.000024	192.168.1.101	192.168.1.103	TCP	1419 > 135 [ACK] Seq=1 Ack=1 Win=17520 Len=0
195	0.000608	192.168.1.101	192.168.1.103	TCP	1420 > 139 [SYN] Seq=0 Win=16384 Len=0 MSS=1460
196	0.000170	192.168.1.103	192.168.1.101	TCP	139 > 1420 [SYN, ACK] Se Open port (139) n=17520 Len=
197	0.000020	192.168.1.101	192.168.1.103	TCP	1420 > 139 [ACK] Seq=1 Ack=1 Win=17520 Len=0
198	0.000955	192.168.1.101	192.168.1.103	TCP	1421 > 156 [SYN] Seq=0 Win=16384 Len=0 MSS=1460
199	0.000195	192.168.1.103	192.168.1.101	TCP	156 > 1421 [RST, ACK] Seq=1 Ack=1 Win=0 Len=0
200	0.001017	192.168.1.101	192.168.1.103	TCP	1422 > 179 [SYN] Seq=0 Wi en=0 MSS=1460
201	0.000147	192.168.1.103	192.168.1.101	TCP	179 > 1422 [RST, ACK] Se Blocked ports Win=0 Len=0
202	0.000446	192.168.1.101	192.168.1.103	TCP	1423 > 371 [SYN] Seq=0 Win=16384 Len=0 MSS=1460
203	0.000139	192.168.1.103	192.168.1.101	TCP	371 > 1423 [RST, ACK] Seq=1 Ack=1 Win=0 Len=0
204	0.001253	192.168.1.101	192.168.1.103	TCP	1424 > 443 [SYN] Seq=0 Win=16384 Len=0 MSS=1460

7. Always look for unusual traffic patterns. Too many ICMP requests, for example, are a good indication for scanning. Look for multiple ICMP requests to clients, ICMP timestamp request, ICMP in ascending or descending order, and so on. These patterns can indicate malicious scanning.

- ❑ When you suspect a scan, click on the title of the destination (address), and you will get the packet list sorted by the destination address. In this way, it will be easier to see the scan patterns.

- ❑ In the following screenshot, you see an example of this scenario:

No.	Time	Source	Destination	Protocol	Info
21437	536.859855	10.0.0.1	194.90.15.152	ICMP	Timestamp request id=0x2885, seq=0/0, ttl=47
21595	536.943169	10.0.0.1	194.90.15.152	ICMP	Timestamp request id=0x4eb7, seq=0/0, ttl=41
10749	524.213695	10.0.0.1	194.90.15.153	ICMP	Echo (ping) request id=0x5cf, seq=0/0, ttl=46
11715	525.318336	10.0.0.1	194.90.15.153	ICMP	Echo (ping) request id=0xec57, seq=0/0, ttl=44
25000	543.548790	10.0.0.1	194.90.15.153	ICMP	Timestamp request id=0x12b7, seq=0/0, ttl=54
25112	544.107653	10.0.0.1	194.90.15.153	ICMP	Timestamp request id=0xc371, seq=0/0, ttl=38
10750	524.213751	10.0.0.1	194.90.15.154	ICMP	Echo (ping) request id=0xa Four ICMP requests to 4
11716	525.318361	10.0.0.1	194.90.15.154	ICMP	Echo (ping) request id=0x0 each destination: 0
28770	551.905402	10.0.0.1	194.90.15.154	ICMP	Timestamp request id=0x3 • 2 echo requests 5
28838	552.007147	10.0.0.1	194.90.15.154	ICMP	Timestamp request id=0x3 • 2 timestamp request 7
10751	524.213802	10.0.0.1	194.90.15.155	ICMP	Echo (ping) request id=0x902e, seq=0/0, ttl=52
11717	525.318387	10.0.0.1	194.90.15.155	ICMP	Echo (ping) request id=0x25d4, seq=0/0, ttl=43
31470	560.457512	10.0.0.1	194.90.15.155	ICMP	Timestamp request id=0xfb5a, seq=0/0, ttl=49
31557	561.591617	10.0.0.1	194.90.15.155	ICMP	Timestamp request id=0xb244, seq=0/0, ttl=42
10752	524.213836	10.0.0.1	194.90.15.156	ICMP	Echo (ping) request id=0xd657, seq=0/0, ttl=45
11718	525.321236	10.0.0.1	194.90.15.156	ICMP	Echo (ping) request id=0x289e, seq=0/0, ttl=59

Click here for ascending/descending order

8. In the case of application scanning, you can have various types of scans:

   ❏ **NetBIOS scans**: It looks for massive scanning of NetBIOS ports

   ❏ **HTTP**: It looks for SYN requests to HTTP port 80 with HTTP requests later on

   ❏ **SMTP**: It looks for massive scanning on the TCP port 25

   ❏ **SIP**: It looks for massive requests on port 5060

Other types of applications are scanned according to their port numbers

How it works...

The majority of scanners work in several steps: ARP scanning, ICMP, and then TCP or UDP. The principle is simple:

▶ If the scanner is on the LAN, it sends an ARP broadcast to the entire LAN.

▶ The scanner sends ICMP requests. Some of the ICMP requests will be answered.

▶ When someone answers the ARP or ICMP request, it goes up to TCP and UDP and starts scanning the layer-4 ports. When the scanner finds out that a port is open, it starts with application scanning.

▶ In application scanning, the scanner sends commands to the applications, trying to get the application to answer, and in this way, try to break into it.

There's more...

Most of the modern intrusion detection/prevention systems (IDS/IPS) in the last several years know how to deal with ICMP scans, TCP SYN scans, and various types of scans that generate massive traffic of standard, well-known attack patterns. In case you have such a system and you connect to the Internet with an ISP that has their systems, you are probably protected from these simple types of attacks.

These systems usually work in two ways:

▶ NetFlow/Jflow-based IDS/IPS that identifies massive traffic coming from several sources; they neutralize it by blocking it or changing the routing tables to disable these packets from getting to the ISP network

▶ Content-based IDS/IPS that looks at the traffic patterns and accordingly decides whether to forward it or not

Attacks coming from the internal network are not filtered by the external devices, and therefore, are even more common. There are more sophisticated types of attacks that will be discussed in the *Locating smart TCP attacks* recipe later in this chapter.

The way to prevent attacks coming from the Internet is to connect through an ISP with efficient IDS/IPS systems along with using one of your own. The way to prevent attacks coming from the internal network is to implement organizational security policy along with appropriate protection software such as antivirus and personal firewalls.

See also

In the previous section, I've mentioned the issue of organizational security policy, that is, how to implement a set of rules for securing your organization. Further information on this subject is widely available on the Internet. Some interesting websites that cover this area are:

▸ http://www.cert.org/work/organizational_security.html

▸ http://www.praxiom.com/iso-17799-4.htm

▸ http://www.sans.org/reading-room/whitepapers/policyissues/1331.php

▸ http://www.sans.org/security-resources/policies/

Discovering DoS and DDoS attacks

Denial of Service (DoS) and **Distributed Denial of Service (DDoS)** are attacks that intend to deny users from accessing network services. Services that can be denied to users can be:

▸ **Communication lines**: This will usually be done by generating traffic that floods and blocks the communications line

▸ **Applications and services (web services, mail services, and so on)**: This will usually be done by loading a server to a point at which it will not be able to serve clients' requests

DoS/DDoS attacks can be a result of scanning that we talked about in the previous recipe. The difference is that DoS/DDoS is a scan that slows down a server or a network in a way that denies user access.

In this recipe, we will see some common DoS/DDoS patterns, and learn how to identify and block them.

Getting ready

DoS/DDoS are usually discovered when one of the network resources, that is, communications lines or servers becomes very slow and is also not functioning.

When you identify such a resource, connect Wireshark with port mirror to this device and start packet capture. In this recipe, we will go through some common DoS/DDoS attacks and their signatures.

How to do it...

Connect Wireshark to the network with port mirror to the port of the resource that you suspect is exposed to DoS/DDoS. Usually, it will be a server that becomes very slow, a communication line that becomes very loaded, or any other resource that stops functioning or becomes very slow.

1. When a communication line becomes very slow, for example, a connection to the Internet, connect Wireshark with port mirror to this line.

    1. Try to locate where the traffic comes from.

    2. I've port mirrored the server, and this is what I got:

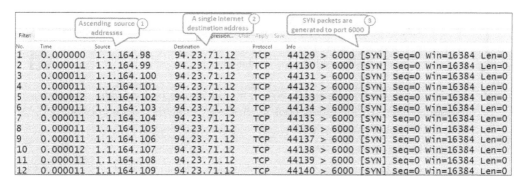

No.	Time	Source	Destination	Protocol	Info
1	0.000000	1.1.164.98	94.23.71.12	TCP	44129 > 6000 [SYN] Seq=0 Win=16384 Len=0
2	0.000011	1.1.164.99	94.23.71.12	TCP	44130 > 6000 [SYN] Seq=0 Win=16384 Len=0
3	0.000011	1.1.164.100	94.23.71.12	TCP	44131 > 6000 [SYN] Seq=0 Win=16384 Len=0
4	0.000011	1.1.164.101	94.23.71.12	TCP	44132 > 6000 [SYN] Seq=0 Win=16384 Len=0
5	0.000012	1.1.164.102	94.23.71.12	TCP	44133 > 6000 [SYN] Seq=0 Win=16384 Len=0
6	0.000011	1.1.164.103	94.23.71.12	TCP	44134 > 6000 [SYN] Seq=0 Win=16384 Len=0
7	0.000011	1.1.164.104	94.23.71.12	TCP	44135 > 6000 [SYN] Seq=0 Win=16384 Len=0
8	0.000011	1.1.164.105	94.23.71.12	TCP	44136 > 6000 [SYN] Seq=0 Win=16384 Len=0
9	0.000011	1.1.164.106	94.23.71.12	TCP	44137 > 6000 [SYN] Seq=0 Win=16384 Len=0
10	0.000012	1.1.164.107	94.23.71.12	TCP	44138 > 6000 [SYN] Seq=0 Win=16384 Len=0
11	0.000011	1.1.164.108	94.23.71.12	TCP	44139 > 6000 [SYN] Seq=0 Win=16384 Len=0
12	0.000011	1.1.164.109	94.23.71.12	TCP	44140 > 6000 [SYN] Seq=0 Win=16384 Len=0

    3. We see source addresses in the ascending order, generating traffic to the Internet address **94.23.71.12**.

When you look at the time column that is configured with "time since the previously displayed packet", you see that there are 11-12 micro-seconds between frames. When you see TCP-SYN coming at this rate, something is wrong. Check what it is!

4. Since the source addresses are unknown, I've checked their MAC address. What I got was:

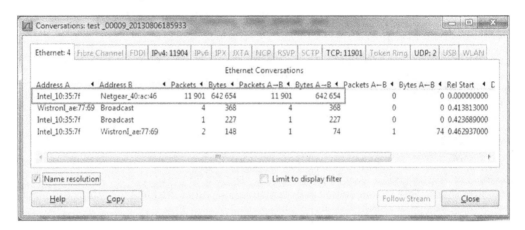

5. The problem was that all source addresses came from a single MAC address; so I checked their MAC addresses, and all IP addresses came from a single MAC address, the MAC address of the server.

Conclusion

Check for SYN scans, and verify which IP and MAC addresses they are coming from. It can be that a worm is generating source addresses that are not the addresses of the host.

2. Another example can be a simple SYN scan that comes from a single attacker, as seen in the next illustration. Look for SYN and watch the port numbers that they are scanning. You might see:

   ❑ No response

   ❑ Reset packet

   ❑ SYN-ACK response

3. There can be various consequences to this type of attack:

   ❑ In case of no response or reset response, the attacked server is functioning well. In case the server answers with a SYN-ACK response, it might be a risk to the server.

❑ The risk is that if too many connections will be opened (SYN/SYN-ACK/ACK) or half opened (SYN/SYN-ACK), the server might get slow due to these connections.

❑ You can see a typical TCP SYN attack in the following illustration. A SYN attack becomes DoS/DDoS when it blocks a communication line or loads a server to the point that it stops functioning.

No.	Time	Source	Destination	Protocol	Info
55371	0.000023	10.0.0.103	10.0.0.10	TCP	33928 > 1080 [SYN] Seq=0 Win=1024 Len=0 MSS=1460
55372	0.000025	10.0.0.103	10.0.0.10	TCP	33928 > 1082 [SYN] Seq=0 Win=1024 Len=0 MSS=1460
55373	0.000025	10.0.0.103	10.0.0.10	TCP	33928 > 15003 [SYN] Seq=0 Win=1024 Len=0 MSS=146
55374	0.000034	10.0.0.103	10.0.0.10	TCP	33928 > 6567 [SYN] Seq=0 Win=1024 Len=0 MSS=1460
55375	0.000025	10.0.0.103	10.0.0.10	TCP	33928 > 458 [SYN] Seq=0 Win=1024 Len=0 MSS=1460
55376	0.000026	10.0.0.103	10.0.0.10	TCP	33928 > 8383 [SYN] Seq=0 Win=1024 Len=0 MSS=1460
55377	0.000035	10.0.0.103	10.0.0.10	TCP	33928 > 2100 [SYN] Seq=0 Win=1024 Len=0 MSS=1460
55378	0.000025	10.0.0.103	10.0.0.10	TCP	33928 > 1721 [SYN] Seq=0 Win=1024 Len=0 MSS=1460
55379	0.000025	10.0.0.103	10.0.0.10	TCP	33928 > 8994 [SYN] Seq=0 Win=1024 Len=0 MSS=1460
55380	0.000025	10.0.0.103	10.0.0.10	TCP	33928 > 6699 [SYN] Seq=0 Win=1024 Len=0 MSS=1460
55381	0.000025	10.0.0.103	10.0.0.10	TCP	33928 > 10616 [SYN] Seq=0 Win=1024 Len=0 MSS=146
55382	0.000025	10.0.0.103	10.0.0.10	TCP	33928 > 2381 [SYN] Seq=0 Win=1024 Len=0 MSS=1460
55383	0.000024	10.0.0.103	10.0.0.10	TCP	33928 > 55555 [SYN] Seq=0 Win=1024 Len=0 MSS=146
55384	0.000025	10.0.0.103	10.0.0.10	TCP	33928 > 8193 [SYN] Seq=0 Win=1024 Len=0 MSS=1460
55385	0.000026	10.0.0.103	10.0.0.10	TCP	33928 > 10001 [SYN] Seq=0 Win=1024 Len=0 MSS=146
55386	0.000025	10.0.0.103	10.0.0.10	TCP	33928 > 5904 [SYN] Seq=0 Win=1024 Len=0 MSS=1460

How it works...

Denial of Service is an attack that denies the use of a network service. The way to do this is by causing the device under attack to allocate hardware resources (CPU, memory, and so on) to the attacker so that nothing is left for the users.

Denial of Service is when there is an attack on a network resource. Distributed DoS is when the attack is coming from multiple sources.

There's more...

DoS/DDoS attacks are sometimes hard to discover since they can simulate a real situation. For example:

1. Ping scans that can also come for management systems.

2. HTTP GET requests that are the normal requests that are accepted by web servers.

3. SNMP GET requests.

These and many others should be monitored for their quantity and sources in order to discover a problem. In the following screenshot, we see what we get when we follow a specific TCP stream.

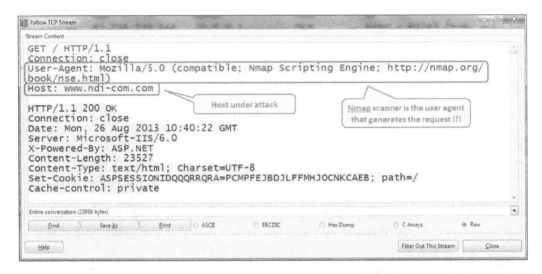

Locating smart TCP attacks

Another type of attack is when you send unknown TCP packets, hoping that the device under attack will not know what to do with them and hopefully pass them through. These types of attacks are well known, and blocked by most of the modern firewalls that are implemented in networks today; but still, I will tell you about them in brief.

Getting ready

What I usually do when I get to a new network is connect my laptop to the network and see what is running over it. First, I just connect it to several switches and see the broadcasts. Then I configure port mirror to critical servers and communications lines and look at what is running over it.

To look for unusual traffic, port mirror communications links and central servers, and check for unusual traffic patterns.

How to do it...

The traffic patterns you should look for are:

- ▶ ACK scanning: Multiple ACKs are sent usually to multiple ports in order to break the existing TCP connections.

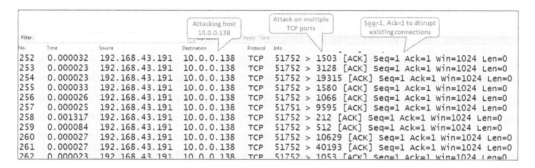

- ▶ Unusual flags combinations: This refers to anything with a URG flag, FIN and RST, SYN-FIN, and so on. Unusual flags combinations are not the usual SYN, FIN or RST, with or without ACK. In the following screenshot, you see an example of this scenario. The operations FIN/PSH/URG are together called Xmas scan.

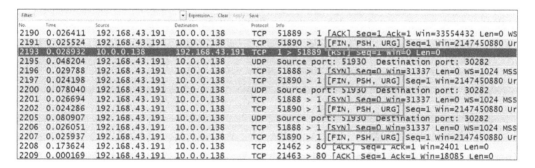

TCP scans with all flags set to "0". This scan is called Null scan.

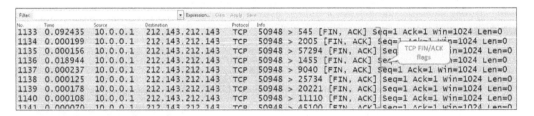

> ▶ **Massive FIN-ACK scanning**: Large amount of packets with FIN and ACK flags
>   set to "1" are sent to multiple ports in order to cause them to be closed or just
>   to flood the network.

No.	Time	Source	Destination	Protocol	Info
1133	0.092435	10.0.0.1	212.143.212.143	TCP	50948 > 545 [FIN, ACK] Seq=1 Ack=1 win=1024 Len=0
1134	0.000199	10.0.0.1	212.143.212.143	TCP	50948 > 2005 [FIN, ACK] Seq=1 Ack=1 win=1024 Len=0
1135	0.000156	10.0.0.1	212.143.212.143	TCP	50948 > 57294 [FIN, ACK] Seq TCP FIN/ACK in=1024 Len=0
1136	0.018944	10.0.0.1	212.143.212.143	TCP	50948 > 1455 [FIN, ACK] Se flags =1024 Len=0
1137	0.000237	10.0.0.1	212.143.212.143	TCP	50948 > 9040 [FIN, ACK] Seq=1 Ack=1 win=1024 Len=0
1138	0.000125	10.0.0.1	212.143.212.143	TCP	50948 > 25734 [FIN, ACK] Seq=1 Ack=1 win=1024 Len=0
1139	0.000178	10.0.0.1	212.143.212.143	TCP	50948 > 20221 [FIN, ACK] Seq=1 Ack=1 win=1024 Len=0
1140	0.000108	10.0.0.1	212.143.212.143	TCP	50948 > 11110 [FIN, ACK] Seq=1 Ack=1 win=1024 Len=0
1141	0.000070	10.0.0.1	212.143.212.143	TCP	50948 > 45100 [FIN, ACK] Seq=1 Ack=1 win=1024 Len=0

How it works...

There are many types of TCP scans based on the assumption that when we send target RST
or FIN flags (with or without an ACK) that scan various port numbers, we will cause the target
to close connections, and when we send unusual combinations of flags to it, it will make the
target busy. This will cause it to slow down and drop the existing connections.

Most of these scans are well known and well protected against firewalls and intrusion
detection/preventions systems.

You can also configure pre-defined filters to catch these types of attacks, but the best thing to do while suspecting such an event is to go through the captured data and look for unusual data patterns.

For scan types, go to the `Nmap.org` web page:

`http://nmap.org/book/man-port-scanning-techniques.html`

Discovering brute-force and application attacks

The next step in network attack is to understand the various types of brute-force attacks. A brute-force attack is a trial-and-error method used to obtain information from the victim, for example, trying to find organizational servers, user directories, and crack passwords.

Getting ready

Brute-force attacks usually will not produce non-standard loads on the network, and the way they are discovered is usually by IDS systems or when there is a suspicion that someone is trying to hack into the network. In this recipe, we will learn how to identify typical brute-force attacks.

How to do it...

When you suspect a brute-force on the network, follow these steps to locate it.

1. Connect Wireshark with port mirror to the port in the server that you suspect is under attack.

2. For DNS brute-force attacks, look for DNS queries that are asking for common names under your domain. For example, in the following illustration, you can see a scan for ISP servers. We can see DNS queries to common names such as dns (1) and dns2—a record for IPv4 (2) and a record for IPv6 (3), and intranet—a record for IPv4 (4) and a record for IPv6 (5).

    a. In the case of **dns.icomm.co** (1), we got a reply; in all other cases, we did not.

b. Many queries with no response can indicate a DNS brute attack, but also indicate someone who is looking for a server that does not exist. Look at the source address to see where it is coming from.

No.	Time	Source	Destination	Protocol	Info
7749	0.127587	10.0.0.1	10.0.0.138	DNS	Standard query 0x0001 AAAA sip.icomm.com
7750	0.023064	10.0.0.138	10.0.0.1	DNS	Standard query response 0x0001
7751	0.128110	10.0.0.1	10.0.0.138	DNS	Standard query 0x0001 A dns.icomm.com
7752	0.026680	10.0.0.138	10.0.0.1	DNS	Standard query response 0x0001 A 81.199.199.199
7755	0.124379	10.0.0.1	10.0.0.138	DNS	Standard query 0x0001 AAAA dns.icomm.com
7756	0.023907	10.0.0.138	10.0.0.1	DNS	Standard query response 0x0001
7757	0.127113	10.0.0.1	10.0.0.138	DNS	Standard query 0x0001 A ns2.icomm.com
7758	0.023341	10.0.0.138	10.0.0.1	DNS	Standard query response 0x0001 No such name
7759	0.005137	10.0.0.1	10.0.0.138	DNS	Standard query 0x0001 AAAA corp.icomm.com
7760	0.000190	10.0.0.1	10.0.0.138	DNS	Standard query 0x0001 AAAA whois.icomm.com
7761	0.000640	10.0.0.1	10.0.0.138	DNS	Standard query 0x0001 AAAA ns2.icomm.com
7762	0.001602	10.0.0.138	10.0.0.1	DNS	Standard query 0x0001 AAAA ns2.icomm.com
7763	0.023563	10.0.0.138	10.0.0.1	DNS	Standard query response 0x0001 No such name
7764	0.088002	10.0.0.1	10.0.0.138	DNS	Standard query 0x0001 A intranet.icomm.com
7765	0.024316	10.0.0.138	10.0.0.1	DNS	Standard query response 0x0001 No such name
7766	0.134785	10.0.0.1	10.0.0.138	DNS	Standard query 0x0001 AAAA intranet.icomm.com
7767	0.023727	10.0.0.138	10.0.0.1	DNS	Standard query response 0x0001 No such name

3. Another brute-force attack to watch out for is HTTP trying to find resources on the server.

a. To look for HTTP scanning, look for the scanner's signature in the packet details, as seen in the following screenshot.

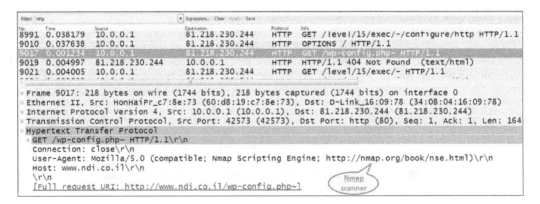

b. Also, look for too many HTTP error messages. Some examples are illustrated in the following screenshot. Choose **Statistics | HTTP | Packet Counter | PC**. If you get too many error messages, check for their source.

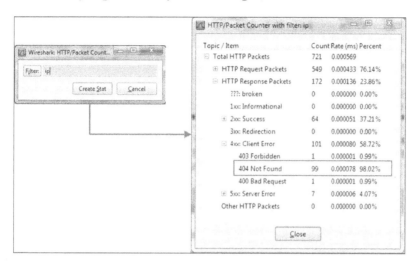

How it works...

Brute-force attacks are trial and error attacks that send requests to the destination, hoping that some of them will be answered. Since most of these requests will be denied (if you've configured your servers properly), a large amount of **Not Found** messages, forbidden messages, and other error codes can be some of the syndromes for such an attack.

There's more...

For discovering HTTP error codes, configure the display filter `http.response.code >= 400`. The same applies to SIP and any protocol that uses HTTP-like codes. To find known scanners, you can simply use the **Edit | Find** packet feature and look for common scanner names. In the following screenshot, you can see an example for Nmap, which is one of the common ones. We chose the string **nmap.org** (1) in **Packet bytes** (2).

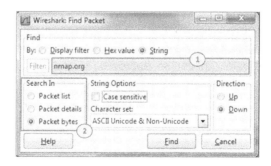

And this is what we got:

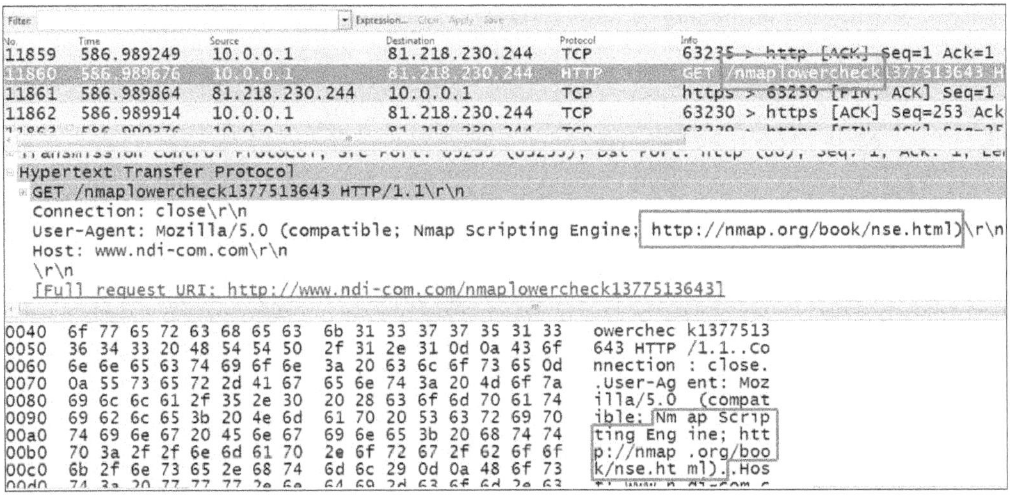

Another important issue is brute force attack, that is, when the attacker tries to guess the password in order to break into a server.

In the following screenshot, you'll see what happens when an attacker tries to break into a well-protected FTP server.

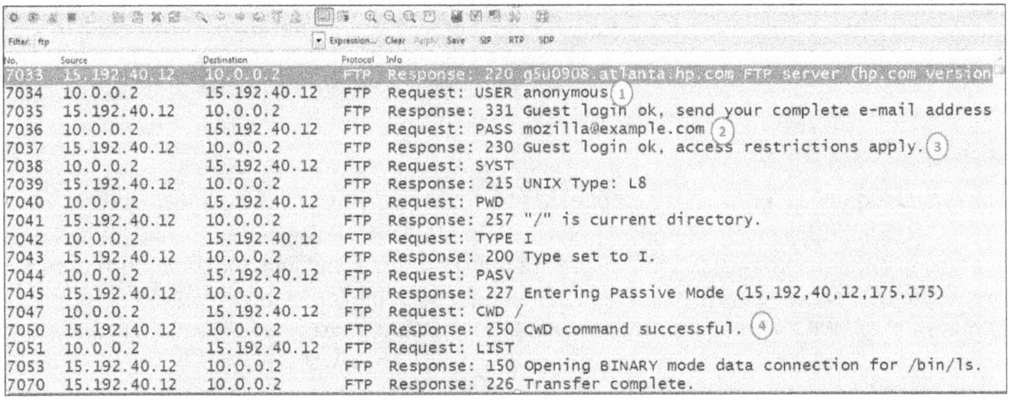

1. Since it is FTP, the first trial is with username anonymous (1), a password chosen by the attacker (2), login is, of course, approved (3), and the attacker gets in (4).

2. In the following screenshot, you see what happens when the attacker tries other usernames that are not authorized.

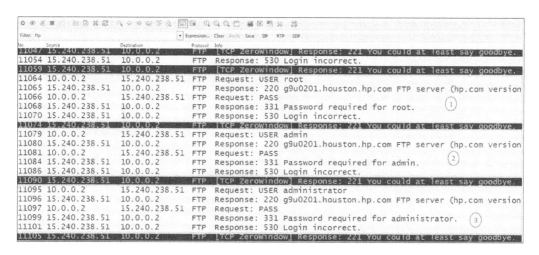

3. Here, you can see that the attacker is trying to login with the usernames **root** (1), **admin** (2) and **administrator** (3).

4. The attacker is blocked, and the server sends a **TCP Zero-Window** message and even answers by saying **you could at least say goodbye**.

Links, Tools, and Reading

In this appendix I would like to refer to some useful links from which you can get further information about Wireshark: learning sources, additional software, and so on.

Useful Wireshark links

The main Wireshark link is of course http://www.wireshark.org. Here you can find:

- The downloads page at http://www.wireshark.org/download.html.
- The learning page at http://www.wireshark.org/docs/.
- And what is called the **Enhancement** area at http://www.riverbed.com/ products-solutions/products/performance-management/wireshark-enhancement-products/. This is a link to Riverbed, who acquired CACE Technologies, the primary sponsor of Wireshark, and became the main sponsor; they now develop and sell commercial add-ons.
- As open source software, Wireshark development resources are located under http://www.wireshark.org/docs/wsdg_html_chunked/ or http://www.wireshark.org/develop.html

Also some other useful links are:

- The Wireshark graphical user interface was created using GTK+, or the GIMP toolkit, an open source kit that can be found on the GTK+ project web page at http://www.gtk.org/
- For WinPCap (the Windows capture driver), go to www.winpcap.org, and for remote monitoring go to http://www.winpcap.org/docs/docs_40_2/html/ group__remote.html#Config

tcpdump

tcpdump is free Unix-based software that runs under the Unix/Linux command line. Some of the useful resources for it are:

- The tcpdump website: `http://www.tcpdump.org/`
- The Windows version of tcpdump (Windump): `http://www.winpcap.org/windump/default.htm`
- A friendly tutorial: `http://danielmiessler.com/study/tcpdump/`
- The official man page: `http://www.tcpdump.org/tcpdump_man.html`

Wireshark can open tcpdump files, so when you capture packets with tcpdump, you can later open it with Wireshark or any other graphical tool.

Some additional tools

Although Wireshark is by far the most common network analysis tool on the market, there are also many other network troubleshooting tools that I use a lot. Before getting into the details, I would like to go back some years to one of the funniest network problems I've ever had. The case itself was very simple, but it comes with an important lesson. It had to do with a network in a warehouse of a big hospital. The warehouse workers were equipped with wireless terminals, taking medication as needed and conveying it to the various departments of the hospital. The problem was that all the terminals worked very slowly. They called an integration company to help them with the problem, and these guys came in with every piece of troubleshooting equipment ever made. They came with Wireshark, Sniffer, wireless analyzers, spectrum analyzers, and many other boxes. I went there, and when I saw what they were doing, I told them that they forgot to bring one important thing, their heads. If they had used them, they would have discovered that the problem was a bad RJ45 cable from the warehouse to the hospital's main network 50 meters from there.

The conclusion is very simple of course. Tools are just tools. Without the knowledge of networking and where to use them, they will not help you. In this section I would like to bring in some additional tools, and where to use them.

What I bring here, along with other examples in the book, are devices and software tools that I've worked with over the years. Some of them are freeware and some are commercial products. It is important to note that their descriptions come from my own experience. I don't have a commercial or any other interest in any of them.

SNMP tools

The first sets of tools that I usually use to solve a problem are SNMP tools. There are tools with strong mapping capabilities, there are some with good statistical capabilities, and there are some with good logging and events capabilities.

First, in order to just monitor SNMP counters, you can use simple free MIB browsers and graphical tools such as:

Vendor	Software name	Where to download	Notes	License
Manage engine	MibBrowser	`http://www.manageengine.com/products/mibbrowser-free-tool/`	Very friendly with minimal configuration.	Free
Open source	MRTG	`http://oss.oetiker.ch/mrtg/`	Requires time and knowledge to install and configure. Good for long-term statistics. Commonly used by ISPs as a console for their customers.	Free with up to 10 sensors (*1); Commercial from 11 sensors
SolarWinds	Network device monitor	`http://www.solarwinds.com/products/freetools/network-device-monitor/`	Solarwinds is one of the leaders in network management tools, and along with the commercial stuff, you can find many free tools.	Free
SolarWinds Engineering toolset	Engineer's Toolset	`http://www.solarwinds.com/engineers-toolset.aspx`	Various tools for network monitoring, discovery, SNMP, configuration, basic scanners and more.	Free with limited capabilities; Commercial with full capabilities

SNMP platforms

SNMP platform are pieces of software that provide a central console that shows a map of the network, collects information and presents statistical reports, and collects SNMP events and presents them by severity and other parameters.

Some of the common tools in this category are:

Vendor	Software name	Where to download	Notes	License
Castlerock Computing	SNMPc	`http://www.castlerock.com/`	This is one of the friendliest SNMP tools that I have worked with for more than a decade. The SNMP management platform is very easy to use and is great for network debugging.	Commercial
SolarWinds	Assorted	`http://www.solarwinds.com/network-management-software.aspx`	SolarWinds has various tools that provide monitoring, mapping, configuration management and other network management capabilities. These are some of the best options available but are expensive.	Commercial
Manageengine	Assorted	`http://www.manageengine.com/network-performance-management.html`	Various tools that provide monitoring, mapping, configuration management and other network management capabilities. One of the best but expensive.	Commercial

Vendor	Software name	Where to download	Notes	License
HP	IMC, NNM, and so on	`http://h17007.www1.hp.com/us/en/networking/solutions/network-management/index.aspx#.UkgqGT8YhyI`	This is a great platform. HP made it much friendlier than previous Network Node Manager (NNM) software. It is definitely worth checking out.	Commercial
OpenNMS	OpenNMS	`http://www.opennms.org/`	It is open source but requires know-how of how to configure it.	Free
Nagious	Nagious	`http://www.nagios.org/`	It is open source but requires a knowledge to configure it.	Free

There are many others tools, such as:

 ▸ The open source Cacti (`http://www.cacti.net/`)

 ▸ Zabbix (`http://www.zabbix.com/`)

 ▸ MRTG (`http://oss.oetiker.ch/mrtg/`)

 ▸ Some others (some under the GNU public license).

There are the "heavyweight" suites, such as:

 ▸ The HP OpenView suite of management applications (`http://www8.hp.com/us/en/software-solutions/software.html?compURI=1174702#tab=TAB1`)

 ▸ CA Unicenter (`http://www.ca.com/us/network-performance-management.aspx`)

There are also other medium-sized platforms, various tools from Plixer (`http://www.plixer.com/`), and many others.

For network monitoring and troubleshooting you will need the very basic tools, while as a platform you will need a more sophisticated one. You can find a nice comparison of management platform on `http://en.wikipedia.org/wiki/Comparison_of_network_monitoring_systems`.

The NetFlow, JFlow, and SFlow analyzers

NetFlow from **Cisco** (www.cisco.com/go/netflow) and JFlow from **Juniper** (http://www.juniper.net/techpubs/software/erx/junose82/swconfig-ip-services/html/ip-jflow-stats-config2.html) provide a method for collecting TCP/IP traffic flow statistics on your routing devices.

SFlow (http://en.wikipedia.org/wiki/Sflow and http://www.sflow.org/index.php) is an industry standard technology for monitoring high-speed switched networks.

The differences between them are:

 ▸ **NetFlow** applies to Cisco routers and L3 switches. In layer-3 switches make sure that they support NetFlow (depends on software version and hardware). In some cases, you will need additional software/hardware for this. It was standardized by RFC3954 (http://www.ietf.org/rfc/rfc3954.txt).

 ▸ **JFlow** applies to Juniper routers and L3 switches.

 ▸ **SFlow** is a standard for monitoring LAN switches and was standardized by RFC3176 (http://tools.ietf.org/html/rfc3176).

 ▸ **IPFIX** (RFCs 5101 and 5102) is a standard developed from **NetFlow** v9, and standardized by the **IETF**.

All Flow/IPFIX technologies are based on the communications device that collects the flow data from the interfaces and sends them to the management station. They require a simple configuration on the router or switch and software to collect the data and present it.

This software can be used for monitoring which users are causing a load on the network (displayed according to IP addresses or DNS names), on which applications (HTTP, SMTP, and so on, displayed according to their port numbers), web pages (displayed according to their IP addresses, translated to DNS names), and other such criteria. While Wireshark is usually used for this purpose in short-term monitoring (the **Conversations** feature), these tools can be used for long-term monitoring as well.

Some common software options include:

 ▸ http://www.plixer.com/Scrutinizer-Netflow-Sflow/scrutinizer-flow-analyzer.html from **Plixer**

 ▸ http://www.sevone.com/technologies/NetFlow-analysis from **SevOne**

There are freeware tools, and there are commercial tools with free limited capabilities versions (usually limited by the number of interfaces they can monitor); in commercial SNMP platforms, you usually have a free license for two to five interfaces.

HTTP debuggers

HTTP debuggers are tools that provide statistical and detailed data about HTTP. Here are some tools for this:

Vendor	Software name	Where to download	Notes
Eric Lawrence and Telerik	Fiddler	`http://fiddler2.com/`	The most common freeware HTTP debugging tool, this works as a separate software that captures packets and analyzes them (such as Wireshark).
Simtec Limited	HTTPWatch	`http://www.httpwatch.com/`	This is available in basic limited and commercial editions. Available as an add-on to Firefox or Internet Explorer. Files can be opened with HTTP Watch Studio. Available also for iPhone iOS.

What you will get with these tools is HTTP statistical and performance information, for example, how much time it took to open a web page, the reasons for delays, and error summaries.

Syslog

Syslog (`https://tools.ietf.org/html/rfc5424`) is a protocol for message logging. There are many parameters on communication devices that can be configured, so in cases where a problem occurs, a message will be sent to the Syslog server. These are usually hardware- and- software- based problems that are not always covered by SNMP.

A great Syslog server (that receives the messages and presents them) can be found at `http://www.kiwisyslog.com/free-edition.aspx`. There are many other tools, and they are available for free in many management platforms.

Other stuff

Some other tools you might need to get for working with networks are:

▸ A neat tool, **Xplico**, for extracting application data contained in capture files: `http://www.xplico.org/about` (freeware)

▸ **Nmap** security scanner: `http://nmap.org/`

▸ **Netcat** (nc) for Linux: `http://nc110.sourceforge.net/`

Network analysers

While Wireshark is by far the most common network analysis tool, there are also some other tools that can be used in times of trouble. Some of them are:

- ► **Riverbed Cascade suite of tools**: This is developed by the Wireshark guys and provides a graphical analysis of Wireshark files. It can be found at `http://www.riverbed.com/products-solutions/products/performance-management/`

- ► **WildPackets OmniPeak**: I've used this in some cases for heavily loaded networks, which my laptop with Wireshark couldn't handle. It has great statistics tools and works well under heavy loads. It can be found at `http://www.wildpackets.com/products/omnipeek_network_analyzer`.

There are probably more, but these are the two I've worked with and both do a great job.

There is a simple analysis tool in some Cisco devices that comes as a part of the IOS. Cisco calls it **Mini Protocol Analyzer**, and you can find it at `https://www.cisco.com/en/US/docs/routers/7600/ios/12.2SR/configuration/guide/mpa.html`.

Interesting websites

Here are some interesting websites that I use a lot:

- ► First and most useful is `http://www.cisco.com`, from where you can learn the technologies along with how to configure them in Cisco

- ► Many Wireshark files, exercises, and challenges can be found at `http://www.honeynet.org/`

- ► A summary table of Wireshark filters can be found at `http://packetlife.net/media/library/13/Wireshark_Display_Filters.pdf`

- ► Captured and filed examples can be found at `http://wiki.wireshark.org/SampleCaptures`

- ► Another interesting Wireshark filter page is `http://www.packetlevel.ch/html/tcpdumpf.html`

- ► Some Perl stuff can be found at `http://perldoc.perl.org/perlre.html`, and Perl regular expressions can be found at `http://perldoc.perl.org/perlre.html#Regular-Expressions` and `http://www.regular-expressions.info/perl.html`

Books

Here is a list of some of the books I've used over the years:

▸   To understand TCP/IP basics: *TCP/IP Illustrated, Volume 1: The Protocols (Second Edition)* (by *Addison-Wesley Professional Computing Series*)

▸   A comprehensive, illustrated internet protocol reference, free on the Internet: *The TCP/IP Guide* (`http://www.tcpipguide.com/`)

▸   Many books from Cisco press are worth reading, both the technology and certifications books: `http://www.ciscopress.com/`

▸   Cisco design guides: Just Google the subject you're looking for

Index

D

data
  capturing, starting 14
  part of file, saving 31, 32
  printing 34
  saving, in different formats 32, 33
  whole file, saving 31
Database Administrator (DBA) 196
database traffic
  issues, analyzing 320-323
Datagram distribution service (port 138) 313
Date and Time of Day 27
DDoS
  about 388
  attacks, discovering 398-401
decode_error 282
decompression_failure 282
decrypt_error 282
decryption_failed 281
Deep Packet Inspection (DPI) 373
delay
  about 376
  monitoring, Wireshark used 374-377
  problems, discovering 377-381
DELETE 264
Denial of Service. *See* **DOS**
details tab 142
DHCP
  about 207
  problems, analyzing 207-210
DHCP Ack 209
DHCP Discover 209
DHCP Offer 209
DHCP Request 209
Differentiated Services (DiffServ) 40, 78
Dir (direction) qualifiers 47
displayed data
  saving 70
display filters
  about 43, 63
  configuring 64-67
  parameter, selecting in packet pane 68, 69
  syntax, writing 68
display filter toolbar 22
Display window 89

Distributed DoS. *See* **DDoS**
DNS
  about 245
  issues, analyzing 254-261
  namespace 251, 252
  operations 250, 251
  operations, analyzing 249, 250
  servers, using 252
  slow responses 257, 258
  traffic, filtering 246-249
DNS Benchmark
  from GRC, URL 253
DNS display filters 81
Domain Name System. *See* **DNS**
DoS
  about 388
  attacks, discovering 398-401
dst host <host> filter 51
dst net <net> filter 52
dst net <net>/<len> filter 52
dst net <net> mask <netmask> filter 52
dst port <port> filter 54
duplicate ACKs 232-234
duplicate IPs
  finding 203-207
Dynamic Host Configuration Protocol. *See*
  DHCP

E

e-mail traffic
  issues, analyzing 298-309
End Bytes field 91
End Mbit/s field 91
End Packets field 91
Endpoints tool
  using, from statistics menu 96-98
Enhancement area
  URL 411
Enterprise Resource Planning (ERP) 312
Eric Lawrence and Telerik
  URL 417
error codes filters 263
error events 147, 148
error storms
  about 154
  discovering 155

I

Thank you for buying
Network Analysis Using Wireshark Cookbook

About Packt Publishing

Packt, pronounced 'packed', published its first book "*Mastering phpMyAdmin for Effective MySQL Management*" in April 2004 and subsequently continued to specialize in publishing highly focused books on specific technologies and solutions.

Our books and publications share the experiences of your fellow IT professionals in adapting and customizing today's systems, applications, and frameworks. Our solution based books give you the knowledge and power to customize the software and technologies you're using to get the job done. Packt books are more specific and less general than the IT books you have seen in the past. Our unique business model allows us to bring you more focused information, giving you more of what you need to know, and less of what you don't.

Packt is a modern, yet unique publishing company, which focuses on producing quality, cutting-edge books for communities of developers, administrators, and newbies alike. For more information, please visit our website: www.packtpub.com.

About Packt Open Source

In 2010, Packt launched two new brands, Packt Open Source and Packt Enterprise, in order to continue its focus on specialization. This book is part of the Packt Open Source brand, home to books published on software built around Open Source licenses, and offering information to anybody from advanced developers to budding web designers. The Open Source brand also runs Packt's Open Source Royalty Scheme, by which Packt gives a royalty to each Open Source project about whose software a book is sold.

Writing for Packt

We welcome all inquiries from people who are interested in authoring. Book proposals should be sent to author@packtpub.com. If your book idea is still at an early stage and you would like to discuss it first before writing a formal book proposal, contact us; one of our commissioning editors will get in touch with you.

We're not just looking for published authors; if you have strong technical skills but no writing experience, our experienced editors can help you develop a writing career, or simply get some additional reward for your expertise.

GNS3 Network Simulation Guide

ISBN: 978-1-78216-080-9   Paperback: 154 pages

Acquire a comprehensive knowledge of the GNS3 graphical network simulator, using it to prototype your network without the need for physical routers

1. Develop your knowledge for Cisco certification (CCNA, CCNP, CCIE), using GNS3

2. Install GNS3 successfully on Windows, Linux, or OS X

3. Work your way through easy- to- follow exercises showing you how to simulate your test network using Cisco routers, Ethernet switches, and Virtual PCs

Network Graph Analysis and Visualization with Gephi

ISBN: 978-1-78328-013-1   Paperback: 116 pages

Visualize and analyze your data swiftly using dynamic network graphs built with Gephi

1. Use your own data to create network graphs displaying complex relationships between several types of data elements

2. Learn about nodes and edges, and customize your graphs using size, color, and weight attributes

3. Filter your graphs to focus on the key information you need to see and publish your network graphs to the Web

Please check **www.PacktPub.com** for information on our titles

www.ingramcontent.com/pod-product-compliance
Lightning Source LLC
Chambersburg PA
CBHW080142060326
40689CB00018B/3817